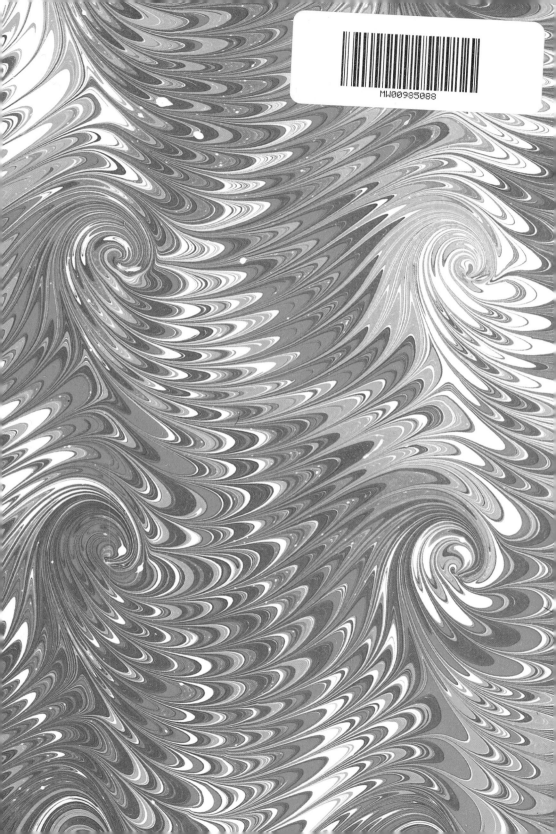

Retreat from Leningrad

Steven H. Newton

RETREAT FROM
LENINGRAD

Army Group North
1944/1945

Steven H. Newton

Schiffer Military History
Atglen, PA

Book Design by Robert Biondi.

Printed in the United States of America.
ISBN: 0-88740-806-0

We are interested in hearing from authors with book ideas on related topics.

Published by Schiffer Publishing Ltd.
77 Lower Valley Road
Atglen, PA 19310
Please write for a free catalog.
This book may be purchased from the publisher.
Please include $2.95 postage.
Try your bookstore first.

Contents

INTRODUCTION

he massive debriefing of German Army officers conducted by the United States Army Historical Section following V-E Day concentrated not too surprisingly on campaigns in which the Americans had fought. The interviews, reports, and monographs are heavily weighted toward coverage of D-Day, the Battle of the Bulge, or the war in Italy. But as the political climate between the victorious Allies began to chill, the interests of the interrogators turned more and more toward an examination of the Russian front. There was a frantic, almost millennial intensity to this secondary effort, which took place in an atmosphere that it was only a matter of time before the Red Army spilled out of East Germany onto the central plains of Europe.

The problem with the Russian front projects was that the Americans had only a rather spotty collection of officers with experience in the East on which to rely. At the highest levels the captured Germans included three chiefs of the army general staff - Franz Halder, Kurt Zeitzler, and Heinz Guderian - plus a number of army group commanders from the latter part of the war, such as the virulently anti-communist Lothar Rendulic. These men provided the overall framework for an understanding of the major campaigns against the Soviets, but - with the exception of Rendulic - very little detail at the tactical or operational levels. Among senior staff officers and division commanders there was a random sampling of leaders who had served in Russia up to mid-1944. Unfortunately for the Allies, this was a rather mixed bag, and the reports they produced were rather spotty in terms of their coverage. Most of them could be considered tactical snapshots at the regiment or division level, produced from memory without the aid of maps or other supporting documents. They were therefore intriguing but often inaccurate; many have not ever been translated into English, and languish unread in the

Capture German Documents section of the National Archives.

There are some exceptions. A few larger projects were supervised by senior staff officers who gathered together representatives from all the major commands of an army or army group to create a coherent monograph on a particular campaign. Hans von Grieffenburg, former chief of staff to Army Group Center in 1941, supervised the team which recreate the battle of Moscow. One Manstein staffer, Theodor Busse, coordinated the Kursk project, while another, Friedrich Schulz, edited the monograph concerning Army Group South's operations after Stalingrad. The first two of these have been reprinted in English by Garland Press, the third has been commercially published in German. Several other first-rate operational/tactical narratives have never seen the light of day, except in the bibliographies of general histories of the war.

One of the best such unpublished works is the Army Group North Project, which chronicled in detail the operations of German forces in the Baltic states from the point at which the Russians pushed them away from Leningrad to the final surrender in Courland. It was initiated by Franz Halder, who had by 1948 become a full-time employee of the United States Army. He assigned former Major General Burkhardt Müller-Hillebrand as team leader. Müller-Hillebrand was a scholar-soldier who began the war as the Operations Officer of the 93rd Infantry Division and advanced to a post on the general staff of the XVII Corps in July 1940. After the fall of France, he was named as Halder's adjutant, where he remained until April 1942, being then named as the Chief of the Organization Detachment at OKH. His first field command came in early 1943: after a temporary stint as acting commander of the 16th Panzer Division, Müller-Hillebrand spent ten months as the commander of Panzer Regiment 24. In April 1944, he became Chief of Staff to the XLVI Panzer Corps, rising to the same position in the Third Panzer Army that September. With the last two assignments Müller-Hillebrand participated personally in the desperate attempts to keep Army Group North from being isolated in Courland. After the war, Müller-Hillebrand wrote extensively - his work on the problems of coalition warfare is available in English though currently out-of-print, and his *Das Heer*, while it has not been translated, remains one of the standard statistical sources on the Wehrmacht. In 1956, he became a Brigadier General in the recreated Bundeswehr.

Müller-Hillebrand assembled an impressive array of senior staff officers and commanders to author the reports. These included Oldwig von Natzmer, the army group's chief of staff under Field Marshal Ferdinand Schörner; Herbert Loch, commander of the Eighteenth Army; Paul Hermann, Chief of Staff to the Sixteenth Army; Paul Reichelt, Chief of Staff to *Armeeabeilung* Narva; and William Heinemeyer, the officer responsible throughout 1944 for maintaining the army group's war diary. These men had lived through the events they described, and because of their extended service on what had long been a static front enjoyed a better grasp of the geography than many others. Likewise, due to the fact that many of the units which fought in the Baltic theater remained their throughout their existence, there were far fewer errors in unit identification made in this study than in others.

The resulting study is a masterful account of an extended defensive campaign under adverse circumstances. It includes the only complete history of the origin and campaigns of *Armeeabteilung* Narva available in the English language, as well as a detailed description and commentary on the construction of the Panther Line through eastern Estonia. The authors provide a thorough examination of the motley assemblage of foreign volunteers employed by the German Army, including Danes, Dutchmen, Estonians, Lithuanians, Norwegians, Spaniards, and Swedes. (There is a special emphasis on the role of the Estonians in the defense of their own borders.) The reader is treated to blow-by-blow accounts of the plans, messages, and recriminations passing back and forth between the OKH and the army group headquarters, alongside considerable tactical detail on fighting in swamps, on the Baltic Islands, and in the hills east of Pskov.

To this original study have been added considerable amounts of technical information gleaned from Army Group North records in the National Archives. For example, as an appendix this edition presents the most detailed battalion level order of battle for Army Group North in January 1944 available in any language (including, for example, indigenous police and security forces as well as the order of battle of all Luftwaffe Flak units in the area). Detailed statistics on the infantry strength of the army group - battalion by battalion - as well as artillery, anti-tank, and armor holdings have been included in the notes. Literally every unit mentioned in the original text has been correctly identified, and the names of unit commanders provided for over 90% of them. In addition, a complete set of maps has been created for this publication, drawn from the original German situation maps.

Finally, a completely original final chapter has been written, which assesses the reasons underlying the tactical success of Army Group North. For this essay a considerable amount of primary data have been unearthed to illustrate the means and methods employed by the army group's commanders to keep up the fighting strength of its divisions until the very end of the war. Among other arguments presented there, this chapter explores the questions of the effectiveness of foreign volunteers and the ways in which Army Group North actually benefitted from the peculiarities of the Wehrmacht's replacement system. This essay provides the conclusions that I believe Müller-Hillebrand himself might have wanted for the study.

It should be noted in closing that this study should be read with an understanding of the personal motivations of the authors taken into account. Hitler was always inflexible, German troops were always heavily outnumbered, and the front-line soldiers followed a different morality than the "Golden Pheasants" of the rear area, at whose feet massacres and atrocities should be laid. But it should be recalled by the reader that, at least in the case of the Baltic, Hitler's "political" considerations were often correct if his tactical conceptions were unsound. The German troops of Army Group North *were* usually outnumbered, but also enjoyed far better scales of equipment and replacements than their comrades further south. Nor was it possible, when every possible police and security unit was being dispatched to the front, to so precisely separate the *frontkämpfer* from the rear area commandoes. These shadings will be made apparent in the notes, and are not especially the sole province of German officers writing German military history - they tend to be the common failings of most officers in any army recalling their own operations.

CHAPTER 1

A Brief Review of the Battles of Army Group North from the Beginning of 1943 to the end of 1945

Oldwig von Natzmer

The Battles of 1943 and the Resultant Composition of the Army Group in the Beginning of 1944

The Composition of the Army Group

Army Group North had been committed on the northern flank of the German East Front, which extended from Nevel to Leningrad.

Army Group North, as were all army groups on the Eastern Front, was under the direct command of the OKH [*Oberkommando der Heer* - Army High Command], that is to say, under Adolph Hitler. The command functions for the Eastern Front - and only for this front - were in the hands of the Chief of the Army General Staff; thus all orders to the army group were issued by the Chief of the Army General Staff and all requests of the army group had to be filed there. Hitler had reserved the right to make all basic decisions; the Chief of the Army General Staff was merely the executive organ of the instructions issued by Hitler.

The adjacent unit on the right - to the South - was Army Group Center, on whose left flank the Third Panzer Army was employed linking up with Army Group North. The left - or northern - flank of the Army Group North was anchored on the coast west of Leningrad. No local contact was maintained with the Finnish front northwest of this city. The Russians held an extensive bridgehead west of Leningrad, around Kronstadt and Oranienbaum.

The Sixteenth and Eighteenth Armies were assigned to Army Group North. Their fronts were separated by Lake Ilmen. The strength of both of these armies varied in accordance with the point of main effort of the operations. In the beginning of 1942, for instance, the Sixteenth Army had three corps with a total of sixteen divisions, and the Eighteenth Army had seven corps with twenty-two divisions. The total number of divisions in the sector of the army group varied very little during the course of the 1943 battles.

The Russians faced the army group with a far greater number of units; at the beginning of 1943, seven Russian armies[1] with about forty-eight divisions and forty independent brigades were committed opposite the Sixteenth Army, while the Eighteenth Army had to face ten Russian armies[2] with thirty-three divisions and twenty-six brigades.

The Situation

The front of the army group was not in a straight line but bore the mark of previous battles; it was established during and as a result of the fighting. The biggest salient, as shown on the situation map, was the salient at Demjansk; the fighting which took place at this point will be discussed later.

The conduct of the operations of the army group had become more or less a tactical routine; important operational decisions could no longer be made. The order was to hold the front. The execution of this order was to be viewed with the overall situation prevailing at that time in mind; Hitler alone was in "command," and even the commanders of army groups had been reduced to mere "receivers of orders." All proposals and suggestions submitted by the army group to the OKH - that is, to Hitler - were concerned almost exclusively with such "vital" questions as the straightening of the front line by a few kilometers at various places, or permission to exchange divisions. Even a request like this assumed often the proportions of an "affair of state," and the solving of the problem frequently required day-long discussions and great diplomacy. Conduct of the operations of the army group by its commander or his staff in the old Moltke tradition of assigning missions had become obsolete.

Ideas on a strategic level were out of the question, owing to the extremely rigid regulations in regard to secrecy contained in "*Führer* Order 1." The tactical situation of the adjacent units could still be ascertained by means of telephone conversations. The situation at other fronts and in other theaters of operations, however, as well as information concerning economic conditions and the political situation was kept secret even from the commander of an army group. The blinders which the supreme command had intentionally put on every soldier were not to be removed by any rank. The gathering of news through illegal channels was a tedious job. This was the only way by which an approximate idea could be obtained as to the overall German situation.

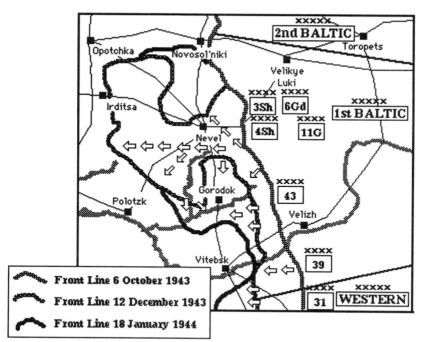

Map 1: The Battle of Nevel, Oct-Dec 1943

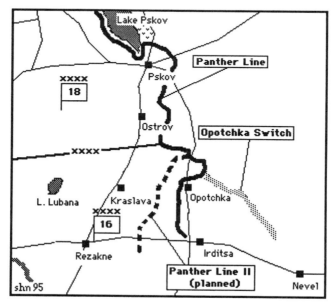

Map Two: The Panther Line, Jan 1944

The only intelligence the army group received at all times, solicited or unsolicited, was that no substantial support of any kind could be given it. The army group had no reserves at its disposal, either in the form of troops or material. The only mission with which the command was charged was the skillful juggling of available units so that troops could always be committed at the focal danger point by removing them from some other point along the front. Owing to these conditions, the command was forced to leave the initiative to the enemy. It was always a very great problem to find a section of the front from which a division could be removed, and to find a good reason with which to combat the understandable arguments which the deprived army advanced.

That such measures, this "eternal war of the poor man," put a strain on the nerves of all concerned is obvious. The war diaries of the Sixteenth and Eighteenth Armies disclose that at that time the commanders of these armies intentionally prohibited - even during calm periods - the detaching of a unit from the front for the purpose of granting it a rest. It was better to keep the divisions at the front and assign them to narrow sectors. This was in no way due to a lack of interest in the men's welfare, but rather it was a precautionary measure. A reserve unit removed from the front was certain to be taken by the supreme command within a day and assigned to the always existing pressure points at some other front. Another reason was the experience that Russian attacks could be easier repulsed by the narrow and deep echeloning of a division than by throwing available reserves into battle. It was imperative to feed the battle from the rear. By applying these tactics, the local commander would still have a small reserve at his disposal, which had the advantage of being familiar with the locality and which, in addition, was a component of the unit.

The position of the commander of the army group was such that he had to face a constantly attacking enemy without reserves. This enemy had an almost unlimited supply of men and material at his disposal, while the German forces were being gradually reduced and their units were disintegrating. The commander had to take from Peter to feed Paul, and was always too late in spite of these tactics. He was constantly troubled by the thought that an enemy penetration at any point of the already thin front would spell disaster for both armies. His superiors had nothing but cheap words of consolation for him, and ignored his suggestions on principle. He continually had to make greater demands upon his troops, although he was fully aware that they could hardly be fulfilled. Knowing these things, it becomes easy to realize the responsibility which rested upon the shoulders of such a man and his aides!

Only two factors tended to facilitate the command of the army group to a certain extent; firstly, its excellent signal intelligence and air reconnaissance, which permitted in almost every instance an early knowledge of major Russian attacks, and allowed timely counter-measures to be taken, and secondly the well-known inflexibility of Russian attack methods. Once the Russians had made a decision to attack, they seldom changed their plans even after their first attacks had been repulsed with heavy losses. In the end, it was only a matter of holding out.

The German command did not have to expect tactical or strategic surprises by the enemy. The large-scale battles of attrition, fought of the pattern of the *"Todesmühle von Verdun"* ["Death-mill of Verdun"] in World War I, came to an end only after the unusually high losses had made continuation of of the battle impossible, even according to Russian standards, or if a breakthrough had been successful. How critical the situations often were, how often the Russians were close to breaking through, and how the last company or battery brought up decided the situation in our favor in the nick of time, will be shown later. This will show again the almost superhuman demands which were made upon the troops and the command in situations of this kind.

Cooperation between the three branches of the Wehrmacht during the defense against Russian attacks was good. *Luftflötte* [Air Fleet] 1, which was committed in the sector of the army group, gave the ground troops excellent support in spite of the weakness of its units and the fact that flying conditions were frequently unfavorable. The Russians, although considerably superior in this field, had never been able to achieve local air superiority for more than a few hours. Having chosen two of the most remarkable months as an example, the ratio of the German and Russian air force units employed in this area show that in [month omitted in original manuscript] 1,972 sorties were flown by the German bombardment and fighter airplanes, as compared to 7,343 sorties flown by the Russians; in September, the Germans made 3,091 sorties, while the Russians flew 5,747 missions. The number of German sorties includes escort flights, which on many occasions were flown in support of German Navy mine-layers and mine-sweepers.

Elements of the Navy considered the securing of the coast and the fight against in the Leningrad-Kronstadt area to be a common cause of the three branches of the Wehrmacht. There was no supreme Wehrmacht agency in command of this joint conduct of the war; the branches of the Wehrmacht were merely instructed to collaborate with each other. The reason for this fruitful collaboration without a joint high command was the friendly relations between the men in command of these branches. The principal task of the Navy consisted in blocking the ports of Leningrad and Kronstadt, and keeping clear the waterways essential for the supplying of troops.

One peculiarity of this theater of operations caused considerable difficulties, namely the presence and active participation of numerous guerilla bands in the rear area of the army group. The army group was in no position to muster sufficient troops to combat the bands; not even the protection of the most important installations could be guaranteed. Individual operations against the bands with hastily assembled forces were undertaken, but failed to produce a decisive success at any point. The deep and swampy forests afforded the bands sufficient protection and made it impossible for smaller units to combat these bands successfully. An apparently well-devised network of communications connected individual bands with each other, as well as with the Russian forces. Raids on farms as well as the supplies which were dropped by the Russian Air Force not only provided them with necessary food, but even permitted the setting-up of sizeable food supply and ordnance depots. Although the damages actually caused by the guerilla bands did not reach large proportions, frequent interruptions of rail traffic, raids on supply trains and general insecurity in the rear areas proved to be a disturbing factor. In December, 1943, the total number of guerillas in the area of the army group was estimated at more than 20,000 men.[3]

How seriously the guerilla raids affected the overall situation is indicated by a compilation of the disruptions of rail traffic in the area of the army group in 1943. The partisans carried out 9,768 demolitions and fifty-one raids, resulting in the death of 208 Germans, the wounding of 773 men, and destruction and damage to 1,139 locomotives and railway cars. The numerous surprise attacks on road traffic by means of fire and mines must added to this list. As a result, the supplying of the army group became more difficult, and was even endangered at times.

The action against the city of Leningrad, whose armaments plants continued operations on an emergency schedule, was a task assigned to the Luftwaffe and a special "artillery group of the heaviest flat trajectory fire" employed in the area southwest of Leningrad. This artillery group comprised fifteen medium-heavy and heavy batteries which covered almost the entire city proper. Their number and ammunition, however, did not suffice to achieve a destructive effect. The dauntless attitude of the inhabitants, particularly that of the working men of Leningrad, must be fully appreciated, although it was more or less forced upon them by an extremely energetic military command in the city. Although an encirclement of Leningrad by German and Finnish troops was not achieved and the supply route across Lake Ladoga remained open during the summer and winter, living conditions in the city, which was constantly under enemy fire, were very bad. In spite of this, the Russian command succeeded in supplying the armies employed in the defense of the city with the necessary war equipment from the Leningrad plants and in replacing, at least in part, the losses by drawing from the manpower within the city.

The Events

The year 1943 was a year of almost continued heavy fighting for Army Group North, as well as for all other army groups at the Eastern Front. This year was characterized in particular by four major defensive battles:

1. The battle south of Lake Ilmen for the Demjansk front sector (1 January-19 March) which extended far to the east;

2. & 3. The two defensive battles south of Lake Ladoga and south of Leningrad (12 January-5 April and 22 July-24 September);

4. The battle at Nevel on the right flank of the army group (6 October 1943-5 January 1944).

The Winter Battle South of Lake Ilmen, 1 January to 19 March 1943

The salient at Demjansk, which protruded far to the east, was a left-over from the year 1942. After their successful breakthrough at the boundary between Army Group Center and North, the Russians had attempted in vain through renewed attacks to break down the remaining bastion of the Sixteenth Army around Demjansk. The numerous attacks against the narrow strip of land had cost the Russians unusually high losses without achieving a decisive success. The Russians started a new major attack in the beginning of January, 1943. The result again was an unusually high consumption of manpower on both sides. A great number of divisions of both armies of the army group moved through Demjansk, the combat area; the "hill" was grinding and in a short while reduced every newly committed unit to the point where it became necessary to replace it. The repeated requests of the army group for permissions to straighten the front south of Lake Ilmen were turned down by the supreme command. This was never understood by the combat troops, although the refusal was not entirely unreasonable, because no matter how high our own losses were, the Russian losses were still considerably higher, which justified our own casualties. Hitler's hope to be able to straighten the German front from the difficult to defend bastions of Demjansk and Rshev[4] was one of his many misjudgments of the situation, and a gross overestimation of the German strength.

The battles developing simultaneously in the area south of Leningrad and the Zwang River in January, which also had to be supported by the army group, finally brought permission for the army group to evacuate the salient at Demjansk.[5] The retreat by bounds, starting on 17 February 1943, resulted in an immediate reorganization of the Russian forces and renewed heavy attacks against the narrow strip of land. This weakest point of the front was once more subjected to an unusual test; often a Russian breakthrough from the south and the north was prevented only by actually committing the last soldier. The disengagement - carefully and accurately prepared and carried out according to plans up to the last minute - was concluded on 26 February, and ended in a position east of the Lovat River bank.[6] This position could not be firmly held, but served at first as a line of defense. In spite of every effort, the enemy failed to prevent the withdrawal; nor was he able to harass the movement in the least. The distances of the individual intermediate positions (approximately six to nine kilometers) were commensurate with the troops' capacity; besides, they were dictated by the difficulty which was encountered while moving the elements through the narrow strip of land.

Without letting up, the Russians continued their attacks against the new position, and against the flanks of the slight salient which still existed after the disengaging movement, until - about the middle of March - they were completely exhausted. From 23 February to 19 March, fourteen Russian rifle divisions and three rifle brigades were destroyed, an additional twenty-eight units suffered very heavy casualties, 290 tanks were destroyed, almost 3,000 prisoners were taken, and more than 50,000 enemy dead were counted. Although our own losses counted heavily because of the constantly worsening overall situation in Germany, the battle ended in a definite victory for the German side.

The figures mentioned here and elsewhere also explain the unusually high losses of the Russians during World War II. The gathering of accurate figures was as good as impossible. Almost during the entire war the Russian command squandered manpower to a degree virtually unthinkable in the West. This reckless expenditure can only be explained by the fact that the Russian does not value life too highly - because it does not pay for the masses of the Russians to live, and because bondage or political fanaticism leads to self-sacrifice. With a grin or a murmured "*nitchevo*,"[7] the Russian sacrifices his life as he would discard a superfluous garment. To understand the Slavic mind in all its complexity is almost impossible for a man of the western world.

The Defensive Battles South of Lake Ladoga and South of Leningrad (12 January to 5 April and 22 July to 24 September 1943)

The attempt of the Russians to destroy the salient south of Lake Ilmen and to advance in the direction of Pskov to unhinge the northern flank of the German Eastern Front had been prevented by the failure at Demjansk. As this fighting neared a climax, the Russians simultaneously started an additional large-scale attack, which this time was to free Leningrad. This long-aspired objective - the throwing back of the German northern flank - was now to be achieved by force for military, economic, and ideological reasons. The isolation of Finland, the re-activation of Leningrad's war industries, and the freeing of the entrances to the Baltic Sea were to be the prizes for the operation.

The first of these two battles comprised two phases, the attack against the German positions south of Lake Ladoga, and the subsequent attempt to roll up the new German positions from both flanks to free the outpost area of Leningrad once and for all. The first Russian attack (12 January to 9 February), launched from two sides - which was tactically correct, but whose objective was too limited - resulted in the withdrawal of the German positions. The weak German forces had neither the men nor the materiel to meet this mass attack. The execution of their original intent - never to let the German front settle down again once it had wavered - was denied the Russians; an eight-kilometer-wide corridor south of Lake Ladoga which was covered by German artillery fire in its entire width was the final result. To achieve this end, the Russians had employed twenty-nine divisions, thirteen brigades, and eighteen tank units during this first phase alone.[8]

The second phase (10 February to 5 April), which was also an attempt to unhinge the northernmost German salient from the deep flank, brought no appreciable success. A few hundred meters of ground, for which the attacker had paid dearly, remained in his hands. The losses of the Russian forces during this battle were again very high because of their inflexible combat tactics, a fact which has been mentioned previously. According to reliable data, the losses could be estimated at approximately 200,000 dead and wounded.

The superiority in personnel and materiel during this battle was without a doubt overwhelmingly on the side of the Russians. It would, therefore, be of interest to examine closer the reasons for the successful defense by the Germans. Three factors were decisive:

1. The system of relieving the troops.
2. The commitment of the artillery.
3. The terrain.

The "centrifugal pump" began to show its effect during the very first days of the battle. Battered German units were pulled out and committed again at a calm sector of the front and replaced by the unit which had been freed. One may be inclined to think that this is a solution for anyone without reserves. The difficulties encountered while carrying out such a maneuver, however, can only be realized by someone who is fully acquainted with the thousand exigencies and contingencies of a battle. Units are in danger of becoming quickly disorganized, promised relief does not arrive, relieved elements must be committed again 500 meters to the right or the left of the old battlefield to intercept a new attack, there are frictions at several places simultaneously; finally, improvisation is the order of the day. Sixteen German divisions were moved during this battle alone. Only two of these came from the adjacent Sixteenth Army; three units - without combat experience - were attached to the Eighteenth Army to relieve experienced divisions.[9]

The artillery must be credited with an equally large part in the successful defense. A remarkable artillery point of main effort was formed by recklessly stripping those front sectors which were not immediately affected by this battle; sufficient amounts of ammunition were available. As far as it was possible, the "group for heavy flat-trajectory fire," which had been committed against Leningrad was brought forward so that the number of pieces available increased further. An astonishingly flexible artillery command increased the effect of the fire by concentrating its guns at the respective points of main effort. On the whole, the artillery was employed to greatest and most successful advantage.

The third factor which aided the defense was the terrain. It was unsuitable for any type of warfare in the area southeast of Leningrad and Lake Ladoga. Swampy areas, extensive woods with dense underbrush, very few roads and highways, which forces all traffic into certain channels, are characteristic of this terrain. Tanks - even the Russian T-34's known for their cross-country mobility - lost their importance in this terrain; time calculations as far as the infantry is concerned were completely undependable. Even regular percussion fuses were in many cases (particularly north of Ssinjavino and Mga) useless because the shells sank into the swamps without exploding. What difficulties were encountered by the defense in this terrain and how it interfered with the proper functioning of the "centrifugal pump" does not need further illustration.

The description of the second battle south of Lake Ladoga (22 July-24 September 1943) has been omitted since it would be repetitious. The renewed attempt by the Russians to finally bring the northern salient of the German front to a collapse was also unsuccessful this time. The main effort of these battles centered on the only elevated terrain in the are, namely the hill at Ssinjavino. This hill had been attacked time and again, resulting in a great loss of men, while the successful defending units suffered at least the same number of casualties. The pattern of the battle resembled that of the previous struggle. The tactics of the defense, which had proven themselves earlier, were also adhered to in this case.

The Battle of Nevel (October-December 1943)

Toward the end of 1943, the main effort of the battle shifted to the southern flank of the army group. After their failure south of Lake Ladoga the Russians now made an attempt to push through into the Baltic area, along the boundary between Army Group Center and Army Group North, to roll up the front of Army Group North from the south.

The previous battles at the northern flank of the army group (described above) had required a great number of forces; other parts of the front, among them the right (southern) flank, had to be considerably weakened in favor of the point of main effort in the north. Thus, the XXXXIII Corps, with only three weak divisions, was committed directly north of the boundary of Army Group Center on a front of more than eighty kilometers; each division had thus to cover approximately twenty-seven kilometers. Considering the condition of the German divisions at that time and the extent of the front they had to cover, only very small local reserves could be detached and these only in very rare cases exceeded the strength of a company. Conditions at the adjacent unit, the northern flank of the Third Panzer Army (which belonged to Army Group Center) were just as unsatisfactory. There, at the left (northern) flank, the II Luftwaffe Field Corps[10] was committed, with three Luftwaffe Field divisions one next to the other. The Luftwaffe Field divisions had but limited combat value; they were composed of officers and men from the Luftwaffe and were well-armed, but had no experience and were insufficiently trained.

On 6 October 1943 the major Russian attack, which had been expected, although not on such a scale, was launched under these tactically very unfavorable conditions. This attack, in which weaker elements attacked the left flank of Army Group Center and in which the main thrust was directed against the southern flank of Sixteenth Army, succeeded immediately in opening a gap between the two army groups and, on the first day, the enemy advanced as far as Nevel and even beyond. Both army groups were in great danger; the breakthrough through the front line of both armies was a success, and the Russians prepared to envelop both flanks. But no matter how far the Russians immediately pivoted south and north after the breakthrough, they repeatedly encountered blocking positions and quickly brought-up German forces. Although the numerous German counterattacks failed to regain the lost ground and the gap could not be closed at first, the Russian troops which had broken through were tied down time and time again, and were unable to gain freedom of action.

After the *coup de main* against Nevel, in which the Russians surprisingly succeeded, the battle itself (which lasted three months) had three phases:

1. The renewed attempt by the Russians to break through the bastion of the German front northeast of Nevel and thus free the Velikie Luki-Nevel-Gorodok railway line.
2. The deep penetration of the Russians into the open flank of the German front to interrupt the important Idrizia-Novossokoniki supply route and later roll up the German front northward from the south.
3. The renewed attempt from two sides to effect a collapse of the bent German flank northwest of Nevel.

All three attempts, which had been undertaken with strong forces, were frustrated time and again by the German defenses, which were frequently organized in the nick of time.

On the German as well as the Russian side, the battle had marked characteristics. The Russian side showed a clear-cut tactical organization which heretofore had not been so apparent during attacks. The First Baltic Front,[11] consisting of two armies, was to envelop the northern flank of Army Group Center, while the Second Baltic Front, likewise consisting of two armies, had the identical mission as far as the southern flank of Army Group North was concerned.[12] In addition, the Russian Air Force maintained close and well-organized collaboration with the ground forces; almost all Russian attacks had been excellently supported by the air force, although the strength of the air forces committed was not commensurate with the actual successes achieved. (Experience had taught the German troops not to fear the Russian Air Force, because of its ineffectiveness; units which had been transferred to the East, after having fought the Western Allies, were even more unimpressed by the Russian Air Force.) The stubbornness with which the Russian command adhered to a decision once it had been made, even if the situation took an entirely different turn from what had been expected, was also characteristic of this battle. The Russian Third Shock Army, in particular, again and again repeated its attempts to outflank the German defenses in order to develop its forces in the enemy-free territory. The reason why this final objective was not reached was the rapid decrease in the fighting power of the attacking units, which suffered severe casualties, and the "muddy period"[13] which affected both men and materiel. The muddy period also hampered of course the German defense, but it was of still greater disadvantage to the attacking forces.

On the German side, the offensive conduct of the defensive was especially remarkable. As long as the northern flank of Army Group Center was still within reach, the plan to close the gap by means of an attack was adhered to in spite of unfavorable conditions. Although this repeatedly launched attack, which was necessarily carried out with insufficient troops, failed to reach its objective - just as numerous German counterattacks at other points did - the Russian attack thus lost a decisive amount of striking power. The defense itself had the same characteristics as other defensive battles: the "centrifugal pump" was again put into action, and other parts of the front had to be further weakened in favor of the southern flank. Again a great number of divisions were exchanged during the battle. In addition, individual panzergrenadier battalions, assault gun battalions, anti-aircraft batteries and the like were assembled and inserted in the ever-expanding defensive front.[14] Noteworthy, for instance, was the order which was issued by the army group on 2 November to Eighteenth Army to pull six battalions and two to three regimental staffs out of the front line and transfer them to Sixteenth Army. To free an entire divisions for this purpose was already an impossible task; one had to be satisfied with individual elements.

Rigid organization was also an outstanding feature on the German side. Shortly after the beginning of the battle, both flank corps were assigned to *Gruppe* "Loch" (name of the commanding general), which had been specifically organized for the purpose of coordinating the combat command.[15] This measure, frequently applied by the German command at points of main effort during battle, also proved itself to the fullest in this case. *Gruppe* Loch did not lose its grip on the situation in spite of the almost continuous crises, and it retained its capability of improvising.

The following figures are mentioned in order to show the extent of the battle: The German I Corps, which had to bear the brunt of the battle and to which seven divisions had been assigned in the course of the fighting, was opposed by two Russian armies, twenty-five rifle divisions, two rifle brigades, eleven independent tank units, two artillery divisions, and one mortar division, in addition to numerous GHQ artillery regiments. In the course of the battle, the attrition of these enemy units was extremely high; 305 Russian tanks were destroyed, more than 1,300 prisoners were taken, and the Russian losses in dead and wounded were estimated to amount to approximately 70,000 men.

When, at the end of December, the Russian striking power began to lose force, the German I Corps was withdrawn during the early part of January from its front salient protruding far south. A new front was established, and contact with Army Group Center was re-established by bending back its flank. Approximately eight kilometers of terrain, measured at its greatest width, had been given up. The German units had likewise suffered heavy casualties, but the breakthrough planned by the Russians had been prevented.

The Situation of the Army Group at the End of 1943

Although the Russians had been unable to carry out their intention during the battle at Nevel, as well as during previous major engagements, the German defensive successes had been paid for dearly. The local reserves had been used up to the last man, and the possibility of pulling additional units out of the front without considerably jeopardizing the cohesion at the front no longer existed. The divisions had dwindled, their fighting power had been reduced to the danger point. Although replacements from the Zone of the Interior, which were quite adequate, offered a certain compensation, the loss of combat-experienced soldiers and the strong intermixture with foreign (Latvian, Estonian, Spanish, and so forth) troops and inexperienced units represented a considerable reduction in fighting power. The situation is elucidated, just to mention one example, by the report of General of Artillery Georg Lindemann, the Commander of Eighteenth Army, to the army group, dated 16 November 1943:

"1. I report the following:

"a. Eighteenth Army has made available seven divisions, two battalions, artillery, Tiger tanks, mortars and assault guns since its victorious third defensive battle south of Lake Ladoga.

"b. In accordance with order # . . . . dated 15 November 1943, the 5th Mountain Division will also be transferred without replacement.

"c. By order of the *Führer* the army is to hold its present line. However, the army is no longer in a position to cope with the situation in case of strong enemy attacks.

"2. Request permission for a personal report to the *Führer* to acquaint him with the situation of the army and the consequences which the transfer of the 5th Mountain Division will have."

Such a report was not rare, and repeated at almost regular intervals. Actually, the overall situation of the army group had reached a dangerous point because of the transfer and consumption of troops, especially, since new enemy attacks had to be anticipated at any time. These could be launched not only at the former points of main effort, but also from the "Oranienbaum pocket," an island almost in the rear of the Eighteenth Army. For this reason the plan for an early withdrawal of the front gained more and more prominence. The army group and Hitler had already argued over this problem for quite some time. Since autumn 1943 a troop economizing line - the "Panther Line" - had been established in the rear area of the army group, which made use of Lake Peipus. This position was gradually nearing completion.

Opinions concerning the time at which this position was to be occupied varied greatly from the armies and the army group on the one hand, and the high command of the army group and OKH on the other hand. The request of the army group to be permitted to occupy this position late in autumn 1943 - which was prompted by the first Russian successes in connection with the battle at Nevel - and thus gain urgently needed reserves, was strongly rejected by Hitler. In December, however, new decisive measures had to be taken as a result of the situation.

On 30 December the commander-in-chief of the army group, Field Marshal Georg von Küchler, again requested permission to occupy the Panther Line. After the conclusion of the retreating movement, the army group would then have three divisions in reserve, and could also make eight divisions available to the OKH for employment at other fronts. In spite of this offer, which would have been beneficial to the overall situation, Hitler's misgivings (the isolation of Finland, the restoration of Leningrad's industries, the violation of his principle never to withdraw unless forced to do so) had again come to the fore so that a clear-cut decision could not be made at this time. The Russians, however, finally forced this decision several weeks later.

The occupation of the Panther Line had to be carried out under enemy action, particularly by the Eighteenth Army, and thus under considerably more unfavorable conditions. The fatal "too late," the most outstanding weakness of the German supreme command during the second half of World War II, again gained prominence. The foundation for the complete isolation of the army group, which occurred several months later, was already laid at this time.

The lessons learned during the battles described have been mentioned in the text. These lessons, however, must not be regarded as valid for all cases, because they are one-sided and based upon the "poor man's war" which Germany waged at that time. It is improbable that an armed force would be asked to fight the Russians again with such inadequate means. Such an attempt would probably be doomed to failure, as was the one undertaken during World War II. Only this lesson is generally valid: namely, that a war against Russia can only be fought with a definite superiority in men and materiel or, if sufficient manpower is lacking, the shortage should be compensated for by a corresponding superiority in materiel.

A special lesson taught by the fighting in 1943 was the increased value of the artillery in defense. The Germans utilized the artillery whenever other implements of war were lacking. The quick formation of a concentration of artillery; the uniform command of larger artillery units; close collaboration between air and ground reconnaissance and timely fire concentrations on the enemy attack while it was still in the process of developing; these were the basic principles for this way of utilizing the artillery, which was made possible by sufficient artillery ammunition.[16] The efficient employment of pieces assembled from the entire area of the Eighteenth Army in the course of the defensive battles south of Lake Ladoga and Leningrad, is particularly impressive. The Sixteenth Army, by comparison, had not been able to employ its artillery to the same extent and with the same effort. The reason for this was not only the lack of initiative to fully exploit the artillery's possibilities, but also the tying down and the belated release of the batteries south of Lake Ilmen, which had been concentrated there by order of OKH. Both armies suffered equally from lack of troops, and the strength of the enemy's attacks can likewise be regarded as almost equal. A study of the table provided in the notes will furnish the answer to the question of why the Eighteenth Army was successful in repulsing the enemy attacks almost without loss of territory, while the same success could be achieved by Sixteenth Army only after considerable terrain had been lost.[17]

The Operations in 1944

The operations of Army Group North during 1943 were followed by the fierce battles of 1944. In order to facilitate a proper evaluation and review of these operations as a whole, the following brief summary of the pertinent events is given.

As early as 15 January 1944, the Russians continued their attempt to destroy the northern flank of the German Eastern Front, and to advance in the direction of Narva and Riga. Due north of Lake Ilmen, the Russian attacks were directed against Novgorod and simultaneously against the northernmost front salient south of Leningrad as well as against the holding line of the "Oranienbaum pocket" south of Kronstadt. Owing to their numerical superiority in men and materiel, the Russians now succeeded in all three attacks; the German lines were pierced at several points and a wide gap developed between the Sixteenth and Eighteenth Armies. As a result, a coherent front no longer existed on 26 January.

Although the Russians failed in their attempts aimed at pocketing the individual combat groups, and although it was possible to close the gap at the flank of Sixteenth Army through the commitment of *Gruppe* Friessner - comprising five divisions - at the boundary, the destruction of the Eighteenth Army left the German command no other choice than withdrawal into the prepared Panther Line.[18] Only thus could the German command hope to prevent the destruction of the individual units and to organize a new coherent front line.

This time, Hitler could not possibly fail to realize the necessity of the withdrawal; on 15 February - several weeks too late - the order was signed to occupy the Panther Line. Luck, always the most essential factor in warfare, favored the German command; in this seemingly hopeless situation, the following four factors enabled the German command to still conduct a withdrawal, which, though it could not be called and orderly one, was carried out according to plan, and finally to occupy the Panther Line without suffering substantial losses in men and materiel.

     1. The northernmost flank of the army group - wheeled back from the point where the breakthrough had occurred toward the south and with its left flank anchored on the coast - was able to beat off all further Russian attacks, to conduct a fighting withdrawal and to reach the northern sector of the Panther Line, the Narva front, in good order. In the course of the subsequent operations, this northern sector of the front was organized as the independent *Gruppe* "Sponheimer" and, at a later

juncture, like the other two armies, was placed under the command of the army group as "*Armeeabteilung* Narva."[19]

2. The center of the army group, which had not been attacked as fiercely as the other sectors, conducted an orderly withdrawal toward Luga; it was able to beat off numerous Russian enveloping attacks.

3. The army group's split-up southern sector was adequately supported by *Gruppe* Friessner (group committed at the boundary).

4. The decisive factor, however, was the failure of the Russian command to realize the potentialities of the situation in time as well as the fact that its attempts to push into the open gaps in the German lines and to develop and destroy the individual combat groups were carried out either too late or with inadequate forces. German *kampfgruppen*, speedily organized in a makeshift manner, were able to frustrate nearly all of these attempts to envelop elements of the army group. On 1 March 1944, the Panther Line was occupied along almost its entire length and a withdrawal movement covering almost 300 kilometers had been carried out under the most difficult conditions. Once again, the operational intentions of the Russian command had been frustrated, and the command of the army group had gained time for the reorganization of its units.

Some data concerning the Panther Line, which so frequently is referred to in these pages, may be given here in order to provide the reader with an idea of the great length of time which was required for the construction of such a position, owing to the transportation and road conditions then prevailing in Russia.[20]

After determination of its course on the terrain, the construction of the position began on 7 September 1943; the most essential part of the work was completed toward the end of December 1943; however, the work, as it was planned according to the blueprints, was not quite finished by the time of the occupation of the position about the beginning of March 1944. The position could be organized only in a field-type manner; that is, without armored cupolas and with only a few concrete bunkers.

The length of the position was roughly 500 kilometers. Along a sector covering approximately 160 kilometers the positions was protected by Lake Peipus. For its development, the position was subdivided into several sectors which were provided with building material in accordance with their technical importance.

During the period from 7 September to 31 December 1943, the following installations were constructed in the position (figures in brackets refer to work still in progress on 31 December):

Tank obstacles: 37 kilometers
Wire entanglements: 250 (380) kilometers
Emplacements for machine guns,
Anti-tank guns, etc.: 1,345 (100) kilometers
Shelters: 5,460 (3,000) kilometers
Concrete shelters: 645 (180) kilometers
Steel shelters: 75 (40) kilometers
In addition, 13 (30) kilometers of roads and 1,160 (2,100) road bridges had been constructed or were under construction.

Toward the middle of November (to give an example) the following labor force was available for the construction work: approximately 30,000 workers recruited from the civilian population, 17,000 soldiers and 7,000 members of the "*Organization Todt*" (German construction organization into which technicians and men of older age classes were drafted).[21] There were in use at the time referred to above twenty-five concrete mixers, thirty-five excavators, and forty-five large-size plows. The lack of equipment as well as transportation difficulties prevented the employment of machines to a greater extent. The building material, principally wood (as far as it could not be obtained on the spot), had been shipped to the area in 8,000 railroad cars and 170 boats during the period from 7 September to 31 December 1943.

The communications net set up in the position provided wire communications down to the prospective command posts of the divisions; 2,260 kilometers of wire had been used for purpose.

Continuation of the Operations

The German command was not given much time to organize the defense of the Panther Line. As early as 4 March, only a few days after the occupation of the Panther Line, the Russians began their attacks against that position. Once more, the attacks were directed against the sector of the Eighteenth Army and, within that sector, particularly against the hilly terrain in the Pskov area and the salient pointing east. The German outpost lines were pushed back toward the main line of resistance. During the heavy fighting in March and April 1944, the Russians achieved several penetrations into the German positions; at some points the German lines were withdrawn in a flexibly conducted defense, but all Russian attempts to achieve a decisive breakthrough failed. The position proved its value, and facilitated the German defensive operations in an extremely effective manner.

Toward the middle of June, the Russians discontinued their attempts to break through the Panther Line and concentrated their attack forces in the area south of the sector held by the army group for action against an operational objective of major importance. As a result of this large-scale offensive against the northern sector of the adjacent Army Group Center, the position of Army Group North became untenable. The units of Army Group Center were destroyed within a few weeks. The execution of the plan of the Russian command - to tear open the German Eastern Front, to advance toward Riga and to pocket Army Group North - approached its final stage.

The command of the army group had to base its actions on the fact that, in the area hitherto held by Army Group Center, only isolated *kampfgruppen* were still attempting to stop the Russian breakthrough in individual encounters and that, therefore, the army group, with its three armies, had to rely solely on its own strength. The extension of the southern flank, which was now anchored on the Daugava River,[22] as well as the make-shift establishment of a thin defense line along the Daugava, were merely stopgap measures which could not be regarded as a final solution. However, in spite of repeated requests and presentations, Hitler was unable to reach a far-reaching operational decision through which the situation might have been restored. Much, though not everything, could have been saved at that juncture through a major and timely withdrawal. Instead, inefficient measures continued to be employed, but these measures - taken in a day-by-day basis - could not possibly eliminate the danger. Every day additional units were withdrawn from the northern flank, which hitherto had not been attacked, in order to extend the army group's southern flank, or to support the fighting remnants of the Third Panzer Army. The available means were inadequate. In August, the Russians drove forward in the area between the two army group sectors west of Riga, and reached the Gulf of Riga. For the first time, Army Group North was pocketed, its communications with the Zone of the Interior severed.

Toward the end of August, the army group succeeded in restoring these communications for a short period of time. Advancing from the west, weak armored forces, supported by the fire of the heavy guns of the heavy cruiser *"Prinz Eugen,"* broke through the Russian lines in the direction of Riga, while reorganized elements of the Third Panzer Army established loose contact with the army group's western sector in the area south of Jelgava, and once more blocked the Russian advance toward the coast of the Baltic Sea.

Meanwhile, the situation at the army group's northern flank deteriorated from day to day. The Russians pierced the German lines at several points; toward the end of August, Tartu was lost. *Armeeabteilung* Narva was in grave danger of being cut off and destroyed. Everything possible was done to convince Hitler that Estonia could no longer be held, particularly in view of the fact that, toward the beginning of September, the army group's northern flank too had become exposed as a result of the conclusion of the Finnish-Russian armistice.

However, even this decisive turn of events failed to induce Hitler to take the appropriate action as fast as the situation demanded it. The order to hold the line remained the army group's mission for the time being. In spite of Hitler's opposition, the army group's command had already made preparations for the evacuation of Estonia. Acting on orders issued by the army group, the troops started carrying out the first preparatory measures for the evacuation early in September. Toward the middle of September, the situation at the two most critical points, the Riga and Lake Virts areas, deteriorated to such extent that a splitting-up of the army group could no longer be prevented unless the withdrawal movement was started immediately; finally, a withdrawal toward a position east of Riga was authorized and began on 18 September. Again, the measures taken by the German command were inadequate. The suggestion of the army group command to abandon the Baltic area and to concentrate all available forces in East Prussia for the protection of the Zone of the Interior was not even taken into consideration.

The well-prepared withdrawal movement was carried out according to plan. Halting and fighting in the daytime and marching at night, the troops withdrew in exemplary order. Speed was the secret of the success. Although the units retreating from the Narva front had to cover nearly 400 kilometers, the new position east of Riga was occupied on 27 September - that is, within eleven days. It was not possible to carry out the evacuation of Estonia according to plan; however, the Navy, making use of every available craft, succeeded in evacuating more than 70,000 men, as well as 30,000 tons of goods from the ports of Tallinn and Paldiski.

However, the real purpose of the withdrawal, namely the freeing of forces for the launching of an attack against the Russian forces southwest of Riga in connection with the panzer units of the Third Panzer Army, had not been achieved. The Russians immediately attacked the new position so fiercely that it was necessary to commit all available forces in its defense. The evacuation of Riga was therefore accelerated. Toward the end of October, the army group abandoned Riga and continued the withdrawal movement toward the new "Courland Line." During these days the army group's communications with the Zone of the Interior were cut. The Russians broke through the German lines between Memel and Liepaja and reached the coast; the weak German forces stationed in that area were thrown back and the Third Panzer Army had to rally its forces in East Prussia.

As a result of this inevitable development of the situation, the "Courland Fortress" now came into being; both in length and width this area measured 150 kilometers. The distance between this area and the town of Memel, which was still defended, was only sixty kilometers; however, the isolation of the area became gradually tighter. The battle for East Prussia had begun, and the chances of bridging the distance between the pocketed Army Group North and Army Group Center - which was fighting in East Prussia - became increasingly dim. A front of more than 200 kilometers had to be defended, and a coastal front covering more than 300 kilometers had to be guarded.

The 1944 operations, which have been dealt with here in a summary manner, are thoroughly discussed in the following parts of the study, so as to enable the reader to follow the course of the individual phases of the operations. These reports not only may be regarded as excellent accounts of the events, but also serve as a textbook for the study of measures employed in defensive operations with inadequate forces against a superior enemy. Attention is drawn to the valuable reports based on personal experiences which are attached to the individual parts. However, it is necessary once more to point to the fact that these experiences were gained during a specific phase in the development of Russian combat, and that they are applicable only in a situation such as faced by the German Wehrmacht, which - numerically inferior in men and materiel - had to conduct operations against the Russians, who were able to draw freely from an abundance of manpower and materiel. In the final phases of the war, the Russian command displayed a higher degree of flexibility, as was evidenced by the manner in which its offensive operations were conducted during the last months of the war.

However, the experiences of the German Wehrmacht described in these pages clearly proves that forces which are considerably numerically inferior are able to successfully resist a numerically superior enemy as long as the difference in comparative strengths does not assume such proportions as to render continuation of the operations absolutely impossible for the inferior side. This lesson, as well as the tactics employed in defensive operations in the Russian area, are likely to remain applicable. The basic tactics employed by the Russians in offensive operations are also unlikely to undergo major changes; these tactics will merely be modified in a constant development which will continuously produce new and improved variations.

The Last Phase and Concluding Remarks

Soon after the "Courland Fortress" front had been established, it was attacked by strong Russian forces. The Russian command was disturbed by the fact that Army Group North (re-named "Army Group Courland" in January 1945) threatened the flank of the Russian forces employed in the offensive against East Prussia and the General Government of Poland. Repeated requests of the army group command demanding the launching of an attack from Courland along the coast of the Baltic Sea in the direction of East Prussia failed to receive consideration even at this juncture. All plans prepared and submitted for this purpose were rejected.

In fierce battles, known as the "Battles for Courland," the army group's divisions repulsed continuous Russian attacks. It was not until March that the Russian attacks diminished in fierceness. The commitment of the forces in these attacked was no longer warranted in view of the development of the general situation. With the German surrender, on 9 [sic] May 1945, this army group also ceased to exist.

In accordance with the war situation prevailing at the time under review, the accounts of events given in these pages deal with the defensive operations and withdrawal movements of the German Wehrmacht. However, many offensive actions are also dealt with in these accounts; particular reference is made to these accounts because the significance of these offensive actions as part of the large-scale defensive operations is not very conspicuous. These counterattacks on a minor, but also on a larger scale, which were carried out everywhere along the entire front, did not result in the scattering of forces. However, they could not be coordinated in a joint offensive operation on a large scale because the situation never permitted the establishment of an adequate focal point.

Nevertheless, these attacks constituted the most essential parts of the German defense. Even when they did not result in the recapture of lost terrain, they served to wear down enemy strength, and deprived his attacks of their vigor. Actually, the skillful commitment and the flexible command of the artillery and anti-tank weapons, as well as rapidly launched counterattacks, constituted the backbone of the defense.[23] In cases where it was possible to commit a panzer unit in these counterattacks, such action always was particularly effective. The commitment of adequate air forces would have substantially facilitated the defense against the Russian attacks, but such air forces were not available. However, in modern warfare the air force will be not only the principal arm in offensive operations, but also the backbone of the defense.

This comprehensive account, covering more than two years of warfare, shows that in spite of all difficulties, which can hardly be overrated, the German command, with well-disciplined troops of high fighting morale at its disposal, was able to carry on defensive operations as long as this was humanly possible. The fact that the orders issued by the supreme command went far beyond anything that could possibly be accomplished is not the fault of the front-line commanders; the inevitable final collapse of the defense was the result of Hitler's limitless political aspirations.

NOTES

[1]Note in original: "First and Third Main-Attack [Shock] Armies, Second Guard Army and Eleventh, Twenty-seventh, Thirty-fourth and Fifty-third Armies."

[2]Note in original: "Second Main-Attack [Shock] Army, Fourth, Eighth, Twenty-third, Forty-second, Fifty-second, Fifty-fourth, Fifty-fifth, Fifty-ninth and Sixty-seventh Armies."

[3]Here von Natzmer may well have underestimated the number of partisans operating in the Leningrad area. John Erickson estimated that there were at least 35,000 active paritsans in ten bands in January 1944; this figure is also echoed by German sources. The number appears to have been derived from official Russian sources identifying thirteen distinct brigade organizations. John Erickson, *The Road to Berlin, Continuing the History of Stalin's War with Germany* (Boulder CO: Westview, 1983), p. 173; S. P. Platonov, *Bitva za Leningrad, 1941-1944* (Moscow : Ministry of Information, 1964), pp. 273-274. Wolfgang Schumann and Olaf Gröhler, eds., *Deustchland im zweiten Weltkrieg,* 6 volumes, (Köln: Pahl-Rugenstein Verlag, 1981-1985), V: p. 595.

[4]Note in original: "Rshev, a front salient of Army Group Center protruding toward the north, approximately 200 km southeast of Demjansk and 250 km east of Nevel."

[5]Permission from Hitler to withdraw the twelve divisions in the Demjansk pocket had more to do with the Stalingrad debacle at the far end of the Russian front than events around Leningrad. Earl F. Ziemke, *Stalingrad to Berlin, The German Defeat in the East* (Washington DC: Center for Military History, 1968), pp. 111-113.

[6]Tactical responsibility for the conduct of the retreat fell upon General of Infantry Paul Laux, commander of the II Corps. Among the divisions involved in the withdrawal—either inside the salient or holding open its neck—were the 12th, 30th, 32nd, 58th, 122nd, 123rd, 126th, 254th, 290th, and 329th Infantry, 5th Jaeger, 18th Motorized, and 21st Luftwaffe Field Divisions. Paul Carell, *Scorched Earth, The Russian-German War, 1943-1944* (New York: Ballantine, 1966), p. 300.

[7]Literally "no matter," or "it doesn't matter."

[8]Natzmer's narrative is here should be considered a secondary source—he was not present during the vents he is describing—and he tends to present the results in overly favorable terms. For example, he omits any mention of the near-annihilation of *Kampfgruppe* Hühner, under the command of Lieutenant General Werner Hühner of the 61st Infantry Division. The German tactical commander during these operation was General of Infantry Carl Hilpert of the LIV Corps. Carell, Scorched Earth, pp. 259-282.

[9]This is a reference to the arrival of the Luftwaffe Field Divisions.

[10]Note in original: "Fighting as ground force with the Army."

[11]Note in original: "Russian equivalent of 'army group.'"

[12]Popov's First Baltic Front attacked with the Forty-third and Thirty-ninth Armies, keeping the Eleventh Guards Army in reserve. The Second Baltic Front (Yeremenko), employed the Third and Fourth Shock Armies in the main attack, supported by the Sixth Guards Army. Ziemke, *Stalingrad to Berlin*, pp. 196-199.

[13]Note in original: "Muddy period—the rainy season in autumn."

[14]Natzmer glosses over the point that Hermann Göring, embarassed at the rout of the 2nd Luftwaffe Field Division, funneled a significant number of flak batteries and over 600 aircraft into the area. Albert Seaton. *The Russo-German War* (New York: Praeger, 1971). p. 389.

[15]The commander was fifty-seven-year-old General of Artillery Herbert Loch, then commander of the XXVIII Corps, and later the commander of the Eighteenth Army, and one of the authors of this volume.

[16]Note in original: "In comparing the consumption of ammunition of both armies it should be borne in mind that the Eighteenth Army had been particularly lucky because of the assigning of a special artillery group which was to take targets in Leningrad under fire. This heavy artillery especially affected the consumption by tons because of the weight of its ammunition. Besides, the great range of this artillery facilitated its bringing up for participation in the defensive battles east of Leningrad."

[17]This emphasis on artillery as the backbone of the defense is further supported by the extensive and systematic use made of captured weapons by the German Army in Russia throughout the war. In mid-January 1944, army group records reveal the following statistics concerning the Soviet heavy mortars and field pieces placed into the line:

Type	Eighteenth Army	Sixteenth Army
Light Field Pieces	54	229
(75mm, 105mm)		
Anti-tank Guns (76.2mm)	15	43
Medium Field Pieces	36	44
(122mm-152/155mm)		
Light Mortars (77mm)	65	46
Heavy Mortars	—	26
(280mm, 305mm)		
Totals:	150	387

Source: *Heeresgruppe Nord Ia Kreigsgliederung*, T-311, Reel 70, 16 January 1944; National Archives, Washington DC.

[18]Von Natzmer's reference to the "destruction" of the Eighteenth Army is a bit severe, although the retreat from the line of 14 January could hardly be characterized as anything other than a devastating defeat. Of twenty-one divisions and brigades in the Eighteenth Army at the beginning of the Soviet offensive, eight were reduced to *kampfgruppen*, and two were destroyed outright. Schumann and Gröhler, *Deustchland im zweiten Weltkrieg*, V: p. 70.

[19]Note in original: "A reinforced corps, commanded by a Corps commander with a Corps Staff."

[20]The Panther Line was completed under the command of Major General Erich Abberger, commander of the 3d Engineer Staff. Abberger, who had served as a senior engineer officer in Army Group North since 1941. He was responsible for

the design of many of the linear defenses which stymied the Russians outside Novgorod for two years. He is also interesting in having been one of the few senior officers during the first wave of mass murders of Jews by the *Einsatzgruppen* in 1941 to have filed a formal complaint with his superiors. Abberger survived the war, was captured by the Americans, and wrote several manuscripts for the military history series, including MS#D-076. An Army Engineer in Russia (1942). Wolf Keilig, *Das Deutsche Heer*, 3 volumes, (Frankfurt: Podzun Verlag, 1958), III: 211/p.2; Gerald Fleming, *Hitler and the Final Solution* (Berkeley: University of California, 1984), pp 81-86.

[21]The best concise history of Organization Todt is found in Nigel Thomas, Carlos Caballero Jurado, and Simon McCouaig, *Wehrmacht Auxiliary Forces* (London: Osprey, 1992), pp. 15-22.

[22]This is the German spelling of the Dvina River; German spellings for German and Russian locations have been retained throughout, for the sake of consistency.

[23]One of the areas which the authors of this study pass over without much comment is the relative strength of the German Army in terms of the anti-tank guns. The following table represents the numbers of towed anti-tank guns in Army Group North at the beginning of the Soviet offensive in January 1944:

Unit	Anti-tank guns
18th Army	
III SS Panzer Corps	
11th SS PG	19
4th SS Brig.	11
61st Inf.	17
9th LWF	15
10th LWF	11
Corps troops	23
Corps total:	96
L Corps	
126th Inf.	15
170th Inf.	15
215th Inf.	20
Corps troops	64
Corps total:	115
LIV Corps	
11th Inf.	24

24th Inf.	23
225th Inf.	18
Corps troops	17
Corps total:	82
XXVI Corps	
227th Inf.	16
212th Inf.	15
Corps troops	8
Corps total	39
XXVIII Corps	
21st Inf.	14
121st Inf.	23
12th LWF	9
13th LWF	12
KG 4th SS PG	10
Corps total:	68
XXXVIII Corps	
2nd SS Lat. Brig.	—
28th Jgr.	16
1st LWF	15
Corps troops	5
Corps total:	36
Army troops:	25
Army total:	461
16th Army	
X Corps	
30th Inf.	18
8th Jgr.	14
21st LWF	8
Corps total:	40
II Corps	
93rd Inf.	—
218th Inf.	10
331st Inf.	14
Corps total:	24
XXXXIII Corps	
15th SS	—
23rd Inf.	16

69th Inf.	8
83rd Inf.	26
205th Inf.	8
Corps troops	9
Corps total:	67
VIII Corps	
58th Inf.	27
81st Inf.	17
263rd Inf.	18
329th Inf.	19
Corps troops	8
Corps total:	89
I Corps	
32nd Inf.	27
122nd Inf.	19
132nd Inf.	11
Gr. Jeckeln	12
Gr. Gottberg	—
Corps total:	69
Army troops	24
Army total	303
Army Group reserves	
388th Field Training	—
207th Sec.	6
281st Sec.	17
285th Sec.	12
290th Inf.	22
Reserve total:	57
Army Group grand total:	821

These figures represent 40mm (although very few of them), 75mm, and 88mm towed anti-tank guns, not including assault guns: a "division slice" of 19.65 anti-tank guns per division. Admittedly, this strength was below the organizational assignments, which varied from 36-48, depending on which table the particular division was established; but it should be noted that during March 1944 the average divisional anti-tank strength in Army Group South was only 8.2. In other words, the anti-tank strength of Army Group North relative to the Red Army in its front was far higher than the other army groups in Russia. *Heeresgruppe Nord, Zustand der Divisionen,* 19 December 1943, *Heeresgruppe Nord,* Weekly Report of Armored Strength, 10 January 1944, T-311, Reel 73; Alex Buchner, *The German Infantry Handbook,*.

CHAPTER 2

The Operations of the Sixteenth Army During the First Half of 1944 to the Occupation of the Panther Line

Paul Hermann

The Withdrawal Actions up to the End of February 1944

Upon the conclusion of the fierce fighting for Nevel, and following the subsequent defensive action up to December 1943 - conducted to frustrate the attempt at a breakthrough undertaken by the Russians on both sides of the boundary between Army Groups Center and North - the Sixteenth Army's southern flank already occupied positions west of the Panther Line along a line extending from a point east of Polotzk up to a point east of Pustochka. The center and northern sectors of the Sixteenth Army continued to hold the positions they had occupied during the preceding year.

The entire length of the Sixteenth Army's front ran for roughly 500 kilometers. Under the command of six corps headquarters, a total of twenty infantry divisions and two police units were employed.[1]

Composition of Sixteenth Army (beginning at the right):

I Corps (width of sector 90 kilometers):
122d Infantry Division, elements of 22d and 87th Infantry Divisions (latter not ready for employment), Police *Gruppe* von Gottberg, 132d Infantry Division, Police *Gruppe* Jeckeln.[2]

VII Corps (width of sector 85 kilometers):
58th, 81st and 329th Infantry Divisions.

XXXXIII Corps (width of sector 75 kilometers):
331st, 93d, 218th and 290th Infantry Divisions.[3]

X Corps (width of sector 160 kilometers):
21st Luftwaffe Field Division, 8th Jaeger (light infantry) Division, 30th Infantry Division.

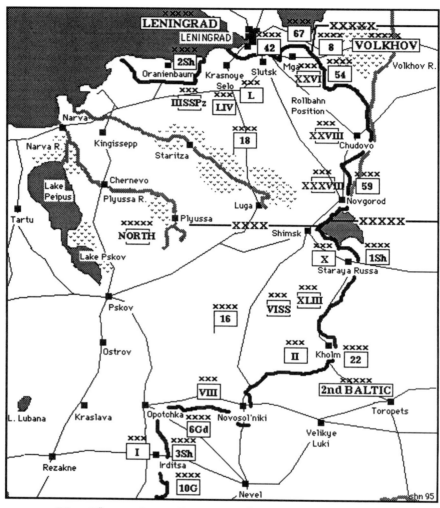

Map Three: Army Group North, 14 January 1944

Behind the left flank of the XXXXIII Corps, the headquarters of VI SS "Volunteer" Corps, with the 15th SS Latvian Waffen Grenadier Division, was kept as a supporting force.[4] No reserves were available except the small local reserve forces that the divisions in the front line had themselves formed.

The fierce fighting from October 1943 to the end of the year had taxed to the utmost the strength of both sides. As a result of reckless employment of units, the Russians had suffered staggering losses in men and materiel. This alone was sufficient to force them to temporarily discontinue the operations, apart from local attacks. However, on the basis of intelligence reports concerning the enemy intentions, it was to be expected that the breakthrough attempts aiming at a thrust into the Baltic countries would be continued after rehabilitation of the attack units. It was intended to coordinate this thrust, which was to be conducted approximately in the area on both sides of the boundary between Army Groups Center and North in the general direction of Daugavpils, with an enveloping attack to be launched simultaneously from Leningrad against the northern flank of Army Group North. The reorganization and rehabilitation of the First Baltic Front (comprising the Forty-third and Eleventh Guard Armies and the Fourth Shock Army) for this purpose in the areas in front of the southern sector of the Sixteenth Army became evident.

The strength of the German troops, which had been engaged in ceaseless combat operations for several months and were experiencing their third Russian winter, was also taxed to the utmost. The positions occupied by them - particularly in the southern sector of the Sixteenth Army - were inadequately organized and located on unfavorable terrain. The German command fully realized that, in view of the condition of the troops and the positions, it would not be able to ward off renewed Russian attacks on a major scale unless it was reinforced by the assignment of combat-worthy units and adequate reserves. Headquarters of Sixteenth Army had repeatedly requested that this army should be withdrawn along its entire sector to the prepared Panther Line. The request had been supported by the headquarters of the army group. If the request had been granted, the sector of Sixteenth Army alone would have been shortened by roughly 250 kilometers - that is, half of the width of its entire sector at that time. Thus at least four or five divisions would have been freed and made available as reinforcements for the southern sector of the army and as reserves. The requests submitted by the Field Marshal von Küchler concerning withdrawal to the Panther Line and the authorization to order such a withdrawal were brusquely rejected by Hitler. The assignment remained unchanged, and read as follows: "The operations will be conducted along the positions occupied at the present time; every inch of ground will be defended."

Since the beginning of January 1944 it had become increasingly evident that a renewed Russian attack on a major scale, with the point of main effort opposite the right sector of the Sixteenth Army and on both sides of the boundary of the army group's sector, was imminent. The activity of the partisan groups operating behind the front line, as well as the constant air traffic from the enemy-held area to these partisan groups, became very lively.

On 14 January 1944, the Russians launched the expected large-scale attack with strong massed forces. Employing great masses of artillery, concentrated armor and close-support air groups, the enemy jumped off in the area due south of the boundary of the army group's sector as well as in the direction of Vitebsk and against the sector west and northwest of Velikie Luki, while simultaneously advancing in the sector of the Eighteenth Army north of Lake Ilmen, near Novgorod and from the Leningrad area. In a fierce struggle, the adjacent Third Panzer Army was able to hold Vitebsk and thus to prevent a thrust into the southern flank of the Sixteenth Army. The Sixteenth Army succeeded in holding its positions, except for some minor local penetrations which were sealed off. However, owing to the destruction of the Eighteenth Army near Novgorod - as well as in the Leningrad area - the northern flank of the Sixteenth Army was greatly endangered. The inevitable result was the shifting of forces from the Sixteenth Army to support the troops fighting in the Eighteenth Army area. Since, in the Sixteenth Army sector, the point of main effort was near this army's southern flank, which was continuously attacked, and since - on the other hand - a gap threatened to develop between the Sixteenth and Eighteenth Armies as a result of the enemy thrust of north of Lake Ilmen in the general direction of Pskov, headquarters Army Group North inserted *Gruppe* Friessner here to cover the area of the boundary. The Sixteenth Army transferred to *Gruppe* Friessner the X Corps with 15th SS Latvian Waffen Grenadier Division, 21st Luftwaffe Field Division, 30th Infantry Division and 8th Jaeger (light infantry) Division. In addition, the 58th Infantry Division had to be released from the VIII Corps area and the bulk of the GHQ anti-tank units and the GHQ motorized artillery, as well as nearly all construction units, had to be shifted to the Eighteenth Army. Moreover, the Sixteenth Army also had to withdraw the bulk of the police units of Police *Gruppen* von Gottberg and Jeckeln from the front line and employ them in the communications zone in actions against the partisans. Thus the forces engaged in the task of halting the Russian onslaught were substantially weakened in a critical situation.[5]

In view of the critical situation of Army Group North, which was confronted with the ever-growing threat of being split up, Field Marshal von Küchler renewed his request for authorization to withdraw to the Panther Line. Again this request was rejected. Field Marshal von Küchler was relieved from his post. On 31 January 1944, Colonel General Walter Model assumed the command of Army Group North.

At first, General Model attempted to carry out the order demanding the defense of every inch of ground. For this purpose, far-reaching plans were laid concerning the construction of tactical rear and switch positions, as well as roads; however, owing to the lack of construction units, only a very small part of that project could be carried out. However, the events in the sector of the Eighteenth Army, which was engaged in a hopeless struggle in the wooded and swampy terrain around Luga, finally made the decision to withdraw to the Panther Line imperative. The authorization for the start of this movement was granted effective 15 February 1944.

The main task of the Sixteenth Army, which had stripped its front in the area between Cholm and Lake Ilmen to a far-reaching extent while engaged in fierce defensive combat east and northeast of Pustochka, was the holding of its own positions in order thus to cover the withdrawal movement of the Eighteenth Army to the Panther Line and to secure that army's southern flank. The German command relied solely on mobile infantry reserves, which were kept in readiness, and on motorized anti-tank units and GHQ artillery.

On 22 February 1944 the Sixteenth Army also started a systematic withdrawal to the Panther Line. Cholm, a town which had been fiercely fought over during the winter and in the spring of 1943, and Staraya Russa, which had be successfully defended in numerous battles since 1941, were evacuated. The withdrawal movement was carried out along several withdrawal routes without enemy interference and, toward the beginning of March 1944, the Sixteenth Army was entrenched along its entire sector in the well-organized and tactically favorable Panther Line.[6] Along a front line covering roughly 250 kilometers, the army was disposed as follows:

I Corps:
205th and 87th Infantry Divisions and elements of the 132d Infantry Division; the 281st Security Division was stationed to provide security in the town of Polotzk, which had been declared a "fortified locality."

X Corps:
290th, 263d, 24th and 81st Infantry Divisions.

II Corps:
329th Infantry Division and 28th Jaeger (light infantry) Division.
L Corps:
93d and 216th Infantry Divisions, 13th Luftwaffe Field Division, elements of 69th and 132nd Infantry Divisions.
VI SS Corps:
15th and 19th SS Latvian Waffen Grenadier Divisions.

Until the establishment of a stable front, the individual divisions were not able to make forces available as reserves beyond the approximate strength of one reinforced regiment.

On 27 February 1944, headquarters of the army was withdrawn to Valnavn. While these withdrawal movements were carried out, the enemy advanced, but in part only hesitantly and very cautiously. His movements were considerably hampered as a result of the destruction of the communications and sheltering facilities in the evacuated area, which had to be carried out for tactical reasons. From statements made by prisoners and deserters, it was evident that the losses in men and material sustained by the Russians in the course of the preceding operations had again been heavy; an early renewal of enemy mass attacks was therefore not anticipated. This opinion seemed to be justified also in view of the fact that, immediately after the occupation of the Panther Line, the muddy period set in, rendering large-scale movements in the combat area impossible.

The Defensive Fighting on the Panther Line from March to June 1944

On the Panther Line, which proved to be a tactically well-organized and technically well-prepared position, the German forces were able to recover very speedily. No fighting of operational importance took place in the sector of the Sixteenth Army during the months from March to May inclusive, except for some local scouting raids carried out by the enemy and local enemy attacks launched to improve his positions (capture of important observation points and the like).

After the end of May, however, Russian preparations for a large-scale attack could again be observed. Statements made by prisoners and deserters indicated that the enemy units were being rehabilitated. The reconnaissance activity became increasingly lively. From the German positions, it was possible to observe detachments being guided into positions. Major units could also be seen training close behind the front, where they made use of artillery, tanks, and live ammunition. In spite of the excellent camouflage, an art in which the Russians are masters, radio intelligence revealed with ever-increasing clearness the organization and bringing up of new units. Headquarters, Sixteenth Army, as well as Headquarters, Army Group North, fully realized that the large-scale attack which the enemy was expected to launch soon would strike in particular at the sector of Army Group Center, but at the same time at parts of the sector held by Army Group North. Here, indications pointed to the sectors on both sides of the boundary between Army Groups Center and North, the Sixteenth Army's left wing in the area northeast of Opotchka and the Pskov area as the prospective points of main effort. Toward the middle of June 1944, the rehabilitation of personnel and materiel of the Sixteenth Army was completed; fourteen divisions were employed in the front line and two divisions held in reserve.[7] The supply situation could be regarded as very favorable.

Experience

Command

Since the beginning of 1942, the initiative in conduct of operations in the northern sector of the Eastern Front had shifted more and more to the enemy, and the operations of Army Group North had been restricted to purely defensive actions. During 1943 the development of the enemy situation and reports received from "reliable sources"[8] revealed clearly that the Russians would soon also launch a large-scale attack in the northern sector with the following objectives: relief of beleaguered Leningrad and subsequent destruction of Army Group North; followed by a thrust through the Baltic countries into the deep flank of the entire Eastern Front, aiming at bringing about its collapse. In order to be able effectively to counteract such an operation and to spare manpower, Army Group North had repeatedly requested the organization of an operationally and tactically favorable rear position and the authorization to make the decision concerning occupation. Since Hitler was of the opinion that the existence of an organized position in the rear area would adversely affect the will of the troops and the command to put up stubborn resistance in the fight for their present position, this request was entirely disregarded in the fight for their present position, this request was entirely disregarded at first. It was not until Summer 1943 that he gave his approval for the organization of the Panther Line, but the right to order a withdrawal to that position, however, he reserved.

In view of previous experiences according to which the decisions of Hitler usually were made too late, Field Marshal Küchler, in agreement with the Commanders-in-Chief of the armies, began with the organization of the Panther Line as approved by higher headquarters, and simultaneously also with preparations for a possible withdrawal to that position. The principal reason for this was the fact that the withdrawal of a battle front toward a position in the rear area under enemy pressure constitutes one of the most difficult operations. This is true particularly when forces which are overstrained and weakened as a result of losses in men and material face an enemy with superiority in armor and air forces.

The task is difficult even in a theater of operations with a good road net such as found in Western Europe; it is nearly impossible, however, to carry out such a task in the vast spaces of Russia, where the friendly troops are confined to the few existing roads, while the enemy - thanks to his numerical superiority, his better winter equipment, and his familiarity with prevailing conditions - is able to move also outside the normal communications routes and thus to arrive in the area to be controlled earlier than the friendly forces. If, moreover, a disorganized stream of refugees moving along the paths and roads clogs up defiles and localities, the conduct of operations is made extremely difficult and sometimes even impossible. The withdrawal would then turn into a rout, the combat morale is bound to decrease, and the destruction of the troops and the loss of weapons and equipment would be the inevitable result. Precautionary measures had to be taken against such dangers.

The essential measures taken for this purpose consisted of the following orders:

1. Orientation of headquarters personnel (corps and divisions) and combat troops (particularly artillery and anti-tank units) into their prospective new sectors.
2. Improvement and marking of the generally inadequate road net (in the operational zones of the individual corps at least one through-road and, if possible, one for each division).
3. Preparation of intermediate positions, to be organized in a makeshift manner, on both sides of the withdrawal routes.
4. Preparation of the thorough destruction of all communication routes between the positions, sheltering facilities which could be of use to the enemy - airdrome installations, railroad stations, and so forth.
5. Removal of all equipment no longer useful to the troops (particularly vehicles).[9]

6. Removal of all not vitally needed supplies from the depots located between the positions.

7. Establishment of small supply dumps with stocks of ammunition, rations, and fuel between the positions in order as far as possible to restrict traffic to one direction during the evacuation of the withdrawal action.

8. Creation of a scorched-earth area extending several kilometers in front of the Panther Line.

9. Evacuation of the sick and wounded to new establishments located far behind the Panther Line.

10. Development of a dense signal communication network.

11. Preparation for evacuation of the civilian population, since this usually turns into a disorganized stream of refugees clogging up the roads at the start of a withdrawal movement (organization of collecting points on roads and railroads).

12. Establishment of receiving centers for the civilian population behind the Panther Line with facilities to feed and shelter refugees and give them medical aid.

13. Determination and procurement of the rolling stock require for the troops and the civilian population.

For the preparation and execution of these measures, army headquarters organized a special staff headed by the chief of staff. The execution of the measures carried out in the field was conducted by an appropriate staff headed by a commanding general, who was relieved of other duties. Close cooperation between the Army Rear Area Commander (Korück 501) and the Rear Area Commander, Army Group North was ensured. Later, these precautionary measures proved decisive for systematic execution and success of the withdrawal movements toward the Panther Line in the zone of Sixteenth Army.

In the course of the withdrawal movements, the command benefitted time and again from the fact that it had kept in readiness the necessary tactical reserves, made up of companies equipped with great numbers of anti-tank weapons. The rear guards, also, were equipped with mobile anti-tank weapons; some tanks or assault guns were attached to them for the execution of counterthrusts.[10] In principle, operations were to be conducted aggressively. It was of particular importance to provide the rear guards with radio equipment in order to enable the command to conduct the tactical withdrawal movements in a rigidly synchronized manner.

Both organization and tactical movements were conducted according to a time schedule. Only thus was it possible to prevent a breakthrough by rapidly pursuing enemy armor or motorized artillery.

Impression and Experiences Regarding the Conduct of Operations by the Russian Command

Command

In the course of the 1943 operations and, increasingly so, during the first half of 1944, it was seen that the enemy - who continued to throw his infantry units into battle regardless of losses - attempted to push the German lines back and to achieve success by committing numerically superior forces in a small sector of the front. His attacks, whether he launched local thrusts or attacks along a wide front, were always preceded by an unusually heavy preparatory fire from all ground weapons.

Characteristic of the reckless manner in which the Soviet command conducted operations was the fact that sometimes exhausted divisions were kept in the front line, their remnants rigidly organized, and had to continue the fight - frequently together with fresh troops which had been moved up, until they were bled white. If the reserves were not available, the enemy did not hesitate to strip adjacent sectors to a great extent.

For the purpose of piercing the enemy main line of resistance and the main defensive area, the rifle divisions were first committed; they received the strongest artillery and air support. Only after a penetration of the front line had been achieved, were major tank units committed in the task of advancing through the gap in the enemy line toward operational objectives. Infantry moved with makeshift transportation was brought up close behind to hold the ground gained. The tank units usually were accompanied by numerous self-propelled guns, anti-tank weapons, and strong anti-aircraft batteries. While the tank forces carried out their thrust into the deep rear, the infantry wheeled toward both sides in order to roll up the main line of resistance from the flanks and, if possible, to destroy the enemy forces through an enveloping attack. All these operations were supported by the continuous commitment of close support air units in bombing and strafing missions. Observation of the employment of the Soviet air forces, which frequently was not coordinated with the ground action, often revealed the enemy's operational intentions prematurely.

The enemy's disregard of the possibility that his advanced elements might be cut off was remarkable; on the other hand, he always attempted to prevent the destruction of endangered forward elements by the reckless commitment of additional forces. If the Bolshevists were forced to assume the defensive, they put up tenacious resistance in their positions. Rapid organization of the anti-tank defence lines, in front of which many a German counterattack came to grief, was particularly noteworthy.

Infantry

The combat efficiency of the infantry was definitely not above average. The brutal measures employed by the Soviet command in driving the attack units forward frequently created the erroneous impression that the troops were imbued with a fighting morale which actually did not exist in most of the units. This became particularly evident when, in the course of the operations, the infantry could no longer be rigidly controlled by the command, and the troops had to accomplish their assigned missions as isolated combat groups or even as individual fighting men. In defensive action the enemy put up very stubborn resistance. This was evident particularly in his counterthrust, which usually were launched rapidly.

Offensive operations on a major scale were preceded by intensive training. This training, which was conducted in the form of maneuvers in which all arms participated, frequently took place in the zone close behind the front line; therefore it could be observed from the German positions and taken under fire. In numerous instances, the Soviets did not pay too much attention to this interference, and seemed to regard it merely as a realistic representation of the enemy.

Artillery

Through the employment of strong massed artillery in a narrow sector, the enemy decimated the German forces - the infantry components of which were weak - in their positions, which lacked depth and thus usually succeeded in bringing about a tactical penetration or breakthrough.

Prior to the launching of major offensive operations, the Russians camouflaged the build-up of their artillery primarily by reducing the activity of that arm and by moving the artillery into firing positions only at night time; reliable information could therefore be obtained only through aerial photographs, which were compared with previous pictures. Shortly before the start of the attack, however, the artillery fire increased. Sometimes the moving up of batteries in great numbers and the adjustment fire, particularly of the heavy batteries, could be observed through ground observation.

Generally the Russian artillery command lacked flexibility. This became evident particularly through its inability to lend effective support to the infantry in the advanced stages of an attack, and to smash German counterthrusts. The Russian artillery was incapable of taking the German artillery under systematic fire.

Tanks

The tank units employed in offensive operations, like the artillery, were concentrated in the respective front sectors only a short time before the launching of a large-scale attack, usually as late as the night preceding the jump-off. They were employed against operational objectives located deep in the rear of the German lines.

The tanks committed in direct support of the infantry served primarily as mobile artillery and as anti-tank guns.

Air Force

From the fall of 1943, close-support units and bomber formations were employed in the support of ground attack to a considerably increased extent. Nearly all offensive actions, both those of a local nature and those on an operational scale, were supported by missions flown on a continuous basis by close-support planes and bombers. Almost invariably in such cases, only anti-aircraft guns were used in defense, while the employment of fighters for this purpose was prohibited.

Major offensive operations were preceded by a lively air traffic to the Soviet partisans operating behind German lines; at night time this traffic, carried out partly by cargo-carrying gliders, served to provide partisan units with supplies, in the day time to support them in their guerilla activities.

Shortly before the launching of large-scale attacks, as well as in the course of these operations, the Russian air forces engaged in widespread nuisance raids in the area immediately behind the German lines. These raids were directed against localities, railroad stations and road junctions; usually, however, only little damage was caused by them. Generally it can be stated that even the large-scale employment of Russian air forces failed to produce decisive results.

NOTES

[1] For a more complete organization of the army, compiled from the *Kriegtagebuch* of the Army Group Operations Officer, see Appendix.

[2]The strength of the two *Gruppen* of *Polizei* should not be discounted. Each was composed of several regiments of SS, Latvian, and Estonian policemen (see Appendix for a detailed organization), who were armed with infantry weapons and even light infantry guns. Army Group North records from early January indicate that *Gruppe* Jeckeln had a front-line strength of at least 3,670 men. Given that almost none of the men counted in this figure represented supply of support troops, this unit was actually able to put as many men on the line as most of the infantry divisions in the army group. *Gruppe* von Gottberg could put 4,334 men into the front lines. *Heeresgruppe Nord Ia Kriegsgleiderungen*, 10 January 1944; *Heeresgruppe Nord*, Ia, 159/44, 17 January 1944, T-311, Reel 70, National Archives, Washington DC.

[3]This division was actually in the army group reserve behind the corps. See Appendix.

[4]This division was composed of veterans of the original Latvian Legion augmented by Latvian *volksdeutsche*. It was still in the process of organizing (with a total strength of about 15,000 and an infantry strength of 3,485) when the Soviet offensive opened, and was deployed in small packets around the front. The VI SS Corps commander, General of Police Kurt Pfeffer-Wildenbruch, wrote a vituperative letter complaining of this practice on 9 February 1944. He argued that his division had essentially been gutted by being placed under five different divisions in three separate corps and commanded by German officers who considered Latvian SS volunteers as nothing better than cannon fodder. In the first three weeks of the Red Army's attack, the division had taken over 1,600 casualties—SS Grenadier Regiment 34 alone lost 50% of its men. The division also lost nearly 80% of its assigned transport and 15% of its horses. The unit was so weak by late February that it was no longer carried on the Order of Battle as a separate formation, although during March the unit was rebuilt. *Heeresgruppe Nord*, Ia, 159/44, 17 January 1944; *VI SS Corps*, Ia, 32/44, 9 February 1944, T-311, Reel 70; see also J. Lee Ready, *The Forgotten Axis, Germany's Partners and Foreign Volunteers in World War II* (Jefferson NC: McFarland & Co., 1987), pp. 301, 304.

[5]Though Hermann does not mention it, these two units disappear from any further consideration in his narrative and in the operations of Army Group North due to their transfer, during February, to the rear area of Army Group Center. Jeckeln himself remained in the Baltic as *Hohere SS und Polizei Führer "Ostland."* *Heeresgruppe Nord Ia Meldungen*. T-311, Reel 68, entries for 7-11 February 1944.

[6]The campaign and subsequent withdrawal were not cheap in terms of casualties. The Sixteenth Army took 904 officer and 26,800 enlisted casualties in January and February 1944. *Heeresgruppe Nord, Feldersatz*, 1 March 1944, T-311, Reel 73.

[7]The rehabilitation of the Sixteenth Army had in fact begun much earlier—even before the retirement to the Panther Line. Unlike the Eighteenth Army, which took over 60,000 casualties in January and February, receiving less than 30,000 replacements, the Sixteenth Army's 27,704 casualties during those two months were nearly matched by 21,760 replacements (78.5%). *Heeresgruppe Nord, Feldersatz*, 1 March 1944, T-311, Reel 73.

[8]Note in original: "Designation used in references to radio intelligence."

[9]Note in original: "Conditions in Russia (weather and road conditions) as well as the lack of motor vehicles and fuel forced the troops to use great numbers of of the light vehicles found in these areas, which are drawn by the hearty Russian peasant horses."

[10]There could not have been many AFVs attached to these rear guards. The reports of the Operations Officer of the Army Group indicated that on 17 January the Sixteenth Army possessed only 35 Assault Guns, 17 Tigers, and 4 captured T-34s. By 24 January the Tigers had been transferred to the Eighteenth Army, and 9 of the Assault Guns had been destroyed in combat. *Heeresgruppe Nord Ia Meldungen*, T-311, Reel 68, entries for 17, 18, 24 February 1944.

CHAPTER 3

The Operations of the Eighteenth Army During the First Half of 1944 to the Occupation of the Panther Line

Herbert Loch

Prefatory Remarks

For this report the author had at his disposal only a few situation maps and some very brief and sketchy war-diary entries, which are strictly confined to the zone of the Eighteenth Army. The adjacent units, as well as units which, in the course of the operations, were shifted to the adjacent army (XXXVIII Corps) or became independent units (*Gruppe* Sponheimer) no longer appear on the situation maps and in the notes after the time of their transfer. This is unfortunate, particularly in view of the fact that many considerations and decisions of the Eighteenth Army's command often were decisively influenced by the events which took place in the zones of adjacent units.

As far as the enemy situation is concerned, only the following information was available to the author:

1. For the period from 14 January to 31 March 1944, a chart dated 31 December 1943, showing the deployment of the Russian units - that is, at a time prior to the launching of the Russian attack.

2. For the period from 1 April to 30 June 1944 only a general estimate of the enemy forces committed in the attack south of Pskov.

No records concerning the considerations and decisions of the army headquarters and information on enemy strengths and the measures which influenced these considerations and decisions are available. As far as considerations of the German command are discussed, the opinions expressed are those of the author, formed on the basis of the information found in the available situation maps and war-diary entries and, with regard to the defen-

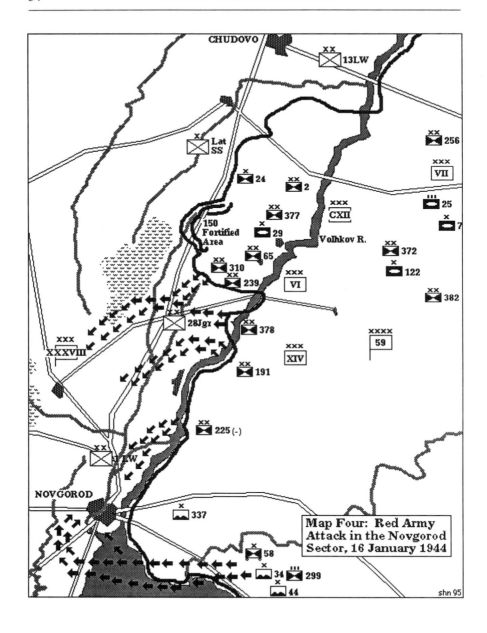

CHUDOVO

13LW

256

VII

Lat
SS

24   2

25

CXII

7

377

150
Fortified
Area   29   Volhkov R.

372

65

122

310

239   VI

382

28Jgr

378

XXXVIII

59

XIV

191

225 (-)

LW

NOVGOROD

337

**Map Four: Red Army
Attack in the Novgorod
Sector, 16 January 1944**

58

34   299

44

shn 95

sive operations in the Panther Line, on the basis of his personal experiences.

Owing to the complete lack of pertinent records, no statements are made in this report concerning the air situation, combat strengths, losses, expenditure of ammunition, and so forth.

Large sections of the combat area in which the army conducted its fighting withdrawal are familiar to the author, who was in the Eighteenth Army for nearly three years; the area of the defensive battle that started on 4 April - in the course of which the author, for the first four weeks, was in command of the most crucial sector and then in command of the whole front - is thoroughly familiar to him from personal experience. He therefore was able to point out certain discrepancies between the entries on the maps and the actual terrain conditions, which are of decisive importance for the proper evaluation of the operations.

The Army's Withdrawal During the Period from 14 January to 1 March 1944

Since the fall of 1943, the army group had been convinced that the Soviet forces massed in front of its sector would soon launch offensive operations aimed at the destruction of the northern flank of the German Eastern Front. The friendly forces available for the expected defensive operations were far inferior to those which the enemy command had at its disposal. The assignment of reinforcements by the OKH could not be regarded as likely. On the contrary, although the army group constantly pointed to the imminence of a major enemy attack, forces were continuously withdrawn from its zone.

Conscious of the fact that, along the extensive and only thinly manned front, resistance against a major enemy attack could not last very long, and that this front was bound to collapse, Field Marshal von Küchler requested the OKH to order the organization of a suitable position to the rear, one protected by natural terrain obstacles to the greatest possible extent, between the northern flank of Army Group Center and the Baltic Sea north of Narva, and to employ GHQ forces in this task. The Field Marshal pointed out that no forces could be withdrawn from the army group's units to be employed in the development of this position because the enemy attack might be launched at any moment. The army group also requested authorization to order withdrawal to the new position as soon as it was to some extent ready for defensive action, the withdrawal movement to be carried out at an early moment - that is, not as a fighting withdrawal or under enemy pressure.

In the Eighteenth Army's zone the proposed position extended in front of the Velikava River from Puchkinekiye-Gory, east and north of Pskov toward the southern tip of Lake Pskov, from there along the western shore of Lake Pskov and Lake Peipus up to the Naroova River and along the western bank of that river up to the Baltic Sea. The total length of this position, called the Panther Line, amounted to 425 kilometers, of which 215 kilometers were "land fronts" and 210 kilometers "lake fronts." The latter could be guarded by a few security units. In comparison with these figures, the old position comprised 400 kilometers of "land fronts" and fifty kilometers of "lake fronts." Disregarding the "lake fronts," the shortening of the front sector held by Eighteenth Army would therefore have amounted to nearly 200 kilometers. As a result of the occupation of the proposed Panther Line, very substantial elements of the forces employed along the present line would therefore have been freed to serve as reinforcements or reserves in the anticipated defensive battle.

The OKH decided on army group's request that the development of the position should be carried out by the army group's own forces because the OKH was in no position to make forces available for the purpose. The army group's additional request, demanding authorization to withdraw into the Panther Line as soon as the development of that position was completed was bluntly rejected, and the army group was advised to resist along the present front line.

The army group's assessment of the situation, which had prompted the submission of its above proposal, was completely borne out by the large-scale Russian attacks launched toward the middle of January 1944; within a very short time, these attacks led to the collapse of the German front, and the German troops were forced to carry out a costly withdrawal under the most difficult conditions in practically trackless terrain.

Immediately after the OKH's decision had been received - around the middle of September - the army group began with the development of the selected position. Headquarters of I Corps was charged with the task of directing the work within the zone of Eighteenth Army. A certain number of engineer and construction forces of the army were made available to headquarters of I Corps for this purpose. In addition to the Panther Line, the "Rollbahn Position" was developed and linked with an existing rear position around Tchudovo.

This position was organized for the protection of the important Rollbahn[1] and the Tchudovo-Tossno railroad as well as for the purpose of making strong forces available as tactical reserves through the substantial shortening of the line resulting from the occupation of the position.

As a further measure, the army began with the improvement of the road net, a task the completion of which could decisively influence a future withdrawal movement, in view of the fact that the army's communication area consisted largely of swampy, wooded, and trackless terrain. In view of existing street and road conditions, it was absolutely impossible to meet, even approximately, the ideal minimum requirement according to which one march route should be available to every division, or at least to every corps. Particularly unfavorable conditions prevailed deep in the rear of XXVIII Corps, which was committed on the army's eastern front. Here, an absolutely trackless area of swamps extended over a width of forty to fifty kilometers; as this area would have to be crossed in case of a withdrawal, it had to be bridged by a corduroy road.

All operational measures necessitated by a possible withdrawal movement were thoroughly investigated by the army's general staff and other higher commands, and records and maps containing the results of this investigation, supplemented by data obtained through reconnaissance, were arranged in files. Special attention had to be paid in this connection to the enormous difficulties resulting from the fact that, in the course of a withdrawal movement from the present front, the bulk of the army would have to depend on one single march route, the Luga-Pskov road. It was therefore necessary to consider at a very early moment what measures would have to be taken to relieve the burden on this Rollbahn and to protect this vital artery of the army against flank attacks, disruption, mining, and so forth by the partisans. One of the results of these considerations was the order, issued as early as the end of 1943 or the beginning of 1944, to the effect that the army's units were to evacuate all vehicles not vitally needed, and all surplus equipment.

Toward the end of 1943 or the beginning of 1944, it became increasingly evident that a large-scale enemy attack was imminent. According to the information obtained by the German command through reconnaissance, the enemy had assembled thirty divisions, three brigades, five ski brigades, ten tank brigades, eight tank regiments, two tank battalions, and numerous other units in the area opposite the sector held by Eighteenth Army, in addition to the twenty-five divisions, nine brigades, and nineteen machine-gun battalions committed on the front line. Toward the beginning of January 1944, the forming of the enemy points of main effort could also be clearly observed. It took place in the sector east of Novgorod, south of Leningrad, and in the area of the Oranienbaum pocket. The front salient protruding into the sector held by XXVIII Corps - created in the course of the Russian attacks in the spring of 1943 - the tip of the so-called Pogostje pocket, was another point where an attack had to be anticipated, aimed at the disruption of the Rollbahn and the Novgorod-Tossno-Krassnogvardeisk (Gatschina) railroad, communication routes of particular importance for movement of supplies. The German command attached special significance to the fact, ascertained early in January 1944, that headquarters of the Russian Forty-second Army, which was regarded specifically as an attack staff, had been shifted to the Oranienbaum sector.[2] On the basis of this fact, it was assumed that the major enemy offensive would include also a thrust from the Oranienbaum pocket.

In spite of all these alarming signs, three more seasoned divisions were withdrawn from the Eighteenth Army's sector for employment elsewhere during the period from 1-13 January 1944; to replace these divisions, the 11th SS *"Nordland"* Panzergrenadier Division and the 4th SS *"Nederland"* Panzergrenadier Brigade were assigned to the army.[3] For the time being, therefore, it appeared impossible to make adequate operational reserves available for the imminent major enemy attack. Only one single division, the 61st Infantry Division, could be freed at the front south of Lake Ladoga, where no major attack was anticipated.[4] By enlarging the sectors of the adjacent divisions this division was shifted to the area between Krassnogvardeisk and the Oranienbaum pocket to serve as operational reserve of the army. The forming of additional reserves at this juncture was absolutely impossible without completely stripping the very thinly manned front. The forming of additional reserves therefore had to be postponed until such time as - after the launching of the major enemy attack - the enemy points of main effort could be clearly ascertained. At that time it would be possible in particularly urgent cases to free individual regiments and - if possible - divisions at comparatively quiet sectors and to shift them as reserves to sectors which were particularly threatened. In view of the vastness of the battlefield, it was necessary to keep adequate means of transportation ready in order to enable the command to carry out such relief measures and shifts as speedily as possible. However, the forming of additional reserves in the above manner could be regarded only as an emergency measure, entailing numerous disadvantages.

As has already been mentioned, the Eighteenth Army had received strict orders from the OKH to the effect that resistance against the anticipated large-scale attack of the Soviet forces was to be put up in the army's present positions. Otherwise, the army perhaps would have ordered the shortening of its eastern front through the withdrawal of the XXVIII and XXVI Corps into the Rollbahn Position, the organization of which had been completed in the meantime. Through this measure at least three divisions would have been freed to serve as operational reserves. Moreover, this measure certainly would have been of the greatest and perhaps even of decisive importance with respect to the outcome of the fighting.

On the basis of combat reconnaissance it was evident to the German command that in addition to the sector south of Leningrad, the points of main effort of the enemy offensive would be situated near Novgorod and the region of the Oranienbaum pocket, and it was anticipated that the main attack would take place in the eastern section of the area. However, the army failed to replace with other units the Luftwaffe Field divisions which were committed in these particularly threatened front sectors, although on account of their composition and their lack of combat experience such divisions usually were committed only in quiet sectors. This fact, undoubtedly, was known to the Russian command, too, and it appears safe to assume that it influenced to a certain degree the planning of its offensive operations. It can be taken for granted that an exchange of these Luftwaffe Field divisions with other infantry divisions committed in less threatened front sectors would have produced only favorable results. It is unknown to the author whether the army had taken such measures into consideration or whether the failure to take such steps was perhaps due to an order of the OKH, which frequently reserved to itself the right to authorize such shifting of units.[5]

According to the operational plan of the Russian command, the German front was to be pierced at Novgorod and at Leningrad, and the breakthroughs were to be followed by a drive of the Novgorod attack group toward the west, while the Leningrad attack group was to advance in a southerly direction, with elements of this attack group wheeling toward Narva as soon as the breakthrough had been accomplished. The first objective of the operation was to sever all rear communications of the Eighteenth Army and thus - by cutting the Rollbahn and the Luga-Leningrad and Narva-Leningrad railroads, to prevent any reinforcement of that army's fighting power. The next objective was to envelop, pocket, and destroy Eighteenth Army in a giant pincer movement carried out by the Novgorod attack group and the bulk of the Leningrad attack group in the wooded and swampy terrain between Volkhov and the Rollbahn.

The terrain in which these attacks were to be carried out, particularly the area south of Leningrad, favored the commitment of tank units on a major scale, and thus offered the opportunity to increase the vigor and the speed of the drive.

Those elements of the Leningrad attack group which were to advance toward Narva were to drive forward first beyond Narva and toward Estonia.

It seems that originally an advance of this group into the deep western flank and rear of the Eighteenth Army, restricting its far-reaching mission in the area east of Lake Peipus, was not planned.

Early on the morning of 15 January 1944, following a very heavy artillery barrage, the large-scale enemy offensive was launched on both sides of Novgorod, as well as from the Oranienbaum pocket in the area around Gostilizi, twenty-two kilometers southwest of Peterhof. South of Novgorod, the enemy - in a surprise thrust across Lake Ilmen - broke through the lines of the German security forces (1st Luftwaffe Field Division) and drove forward as far as the Rollbahn. North of Novgorod, fierce attacks launched against the entire front of the 28th Jaeger (light infantry) Division resulted in a deep penetration near the left flank. Strong holding attacks were launched along the adjacent front sector held by the XXVIII Corps as well as at the eastern front of the sector held by the XXVI Corps; however the German command, realizing the real nature of these attacks, did not pay undue attention to them, but - acting in accordance with previously laid plans, ordered the immediate shifting of an infantry regiment belonging to the 24th Infantry Division (LIV Corps) to the Novgorod sector to reinforce the XXXVIII Corps there. In addition, the army group assigned one regiment of the 290th Infantry Division (*Kampfgruppe* Fürguth[6]) to the XXXVIII Corps.

The entire sector of the I Corps between Pushkin and Urizk was subjected to incessant destructive fire by the enemy. In view of the fact that this sector, which extended over a terrain consisting of dry land without swamps, protected the Rollbahn and the railroad, it was particularly well developed; an enemy attack against it therefore had to be preceded by a heavy artillery barrage. However, the enemy launched only minor thrusts on this day.

Instead, following a heavy artillery preparation, the enemy mounted an attack from the area of the Oranienbaum pocket against the sector held by the two Luftwaffe field divisions (9th and 10th Luftwaffe Field Divisions) whose low combat efficiency, no doubt, had not remained concealed from him. The objective of the attack was the piercing of the front and a subsequent drive into the rear of the German front southwest of Leningrad. It can be assumed that the enemy was prompted to launch his attack here at this early moment by the fact that his air reconnaissance had revealed the shifting of 61st Infantry Division from its previous sector to the area of the Oranienbaum pocket. The enemy attack was successful; two additional penetrations into the German front were effected, and only the advance regiment of the 61st Infantry Division could be immediately committed in the task of sealing off these penetrations.

On 15 January the enemy continued his attacks along the entire front. While it was possible, through the commitment of *Kampfgruppe* Fürguth, to reduce the area of penetration south of Novgorod, the enemy was able to push the German forces fighting in the area north of Novgorod (28th Jaeger Division) back as far as, and at some points beyond, the Rollbahn and the railroad. In order to reinforce the 28th Jaeger Division, army headquarters therefore directed the XXVIII Corps to withdraw one regiment of the 121st Infantry Division[7] from its present front sector, and to shift it to the sector of the XXXVIII Corps by motor transport.

South of Leningrad, the area between Pushkin and Urizk, the large-scale enemy attack began with the Russian command committing tank units and close-support planes in great numbers; the enemy succeeded in achieving a deep penetration in the area west of the Krassnogvardeisk-Leningrad Rollbahn. Simultaneously, the enemy continued his attacks from the Oranienbaum pocket and succeeded in enlarging the area of penetration at Goutilizi. No forces were available to the German command to take immediate countermeasures against the great threat developing here. All the German command was able to do at this juncture was to place the entire Goutilizi combat sector under the unified command of Lieutenant General Güntherr Krappe, the commander of the 61st Infantry Division, who had just arrived.

On 16 January, the fighting generally followed the same pattern as on the preceding day. The enemy continued his attacks at the original points of main effort with undiminished violence, and was able to deepen the penetrations previously effected by his forces in spite of the tenacious resistance put up by the German troops. Another critical situation seemingly developed at the army's eastern front, where heavy enemy attacks against the sector held by the 121st Infantry Division (XXVIII Corps) led also to local penetrations. The weakening of this front sector through the withdrawal of substantial elements of the division - which had been shifted to the XXXVIII Corps - apparently had not escaped the enemy's attention.

In its assessment of the overall situation, Headquarters, Eighteenth Army, regarded the combat sector south of Leningrad as the most critical point; the situation there called for speedy action. Army headquarters therefore decided to further weaken the sector of the LIV Corps, which had not been under attack thus far, through withdrawal of the East Prussian 11th Infantry Division, a unit of particularly high combat efficiency, and to shift this division to the L Corps.[8] In view of the threatening development of the situation, this measure was inevitable, although the enemy could be expected to extend his offensive to include the sector of 11th Infantry Division, which was directly adjacent to Pushkin at any moment. The Oranienbaum sector, for the time being, had to rely on the support received from the remaining elements of the 61st Infantry Division, which had arrived in the meantime. Furthermore, the withdrawal of the "heaviest flat trajectory artillery group" (*Gruppe "Schwerster Flachfuer"*) from its position at Kronstadt Bay had become a matter of the utmost urgency if this unit was to be saved from falling into the hands of the enemy.

During the following three days, from 17-19 January 1944, the fighting at the points of penetration went on with unabated fury. In the sector of XXXVIII Corps, strong enemy forces continued to attack the positions held by the 121st Infantry Division. The enemy penetrations at Novgorod - south of Leningrad and in the area of the Oranienbaum pocket - constantly became deeper. The Novgorod garrison was in imminent danger of being cut off. The front on the army's right sector at some points consisted only of isolated resistance groups with wide gaps between the individual units. The gap in the front south of Leningrad was constantly widening. Committing strong tank forces, the enemy succeeded in deepening his penetration along a front extending over twelve kilometers up to a depth of eight to twelve kilometers. The front of the 170th Infantry Division now consisted only of individual strongpoints.[9] In the penetration area at the Oranienbaum front, to, the enemy was able to achieve substantial successes. The moment seemed to be approaching when the two penetration areas would be consolidated into a single one, and when, consequently, the German forces committed at Kronstadt Bay and on its right and left would be cut off.

An estimate of the army's overall situation led to the realization that it would no longer be possible for the army's center (XXVII, XXVI and LIV Corps) to hold present positions as ordered by the OKH because of the ever-growing threat of a double envelopment resulting from the progress made by the enemy assault groups in the two penetration areas at Novgorod and Leningrad. In addition, a withdrawal of the army's center toward the prepared position along the Tchudovo-Ljuban-Uljanovski Rollbahn would free substantial forces which were urgently needed to halt the principal enemy assault wedge south and southwest of Leningrad. The OKH finally had to admit the logic of these considerations, and approved the following measures:

1. Evacuation of Novgorod and withdrawal of the army's right flank in conjunction with a withdrawal of the Sixteenth Army's left flank[10] in order to restore a coherent defense line.

Where Do They Get Their Strength?

F YOU take a close look at the butterfly in this photo, you will see that one of its four wings is completely useless. Yet, the butterfly continues feeding and flying. This is not an isolated case. Butterflies have been observed going about their daily activity with 70 percent of their wing surfaces missing.

ness from the world was the best course. —James 4:4.

Hisako states: "I decided to study with her the basic doctrines in the *Live Forever* book again on a daily basis. At first we could only study for a few minutes, with my daughter often complaining of severe stomachaches and headaches when it was time for the study. But I had the study regularly. After a few months, her spirit greatly improved, leading in just a short time to her dedication and baptism." Now Hisako is enjoying the full-time ministry together with her daughter.

Pioneering fathers also need to be careful that they do not become so wrapped up in caring for interested ones in the field and for their congregation duties that they fail to give their growing children the strong emotional support and direction they deserve. This is not something that a

ing this good counsel, many pioneers have been able to remain in full-time service for years, and Jehovah has blessed their efforts to obtain 'bread for each day.'—Matthew 6:11.

The apostle Paul counseled fellow Christians to 'let their reasonableness become known to all men.' (Philippians 4:5) Surely, reasonableness would require that we take appropriate care of our health. Balanced pioneers make every effort to show reasonableness in their way of life and in their attitude toward material things, knowing that others observe their conduct.—Compare 1 Corinthians 4:9.

Youths who take up the pioneer service should refrain from taking undue advan-

2. Withdrawal of the army's center toward the position extending along the Tchudovo-Uljanovski Rollbahn.

3. Withdrawal of the 126th Infantry Division and the 9th Luftwaffe Field Division from the Urizk sector, Kronstadt Bay, southwest of Peterhof.

All these measures were carried out on 18 and 19 January. The already encircled Novgorod garrison succeeded in fighting its way out in a westerly direction. Attacking from the direction of Krasnoe Selo, the enemy sliced into the retreating columns of the 126th Infantry Division and 9th Luftwaffe Field Division, inflicting heavy losses in men and materiel on the German forces. However, after a fierce fight, the two divisions succeeded in establishing contact with the inner flanks of the L Corps and III SS Panzer Corps.[11] The withdrawal movement of the army's center, as ordered on 19 January, which was carried out partly under strong enemy pressure, was completed on 22 January. The considerable shortening of the front line resulting from this movement enabled army headquarters to withdraw three entire divisions from their respective sectors, and to shift two of them - the 225th and 227th Infantry Divisions[12] - to the most seriously threatened front sector, the penetration area south of Leningrad, and another one, the 4th SS *"Polizei"* Panzergrenadier Division, to the XXXVIII Corps in the Novgorod sector.[13]

On 20 January, the enemy continued his attacks from the finally consolidated penetration area around Novgorod against the German penetrations, which at some places consisted only of individual strong points. The German forces withdrawing in the area of the Rollbahn and the Novgorod-Luga railroad were subjected to particularly heavy pressure. By the evening of 21 January, the enemy had advanced as far as a point twenty kilometers west of Novgorod. Since the command of the Eighteenth Army no longer had forces available to reinforce this sector (the 4th SS *"Polizei"* Panzergrenadier Division, which was on its way to the XXXVIII Corps, was urgently needed to close the gap which had developed between the XXXVIII and XXVIII Corps) and since, furthermore, the danger of a breakthrough through the army group's front at the boundary between the Sixteenth and Eighteenth Armies had become increasingly grave, the army group shifted the 8th Jaeger Division from the Sixteenth Army to the Eighteenth Army (XXXVIII Corps).[14]

South and southwest of Leningrad, the enemy continued to throw fresh forces into the battle in order to rip up the Eighteenth Army's front, and subsequently to destroy the bulk of its forces. The German command, after the commitment of the 11th Infantry Division, which had arrived in the meantime, succeeded in establishing a new defensive line in the Taizy sector and west of it; however, the German defenders were unable to hold this line against the relentless attacks launched by the Russians on 21 and 22 January; they were pushed back along the entire front. Southwest of the road junction at Kipen (fifteen kilometers west of Taizy), a gap ten kilometers wide developed between the 126th and 61st Infantry Divisions, and the enemy forces continued their drive through this gap in a generally southwesterly direction. The situation of the III SS Panzer Corps thus became increasingly difficult. All army headquarters was able to do to support this corps was to rapidly move up the 227th Infantry Division, which had been freed at the army's eastern front, to the corps' sector.

On the basis of these successes, the Russian command seemed to consider that the time of decisive action was approaching. Its measures during the period from 23-26 January reveal increased efforts to accomplish the following objectives:

1. The envelopment of the Eighteenth Army's right flank, to be facilitated by a strong holding action coordinated with action to separate the XXXVIII Corps, which was employed in that sector, from the rest of the front.
2. To widen the gap in the German front west of Krassnogvardiesk and thus to bring about the final splitting of the Eighteenth Army into two groups, in order thereafter to carry out a pivoting maneuver with the bulk of the Leningrad attack group, aimed at the pocketing and destruction of the German main forces. This plan could be realized if the Russian command succeeded in seizing the area around Ssiverskaya, since the German forces fighting north of the wooded zone would thus be denied any chance of retreat. In coordinated action with the Novgorod attack group, it would even be possible for the Russian forces to pocket and destroy the entire Eighteenth Army, except for the minor group which was withdrawing toward Narva, provided the Novgorod group was able to advance as far as Luga.
3. Active pursuit of the split-up western group of the Eighteenth Army in order to seize the Panther Line on both sides of Narva as early as possible, and thus to gain unobstructed access to Estonia.

To facilitate the planned continuation of the operations, the German command had to be prevented from shifting additional forces from hitherto quiet sectors to the focal points of the battle. For this purpose it was necessary to mount additional holding attacks against the XXVIII Corps, which was committed at the army's eastern front, and above all against the German forces still employed in the old position at the northern front sector.

Similar considerations occupied the minds of the German military leaders. The Eighteenth Army, which apart from a few assault gun battalions had had no panzer units assigned to it thus far, was assured that the 12th Panzer Division would be shifted to its sector. However, in view of the overwhelming enemy superiority in infantry, and particularly in tank forces, it appeared unlikely that the army would be able to halt the enemy drive through Krassnogvardiesk toward Ssiverskaya for any considerable length of time. As a result, the fate of the XXVI Corps, which was still holding its original front, would be sealed; headquarters of LIV Corps, after the transfer of its sector, had been placed in command on the right of the sector held by the III SS Panzer Corps.

The vast, trackless and nearly impassable area of swamps and woods beginning only a few kilometers behind the front of XXVI Corps made a withdrawal movement in a generally southerly direction impossible. It had to be anticipated that a withdrawal would have to be carried out under strong enemy pressure; adding to the existing difficulties would be the fact that the withdrawal, which had to be started in a southerly direction, would have to be turned into a definite east-west movement before the Tossno-Nyriza road was reached. The army therefore would have to conduct a march along the flank of an enemy who would conducting a relentless pursuit, In view of the difficult situation anticipated by the army, and in view of the uncertainty concerning the situation in the sector of the L Corps, the general situation thus called for speedy withdrawal of XXVI Corps, if that unit was to reach the Rollbahn to Luga, the only remaining route of retreat, in time.

In this situation, which was growing increasingly critical, the assignment of the 12th Panzer Division constituted a particularly welcome reinforcement for the Eighteenth Army. Thus the army, finally, would have a highly mobile and strong tactical reserve available which could provide substantial relief for the fiercely fighting infantry divisions, particularly in their struggle against the powerful armored forces committed by the enemy.[15] Army headquarters now had to determine at which critical points the 12th Panzer Division was to be committed - namely, west of Novgorod, where the enemy tank units were already driving through a gap which had developed between the Eighteenth and Sixteenth Armies, or at the point of penetration south of Leningrad. At this juncture, the Krassnogvardiesk area appeared to be threatened most seriously. General Lindemann therefore decided, for the time being, to assemble the panzer division in the Ssiverskaya area. From this assembly area, the division could speedily be committed in support of the L Corps, as well as the task of covering the withdrawal of the XXVI Corps.

Owing to the existence of favorable communication routes, such as the main road to Luga and the Luga-Novgorod Rollbahn, it furthermore was possible to shift the panzer division rapidly to the army's right sector at a moment's notice.

Here the XXXVIII Corps seemed to face the threat of a double envelopment. On its right, the enemy tank units, followed by a Soviet rifle division, had driven through the Luga Valley as far as the Batezkaya-Utorgoch railroad, where a speedily organized *sperrverband* [blocking force] (*Kampfgruppe* Pohl) was able temporarily to halt their advance on 26 January. The Corps' center (*Kampfgruppen* Speth and Bock), which was conducting a withdrawal toward the Luga River in accordance with orders received, was relentlessly pursued along the railroad and the Rollbahn, The Corps' left (*Kampfgruppe* Schuldt) was enveloped and pushed toward the north and consequently separated from the bulk of the corps; another gap had developed in the front of the Eighteenth Army.[16]

In the sector of the XXVIII Corps, the enemy continued his fierce holding attacks without achieving substantial successes.

The withdrawal movement of the XXVI Corps from the position it had been occupying thus far started on the evening of 23 January. As anticipated, the enemy conducted a relentless pursuit along the entire front; most of the chose intermediate positions therefore could not be held. The corps' withdrawal movement took place under similar conditions during the following days. By 26 January, a coherent front no longer existed. The divisions of the XXVI Corps fought defensive actions along the Uchaki-Michailovka-Ssiverskaya road as three isolated combat teams. There was no longer any contact with the two adjacent units; a twenty-kilometer-wide gap separated the corps' units from the XXVIII Corps and a gap of approximately the same size had developed between the XXVI and L Corps. The enemy attempted to cut the corps' withdrawal route at Kurovizy, four miles north of Ssiverskaya; it therefore was necessary to commit elements of the 12th Panzer Division in the task of halting the enemy forces.

Krassnogvardiesk, south of Leningrad, the Eighteenth Army's former main supply base, was lost after fierce fighting; the German front was pushed back further toward the wooded zone.

In the eastern combat sector, the enemy, attacking with numerically superior forces, succeeded in ripping up the hitherto coherent front of the LIV Corps in the army's right sector, leaving only weak and isolated *kampfgruppen* to continue the fight on the German side. By 26 January, these were pushed back toward a line of strongpoints extending from

Volossovo in a generally northwesterly direction. In order to maintain contact with the LIV Corps, the III SS Panzer Corps had to withdraw its right flank.

Meanwhile the gap between the L and LIV Corps had reached a width of more than twenty kilometers. The enemy had definitely succeeded in ripping up the front of Eighteenth Army. In order to ensure a unified command over the two separated corps of the western combat group, these corps were consolidated into *Gruppe* Sponheimer, and placed under the command of the General of Infantry Sponheimer, the commanding general of the LIV Corps.

The development of the situation in the sector of the XXVI Corps confronted army headquarters with the question of whether a withdrawal of the XXVIII Corps from its hitherto unshaken Rollbahn position had not become necessary in spite of the OKH's express order not to abandon voluntarily any sector of the front. Owing to the fact that *Kampfgruppe* Schuldt, now assigned to the corps, had been forced to yield ground, a gap had developed between the corps' southern flank and the the XXXVIII Corps, through which the enemy was advancing in a westerly and northwesterly direction, thus threatening the only withdrawal route available to the XXVIII Corps. At the army's northern flank, a gap extending over many kilometers had been created through the forced withdrawal of the XXVI Corps. The moment appeared to be approaching when the enemy would have unhampered freedom of maneuver along the corps' entire northern flank, and when he would seize the Tchudovo-Divenskij railroad (fifteen kilometers south of Ssiverskaya), thus disrupting the corps' only supply route. It could be taken for granted that the enemy would attempt to take advantage of the opportunity which offered itself to separate the XXVIII Corps from the rest of the army and to pocket and destroy it. To prevent this, it was necessary to withdraw the corps from the Rollbahn position with the utmost speed. Before the evening of 26 January had passed, therefore, General Lindemann ordered the XXVII Corps to disengage itself from the enemy and to withdraw toward Luga. Later events proved that this order was given just in time. Even a short delay in ordering the corps' withdrawal from the Rollbahn position would have resulted in its encirclement and destruction.

On 27 and 28 January, the enemy continued his efforts to force further withdrawals of the army's southern flank. The attempt at an envelopment carried out by the enemy group which had driven further to the west beyond the Utorgoch-Batezkaya railroad necessitated special measures to protect the Pskov-Luga Rollbahn. For this purpose, the army committed the newly assigned *Kampfgruppe* Karow (one reinforced infantry regiment[17]) in a blocking position along the narrow strip of land between the lakes south of Luga.

In the sector of the XXVIII Corps, the withdrawal movement toward the Tchudovo-Ljuban railroad, its temporary goal, was carried out according to plan in spite of fierce enemy attacks. On 28 January, the enemy committed particularly strong forces in an attack on Ljuban, in an effort to capture this locality and then to launch a drive through the Tigoda Valley into the rear of the XXVIII Corps. However, owing to the tenacious resistance put up by the East Prussian 121st Infantry Division, the enemy succeeded only in capturing the northern section of the town.[18]

The three isolated groups of the XXVI Corps, which had been partly pocketed by the enemy, had to fight their way out of encirclement toward the south under the most difficult conditions, and suffered heavy losses. thus the corps' front had practically disintegrated. Of its divisions, which were placed under the command of headquarters of the L Corps, the 24th Infantry division was committed as a security force on both sides of Novinka. The other two divisions were assembled at the Rollbahn and the railroad south of Ssiverskaya. Headquarters of the XXVI Corps was charged with the task of directing the traffic on the Rollbahn to Luga, which naturally became increasingly unmanageable.

The L Corps, which was being pressed further southward by enemy attacks in superior forces against its northern front and its eastern flank, employed the 12th Panzer Division, which had been assigned to it, in a rear line behind its two front divisions. Then retreating further it was intended to withdraw these two divisions in a big jump through the panzer division, and thus give them a chance to prepare themselves in their position.

In the sector of *Gruppe* Sponheimer, the loosely connected front was continually pressed back by heavy enemy attacks, whose main point of effort was situated at the Rollbahn to Kingissepp. Still, the group succeeded in building up a line of security - discontinuous, it is true - approximately fifteen kilometers east of Kingissepp, on both sides of the railroad and the Rollbahn. Between it and the two divisions of the III SS Panzer Corps, which were retiring southward according to plan, there was a large gap.

An estimate of the overall situation resulted in the following picture:

The presumable intention of the STAVKA [Russian High Command] to encircle the Eighteenth Army in the swampy forest region between the Luga-Leningrad-Volkhov Rollbahn might, on the whole, be regarded as having failed. It was doubtful, however, whether it would be possible to withdraw from this area the XXVII Corps, which was echeloned far in front. The enemy was in a position, both on the right flank of the corps and in the completely open northern flank, to advance on its retirement route, and cut it off.

With its center (I Corps) the army approached the swamp and forest zone, which would no longer allow the enemy to bring to bear his considerable superiority, especially in tank forces. For this reason the situation of the army center would experience a certain relaxation.

Gruppe Sponheimer, hitherto operating independently, approached the fortified Panther Line, in which it would probably be able to check the advance of the enemy.

Although the STAVKA did not achieve the intended encirclement, it could credit itself with having split up the front between Army Group North and the Eighteenth Army. Between the Sixteenth and Eighteenth Armies there was a small gap through which the enemy had already broken with tank forces and infantry, and between the army center and *Gruppe* Sponheimer there was a gap already more than fifty kilometers wide, which allowed the enemy complete freedom of movement in a southerly and southwesterly direction. It was to be expected that the enemy, continuing his attack of his Attack Force Novgorod in the direction of Luga, would launch the forces released in front of the army center for a thrust into the deep flank and rear of the Eighteenth Army. Several good roads leading from Lake Peipus toward the Pskov-Luga Rollbahn would make this easily possible.

The German command was hence obliged to direct its attention mainly to protecting the two deep flanks.

With respect to the time available, the danger at the gap to the Sixteenth Army seemed most acute, since a certain time still had to elapse, because of the great distance to be covered before major enemy forces could appear in the deep western flank of the army. The enemy had already advanced, though with limited forces, to the Rollbahn at the narrowest point of the lake south of Luga. A shift of stronger enemy forces to this point and an attempt to extend the gap to the Sixteenth Army was certainly to be expected.

The situation accordingly required this gap to be closed as soon as possible, and a continuous front to be re-established at the boundary between the Sixteenth and Eighteenth Armies. This would be possible only by employing the highly mobile 12th Panzer Division. The high command - the author does not know whether as a result of a decision by the army or the army group - hence resolved to disengage the 12th Panzer Division from its front and to launch it in an attack to close the gap. In several days of bitter fighting on and after 31 January, the panzer division succeeded in closing the gap and re-establishing contact with the Sixteenth Army (8th Jaeger Division). Its further attempt to push through to the railroad line in order to gain more favorable position abreast of *Kampfgruppe* Speth failed. The division had to shift to the defensive as a result of powerful enemy attacks then beginning.

The presumption of the army that the enemy was going to start a thrust into the deep flank of the Luga-Pskov Rollbahn was confirmed on 31 January. Air reconnaissance observed three attack enemy forward elements crossing the Luga River in a southwesterly direction in the gap between the L Corps and *Gruppe* Sponheimer. The further advance of these enemy columns in the forest, which was very swampy, was likely to proceed along any one of the following four roads:

1. Ossmino-Tolnachevo (fifteen kilometers north of Luga)
2. Sayano (thirty-five kilometers southwest of Ossmino-Plyussa railroad station
3. Gdov-Strugi Krassnye
4. Gdov-Pskov.

Whereas the enemy could soon be expected to appear on the northernmost of these roads, it would presumably take a few days before he did so on the other roads. In any case, the point was to delay and check the enemy's advance as early as possible. Since troops were available for this task only on a limited scale at the time, the enemy had to be intercepted in suitable terrain as far from the Luga-Pskov Rollbahn as possible.

The following measures were therefore taken by the German command:

1. While the 215th Infantry Division was providing cover toward the north, a regiment of this division, which had been sent out to the lake twenty kilometers northwest of Tolmachevo to protect the western flank of the L Corps, was to advance toward Ossmino and block the important crossroads. The 212th Infantry Division was to provide cover along the Luga River for the right flank of the 215th Infantry Division, which had been echeloned far forward.[19]

2. The 58th Infantry Division (minus one regiment diverted to Narva), which had been newly assigned to the army and was just moving up, was unloaded at Strugi Krassnye and at Plyussa Station, and dispatched in a northwesterly direction toward the Plyussa River to block the two large roads in this sector.[20]

3. A *sperrverband* was sent forward directly from the army group from Pskov to Jamm to secure the road from Gdov.[21]

An attempt to recapture Ossmino, which the enemy had already occupied, was unsuccessful.

The 58th Infantry Division march group on the right reached the Plyussa sector on 3 February, whereas the one on the left, which had arrived later, did not reach it until 6 February. On 4 February, the enemy was also approaching the sector.

The *sperrverband* dispatched to Jamm reached its march objective without first encountering the enemy.

There remains to be described the most important events on the other front of the army.

From 29 January-3 February, the XXVIII Corps retreated further westward with the enemy pressing after it. Road conditions were adverse. North of Tessovostrol the troops of the entire corps, while passing the narrow part of the swamp, were crowded together in a one-way corduroy road, forty kilometers long, so that the withdrawal was extremely slow.

The enemy, who undoubtedly knew about this, sought to take advantage of the circumstances. He advanced with strong forces from the gap between the XXXVIII and the XXVIII Corps in a northwesterly direction, and from the north in a southerly direction toward Oredesh to cut the corps off from its route of retreat. For further support, the enemy launched strong forces in an attack on Oredesh. The corps headquarters was aware of the impending danger, and with the aid of trucks and sleds sent the 21st Infantry Division, which had been disengaged, ahead in the direction of Oredesh. In bitter offensive battles, the 21st Infantry Division, which had been reinforced by a few other disengaged units, repelled the enemy forces which had advanced almost as far as Oredesh from a southwesterly direction.[22] Simultaneously with the attack of the 21st Infantry Division, the XXVIII Corps launched the 4th SS *"Polizei"* Panzergrenadier Division (*Kampfgruppe* Schuldt)[23] west of the Oredesh-Batezkaya railroad in a thrust southward to close the gap between it and the XXXVIII Corps, which had established a thin line of security along the railroad. This German thrust was also successful. The enemy advancing from the left flank toward the route of retreat moved rather slowly, presumably on account of difficult terrain conditions. Only his leading brigade came into contact with the blocking position established by the 21st Infantry Division at Cherenna (fifteen kilometers northeast of Oredesh) and was repulsed.

In the evening of 3 February it was definite that the Russian attempt to cut off the XXVIII Corps at Oredesh had failed.

In the army center, the L Corps retired further along the Rollbahn and railroad to the Luga sector in extensive movements, which were facilitated in the beginning by the 12th Panzer Division, which was still assigned to it. The 24th Infantry Division, which was providing cover in a broad formation east of the Oredesh-Vyritza railroad on both sides of Novinka, had to fight its way westward toward the Rollbahn under heavy enemy pressure.[24]

In the left sector of the army, the heavy enemy pressure on *Gruppe* Sponheimer was maintained so that this group did not even succeed in holding the broad Luga sector, and on 1 February had to withdraw to the expanded bridgehead at Narva. For the most part, *Gruppe* Sponheimer now stood on the fortified Panther Line, which, since 30 January, had been occupied by troops of the Narva administrative headquarters.[25] But the enemy did not allow himself to be stopped by the Panther Line, and attacked sections of it from the southwest and northwest.

Whereas north of Narva it was possible to throw the enemy, who had already penetrated, across the Narva River, at the same time destroying a large part of his forces, the enemy penetration southwest of Narva was successful. The foremost elements of the *Feldherrnhalle* Panzergrenadier Division, which were being dispatched to *Gruppe* Sponheimer, had to be committed from the march column against the penetrating enemy units.[26] For the time being they succeeded only in sealing off the point of penetration.

At 2400 hours on 3 February, *Gruppe* Sponheimer, which could no longer be controlled by the army headquarters because of the great distances between them, was separated from the Eighteenth Army and assigned directly to the army group.

As a result of the measures taken by the German command, the whole front of the army - with the exception of the right boundary, had to a certain extent become consolidated. All minor gaps still existing had been closed by German attacks. Now that despite all difficulties the withdrawal of the XXVII Corps had been successfully completed, the army stood in a large semi-circle around Luga, largely in the previously reconnoitered Oredesh-Luga position. By interpolating the 12th Luftwaffe Field Division, which had become free, connection was established between the XXVIII and the I Corps. For greater protection of Luga, which was important to the march movements of the army, the 13th Luftwaffe Field Division, which had likewise become free, was placed at the western flank in the area between the Luga position and the 58th Infantry Division.[27]

On the right flank of the army, the battles proceeded with alternating successes for both sides. It seemed advisable to the army group to place in one hand the control at the boundary between the two armies, which - owing to the development of the situation - constituted a continuous source of danger. It accordingly ordered establishment of *Gruppe* Friessner, which was directly under control of the army group, and to which the left flank corps of the Sixteenth Army and the XXXVIII Corps were assigned. The XXXVIII Corps which, on orders from the army group still was to receive the 121st Infantry Division of the XXVIII Corps, which had become free, thus ceased to be a part of the Eighteenth Army.

While six divisions of the army were still employed in the Oredesh-Luga position, in further withdrawal the semi-circle around Luga had to be tightened again, owing to the increasingly swampy and impassable terrain, chiefly to the west of the Rollbahn, so that four divisions were sufficient to occupy it. These could be controlled by a corps headquarters. On the other hand, it proved advisable to entrust another corps, in addition to the XXVI Corps, with cover of the extensive and deep western flanks. hence, the army ordered the following new chain of command: the XXVIII Corps was to take over the northern front of the L Corps with the 24th, 11th, and 126th Infantry Divisions; Headquarters, L Corps, was to provide protection on the western flank, except for its westernmost section north of Pskov, which remained entrusted to the XXVI Corps.

The forces that had been sent out as flank protection encountered enemy spearheads everywhere. This was the case even in the sector of the 13th Luftwaffe Field Division employed west of Luga, where in the swampy terrain the enemy - taking advantage of any paths, however small - had managed to approach in major strength and to force the advance Luftwaffe regiment to retreat.

The situation of the 58th Infantry Division, which had advanced far out to the Plyussa sector, had developed in a dangerous manner. The two separately advancing groups of regiments had reached the sector and had established a small bridgehead there. They succeeded for some time in blocking the two large approach roads. Then the enemy took advantage of his superiority, started a concentric attack on the two groups of regiments, encircled them, and pushed on in a southeastern direction. These enemy forces then encountered the 24th Infantry Division, newly moved in to reinforce the flank protection. This division had been launched by the L Corps through Plyussa and Strugi Krassnye to relieve the 58th Infantry Division. In spite of hard fighting, however, the 24th Infantry Division gained only little ground so that at first no relief was forthcoming.

There was a wide, still completely open gap between the 24th Infantry Division and the XXVI Corps. In this area the 21st Infantry Division, XXVIII Corps, which had been brought to the scene by railroad and truck, was inserted. Still unclarified and obscure was the situation of the XXVI Corps north of Pskov. There had been no connection for days with the *sperrverband* that had been sent forward to Jamm and had now also been assigned to the army. The possibility existed that it had been encircled or destroyed by the enemy. A security party advancing through Molodi (fifteen kilometers southeast of Jamm) had encountered superior enemy forces, which had forced them to retire. The route to Pskov in the rear of the army seemed to be open to the enemy.

The army headquarters expected strong enemy forces to appear on the eastern bank of Lake Peipus, which the *sperrverband* committed there would not be able to fight off. It was providential, therefore, that the 215th Infantry Division, which had become free as a result of the contraction of the front north of Luga, had been dispatched to the XXVI Corps. Furthermore, the army sent the 12th Panzer Division, which, after having been detached from *Gruppe* Friessner by the army group upon consolidation of the front, had again been assigned to the army, to the XXVI Corps in the area of Seredka (forty kilometers north of Pskov). Immediately upon their arrival, both divisions began their attack and opened the road through Molodi to Jamm, thus relieving the encircled *Sperrverband* Fischer.

Up to 11 February, seven infantry divisions and one panzer division had been committed by the army for the protection of the western flank, while only two divisions remained north of Luga on both sides of the Rollbahn.

During this last phase, the defensive battles of the Eighteenth Army and the adjacent unit on the right, *Gruppe* Friessner, had served the primary purpose of keeping the enemy away from Luga and the Luga-Pskov Rollbahn, since possession of both the Rollbahn and the traffic center of Luga was of vital importance to the Germans. Now the time was approaching when the abandonment of Luga, and following that the desired straightening of the greatly bulging German front, which offered particularly favorable points of attack to the enemy - for instance, in the sector of the XXXVIII Corps - could be considered. Such a step would also release considerable forces which were especially required by the Eighteenth Army for reinforcing its deep western flank. On the basis of these considerations, the army group ordered the withdrawal of the left flank of *Gruppe* Friessner and of the elements of the Eighteenth Army around Luga. Distances and timing of the withdrawal were controlled by the army group. "Green," "Blue," and "Red" defense lines had been selected.

In execution of this order, the divisions of the XXVIII Corps retreated by long bounds, leaving rear guards behind. In doing so they were not much harassed by the enemy, who was retarded by the extensive mining which had been done, and the destruction of the railroads and roads in and around Luga. By morning of 15 February, the "Red" line had been reached. Two divisions were at once pulled through. The 215th Infantry Division was dispatched as a reinforcement to the XXVI Corps; the 11th Infantry Division was dispatched through Pskov into the area west of the narrow part of Lake Peipus - where the enemy had already occupied the island of Piirissar - with the mission to prevent enemy crossing attempts at this narrow part of the lake.

The L Corps joined the withdrawal with its right flank. This could now be done without difficulty because the two groups of regiments of the 58th Infantry Division, which had advanced to the Plyussa sector and had been encircled there, had succeeded in fighting their way eastward to the units committed to their support: the 24th Infantry Division and one regiment of the 13th Luftwaffe Field Division.

The XXVI Corps drew the forces it had sent forward to Molodi and Jamm back, and occupied the "Red" line, in part after having overcome strong enemy resistance. Although the corps itself now had a continuous front, there still was a gap several kilometers wide between it and the adjacent corps, and this corps was unable to close with its own forces.

In the evening of 15 February 1944 the *"Fruehjahrurlaub"* order arrived by teletype from the OKH. It ordered withdrawal of Army Group North to the Panther Line.

The withdrawal was uniformly planned within the army group. In addition to the lines to be reached by specified deadlines - "Bamberg" by 22 February, "Calais" by 24 February, "Darmstadt" by 27 February - the order specified the number of divisions to be employed in the various lines of resistance, and indicated the march destinations for the units to be released. The order also regulated the occupation of the Panther Line, which was to be completed by 1 March.

Withdrawal to the "Bamberg" Line

For the first three days, from 16-18 February, the army had to hold its previous front. It succeeded in doing so, although in the sector of the XXVIII Corps strong enemy forces tried to push in the northeastern bastion of the army at Plyussa on a broad front. In the sector of the XXVI Corps, the enemy also attacked with superior forces in order to break through the front on both sides of the Pskov-Gdov railroad. Although he made a few minor penetrations, the situation was always easily restored. Despite the enemy attacks, the planned relief of the 12th Panzer Division by the 215th Infantry Division, which had arrived at corps headquarters, was carried out, and the 12th Panzer Division was dispatched through Pskov to the Sixteenth Army in the area of Opotchka.

The units entrusted with the protection of the western shore of Lake Peipus - a few smaller units in addition to the 11th Infantry Division and the 207th Security Division - had up to then been controlled by the Rear Area Commander, Army Group North, General of Infantry Kuno-Hans von Both. Since the area controlled by this commander had been shifted to the rear as a result of the withdrawal of the army group to the Panther Line, the L Corps assumed control in his place. The sector of the L Corps, comprising the 24th Infantry Division, 12th Luftwaffe Field Division, and 21st Infantry Division, was taken over by the XXVIII Corps.

The withdrawal to the "Bamberg" line was started on 19 February. In the XXVIII Corps sector, the enemy exerted direct pressure on the whole front, committing particularly heavy forces on both sides of the Rollbahn, and in the sector of the 12th Luftwaffe Field Division. But in general he was unable to interfere much with the withdrawal. Only in the left sector of did the enemy achieve a major success. With three divisions and numerous tanks, he attacked the 21st Infantry Division. He broke through its front in great breadth, and pushed forward to a depth of six kilometers. In a violent, embittered struggle, the division - to which the corps had dispatched all available reserves of infantry and assault guns - succeeded in stopping the enemy.

Further west, in the XXVI Corps sector, violent fighting had flared up again. Major elements of the enemy had infiltrated through the gap to the 21st Infantry Division, and had dug in behind the front. A rapid attack by the 215th Infantry Division succeeded in repelling these enemy forces, and in closing the gap to the 21st Infantry Division by exerting heavy direct pressure in pursuit. On its left flank, the corps was attacked by the enemy in a strength of four divisions. The only success, however, which the enemy was able to achieve was to press back the extreme left flank. The corps expected the enemy to resume his attacks here and perhaps attempt to envelop the left flank across the ice of Lake Pskov. To frustrate this, the engineers started the preparation of an ice barrier on Lake Pskov.

Withdrawal to the "Calais" Line

The withdrawal was carried out on 23 and 24 February. In the sector of the XXVIII Corps, the enemy generally exerted only slight pressure. Only on the left did heavy enemy forces attack the 21st Infantry Division and press it back beyond the specified line of resistance. But the enemy did not succeed in disrupting the front of the division.

In the sector of the XXVI Corps, the enemy continued his attacks against the western portion on 23 and 24 February with strong forces. On 24 February, an enemy battalion crossed the ice on Lake Pskov - without allowing itself to be detained by the still incomplete ice barrier - advanced toward the Pskov-Gdov road, and blocked it for a few hours. Then this enemy battalion was dislodged by German reserves. The enemy was unable to achieve other substantial successes in the sector of the XXVI Corps.

The L Corps had received orders from the army to capture the island of Piirissar at the southern end of Lake Peipus. The decision of the army resulted from the circumstance that this island, only a few hundred meters from the western shore would, after the ice had melted, give the enemy a stepping-stone for carrying operations into the rear of the Panther Line and to Estonia. To forestall this danger, capture of the island seemed advisable, so long as the ice on the lake was still passable for troops. In a hard battle on 24 February, the 11th Infantry Division seized the island, which had been occupied and fortified by the enemy, and held it against violent enemy counterattacks. The enemy in vain repeated his attempt to recapture the island on 25 February.

Withdrawal to the "Darmstadt" Line

The withdrawal was carried out from 25-27 February. On 27 February the Eighteenth Army assumed command of *Gruppe* Herzog (formerly Friessner, now under command of General of Infantry Kurt Herzog); *Gruppe* Haase, commanded by Lieutenant General Wilhelm Haase, with the 21st Luftwaffe Field Division, the 15th Latvian SS Waffen Grenadier Division, and the 30th Infantry Division; and of the XXXVIII Corps with the 8th Jaeger Division, the 121st Infantry Division, and the 2nd Latvian SS Brigade. The withdrawal of the boundary group was delayed by intensive partisan activity. In the sector of the XXVIII Corps only sporadic enemy attacks occurred, while in the XXVI Corps sector the enemy tried to push into the withdrawal movement in all sectors, and particularly west of the Pskov-Gdov road. The enemy achieved no substantial successes.

Withdrawal to the Panther Line

On 26 February, the XXVIII Corps, which had been selected to take command of the Panther Line on both sides of Pskov, took over the sector of the XXVI Corps. The XXVI Corps headquarters was dispatched to *Armeeabteilung* Narva (formerly *Gruppe* Sponheimer).[28]

South of the Pskov-Dno railroad, the withdrawal of *Gruppe* Herzog, which was echeloned toward the front, was continued in a long bound without essential enemy interference to the last intermediate position. North of the railroad, the XXVIII Corps retreated to the combat outpost line under heavy attacks from the enemy on both sides of the Gdov Rollbahn.

On 29 February, *Gruppe* Herzog was to retire further to the line of combat outposts contemplated for the Panther Line, which had been envisaged as a provisional main line of resistance. On the right this was successfully accomplished. In the left sector, at the XXXVIII Corps, however, occupation of the combat outpost line had not been quite completed when two strong enemy attacks set in, which forced the 30th Infantry Division and the 8th Jaeger Division to withdraw their security parties and retire to the Panther Line.

The XXVIII Corps moved into the final position after leaving combat outposts behind. These, however, were pressed back by the enemy at the Luga-Pskov Rollbahn and northeast thereof.

On 1 March, occupation of the Panther Line had been completed on the entire army front. The intention of the enemy to destroy the Eighteenth Army in front of this position had been frustrated.

Battle Experience

Without tank support, the attacking elan of the Russian infantry was not very great during the German withdrawals. The Russian command owed penetrations and breakthroughs almost exclusively to its heavy tank force, against which there was, for a long time, no defense on the German side, except for a few assault guns.

In the case of numerous penetrations, the enemy quickly abandoned his gain in the face of German counterattacks, thus enabling the German troops to eliminate the penetration. In these cases the enemy displayed particular vulnerability on his flanks. The fear of being cut off from the flank was probably the main reason for his retreating from the lines gained in penetration.

No terrain was impassable for the Russian soldier. Guided by natives, the Russian units - both large and small - found their way even through apparently impassable swamps and forests to block the supply routes of the Germans and carry out operations in the rear of the German front; for instance, against the command posts of higher staffs. Hence it was necessary, because of the nature of the combat terrain, which made control difficult, to maintain a large number of assault patrols for quick elimination of minor threats (and also strong reserves in battalion strength) distributed over the front, to be able to meet the attack of major enemy units quickly and efficiently.

The partisan activity in the rear of the German front was very intense throughout the withdrawal. Not only were mines continually being laid by partisans on the railroad, on the Pskov-Leningrad Rollbahn, and on the railroad and Rollbahn to Novgorod in order to paralyze the supply of the Eighteenth Army. Temporarily even the Pskov-Luga Rollbahn was blocked by a strong partisan band. The German command was not surprised by this partisan activity, since the area mentioned had been harassed by this partisan activity, since the area mentioned had been harassed by partisans from the beginning of the German occupation, and since they had given the Germans a great deal of trouble, chiefly through the mining of railroads. Considerable forces for the protection of railroads, roads, and other important objectives from partisan action had accordingly been employed even before the beginning of the withdrawal. they were reinforced during the withdrawal and a divisional staff was entrusted with the exclusive mission of combating partisans on the Pskov-Luga road.

With regard to the speed of withdrawal, it proved advisable to select positions with a distance of eighteen to twenty kilometers between them, and to hold a position for two days. Only in this manner was it possible to allow the great number of units depending on a single road to flow off fairly smoothly, without causing large bottlenecks. Moreover, swampy forests often made it necessary to retreat from a position, especially from flanking positions, first parallel to the front in the direction of the Rollbahn, and later to approach the new position from the Rollbahn laterally along a suitable route. To give the advance detachments dispatched to reconnoiter routes and positions an appropriate lead for their difficult and generally time-consuming task, it was advisable to hold each intermediate position for two days.

The extensive destruction and mining of the Pskov-Luga Rollbahn and railroad and north thereof, as well as of other important roads and tracks in the swampy forest region with its few roads, was of great importance to the success of the German withdrawal. In addition to retarding the enemy's pursuit considerably, these destructions particularly affected the supply of the enemy with rations, munitions, and the like. This is undoubtedly the reason for the great decrease in enemy artillery activity once the enemy had entered the forest zone.

Conclusion

The Russian operation aimed at destroying the Eighteenth Army, which was the main support of the German Eastern Front, and thereby open up the way into Estonia and the German eastern frontier. The Russian high command for the Northwest, which was in charge of the operation, sought to fulfill this double mission simultaneously rather than successively by making it its objective from the very beginning not only to destroy the Eighteenth Army, but also to open up the way into Estonia by committing strong forces in the direction of Narva. The significance attached by the STAVKA to the latter mission appears to a certain extent from the fact that the command of this Narva assault group was entrusted to the Second Shock Army, which was held in particularly high repute. These two parallel operations naturally resulted, from the beginning of the offensive, in a scattering of the main forces, which - as General Eisenhower states in his memoirs, is one of the greatest mistakes in warfare. The two strategic objectives should have been pursued successively; first, the destruction of the Eighteenth Army and only then, if it was still necessary, the way into Estonia should have been opened by force. In all probability, this way would have been open anyway, for it would scarcely have been within the range of possibilities for the OKH to ship considerable forces to the scene in order to prevent the Russian masses from entering Estonia and thus from marching against the German eastern frontier.

Russian strategy provided for breakthroughs through the front of the Eighteenth Army in the two widely separated sectors and a subsequent thrust by two strong attack wedges toward the Pskov-Luga-Leningrad Rollbahn and railroad, while an attack group was to advance on Narva. This strategy was based on the intention of cutting the Eighteenth Army off from all food and ammunition supplies, and of encircling and destroying it in the swampy forest region between Volkhov and the Rollbahn - the historic site of the complete defeat of the Russian Vlassov Army in the spring of 1942.

The first prerequisite for the success of this objective was to break through the German front. The sectors chosen for this purpose - the Novgorod area in the left Russian attack sector, the area southwest of Leningrad, and in close conjunction with it the eastern front of the Oranienbaum pocket in the right Russian sector - were favorably selected in accordance with tactical as well as terrain conditions. They represented the shortest distance to the

Rollbahn, the first strategic objective; favorable road and track connections (at least for Russian conditions), especially in the Leningrad attack sector. They furnished a possibility of employing armored units in broad formation, while on the German side the units for the most part had had little combat experience (Luftwaffe Field divisions). The Russians were successful. They achieved penetrations at both points with surprising rapidity. Southwest of Leningrad the penetration was expanded into a breakthrough on 23 January; the German divisions committed at the Oranienbaum pocket were pushed off in the direction of Narva. The two spearheads were in a position to advance on the Rollbahn, envelop the German main forces from both sides, and thus prepare the encirclement. More than this they were not able to do. The German defensive measures - quick dispatch of reinforcements from other parts of the front to the two flanks, the stubborn resistance of the German troops - increasingly retarded the tempo of the Russian spearheads. The German command managed both to ward off the danger to the Rollbahn north of Luga, its only supply line, and to bring all its troops out of the threatening encirclement. With this the first part of the Russian operations plan had failed.

If, in the subsequent course of the retreat, the German command succeeded in bringing the Eighteenth Army back behind the Panther Line, the reasons for this further Russian failure were probably as follows:

On 23 and 24 January the front of the Eighteenth Army had been disrupted on a large scale; on 25 and 26 January the army was finally split into two parts. The broad gap between the main forces of the Eighteenth Arm and its dislodged elements (*Gruppe* Sponheimer) offered the enemy command - with the far superior forces available to it - a possibility of advancing with strong elements in a general southerly direction against the deep flank and rear of the Eighteenth Army, in order first to cut it off from its sole supply line, the Pskov-Luga Rollbahn and railroad, and then to attack the army in its rear from the southwest. Such an operation, or at least a thrust against the Rollbahn and railroad, the Russians did consider, but too late, and the forces they employed were insufficient. This is the only way to explain, after the German front had been spilt up, between 26-28 January, it was not until 31 January - in other words not until after five days, that three Russian spearheads appeared on the Luga River, and why it was that the enemy forces approaching subsequently in the deep western flank were (by Russian scale) not large, and lacked a common point of main effort. They were held off by a few German divisions. The Russian operations plan should have provided from the beginning for a strong attack force, designed to thrust into the deep German flank to follow the Second Shock Army advancing in the direction of Narva. This thrust should have taken place as soon as possible. The commitment of strong armored forces, which were at the disposal of the Russian Army Command, would have given the thrust increased speed and impact. A prerequisite for a quick and successful thrust into the deep German western flank was to tie down the German front in the Leningrad sector, and to provide cover against *Gruppe* Sponheimer. In view of the Russian superiority, this prerequisite could have been achieved without any difficulty. The German command would in all probability not have been able to disengage more forces from the front to reinforce protection of the western flank.

The German command was decisively handicapped from the beginning by the *"Führerdirectiv"* to meet the enemy's large-scale attack in the old position, and not to abandon any part of the front voluntarily. If this had not been the case, the protruding northern part of the eastern and northern front, composed of the XXVIII and XXVI Corps, would undoubtedly have been withdrawn, probably even before the beginning of the offensive, but in any event sooner than it was, to the fortified, much shorter Tchudovo-Ljuban-Tossno Rollbahn position in order to give the army strategic reserves, of which there was a complete lack. Whether, as a result of this step, the defensive battle would have taken a different course, need not be discussed. As it was, the Eighteenth Army had to be content with inadequate makeshift measures during the critical days at the beginning of the offensive, and at first had to disengage individual regiments from the less heavily attacked parts of the extremely thin-spread front in order to shift them to the most threatened points. Subsequently, whole divisions were disengaged in a similar fashion, and the front was depleted still more. This was possible only on the basis of the unshakeable and justified confidence of the German command in the will of its troops to resist.

The withdrawal of the XXVIII and XXVI Corps was accomplished on 21 and 22 January, in other words, at a time when the penetration at Leningrad had already been extended to a depth of over fifteen kilometers. It would have seemed best to withdraw the salient between the Rollbahn and the penetration point also in order to straighten the front and deprive the enemy of favorable points of attack. Two further reasons spoke in favor of this measure: on the one hand, the extremely thin occupation of this sector of the front (which, after the shift of the 11th Infantry Division, was held only by the 24th and 215th Infantry Divisions) and, on the other hand, the particularly difficult retreating conditions of these two divisions. After the first withdrawal from the present position in a southerly direction, they had to continue the retreat in a flanking march because of the impassibility of the terrain in the deep rear, although the enemy was certain to push west and apply heavy pressure. Nevertheless, army headquarters decided to continue to hold this part of the old northern front. Its abandonment at the present time would have permitted the enemy to advance east of the Leningrad-Luga Rollbahn, and would thus have still more aggravated the situation of the hard-fighting L Corps, and perhaps even made it untenable and caused the whole northern front to crumble. That a later withdrawal of the 24th and 215th Infantry Divisions would be very difficult and attended by heavy losses, as was actually the case, the army headquarters knew. Nevertheless its decision must be regarded as correct.

The other major decisions of the German command have been commented upon in the description of the events. Here we need merely draw attention to the timely withdrawal of the XXVIII Corps, which had been echeloned far forward, and the closing of the gap to the adjacent army through employment of the 12th Panzer Division.

The full extent of the danger threatening the deep western flank of the front after it had been split up was correctly appraised by the army. The army sent the two newly assigned regiments of the 58th Infantry Division and one *sperrverband* in the direction of enemy along the most important potential approach route with the mission of advancing as far as possible to stop the enemy. Although these weak units found themselves in an extremely serious situation and were encircled and almost destroyed by far superior forces, they fully executed their mission. It was to their self-sacrificing action that the German command owed the fact that the enemy was detained for a sufficiently long time to bring up further forces to the scene for the protection of the flanks.

On 1 March 1944 the troops of the Eighteenth Army moved into the Panther Line. Despite the great superiority of the enemy, who was applying heavy pressure, and despite the difficulties incident to the terrain, the German command managed to withdraw the army in an orderly manner without major losses of men and material on a breadth of roughly 300 kilometers, from the old Leningrad front to the new position.[29] Russian strategy had failed. The Eighteenth Army had not been destroyed, and the way to Estonia and the German eastern frontier had not been opened. The STAVKA was confronted with the necessity of attaining its goal by means of a new offensive.

NOTES

[1]Note in original: "Road designated as a main axis of motorized transportation, from which all animal transport and marching columns were normally barred."

[2]The Forty-second Army. commanded by General I. I. Maslennikov, a Party general who turned out to have a flair for operations, was indeed an attack staff. It had been transferred out of besieged Leningrad in November 1941 and directly suborindated to the STAVKA. Since then it had remained on the Leningrad front, of the spearheading Soviet attacks. As such, it was often reinforced with Guards and STAVKA artillery units; for example, in January 1944 it had been reinforced by the crack XXX Guard Rifle Corps with the 63rd and 64th Guards Rifle Divisions. For a complete order of battle for the army in January 1944, see the appendices. Albert Z. Conner and Robert G. Poirier, *Red Army Order of Battle in the Great Patriotic War* Novato CA: Presidio, 1985), p. 57; Seaton, *Russo-German War*, p. 409.

[3]A comparison of the *OKW Kreigsgleiderung* for 26 December 1943 with the Army Group North records for mid-January shows that two units—the 96th and 254th Infantry Divisions—had left the area; both had been transferred to the Ukraine. Loch probably derives the third division by counting the 4th SS *"Polizei"* Panzergrenadier Division. This division was on orders for the Balkans, and about half of it had left the Leningrad area when the Russian offensive began. Victor Madej. *Hitler's Elite Guards: Waffen SS, Parachutists, U-Boats* (Allentown PA: Valor, 1985), p. 42; Victor Madej, *German Army Order of Battle: Field Army and Officer Corps, 1939-1945* (Allentown PA: Valor, 1985), pp. 30, 56.

[4]This division was one of the stronger units available to the Eighteenth Army. At the end of 1943 it was listed as "Category III"—fully capable of defensive combat (the highest rating of any division in the army)—with approximately 2,100 infantry, twelve field and two positional artillery batteries, and seventeen heavy anti-tank guns. *Heeresgruppe Nord, Zustanden der Divisionen,* Ia/Abt III, 19 December 1943, T-311, Reel 70.

[5]What Loch should have been aware of—considering the fact that his corps contained the 12th and 13th Luftwaffe Field Divisions—was that the Army had taken over the Luftwaffe Field Divisions in October 1943, and was in the process of selective replacement of officers and even whole battalions to ring these divisions up to strength with the ranks at least partly filled with veterans. This explains part of the reason why these units were not taken out of line. The other salient reason is that there simply were no "quiet" sectors left by January 1944. There is a considerable

file of organizational data concerning the transition in T-311, Reel 70.

[6]This *Kampfgruppe* was composed of Grenadier Regiment 503 and II/Artillery Regiment 290; see Appendix.

[7]This was Grenadier Regiment 407, designated as *Kampfgruppe* Pohl, to which Loch refers later.

[8]At the end of 1943, the 11th Infantry Division was rated as one of the strongest divisions in the army group (Category III): 2,200 infantry, twelve field and one position artillery batteries, and twenty-four anti-tank guns. *Heeresgruppe Nord, Zustanden der Divisionen,* Ia/Abt III, 19 December 1943, T-311, Reel 70.

[9]The 170th Infantry Division's strength had been reduced to about 350 infantry, fewer than six artillery batteries, and no recorded anti-tank guns. *Heeresgruppe Nord,* Ia, 159/44, 17 January 1944, T-311, Reel 70.

[10]Note in original: "Details unknown to author, probably up to the bend in the Luga River west of Novgorod."

[11]The losses of these two divisions are understated in Loch's narrative. The 9th Luftwaffe Field Division was reduced, by the time it regained contact with the main line of resistance, to an infantry strength of only about 150 men, a handful of anti-tank guns, and no artillery. The 126th Infantry Division had one weak regimental-size *kampfgruppe*, supported by a single artillery battalion. *Heeresgruppe Nord,* Ia, 159/44, 17 January 1944, T-311, Reel 70.

[12]Categorizing these two divisions, both of which were recorded by the Operations Section of the Eighteenth Army as having been reduced to the status of *kampfgruppen*, as "entire divisions" is either an example of wishful thinking on Loch's part or else a comment on the relative weakness of German infantry divisions by late January and early February 1944. *Heeresgruppe Nord*, Ia/Id, 730/44, 7 February 1944, T-311, Reel 70.

[13]Loch here does not take note of the fact that the at least half of the 4th SS had been transferred to Greece.

[14]Considering that the infantry strength of the entire XXXVIII Corps was only about 9,000 men, the addition of the 3,498 light infantrymen of the 8th Jaeger Division

represented a significant reinforcement indeed. *Heeresgruppe Nord*, Ia, 159/44, 17 January 1944, T-311, Reel 70.

[15]The 12th Panzer Division, commanded by Major General Freiherr Erpo von Bodenhausen, was in fact a crack unit that was—as an added plus—no stranger to Army Group North. The division had fought near Leningrad in 1942, before being sent to Army Group Center to participate in the Kursk offensive and the battles for the Dneiper and Dneister Rivers. By 1944 standards it was a strong division, with a reported combat strength of 22 January of 28 tanks (36 under short-term repair) in its panzer regiment, two full-strength panzergrenadier regiments, an artillery regiment with a full battalion of self-propelled guns, a reconnaisance battalion with three companies of armored cars, an engineer battalion with half-tracks, and an army flak battalion with six towed and seven self-propelled heavy flak/anti-tank guns. *Heeresgruppe Nord Ia/Id*, 368/44, 22 January 1944, T-311, Reel 70.

[16]If anything, Loch here underestimates the decimation of the XXXVIII Corps after the first ten days of the Soviet offensive. The three *kampfgruppen* to which he referred were the remnants of the corps's original division. *Kampfgruppe* Schuldt had been formed out of the fragments of the 2nd SS (Latvian) Brigade, combined with the 12th and 13th Luftwaffe Field Divisions—it could put at most 4,500 men into line. *Kampgruppe* Speth was the next strongest, representing the intact infantry of the 1st Luftwaffe Field Division, the 28th Jaeger Division, parts of Cavalry Regiment *"Nord,"* and a few Estonian battalions; it had a strength of just over 2,200 men. Pohl and Bock each commanded regimental-strength groups of roughly 1,200 men each. Thus the total infantry strength for the XXXVIII Corps had been reduced to about 9,100 men with little if any organic artillery. To make matters worse, *Kamfgruppe* Schuldt's displacement would require it to be reassigned to the XXVIII Corps by 30 January, leaving the XXXVIII Corps with only half that number. *Armeeoberkommando 18*, Ia 732.44, 2 February 1944, T-311, Reel 70.

[17]*Kampfgruppe* Karow was built on Grenadier Regiment 322 of the 285th Security Division, and had 1,312 men on 30 January. *Armeeoberkommando 18*, Ia 732.44, 2 February 1944, T-311, Reel 70.

[18]That the 121st Infantry Division maintained its hold on the town was particularly striking in light of the fact that the total infantry strength of the two regiments remaining with the divisions (Grenadier Regiments 405 and 408) had been reduced from 1,400 at the beginning of the offensive to about 630. *Armeeoberkommando 18*, Ia, 732/44, 5 February 1944, T-311, Reel 70.

[19]The infantry strength of the 212th Infantry Division had been reduced to 1,854 officers and men, supported by eight artillery batteries and eleven anti-tank guns. The 215th had only 1,147 infantrymen remaining; the strength of its artillery and anti-tank holdings for that date cannot be determined. *Heeresgruppe Nord,* Ia/Id, 730/44, 2 February 1944; *Armeeoberkommando 18,* Ia, 732.44, 5 February 1944; T-311, Reel 70.

[20]The detached unit was Grenadier Regiment 209. The remainder of the 58th Infantry Division disposed over just 1,024 infantry, nine artillery batteries, and eleven anti-tank guns. *Heeresgruppe Nord,* Ia/Id, 730/44, 2 February 1944; *Armeeoberkommando 18,* Ia, 732./44, 5 February 1944; T-311, Reel 70.

[21]Under the command of 126th Infantry Division commander, Colonel Gotthard Fischer, this *sperrverband* appears to have been composed of various anti-tank, engineer, and support units of the division. *Armeeoberkommando 18,* Ia, 732/44, T-311, Reel 70.

[22]For a detailed description of these battles, see Herbert Gundelach, "21st Infantry Division: Defensive Combat, Disengagement, and Withdrawal from Volkhov to Pskov, January and February 1944," in Steven H. Newton, *German Battle Tactics on the Russian Front, 1941-1945* (Atglen PA: Schiffer, 1994), pp. 159-174.

[23]This description is somewhat deceiving. Schuldt's command had, it is true, been augmented by portions of the *kampfgruppe* of the 4th SS, but this only amounted to slightly more than 800 men in four small battalions. *Armeeoberkommando 18,* Ia 732.44, 2 February 1944, T-311, Reel 70.

[24]At this point, the 24th Infantry Division had been reduced to 1,007 infantry. *Armeeoberkommando 18,* Ia, 722/44, 5 February 1944, T-311, Reel 70.

[25]This also included at least thirty-four flak batteries; see Appendix.

[26]Though there is a tendency to equated "named" divisions in the Wehrmacht (i.e. *Grossdeutschland* or *Das Reich*) with elite status and strength, the *Feldherrnhalle* Panzergrenadier Division was neither. Commanded by Major General Karl-Friedrich Steinkiller, the original unit—the 60th Panzergrenadier Division—had been destroyed at Stalingrad and rebuilt around an infantry regiment from the 93rd Infantry Division. In January 1944 it was described by *Gruppe* Sponheimer as a Category IV

division, fit only for limited defensive combat. The division disposed of only six weak panzergrenadier battalions (each of which had only 70% of its assigned vehicles), three partly mobile artillery battalions, and an understrength engineer battalion. Its striking force centered around twelve StG III assault guns, twelve Pzkw Mark IVs, twelve self-propelled 75mm anti-tank guns, and two batteries of towed 88mm flak. *Gruppe* Sponheimer, Ia, 183/44, 8 February 1944, T-311, Reel 70; *Heeresgruppe Nord,Panzermeldungen,*, 10 February 1944, T-311, Reel 73.

[27]Despite the negative comments sprinkled throughout Loch's narrative, the 12th and 13th Luftwaffe Field Divisions seem to have been reorganized and replenished to some extent by early February. The 12th was one of only two divisions left among the Eighteenth Army's nine which was rated as Category III—fully capable of defensive missions. Both divisions were stronger than the army average in terms of both artillery and anti-tank guns. The 12th had thirteen anti-tank guns and seven full-strength artillery batteries; the 13th had sixteen anti-tank guns and ten batteries. *Heeresgruppe Nord*, Ia/Id, 730/44, 2 February 1944, T-311, Reel 70.

[28]Note in original: "A reinforced corps, commanded by a Corps commander with a Corps Staff."

[29]This statement regarding the absence of major losses during the retreat is as inaccurate as the statements by von Natzmer that the Eighteenth Army was destroyed. In fact, the truth was that the Eighteenth Army had taken heavy losses. During January the army lost 471 officers and 13,257 men; the next month the casualties increased dramatically to 968 officers and 21,981 men. This figure does not take into account 672 officers and 23,291 men assigned to *Armeeabteilung* Narva who became casualties in February (most of these units had been assigned to the Eighteenth Army on 14 January). Thus the total losses of the army were on the order of 60,640, against which only 29,848 (49.2%) replacements were received. *Heeresgruppe Nord, Feldersatz*, 1 March 1944, T-311, Reel 73.

CHAPTER 4

The Defensive Battle of the Eighteenth Army in the Panther Line from 4 March to 28 June 1944

Herbert Loch

In the area of the Eighteenth Army the southern section of the Panther Line ran along the eastern bank of the Velikaya River, whose broad, deep bed was situated close behind the front. The boundary between it and the Sixteenth Army was north of Pushkinske Gory. The northern section ran along the western bank of Lake Pskov and Lake Peipus; the *Armeeabteilung Narva* boundary was at Tammispaese. It would have been best to organize the southern section of the position along the western bank of the Velikaya River, which constitutes a definite obstacle. In the event of such a choice, the dominating heights northwest of Pskov, which afford a good view of the river section itself and the hinterland south and west of Pskov, would in any case have had to be included in the position. Organization of the position on the eastern bank of the Velikaya River had an additional advantage in that behind the front there was a good road for troop movements which was not exposed to the enemy's view - namely the Pskov-Ostrov Rollbahn and the road southeast thereof; that furthermore the terrain for the most part favored the construction of concealed fortifications owing to its ample vegetation; and that finally large sections of the outpost area were swampy, and thus impaired the mobility of the enemy.

While in general the position was on gently rolling terrain, there were in the area between the right army boundary and Lake Pskov major elevations in the southernmost part of the position in the vicinity of Grigorkino (fifteen kilometers northwest of Pushkinske Gory) and the pronounced hills around Dulovo-Gorodez Utkino (twenty kilometers north-northeast of Ostrov) - hereafter referred to as the "Balcony" - in addition to the aforementioned dominating heights northwest of Pskov. The three major elevations cited played a

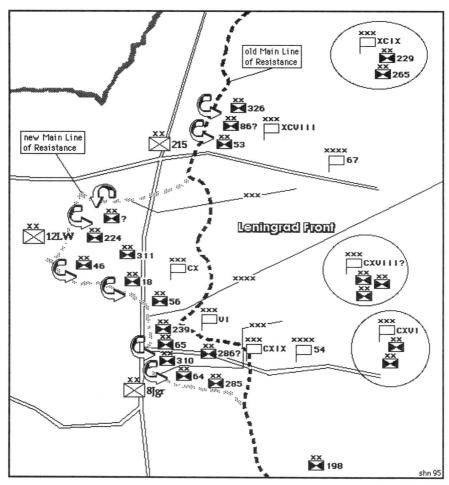

Map Four: Red Army attack, 3 April 1944

great role in the first defensive battles of the Panther Line. The large-scale Russian attack was directed against the sector of the 212th Infantry Division and the adjoining flank of the 215th Infantry Division. This part of the area was completely level in its southern half and without vegetation, while in its northern half it was slightly undulating with alternating thin and dense vegetation.

The Panther Line was a field-type fortification; there were no concrete installations. There was a continuous wire obstacles in front of the whole line from the army boundary to Lake Pskov, as well as anti-tank ditches in front of a few particularly endangered points. There was only one advanced position and one position protecting the artillery. The two towns of Ostrov and Pskov had been reinforced by good fortifications. The position was under construction from September 1943 until the beginning of the attack; by the time the Eighteenth Army occupied it, the construction had to a large extent been completed.

Upon occupation of the Panther Line, three divisions had been set aside as strategic reserves of the army. Of these, the 121st Infantry Division and the [*kampfgruppe* of the] 4th SS *"Polizei"* Panzergrenadier Division were assembled close to the front in line with the Velikaya crossings between Ostrov and Pskov; the 12th Luftwaffe Field Division was assembled further to the rear, at a place where it could be shifted in the direction of Ostrov and Pskov, as well as on the western shore of Lake Peipus, to fight off a potential enemy crossing of the still-frozen lake.[1]

Wherever the terrain permitted, the divisions on the line left behind strong combat outposts.

German headquarters in no way expected the strategic intentions of the enemy to have basically changed as a result of the occupation of the Panther Line. But they were of the opinion that the Russian command - opposite the Eighteenth Army and *Armeeabteilung Narva* it was the staff of the Leningrad Front - on the basis of the experiences gathered in recent weeks, in which, under substantially more favorable conditions the Eighteenth Army failed to be destroyed and retained its power of resistance, would decide to break through the Germans in the strong Panther Line in a systematic attack prepared with all available means, and try to attain its strategic objective in this fashion. Nevertheless, the German command expected that the enemy would at once, without an intermission, start partial operations against the Panther Line in order to establish more favorable conditions for his subsequent attack.

Because of the road and railroad conditions the expected large-scale attack had to take the direction of the Pskov-Irboska-Riga Rollbahn. An attack by the Leningrad Front in the direction of Ostrov was not probable, since - as was know to the German command - its boundary line with the Second Baltic Front, adjoining in the south, passed only a few kilometers south of Ostrov. Moreover, the region north of the boundary line was very swampy and contained only a single fairly good, large road.

On its southern front, however, the Eighteenth Army had to expect an attack from the Second Baltic Front. From the right boundary of the army the Panther Line curved eastward. When terrain conditions were good, the angle thus formed offered an attacker a favorable opportunity for a thrust into the rear of the Sixteenth Army. The prerequisite for such an enemy thrust was that the southernmost part of the Eighteenth Army sector of the Panther Line be neutralized. Hence, the Eighteenth Army also had to expect heavy attacks upon its extreme right flank.

In an offensive by the Leningrad Front with the primary objective of gaining the Pskov-Riga Rollbahn there were essentially two directions to be considered: attack along the Luga-Pskov road and attack from the area northeast of Ostrov and southeast of Pskov. For both directions of attack, the terrain east and west of the Panther Line was - contrary to map indications - swampy only to a limited degree, and for the most part traversable by tanks. For an attack on both sides of the Luga-Pskov Rollbahn, elimination of the block of hills northwest of Pskov, which extended up to two kilometers from the town, and from which the terrain between Pskov and the Panther Line could be seen almost in its entirety, was to a certain extent a prerequisite.

The second attack direction mentioned would initially include a lunge westward toward the Velikaya River. After crossing this river, the attacker had to take a generally northwesterly direction to gain the Pskov-Riga Rollbahn. Owing to the favorable road network, which led across the Velikaya bridges at Shabany, Gorbovo, and Filatova-Gora, the necessary movements would be greatly facilitated. A similar, although not so pronounced significance as in an attack on both sides of the Luga-Pskov Rollbahn, was attributed to the block of hills of the Balcony, situated twenty kilometers north-northeast of Ostrov, in the even of an offensive from the area northeast of Ostrov-southeast of Pskov. From this block of hills, which afforded an excellent view of the open terrain on both sides of the Panther Line, with its sparse vegetation, an enemy attack could be effectively taken under fire. An attack in the direction of the Velikaya crossing at Shabany without prior capture of the Balcony was impossible; an attack on the crossing further north at Gorbovo could, at any rate, be greatly hampered by flanking fire from the Balcony.

The German command expected that the enemy, prior to his large-scale offensive, would try to gain possession of these two blocks of hills, The particularly great efforts made on the Russian side during the recent fighting northwest of Pskov had already given indications of this. The assumption that the enemy would make the direction of his intended large-scale attack dependent upon the outcome of the battles for the hills northwest of Pskov was probable to a certain extent.

This general appraisal of the terrain and presumable enemy intentions, for which there was no further data available at the time the Panther Line was occupied, had induced army headquarters to assemble its strategic reserves as described above. In the Panther Line itself, eight divisions had been placed along the land from from the right boundary of the army to Lake Pskov; three divisions and one security division had been entrusted with providing cover along the western shores of Lake Pskov and Lake Peipus - the "lake front." The fairly strong GHQ artillery assigned to the army was first employed with its point of main effort in the sector of the 126th Infantry Division, northwest of Pskov, and of the 8th Jaeger Division, on the Balcony.

Upon moving into the Panther Line the German divisions had left behind strong combat outposts wherever the terrain permitted, To drive these back and take possession of the terrain directly in front of the Panther Line was the next endeavor of the closely following enemy. To attain his aim, the enemy conducted individual operations on the whole front, and heavy attacks with considerable losses in a few sectors. Judging from the strength of the troops employed, the enemy seemed to attach particular importance to gaining the outpost area in the sector of the 8th Jaeger Division at the Balcony and of the 126th Infantry Division northwest of Pskov. In the southern army sector, the combat outposts were almost everywhere pressed back to the main line of resistance. With the northern divisions, between the Balcony and Lake Pskov, there were some who had to abandon territory; in general, on this part of the army front the combat outposts were able to maintain themselves in the outpost area. The successful fighting against the combat outposts of the two corps on the right - the VI SS Corps and the XXXVIII Corps - induced the enemy on 4 March 1944 to start an attack against the main line of resistance here. He was unsuccessful.

The First Defensive Battle
at Pskov and Ostrov, 4-12 March 1944

Defensive operations Northwest of Pskov, 4-12 March 1944

At daybreak on 4 March 1944 the expected enemy attack, with its point of main effort west of the Rollbahn, began in the sector of the 126th Infantry Division on a broad front between the Pskov-Gdov railroad and the coast, and subsequently achieved a deep penetration. A systematic counterattack pushed the enemy back beyond the old position on 5 March. But in the course of the embittered fighting the German troops were unable to prevent the enemy from again breaking into the position in a breadth and depth of one and one-half kilometers. This was facilitated for the Russians by a fairly large force advancing across the ice of Lake Pskov into the rear of the German front. The 126th Infantry Division did not allow itself to be diverted from undertaking another counterattack, which was completely successful. The position was eliminated, and the enemy forces in the rear of the front pushed back across Lake Pskov.

In view of the importance of the hilly terrain northwest of Pskov in holding the Panther Line, and in view of the vigor of the enemy attacks, a continuation of which had to be expected, it seemed appropriate to the army headquarters to assign further forces to the XXVIII Corps to support the hard-struggling 126th Infantry Division. Hence, out of the army reserves, it assigned to the corps the [*kampfgruppe* of the] 4th SS *"Polizei"* Panzergrenadier Division.

This measure had been taken just in time. On 6 March, the enemy not only extended his attack sector further eastward, but committing fresh forces conducted a new, very strong attack west of the Rollbahn, which resulted in a broad penetration. Through a counterattack of the first elements of the 4th SS *"Polizei"* Panzergrenadier Division - which had arrived in the meantime - it was possible to substantially eliminate this penetration again. Upon continuing his attacks on 7 March, the enemy again broke in here on a rather large front, and in doing so gained possession of a dominating hilltop. For the time being, this hilltop had to be left in the enemy's hands. Only on the day after the next, on 9 March, was the lost hilltop recaptured in a well-prepared German counterattack, which coincided with an enemy counterattack. A renewed enemy attack on both sides of the Rollbahn which pushed through with tanks as far as Abiska - in the rear of the front - was unable to change matters. This attack also was repulsed by the German defenders.

The incessant hard fighting of the past days had naturally reduced greatly the fighting power of the 126th Infantry Division. The XXVIII Corps head-quarters hence felt obliged to consider the question of an early relief for the division. This relief could best be accomplished by an exchange with the 21st Infantry Division, directly adjacent on the right, with battalion being exchanged for battalion without excessively long marches. This relief was facilitated by the circumstance that in the sector of the 126th Infantry Division a few battalions of the 4th SS *"Polizei"* Panzergrenadier Division were at first available, which could temporarily be inserted into the front. On 10 March the 21st and 126th Infantry Divisions exchanged their sectors.

The fighting of the following days revolved chiefly around the possession of the aforementioned position on the hills east of the Rollbahn; it finally had to be left in enemy hands on 11 March. Nevertheless, since 10 March a certain let-down of the enemy offensive, which now was confined to a narrower sector, could be observed. On 12 March the enemy suspended his attacks.

At the end of the first defensive combat operations northwest of Pskov, the enemy had achieved an insignificant gain of territory between the Rollbahn and the lake shore, but he had been prevented by the tenacity of the German defenders from reaching his objective and gaining possession of the dominating hills northwest of Pskov.

From the beginning of the defensive fighting for the hilly terrain northwest of Pskov, the enemy - as had been expected on the German side - conducted more or less heavy attacks also at a number of other points of the army's front. Besides aiming at tying down German troops, the enemy tried, wherever he had previously been unsuccessful, to push back the German combat outposts to the main line of resistance in order to gain possession of the remaining part of the outpost area of the Panther Line. This endeavor was particularly obvious on the right flank of the 215th Infantry Division, where the enemy repeatedly attacked combat outposts with heavy forces on both sides of the road leading to the Velikaya crossing at Filatova-Gora.

From the strategic reserves, composed of three divisions, the [*kampfgruppe* of the] 4th SS *"Polizei"* Panzergrenadier Division - as has already been mentioned - had been assigned to the XXVIII Corps on 5 March. Two days before, the army had been obliged to assign one more division, the 12th Luftwaffe Field Division, to the L Corps. This measure had been necessary since, on orders of the army group, the 11th Infantry Division[2], which had been employed at the front along Lake Peipus, had to be dispatched to *Armeeabteilung Narva* and the further release of the 24th Infantry Division, located on Lake Pskov, had been announced. Thus only one division remained at the disposal of the army. On 6 March the army commander resolved, although the outcome of the fighting northwest of Pskov was as yet uncertain, to release this last division, too, and place it at the disposal of the XXVIII Corps for employment on the Balcony. This decision, which it had not been easy to make, had been prompted by the probability that, according to available reconnaissance results, a heavy enemy attack against the Balcony position was soon to be expected. In view of the great breadth of the front, the 8th Jaeger Division employed there seemed too weak to successfully fight off a sustained attack. Moreover, if the 121st Infantry Division were inserted, it would be possible to shift the right flank of the 8th Jaeger Division beyond the road leading in a northeastern direction from Ostrov, and thus shorten the broad sector of the 30th Infantry division. In view of the two large roads traversing the old sector, which would be of especial importance in an enemy attack in the direction of Ostrov, the reduction of the sector of the 30th Infantry Division and the consequent restriction of its defensive assignments was to be desired.

On 8 March 1944 the 121st Infantry Division assumed control of the left sector of the 8th Jaeger Division and the right one of the 212th Infantry Division as far as north of Panevo, so that the entire Balcony position, including its northern spurs, lay in its sector.

First Defensive Combat Operations Northeast of Ostrov (Balcony), 9-12 March 1944

On 9 March the enemy attacked the Balcony. Simultaneously, the enemy attacked further south in all divisions sectors as far as the boundary of the army. In the course of these secondary attacks, which had to be regarded as holding attacks, and which in heavy degree even continued on 10 March, the enemy temporarily achieved penetrations into the Panther Line in the southernmost army sector, at the 15th SS Latvian Waffen-Grenadier Division[3], and on both sides of the road to Ostrov from the northeast. These penetrations, however, were eliminated through counterattacks.

That the main effort of the enemy offensive begun on 9 March was directed against the Balcony was soon clear. After intensive artillery preparation the enemy, employing strong tank forces, attacked at the southern half of the Balcony position at Susvo-Ivankovo. At two points enemy tanks were able to penetrate two to three kilometers. The reserves kept in readiness, however, soon undertook a counterattack, and eliminated the penetrations, putting a number of enemy tanks out of action. The enemy was not diverted from his offensive intentions by this initial failure, and employing fresh forces started another attack whose point of main effort was directed toward the northeastern sector of the Balcony position at Ivankovo. The enemy entered the position and entrenched himself in it; the 121st Infantry Division was at first only capable of sealing off this penetration.

On 10 March very heavy attacks again began, which in contrast to those of the previous day, extended toward the northern half of the Balcony position at Ivankovo-Panevo. Nevertheless, the 121st Infantry Division carried out the prepared counterattack, aimed at eliminating the penetration at Ivankovo, but the counterattack was unsuccessful. The enemy, on the other hand, in addition to achieving a temporary penetration in the center of the Balcony position at Gorbovo, was able to penetrate the left sector of the 121st Infantry Division at Panevo. The enemy tanks pushed through as far as the Rollbahn, where they were stopped by anti-tank defenses. This deep penetration, which at first looked like a serious menace, was completely eliminated by a counterattack accompanied by assault guns and Tiger tanks, and a large number of enemy tanks were put out of action.

On 11 March the enemy attacks were renewed against the entire front of the Balcony position, the main effort being directed against the center of the Balcony block of hills at Ivankov-Dulovo. The attack was repulsed everywhere. In addition, in a bold and vigorous attack, the 121st Infantry Division succeeded in eliminating the penetration at Ivankovo, which the enemy had achieved on the first day of the attack and which, up to that time, had not been liquidated.

On 12 March the enemy once again attacked the entire Balcony position, with his point of main effort in the center, but did not achieve a result. The enemy then suspended his attacks on the Balcony, as well as northwest of Pskov, probably upon higher orders in both cases. The 121st Infantry Division was able to credit itself with a full defensive success. Upon conclusion of the battles, the division was in full possession of its old position.

In considering the battles for the Panther Line that had so far taken place, it must be observed that, aside from the battles for the outpost area, the enemy did not attain his objective of gaining possession of the block of hills of the Balcony and those northwest of Pskov. In the defensive battles, the German troops achieved complete success. As a natural result of the bitter fighting, the combat power of the participating German units underwent a considerable weakening. If the enemy accordingly pursued attrition tactics with his attacks, it must be said that he attained this goal to a certain extent, and this was of no little importance in view of the difficult German replacement situation, of which the enemy was aware. But a substantially more important result of the the previous operations for the enemy command was the situation that the German army headquarters had been obliged to commit all its available strategic reserves. The establishment of new strategic reserves by disengaging divisions from the front was scarcely feasible for the Eighteenth Army in view of the strained combat situation, as the Russian command was justified in assuming. Conduct of a planned new offensive was favored by this circumstance.

A further result the previous battles were likely to have yielded to the Russian command was with respect to the point from which a new offensive could be launched. An attack on both sides of the Luga-Pskov Rollbahn could hardly be undertaken without possession of the hills northwest of Pskov. The least prerequisite was the launching of very strong forces against these hills, and these forces thus would be lost to the drive in the main direction of attack. Hence, a launching of the offensive further south of the Luga-Pskov Rollbahn seemed more favorable, the southern flank of the offensive remaining at a great enough distance from the block of hills of the Balcony so that in advancing it could not be caught in the flank from them. It may be assumed that the importance of these two hill blocks which were still in German hands decisively influenced final determination of the direction of the offensive.

During the enemy attacks against the hills northwest of Pskov and against the Balcony, the enemy continually engaged in smaller or larger operations in the various sectors of the front, from the right boundary of the army to north of Pskov. Only on Lake Peipus, in the sector of the L Corps, did perfect quiet reign. It was not until the last day of the attack, 12 March, that it was interrupted. The Soviet "Makarov" partisan brigade pushed across the ice on the northern part of Lake Peipus in the the vicinity of the left boundary of the army - where as a result of the thawing weather the ice was already beginning to break up - and penetrated through the thin security line of the 207th Security Division, and made its way some kilometers into the rear. Counteraction was initiated at once, with a view to encircling and destroying the partisan brigade. It split up into several large-size units, shifted from the army area into the sector of *Armeeabteilung Narva*, returned, and was finally crushed on 16 March. Owing to the immediate countermeasures of the 207th Security Division and *Armeeabteilung Narva*, the partisan brigade was unable to do great damage.

Defensive Combat for the Hill Territory
at Grigorkino, 16-18 March 1944

The hill territory located around Grigorkino dominated to a great extent the sector of the VI SS Corps, employed on the right flank of the army. For this reason it had been decided to run the section of the Panther Line on the far side of the Velikaya River over this hill range, from which there was a view extending into enemy territory. It could be assumed that the enemy - as he had done at the Balcony and northwest of Pskov - would try to gain possession of these heights prior to undertaking an attack on this sector. This had already been indicated by the enemy's offensive operations on 9 and 10 March, which had resulted in a temporary penetration at the 15th SS Latvian Waffen Grenadier Division. A repetition of those attacks with stronger forces was expected.

In view of the importance of these heights in holding our own Panther Line, and also in the case of an enemy attack against the adjacent front of the Sixteenth Army, which projected eastward. The Eighteenth Army, once the combat activity northwest of Pskov had subsided, ordered the XXVIII Corps to disengage the temporarily assigned the [*kampfgruppe* of the] 4th SS *"Polizei"* Panzergrenadier Division and dispatch it to the VI SS Corps. Whether this order was occasioned by additional information concerning the enemy know to army headquarters, or whether the defense of this important sector was not to be entrusted solely to Latvian SS units is not known to the author.

On 16 March the enemy attack began, directed against almost the entire front of the 15th SS Latvian Waffen Grenadier Division and the 2d Latvian SS Brigade. In the first assault, the enemy managed to repel the Latvian defenders and capture Koshina, Oshidkovo, and Grigorkino. Through a counterattack with the addition commitment of the [*kampfgruppe* of the] 4th SS *"Polizei"* Panzergrenadier Division, whose fighting power, it is true, was only that of a reinforced regiment, almost all of the terrain lost was regained. The following day there was the same combat picture. In an attack long the whole front, the focal point was directed against the dominating height at Grigorkino, which changed hands several times. In the evening the height was gain in German hands, although its southern spurs - extending as far as Kostima, had had to be left to the enemy.

On 18 March, the enemy changed his offensive tactics. He attacked the right sector of the 15th SS Latvian Waffen Grenadier Division with only few forces, while his main thrust was directed against the height at Grigorkino, defended by the 2d Latvian SS Brigade. After heavy fighting the height was lost. But the enemy could not maintain himself upon it; a quick counterattack threw him off again. The attacking power of the enemy seemed to be exhausted; he did not repeat his attacks during the following days. The defensive battles had found a provisional conclusion. through his attacks, lasting three days, the enemy had achieved only an insignificant gain of territory. He did not succeed in gaining possession of the decisive hill territory around Grigorkino.

Second Defensive Battles Northwest of Pskov

While the fighting for the heights of Grigorkino in the right sector of the army was still in full swing, the enemy surprisingly resumed his attacks on the front of the 21st Infantry Division, with a view to gaining possession of the dominating heights northwest of Pskov. In the early morning of 17 March 1944, after a short, vigorous artillery preparation, strong enemy infantry masses supported by a large number of tanks attacked between the Gdov-Pskov Rollbahn and the lake. In the initial surprise the enemy managed to achieve a few small penetrations, which, however, were quickly eliminated due to the intervention of reserves. On the same day, and on 18 March, the enemy several times repeated his attacks - without success, however.

In the evening of 18 March, the enemy suspended the attacks northwest of Pskov. The dominating heights remained in full possession of the 21st Infantry Division.

Defensive Operations of the Enemy Velikaya Bridgehead Southeast of Ostrov, 26-31 March 1944

When the enemy suspended his attacks against the heights at Grigorkino on 18 March, the German command had no doubt that the enemy would try again in the foreseeable future to gain possession of this territory with stronger forces, since it was of special importance to him. This was also indicated by the local offensive operations that the enemy undertook during the following days at several places along the front of the VI SS Corps. The army group had accordingly ordered the assembly of a boundary reserve composed of one regiment each of the Sixteenth and Eighteenth Armies in the vicinity of the boundary line between the two armies.

On 26 March, after a heavy artillery preparation, the enemy attack began, at first directed against the bend in the Velikaya River, protruding eastward. The enemy succeeded in achieving a broad and deep penetration across the Velikaya River. Despite counterattacks, on our part, the enemy gained more and more ground, so that by evening of the day he had extended his penetration to a depth of four to five kilometers.

On 27 March a systematic counterattack was undertaken by the boundary reserve, composed on one regiment each of the 93d and 30th Infantry Divisions, assigned to the VI SS Corps. After part of the lost territory had been successfully retaken, the counterattack came to a stop. In the meantime the enemy had begun to attack the sector of the 15th SS Latvian Waffen Grenadier Division adjacent to the penetration. Here also success was on his side. The front of the division was pushed back two kilometers south of Grigorkino.

The enemy penetration had gradually been extended to a breadth of approximately ten kilometers and a depth of approximately four kilometers. To drive the enemy out and regain the old line, the forces of the VI SS Corps were insufficient, in view of the enemy's superior numbers. The army headquarters, therefore, ordered our counterattacks to be discontinued. They were not to be resumed until new reinforcements had been received, for which the 13th Luftwaffe Field Division, employed at the southern part of Lake Pskov, and the 12th Panzer Division, employed with the Sixteenth Army, both of whom had been promised by the army group, had been envisaged.

As an immediate supporting measure, the VI SS Corps was relieved of the northern sector of the 15th SS Latvian Waffen Grenadier Division to a point three kilometers northwest of the Velikaya Bend at Terekhova, this sector being assigned to the 21st Luftwaffe Field Division, which itself turned over its left sector to the 30th Infantry Division.

The following three days were taken up by further heavy enemy attacks. They pursued the particular sin of extending the penetration in the sector of the 15th SS Latvian Waffen Grenadier Division, which had been taken over on 28 March by the staff of the Luftwaffe division. The enemy attacks brought about no essential change in the situation, primarily because of the reinforcement of the defenders through the commitment of elements of the 13th Luftwaffe Field Division, which had been brought to the scene by motor transportation.

In the meantime, preparations for the counterattack, intended to eliminate the enemy penetration continued. The conduct of this attack was entrusted to the staff of the L Corps, which had up to then been employed at the front along Lake Peipus, and which now, as *Gruppe* Wegener, took over command of the 13th Luftwaffe Field Division from the VI SS Corps, and the adjacent sector of the 15th SS Latvian Waffen Grenadier Division as far as the Velikaya River. By 30 March the units designated for the counterattack, the 13th Luftwaffe Field Division, elements of the [*kampfgruppe* of the] 4th SS *"Polizei"* Panzergrenadier Division, and the 12th Panzer Division, had been assembled. The fighting power of the last-named division, however, had been greatly weakened; in addition to its two panzergrenadier regiments, it had only twenty-seven combat-ready tanks left.

To ensure a unified command for the battles which, it was anticipated, would take place in close proximity between Sixteenth and Eighteenth Armies, the left flank division of the Sixteenth Army and the 218th Infantry Division of the Eighteenth Army were assigned by the latter to the VI SS Corps.

In the early morning of 31 March the large-scale attack began, its thrust being directed against the southeastern part of the enemy penetration. The attack gained ground gradually in the face of the stubbornly fighting Russians, and several villages that had been converted into strong pockets of resistance were captured. Then the counterattack came to a halt. The superiority of the enemy, who had hurriedly brought reinforcements to the scene, was too great. Part of the regained territory was lost again. The small number of German tanks had to be withdrawn in the face of the far superior enemy tank forces newly thrown into battle. A continuation of the counterattack promised no success. Hence, the army group, also influenced by the enemy large-scale attack that had just begun south of Pskov, ordered the attack to be discontinued and the troops to withdraw to their original position. The 12th Panzer Division was to be disengaged from the front immediately, and dispatched by way of Ostrov to the XXVIII Corps.

On 4 April the L Corps (up to then *Gruppe* Wegener) ceased to be a part of the Eighteenth Army. The Sixteenth Army thus took responsibility for the combat zone of the Velikaya bridgehead off the shoulders of Eighteenth Army headquarters, whose full attention was claimed by the heavy defensive battles south of Pskov.

The Second Defensive Battle South of Pskov, 31 March-17 April 1944

The previous attacks against the hills northwest of Pskov and against the Balcony had probably been undertaken with considerable forces from the Leningrad Front. Nevertheless the German command clung to its opinion that these attacks had been only partial operations, and that the bulk of the Leningrad Front had not yet been employed, but was being kept back for a systematic large-scale attack. The available information on the enemy, gained from prisoners of war and, in addition, chiefly from radio reconnaissance which had observed the presence of a large number of Soviet units east and southeast of Pskov to the level of the Balcony, did indeed provide a clue to the strength of the opposing enemy troops, but not to the direction of the large-scale attack. In order to gain more clarity regarding this point, the army headquarters ordered the XXXVIII and the XXVIII Corps to undertake heavier assault patrol operations with a view to bringing in prisoners. These were carried out on 26 and 27 March without yielding any special results. It still remained entirely uncertain whether the enemy intended to attack in the direction of Pskov, or attack the Panther Line further south. The only thing to be inferred from the statements made by the prisoners who had been brought in by the assault patrols was that an enemy attack on a large scale was soon to begin.

Just as at the beginning of the Leningrad offensive on 14 January the army now had no notable strategic reserves at its disposal, since the three divisions set aside for this purpose had had to be committed in the course of the previous defensive battles for the Panther Line. Only two regiments of the 12th Luftwaffe Field Division had been disengaged from the front along Lake Peipus and placed at the disposal of the army in two separate groups, one southeast of Irboska, behind the center of the Ostrov-Pskov front, and one southwest of Pskov, for prompt commitment in the Pskov sector. The creation of further strategic reserves came to naught as a result of the complete confusion of the situation. This made it impossible to disengage strong units in any sector and weaken the front. Such a thing could only be done after the enemy offensive had begun, and its point of main effort and extent had been discovered.

On 30 March, while in the right sector of the army the fighting for the Velikaya bridgehead was in full swing, a vigorous enemy offensive began on the whole front from east of Ostrov to Lake Pskov. At the Balcony, in the sector of the XXVIII Corps, almost along the whole front of the 212th Infantry Division, and in the adjacent sector of the 215th Infantry Division, as well as north of the Luga-Pskov road at the 126th Infantry Division, these attacks assumed major proportions. German headquarters attached no special significance to these attacks. They could be holding attacks to prevent further reinforcements from being moved to the penetration at the Velikaya bridgehead. But the enemy might also be trying to gain possession of territory important to him. In any case the German command could not infer from this offensive activity that the anticipated large-scale enemy offensive was immediately impending, and that the engagements in the sector of the 212th and 215th Infantry divisions, so to speak, represented the beginning of the enemy breakthrough attempt.

The early morning of 31 March brought sudden and full clarity. With a sustained artillery barrage, the enemy began his large-scale attack, which was directed against the sector of the 212th Infantry Division and the adjoining sectors of the adjacent divisions - the 121st Infantry Division on the right and the 215th Infantry Division on the left. Supported by large numbers of ground-attack airplanes, heavy tank forces and infantry advanced in an attack. At the 212th Infantry Division the enemy first penetrated at four points; then the entire front of the division was made to collapse. In the southern sector of the division the penetration was sealed off east of the Rollbahn in the protective position for the artillery from Naumkovo through Voronino to Pogorelka. In the northern sector the enemy, following the withdrawing infantry, entered the artillery positions, which had been evacuated by the batteries upon the approach of the enemy. It was only west of the Rollbahn, west of a line Stanki-Stremutka, that the enemy was stopped by the infantry of the 212th Infantry Division, effectively supported by the batteries, which had again moved into position.

In the 121st Infantry division sector adjoining on the south, the enemy, while at the same time conducting a holding attack against the eastern front of the Balcony, attacked Panevo and the area on both sides of the road at Vessna, on the boundary line between the 121st and 212th Infantry Divisions, using heavy forces. Russians broke through the front at Vessna and advanced with tanks through to Lobany to a depth of three kilometers close to the Rollbahn at Fedorikha. In see-saw battles the reserves of the 121st Infantry division gradually pressed back the enemy, despite his commitment of new troops, and regained the old position except for a small bulge in the eastern part of Lobany. To the 212th Infantry Division, whose withdrawn right flank was situated at Naumkovo, there was a gap almost three kilometers wide.

The fighting near the right flank of the 215th Infantry Division (to the left of the 212th Infantry Division) proceeded in a similar manner. Here the enemy, in addition to a temporary local penetration on both sides of the large east-west highway leading to the Velikaya River, managed to achieve a penetration of more than one kilometer beyond Krapivinka, which, however, was quickly eliminated by an immediate vigorous counterattack.

The XXVIII Corps, to which the army headquarters soon after the beginning of the enemy large-scale attack had assigned the two Luftwaffe Field regiments that had been kept in readiness as army reserve, launched these regiments for a counterattack at the two most dangerous sectors of the enemy penetration as soon as a general idea of the situation was obtained. The southern *Regimentsgruppe*[4] succeeded in reaching the Lobany-Vanukha line in an attack, and thus in closing the menacing, broad gap between the 121st and 212th Infantry Divisions. The counterattack of the northern Luftwaffe Field regiment pushed back the enemy only a few hundred meters. But at least it was possible to again advance the line here up to Stanki-Stremutka.

At the end of the first day of fighting, the enemy had made his way into the Panther Line on a breadth of ten kilometers and a maximum depth of four kilometers in the northern part of the penetration zone. This was a surprisingly great success for the enemy, which he was bound to try to enlarge with all available means. The countermeasures to be adopted by the German side, if they were to be effective, had to be taken with the greatest possible speed. The most peremptory step seemed to be to relieve the 212th Infantry Division, which had been greatly weakened by the fighting, of a part of its defensive front to enable it to reinforce its remaining sector with the personnel thus released. The XXVIII Corps hence ordered the 215th Infantry Division, though this division had itself been heavily attacked, to assume the northernmost part of the sector of the 212th Infantry Division as far as Stanki. It was, moreover, intended to turn over this sector, in which the situation seemed most menacing because of the depth of the enemy penetration, to the staff of the 12th Luftwaffe Field Division with its particularly energetic and seasoned commander, upon the staff's arrival from the front along Lake Peipus, from which it had been withdrawn.

The German command was aware that the enemy would, without hesitation, throw more forces into battle in order to turn the momentarily sealed-off penetration into a breakthrough. Hence the aim had to be to narrow down the enemy penetration with all means, in order to regain the lost territory, with its better opportunities for a defense, and to take from the enemy the favorable deployment area for commitment of further forces. To enhance the power of resistance it was, furthermore, necessary to immediately disengage forces from the other fronts in order that fresh, compact units could be brought to the penetration site as reinforcement.

As a result, the XXVIII Corps, the Eighteenth Army, and the army group issued the following orders:

1. The 12th Panzer Division, which meanwhile had arrived at the corps, together with a regiment of the 12th Luftwaffe Field Division, to attack from the area around Naumkovo in a general northeasterly direction, gain a line from the fork in the road at Saubje-Yeremino in support of the 121st Infantry Division, thus narrowing the enemy penetration zone in the south.

2. The 12th Luftwaffe Field Division immediately upon arrival of the 212th

and 215th Infantry Divisions to take over the Pogorelka-west of Kryshevo sector.

3. The 8th Jaeger Division to be disengaged from the front by the XXXVIII Corps and be speedily moved to the XXVIII Corps. Its sector to be taken over for the time being by the 30th Infantry Division.

4. Sixteenth Army to disengage the 32nd Infantry division from the front and dispatch it to the XXVIII Corps.

Course of the fighting on 1 April:

In the 121st Infantry Division sector the enemy attacked the left flank without achieving further successes. The division managed to recover Lobany, which had been lost the previous day; as a result of an enemy attack in superior force it was lost again.

Further to the north, in the sector of the 212th Infantry Division, heavy attacks were undertaken against the villages of Voronino and Sidorovo, both of which were captured by the enemy.

In the meantime, the 12th Panzer Division, in accordance with the order of the XXVIII Corps, had begun to attack. The regiment of the 12th Luftwaffe Field Division, advancing on the right, gained the fork in the road at Sagubje, but had to withdraw to its original position in the face of heavy enemy attacks. The 12th Panzer Division drove the enemy out of Voronino, which was captured a short time before, but did not reach its objective of Yeremino.

As was expected on the German side, the point of main effort of the enemy attack was situated at the deepest point of the penetration zone. The enemy, with his far superior forces, gained Stanki, Stremutka and Dakovo. He pushed back the German defenders two to three kilometers to Starossele - west of Uvarovo - and Dakovo. As a result there was a gap three kilometers wide in the German front between Podborove and Letovo; a breakthrough seemed to be imminent. A counterattack led by Colonel Gottfried Weber, the commander of the 12th Luftwaffe Field Division which meanwhile had taken over the Pogorelka-Kryshevo sector, however, succeeded in overcoming this danger and in closing the gap.

In the sector of the 215th Infantry Division, the enemy attacked at the same points as on the previous day, on both sides of the road east of Gavrilova and at Krapivinka. Temporary enemy penetrations were eliminated by counterattacks of the reserves that had been kept ready.

The result of this second day of the large-scale attack was that the enemy in the northern had had extended his penetration zone by three additional kilometers in depth, but that he had not achieved a breakthrough. In the southern half the German defense front was able to maintain its positions; through the counterattack of the 12th Panzer Division the enemy penetration had been narrowed down there, although to no great degree.

On 2 April the enemy endeavored to extend the deep penetration west of the Rollbahn not only the direction of the Velikaya River, but also in the adjoining sectors. To this end, the enemy undertook a surprise night attack against Voronino in the sector of the 212th Infantry Division and captured it. The 12th Panzer Division launched a counterattack to recapture the village, but could not force its way through as a result of the enemy's superiority. At daybreak, the enemy continued to attack in this sector with heavy forces, his main effort being directed toward Vanukha-Volkhovo. The German defenders were forced to abandon their positions, but were again able to entrench themselves on and east of the Rollbahn, and to maintain this line against further enemy attacks. The enemy nowhere succeeded in advancing westward beyond the Rollbahn.

Further north, heavy enemy attacks hit the 12th Luftwaffe Field Division in the penetration salient. While it was able to fight off the attacks on its flanks, its center was thrown back more than one kilometer westward as far as a point east of Sapatkion-Pavlova.

The northern bastion of the penetration zone at Letovo was attacked by heavy enemy forces from a southerly direction, as were Selugina and Krapivinka further to the northeast. Through the first enemy assault the three villages were lost. The 215th Infantry Division counterattacked with the reserves kept in readiness which led to the recapture of Letovo and Selugina, and - after it had changed hands several times - also of Krapivinka.

Through his attacks on this third day of large-scale combat, the enemy had again been able to considerably deepen his penetration west of the Rollbahn. Aside from insignificant territorial gains, he had not been able to achieve the desired broadening of the penetration zone at its flanks.

The 12th Panzer Division, which had only a small number of battle-worthy tanks at its disposal, had lost so much of its combat power during the fighting of the last two days that it had to be withdrawn in the night of 2 April. The division was transferred to the area northeast of Ostrov for rehabilitation.

It was impossible to delay further in disengaging the greatly weakened 212th Infantry Division, which so far had had to stand up against the majority of the enemy attacks. Its sector was taken over by the 8th Jaeger Division, which had arrived in the meantime. The 212th Infantry Division in turn took over the former sector of the 8th Jaeger Division which had temporarily been occupied by the 30th Infantry Division, in addition to its own sector.

Furthermore, for the purpose of increasing the defensive strength of the 12th Luftwaffe Field Division, against which the heavy attacks of the enemy in the penetration bend had continuously been directed, its flank sectors were separated from it, and assigned to the 8th Jaeger Division on the right, and to the 215th Infantry Division on the left. On the left flank of the 12th Luftwaffe Field Division, this measure was to be only a temporary one, since the corps intended to insert the 32nd Infantry Division, which was being moved up, in the northern part of the penetration salient.

On 3 April the enemy attacked, at first only in individual sectors. Then a unified attack conducted by fifteen divisions set in on a broad front, extending from Vernavino in the sector of the 8th Jaeger Division, through Starossele, Sapatkino-Pavlona, and Podborove in the sector of the 12th Luftwaffe Field Division, as far as Letovo and Krapivinka in the sector of the 215th Infantry Division.

Temporarily, the enemy managed to cause the southern bastion of the penetration zone at the railroad east of Bol Ussy to collapse. In the center of the salient there were repeated penetrations at the 12th Luftwaffe Field Division. Around Podborove, which changed hands several times, particularly bitter fighting flared up. With the 215th Infantry Division, the enemy also broke into the front at Letovo and Krapivinka. The will to resist on the part of the German defenders, however, could not be broken by the more than five-fold superiority of the enemy. Along the entire defensive front troops counterattacked again and again. The enemy's unified mass attack failed. In no sector did it achieve success. All enemy penetrations were eliminated. At the end of this day of large-scale fighting, the German front stood firm and unshaken.

From 4-8 April, the enemy continued his attacks on the entire penetration front. But there was no unified attack like that of 3 April, during which the enemy apparently realized that he would not succeed in extending his penetration at its deepest point, even by committing massed forces on a narrow front. Here the enemy continued to attack with only relatively weak forces. However, he shifted his point of main effort to the rear sectors of the penetration zone in an attempt to enlarge these southward and northeastward by committing strong forces. At the southern penetration salient in the sector of the 8th Jaeger Division on 4, 5, and 7 April the enemy tried - by means of particularly heavy attacks, to cause the German defense front at and west of the railroad as far as Starossele to collapse. He repeatedly achieved penetrations, but they were always eliminated again in counterattacks. The fighting in the northern half of the penetration zone proceeded in similar fashion, the enemy endeavoring to extend it to the northwest. Hard fighting flared up here, particularly at Lapinka, Podborove, and Stremutka. The 32nd Infantry Division, which had newly taken over this sector from the 12th Luftwaffe Field Division and the 215th Infantry Division, repulsed all enemy attacks, and temporary penetrations were eliminated. In the 215th Infantry Division sector adjoining on the left, further enemy attacks also occurred during these days with a similar aim of extending the penetration zone, in this case to the northwest. At Letovo and south of Krapivinka, the enemy was initially successful, to a certain extent. But the 215th Infantry Division succeeded in retrieving its old position by means of counterattacks, except for a small area at Letovo.

On 8 April, the last heavy attacks of the enemy occurred, again distributed over the entire penetration front. They achieved no success whatsoever.

Despite the almost complete suspension of the enemy's offensive, the German command did not expect the enemy to abandon his attempts to break through. On the contrary, it took the view that the enemy forces were being rehabilitated by replacements and would resume fighting when this had been done. The main attention of the German headquarters was hence directed toward replacing the units on the defensive front of the penetration zone, which had been greatly weakened by the battles, by fresh, strong divisions. The most peremptory measure was the relief of the 12th Luftwaffe Field Division, whose units had, from the first day, been employed at the focal points of the great defensive battle. To retrieve it, the 21st Infantry Division - whose disengagement from the front northwest of Pskov had been under way since 6 April - had been designated; in addition, the 8th Jaeger Division, which had borne the principal burden of the fighting during the past days, had to be relieved. In accordance with a directive from the army group it was, for the time being, not to be employed with the Eighteenth Army on the front, since its return to the Sixteenth Army had been contemplated. And finally it was impossible to defer a reinforcement of the 215th Infantry Division, which had greatly suffered in its fighting power as a result of the enemy attacks against its right sector since the beginning of the defensive battle.

In order to achieve a properly balanced distribution of forces, particularly in view of the contemplated departure of the 8th Jaeger Division from the army, it could not be avoided that the entire front, form the division on the right flank to lake Pskov, with the exception of the 32nd Infantry Division - which had been at the penetration front for only a short time - was set in motion in a lateral shift.

To facilitate disengagement of the 30th Infantry Division, which had been earmarked to occupy the sector of the 8th Jaeger Division, the 21st Luftwaffe Field Division rook over its right sector, the 212th Infantry Division its left and main sector. The 121st Infantry Division took over three kilometers of front from the left flank of the 212th Infantry Division, which had been greatly weakened by the fighting.

In addition, the 126th Infantry Division had to take over sectors form the adjacent divisions: on the right, the left sector of the 215th Infantry Division (which was thus left with the narrower from necessary to increase its fighting power); on the left, three kilometers from the 21st Infantry Division (which was to relieve the 12th Luftwaffe Field Division at the penetration). A reduction of the sector of the 21st Infantry Division was advisable, since the 12th Luftwaffe Field Division, to which - in line with the redistribution of sectors aimed at restoring strength to the units - the 23d Luftwaffe Field Regiment, which had been employed with the 8th Jaeger Division, was to be reassigned, still had lost too much of its fighting power to take over the whole sector of the 21st Infantry Division.

On 9 April, the 21st Infantry Division and the 12th Luftwaffe Field Division exchanged their areas, and on 11 April the 30th Infantry Division took over the sector of the 8th Jaeger Division, while for the time being the jaeger division was assembled in the area south of Ostrov. On 15 April the 8th Jaeger Division was transferred to the Sixteenth Army.

On the defensive front of the penetration zone, there now were the well-rested strong units of the 30th and 21st Infantry Divisions and the 32d Infantry Division, which had lost relatively little of its fighting power in the previous fighting.

The enemy had availed himself of the intermission on 9 April to restore order to his units, and bring them to full combat strength through incorporation of replacements. According to a number of reports received by the army headquarters from spies, the Leningrad Front had obtained 50,000 replacements to offset the undoubtedly very high losses sustained in previous fighting.

On the morning of 13 April the enemy resumed his attacks in the penetration zone after heavy artillery preparation. With tremendous masses of infantry, supported by a large number of tanks, he attacked the entire sector of the 30th Infantry Division, the adjoining flank of the 21st and the right sector of the 32d Infantry Division, an attack front which extended from Vadrino to Podborove. The right and center of the 21st and the left sector of the 32nd Infantry Division and the adjoining 215th Infantry Division were not attacked - in other words, the front of the enemy attack had been substantially reduced as compared with previous battles. On 14 and 15 April the enemy attacked on a still narrower front, which extended only from Vardino to Lapinka. On 16 and 17 April heavy enemy attacks occurred only against Vadrino. Then the enemy discontinued his attacks, which during these five days had brought him only temporary territorial gains at individual points, which he soon lost again in German counterattacks.

With the conclusion of the fighting on 17 April, the defensive battle south of Pskov had come to an end. In eighteen days of bitter fighting, the enemy had attempted to cause the front of the Eighteenth Army to collapse. For this purpose he had thrown twenty infantry divisions and a great deal of tank forces into battle, which were opposed on the defensive front of the penetration zone by only three to four German divisions. In spite of his great numerical superiority over the Eighteenth Army - which had at its disposal for the defensive battle only its own eight divisions with which to hold the entire remaining portion of the front, plus one weak panzer division assigned for a few days - the enemy achieved only a penetration twelve kilometers wide and eight kilometers deep in a relatively narrow sector. The battle south of Pskov was a full defensive success for the German command and its brave divisions. In the following weeks, and until the beginning of the last third of June, quiet generally prevailed on the Eighteenth Army front, interrupted only occasionally by local enemy attacks and isolated offensive operations, During this period the army reorganized its sectors, chiefly because of the transfer, ordered by OKH, of the 212th Infantry Division to Army Group Center. As was to be expected, the reorganization did not escape the attention of the enemy, who repeatedly tried to learn about the events in the Panther Line by means of reconnaissance thrusts in strength, which he conducted in the various sectors from the right flank of the army to Lake Pskov.

In line with the redistribution of sectors, the 32nd Infantry Division had been employed east and northeast of Ostrov in broad formation. In June, when the swampy outpost area of this part of the position became more and more passable as a result of the sustained heat, and thus an enemy attack in the direction of Ostrov became more probable, army headquarters decided to employ the 215th Infantry divisions, which had been kept at its disposal behind the center of the army, in this section of the front. Through this measure the 32d Infantry Division was limited to the southern half of its former sector, while the 215th Infantry Division received the northern half and three kilometers of front from the 121st Infantry Division, adjoining on the left. In this manner, the two roads into Ostrov from the east and northeast, which were important for enemy attacks, were shared by the 32d and 215th Infantry Divisions.

Immediately after taking over its sector, the 215th Infantry Division was hit by a heavy enemy attack on 22 June. The enemy attacked the area on both sides of the Ostrov road with his southern main force and the village of Troitskaya on the left boundary of the division with a weaker force. The enemy forces attacking in the southern sector of the division succeeded in breaking into the Panther Line, and in gaining a foothold in several villages on both sides of the road. Through counterattacks, the penetrations were eliminated on 23 and 24 June, so that the Panther Line was again entirely in the hands of the division. It can be safely assumed that the primary purpose of the enemy attack on 22 June was to divert the attention of German headquarters from the thrust against the Balcony position, which the enemy planned for the following day, and if possible to induce the German headquarters to draw off reinforcements from this sector for the support of the 215th Infantry Division.

Second Defensive Combat Northwest of Ostrov (Balcony), 23-28 June 1944

On 23 June the enemy began his second large-scale attack against the Balcony position, which - as had been the case during the first attack - was still occupied by the 121st Infantry Division. Whether the objective of the enemy command lay beyond the Balcony, could not be ascertained. There was a possibility that the enemy, after capturing the Balcony, intended to push on in the direction of Ostrov, to gain possession of this important road junction.

With the beginning of his attack, the enemy conducted holding attacks, in part using heavy forces along the whole front of the army north of the Balcony, and in the sectors of the 30th, 21st, and 126th Infantry Divisions and the 12th Luftwaffe Field Division. The first thrust, preceded by heavy artillery fire, was directed against the Voshchinino-Lekhino eastern front. Penetrations were made in the center at Baevo, and at the southeastern corner of the Balcony at Voshchinino. The latter success was exploited by the enemy in an attack with strong forces against the entire southern front of the Balcony position. The front was forced to collapse, and the enemy pushed on as far as the line of Judino-government estate at Kirova-Yermaki-Utkino-

Gorodets. Only in the center of the penetration zone was it possible to re-capture Yermaki through a counterattack.

A systematic counterattack had been prepared for 24 June, which, soon after it had begun, encountered strong enemy forces about to renew their attack, with a view to expanding their penetration. At the same time, the enemy undertook a strong holding attack against the adjacent 30th Infantry Division at Alkhimovo, which resulted in an insignificant local penetration at a salient in the position. The counterattack of the 121st Infantry Division, supported by heavy artillery, by assault guns, and Tiger tanks, pushed the enemy back despite his superiority, and after heavy fighting resulted in re-capture of the old main line of resistance of Judino-Voschchinino-Utkino-Gordoets-Lekhino. A salient in the Panther Line, approximately one and one-half kilometers wide, which jutted eastward from the front, remained in the enemy's hands.

The same battle picture appeared on 25 and 26 June as on the two preceding days. On 25 June, the enemy again attacked Voshchinino-Lekhino with strong forces. The German defenders were pressed back at the south-eastern bastion of the Balcony. The eastern part of Voshchinino and the village of Suevo were lost. A counterattack by the 121st Infantry Division on 26 June pushed back the enemy and again brought all of the old main line of resistance, with the exception of a small section, into German hands.

The severe fighting of the past four days naturally had reduced the strength of the 121st Infantry Division. Reserves to support this division were at the disposal of neither the XXXVIII Corps nor the army. To reinforce the com-bat strength of the division - at least to some extent - army headquarters ordered the 30th Infantry Division of the XXVIII Corps to take over the left sector of the 121st Infantry division as far as south of Panevo.

On 27 June the enemy initially limited himself to attacking the south-eastern corner of the Balcony position again, which he had previously cap-tured and lost several times. While this attack was under way, troops of the 121st Infantry Division started out to recapture the Baevo-Ivankovo section of the position, which had remained in enemy hands on 24 June. But the attacker gained only little ground. An enemy counterattack threw the Ger-man troops back to their original positions. The enemy pressed after them and succeeded in capturing Utkino-Gorodets.

On 28 June the enemy attacks against the southern half of the eastern front of the Balcony were brought to a conclusion. They had been fought off everywhere by the defenders.

In a six-day struggle, the enemy - despite his comparatively great initial success, did not succeed in seizing the dominating heights of the Balcony. The German defense proved to strong for the superior enemy. The counter-attacks of the 121st Infantry Division threw the enemy forces almost entirely out of the penetration zone. When the Russian attacks were discontinued, the entire main line of resistance of the Panther Line, with the exception of a small portion in the part of the Balcony projecting eastward, was again in the hands of the 121st Infantry Division.

The second defensive engagement for the Balcony formed the conclusion of the defensive battles for Ostrov and Pskov. Up to 11 July 1944, the beginning of the retreat from the Panther Line, there were no further major enemy attacks in the area of the Eighteenth Army. Despite the heavy enemy majority, the German command and its brave troops had succeeded in fighting off all breakthrough attempts of the enemy for four months and in maintaining their hold on the Panther Line.

Battle Experience

The Russians were extremely skillful in concealing the troops they had assembled for the large-scale attacks against the Panther Line. Although the German command had been informed by its excellent radio reconnaissance of the number of large units which the Leningrad Front had moved to the scene for the planned offensive, it was unable to draw a conclusion regarding the direction of the attack because of the broad and deep distribution of these troops in the vast assembly area. German air reconnaissance forces were continually sent out in order to obtain clues as to the intentions of the enemy. Although the German planes were scarcely hampered by Russian anti-aircraft defenses in the air and on the ground, air reconnaissance did not clear up the matter. The villages, although undoubtedly densely occupied, were seemingly empty; not the slightest movement - no combat or supply vehicles - could be detected. This was even true of the days immediately preceding the beginning of the large-scale attacks, when the Russians had concentrated twenty infantry divisions and a large number of anti-tank forces in an extremely small area opposite the penetration zone. They had, as it were, vanished from the face of the earth.

Only thus can it be explained that the German command agencies and the German units failed to know about the direction of the enemy attack until the large-scale attack itself began.

During the weeks prior to the large-scale attack, the Russian command tried with all means to obtain an idea of the Panther Line and the troops occupying it. In addition to a great many attacks by small and large units, aimed at pushing back the German combat outposts situated in front of the position, a large number of enemy reconnaissance operations took place in all divisional sectors along the entire army front. It was impossible to discern a point of main effort in this preparatory activity of the enemy so that the presumable direction of the impending large-scale offensive could not be predicted.

Not only did the Russian command know perfectly how to conceal the infantry it had assembled for attack, it also knew how to completely cloak its intentions with respect to the coming battle by distributing its reconnaissance in force over the entire front of the army.

In the large-scale attack south of Pskov the Russian artillery had concentrated its preparatory fire on the penetration zones to an unusual degree. In addition to disrupting the front line the main objective of this artillery fire was the smashing of anti-tank weapons. Each position in which there were such weapons, or in which they were suspected to be, was hit by a separate concentration of fire.

The German batteries, on the other hand, were hardly interfered with by enemy artillery and planes either before or during the attack, although because of terrain conditions they were fairly closely concentrated and for the most part comparatively far forward, so that their positions were bound to be known to enemy reconnaissance agencies. The fact that the German artillery was not taken under fire in the course of the defensive battle is the more striking when one considers that the Russian headquarters were able to observe again and again that the failure of the attack was due largely to the concentrated defensive fire of German batteries and rocket launchers. The reasons for the fact that the German batteries were not fired on at all, or only to a limited extent, must be sought in the absence of observation battalions on the Russian side, and in the shortage of ammunition.

The supply traffic in the rear area, too, was hardly hampered by enemy artillery fire and aircraft. The Velikaya bridges at Gorbovo and Filatova-Gora, for instance, which were highly important for the supply of the defensive front at the penetration zone, were only very rarely attacked by enemy aircraft, The fact that no harassing fire was directed against the area far to the rear was probably due to the lack of long-range batteries.

The enemy owed his initial success in his large-scale attack south of Pskov primarily to his strong tank forces, which - after crushing the forward anti-tank weapons - overran the German positions almost unimpeded. The fact that it was possible nevertheless to stop the enemy a few kilometers in the rear of the Panther Line was due to the anti-tank position in the rear, which - established in line with the Rollbahn - brought the enemy tanks and infantry following behind to a halt by means of its surprise fire. This anti-tank position in the rear included a large number of small-caliber anti-aircraft guns, and at important sectors a few 88mm anti-aircraft guns. The decision to adopt this measure had been made possible because the enemy planes always flew at such a high altitude that they were beyond the range of small-caliber guns, so that these guns could not have performed their proper function of air raid protection in any case.

In the event of a deep enemy penetration the friendly batteries must, at all costs, hold out in their positions, even at the risk of being lost. Only then can they afford support to the retreating infantry, and in addition keep the enemy tanks and the attacking troops following them from pushing through further. An example of the correctness of this principle was offered by the breakthrough in the 212th Infantry division area. In the northern sector of the division, the batteries, in order not to fall into the hands of the enemy who had approached to within a few hundred meters, changed their positions toward the rear upon appropriate orders, with the result that the enemy immediately pressed beyond the abandoned battery positions and extended the depth of his penetration by from two to three kilometers. In the southern sector of the division, the batteries remained in their firing positions, the retreating infantry clung to them and formed another front, and the enemy attack was successfully brought to a halt.

Conclusion

Despite the many circumstances in its favor, the Russian command had not succeeded during the winter offensive of January and February 1944 in destroying the Eighteenth Army, the bastion of the German eastern front. After ending its retreat over 300 kilometers of bad roads and tracks, this army had been able, without having lost much of its combat strength, to prepare for new resistance in the well-fortified Panther Line under substantially better conditions. This was a thing to which the Russian command had to reconcile itself. It undoubtedly realized that a new, thoroughly prepared plan of attack was needed to gain a final victory over the Eighteenth Army. When it nevertheless started relatively large partial operations immediately upon the arrival of its units, it was certainly actuated by psychological considerations, too. It could and would not admit its objective, which was the destruction of the Eighteenth Army had failed.

The partial operations undertaken prior to the planned large-scale attack pursued a double purpose: possession of territory was to be gained that was of importance for the subsequent large-scale offensive. As previously mentioned, the headquarters of the Leningrad Front was likely to have made the choice of the direction for its intended large-scale attack dependent upon whether or not it was previously able to capture the hills of the Balcony and those northwest of Pskov.

Capture of the hills northwest of Pskov and in the Balcony was denied to the enemy despite his commitment of heavy infantry and tank forces. As an objective for the launching of his subsequent large-scale offensive, they were out of the question; the enemy thereupon launched his attack with correct logic against a front sector of the Panther Line which was remote from the two blocks of hills.

The partial operations conducted by the Second Baltic Front near the right flank of the Eighteenth Army were successful. Here the enemy forced a crossing of the Velikaya and was able to hold the captured bridgehead against German counterattacks. To what extent its possession influenced the conduct of the subsequent enemy offensive against the Sixteenth Army is unknown to the author. But such influence must be assumed, since the bridgehead - in conjunction with the front of the Panther Line, which here curved eastward - offered good chances for launching a thrust against the flank and rear of the Sixteenth Army, owing to the favorable and firm terrain.

The partial operations were to force the Eighteenth Army to commit the three divisions which it had kept in reserve upon occupying the Panther Line, so that at the beginning of the large-scale offensive the German command would have no notable strategic reserves at its disposal. This objective was attained. The three divisions that had been kept in reserve were committed in the defense against the Russian partial operations. Their absence at the beginning of the large-scale offensive made itself fully felt. It was due to the lack of these divisions that the extension of the initial Russian success, a surprise success, into a broad, eight-kilometer-deep penetration in the Panther Line must be attributed.

The original right boundary of the Eighteenth Army was shifted twice in the course of the defensive battle; once to the right on 28 March 1944 as a result of taking over the sector of the 218th Infantry Division, then on 4 April 1944 to the left as a result of the separation of the VI SS Corps from the army. These were measures which were considered pleasant neither by the higher headquarters concerned nor the troops, and which should have been avoided. In the description of the fighting for the Velikaya bridgehead, attention has already been drawn to the alignment of the Panther Line, which - at the boundary between the Sixteenth and Eighteenth Armies curved from a generally north-south to an easterly direction. The angle thus formed, with its good terrain conditions, plainly offered the enemy command the opportunity for a thrust against the flank and rear of the Sixteenth Army. On the Russian side, this area was also included in the scope of command of one headquarters, that of the Second Baltic Front, which stood opposite the Sixteenth Army. Analogously, it would have been advisable also on the German side to assign this area in its entirety to one army - from the beginning in this particular case to the Sixteenth Army - which was especially affected by the intentions and measures of the Second Baltic Front.

Although in general one should not allow the enemy to dictate one's measures, it is advisable in many instances during a defensive to adapt oneself to the enemy's command pattern in drawing the boundaries between major army elements. In the case at hand, this was especially valid because the boundary between two armies, which an enemy likes to take advantage of in launching an attack, led through territory which, according to the course taken by the lines, was likely to play a special role in the impending defensive battle.

The large-scale Russian breakthrough attempt against the Panther Line south of Pskov was discontinued as hopeless after eighteen days of hard struggle, although all prerequisites for a successful outcome had been present in the beginning: the Russian command had managed to (1) leave German army headquarters in the dark as to the direction of its attack, (2) to assemble its heavy attack forces unnoticed, and (3) to surprise us with the timing of the attack. It had furthermore managed in the initial assault to cause the German line to collapse along a broad front. Beyond the initial success of the first day, however, for many days the fighting was able to bring only a slight expansion of the penetration, despite continual commitment of fresh forces. The strategic objective of breaking through the German front and clearing the way for a westward thrust was not attained.

This failure would perhaps have been avoided if the Russian command had not stubbornly persisted in the once-chosen direction of attack. It should have become aware in the first days after the beginning of the offensive that the German defensive measures at the penetration zone, after the first surprise had been overcome, would become more and more effective, while the prospect for a successful breakthrough dwindled more and more. On the other hand, the STAVKA undoubtedly realized that once the few reserves of the Eighteenth Army had been committed, further reinforcement of the German defenses could be affected only by weakening the other fronts. The Russian command should have exploited this circumstances and attempted the breakthrough at another sector of the front rather than continue the stalled attack at the original point. With its skill in shifting and concentrating its troops unnoticed by the enemy, the Russian command would not have found it very difficult during the intermission of several days in its attack to shift a strong attack force to another sector and attack this sector by surprise. Such a breakthrough attempt at another point, whether in the direction of the Balcony or aiming at Pskov, would no doubt have had prospects for success. A redistribution of the German defense forces, which would have had to be tied down by strong holding attacks, to the new attack front would in any case have required a certain amount of time on account of road conditions. Attention is drawn especially to the difficulties in redistributing the strong German artillery employed at the penetration zone, and to whose fire the failure of the Russian attacks was to a large extent due. A more flexible conduct of operations than that displayed by the Russians would certainly, after the first attack had stalled, have attempted to achieve the breakthrough through the German front at another point and thus to clear the way for a thrust west.

As already mentioned, the German command had no strong strategic reserves at the beginning of the defensive battle south of Pskov. Only the two regiments of the 12th Luftwaffe Field Division disengaged from the front along Lake Peipus were available, as was the 12th Panzer Division, hurriedly brought to the scene from the Velikaya bridgehead at the beginning of the enemy attack. This division, however, had only about twenty tanks fit for battle. This was an extremely critical situation for the feeding of a strength-devouring defensive battle of presumably prolonged duration. In spite of this, sufficient number of forces had to be continuously furnished to the defensive front for support at the broad and deep penetration zone. This could be done only by ruthlessly weakening the remaining parts of the front to gain battle-worthy units. This was done on a very extensive scale. The headquarters of the XXVIII Corps did not shrink from temporarily weakening sectors to an extent that could scarcely be regarded as bearable in view of the situation. A case in point was the disengagement of the 8th Jaeger Division - whose entire sector had to be taken over for two days by the 30th Infantry Division until the 212th Infantry Division arrived as planned - which was already spread very thin, in addition to its own sector.

In the disengagement of individual divisions for employment at the penetration zone, it was impossible to avoid the lateral shifting of three or four adjacent divisions from time to time. They had to turn over part of their sector to the adjacent units, and in its place take over a new sector on the opposite flank. This measure was necessary to balance the distribution of forces.

During eighteen days of heavy fighting in a small area, twenty Russian divisions, supported by heavy tank forces, had not been able to break through the front of the Eighteenth Army. The far-flung strategic plans of the Russian command had thus for the time being been frustrated.

The battle south of Pskov goes to show that troops animated by a strong will to resist can successfully fight off massed enemy attacks, even if the enemy greatly outnumbers them.

NOTES

[1]The relative weakness of these divisions presents a good profile of the magnitude of the defeat which had been suffered by the Eighteenth Army in January and February:

Unit	Total/Infantry Strength	Artillery Batteries	Anti-tank guns
4th SS	2,847/650	4	7
12th LWF	7,424/1,481	7	13
126th Inf.	7,627/2,689	5	7

Heeresgruppe Nord, Ia/Id, 730/44, 7 February 1944; Ia, no number, 22 February 1944, T-311, Reel 70.

[2]The East Prussian 11th Infantry Division was an example of the fact that—at least sporadically—the German Army replacement system had not completely broken down in early 1944. At the beginning of the year, the division had been at nearly full strength for the 1944 organizational table: 2,250 infantry, twelve field batteries, and twenty-four anti-tank guns, a full-strength engineer battalion, and even a *feldersatz* battalion. After the first two weeks of fighting, used primarily as a fire brigade at the most critical crisis points, the division had been reduced to a *kampfgruppe* with its three regiments totaling only 692 infantrymen, twelve field batteries (missing most of their transportation), and eighteen anti-tank guns. The total losses of the division by the end of February were over 3,600. But the replacement system of Wehrkreis I continued to pump replacements back into the line. The 11th Infantry received nearly 3,000 trained replacements in the same period, bringing its infantry strength back up to 2,303 by 22 February. *Heeresgruppe Nord, Zustand der Divisionen*, Operations Abteilung III, 19 December 1943; *Armeeoberkommando 18*, Ia, 732/44, 5 February 1944; *Heeresgruppe Nord*, Ia/Id, 730/44, 7 February 1944; Ia, no

number, 22 February 1944; *Armeeoberkommando 18*, Ia, 1064/44, 21 February 1944; T-311, Reel 70; *Heeresgruppe Nord, Feldersatz*, 30 January-4 April 1944, T-311, Reel 73.

[3]This division had finally been reconstituted as a complete—albeit weakened—unit; see note in Chapter Three.

[4]Note in original: "A regiment constituted during operations and consisting of men and equipment from various arms."

CHAPTER 5

The Battles of *Armeeabteilung Narva,* 2 February-31 May 1944

Paul Reichelt

Preliminary Remarks

The only reference material available for the preparation of a study on the Narva front consisted of brief notes taken by the author himself, and a map showing the alignment of the front. The study has largely been supplemented from memory. The appraisals and decisions of the *Armeeabteilung* correspond to the situation prevailing at the time. The author had been assigned to the Narva front since the middle of March 1944.

Withdrawal of the Left Flank of the Eighteenth Army After 14 January 1944 as far as the Narva River

The breakthrough attack of the enemy from Leningrad and the Oranienbaum bridgehead, begun on 14 January 1944, had, after a few days, led to withdrawals of the northern sector of the Eighteenth Army, which the enemy - coming from Krassnoe-Solo - hit in the flank. In spite of the fact that it had received reinforcements, the Eighteenth Army was unable to master the situation. The Russians finally forced a breakthrough.

This situation made it necessary to bend back the right sector, composed of the III SS Panzer Corps, which was still in its old position at the Oranienbaum pocket. To ensure firmer control of the endangered sector, the LIV Corps was employed in the sector adjacent to the III SS Panzer Corps. The aim of the enemy, which was to overrun the northern group of the Eighteenth Army in order to gain freedom of action in Estonia, had already become apparent. While the III SS Panzer Corps, beginning on its right was able to withdraw systematically, the LIV Corps remained involved in heavy retreating battles. With his point of main effort at the Rollbahn to

Kingissepp, the enemy pressed forward in pursuit.

On 26 January there was a gap of twenty kilometers between this group and the bulk of the Eighteenth Army. To ensure a unified command of the northern group, the Eighteenth Army combined the LIV Corps and the III SS Panzer Corps under General of Infantry Otto Sponheimer, the Commanding General, LIV Corps, with the designation "*Gruppe* Sponheimer."

Although by 28 January it had been possible once again to form a front in a thin, discontinuous line, approximately fifteen kilometers east of Kingissepp, the immediate penetration of this front by the enemy made a further withdrawal necessary. In the meantime, the enemy had attacked the extreme northern sector, and was pressing after the retreating III SS Panzer Corps, between whom and the adjacent unit there was already a gap. On account of threatening envelopment from the south, the front was unable to hold at the broad Luga sector either.

In heavy and bloody fighting, *Gruppe* Sponheimer immediately withdrew behind the Narva River with the LIV Corps. The garrison headquarters at Narva had already established a rear line and organized the local defense of Narva with emergency alert units. The III SS Panzer Corps, with a few elements ahead of it, was assigned with 11th SS *"Nordland"* Panzergrenadier Division, 4th SS *"Nederland,"* the 20th Estonian SS Waffen Grenadier Division[1], and the remnants of the 9th and 10th Luftwaffe Field Divisions, to the expanded bridgehead, and to the Narva-Hungerburg front; it was able to take up its positions.[2]

Higher headquarters had viewed the development of the situation in the northern area with great concern.

Contrary to expectations, *Gruppe* Sponheimer had been obliged to withdraw surprisingly quickly. By 28 January there was already a gap of fifty kilometers between it and the rest of the Eighteenth Army, which afforded the enemy complete freedom of movement. The quick assault of the Russian Second Shock Army brought with it the danger that *Gruppe* Sponheimer might immediately be overrun even on the Narva River.

As a matter of precaution, the *Feldherrnhalle* Panzergrenadier Division, which was just being moved to the scene, had been sent on to Narva. A reinforced regiment of the 58th Infantry Division was also dispatched there by way of Tartu; its arrival could not, however, be expected before 5 February.[3]

Situation and condition of the troops required controls close to the front. The Eighteenth Army headquarters, which had its hands full southeast of Lake Peipus, was no longer able to exercise a responsible control over the

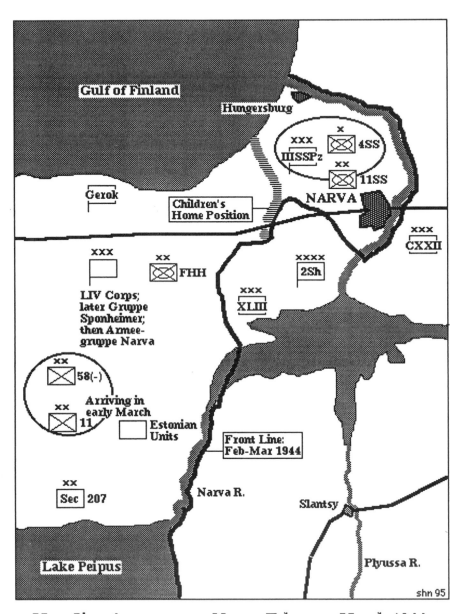

Map Six: Armeegruppe Narva, February-March 1944

remote *Gruppe* Sponheimer, chiefly because of the lack of signal communication. As of 0001 hours, 4 February, *Gruppe* Sponheimer was therefore assigned directly to the army group.

The Narva Front

Organization of *Armeeabteilung Narva.*

At the request of the army group, a new army headquarters[4] was organized and given control of the northern sector of the army group. The former staff of the LIV Corps formed the foundation for the organization of the staff. In a short time, the staff itself, the signal troops, and the rear services were brought up to the minimum strength necessary for the operation of an army. The army group headquarters and the Eighteenth Army headquarters made the largest contribution.

The commander of *Armeeabteilung Narva* had no command authority in the communications zone - that is to say, General of Infantry Sponheimer did not hold the executive authority within the area under his command. In 1941 a German civil administration had been established in Estonia. It was headed by a general commissioner whose official seat was in Tallinn. Estonian authorities, with a first and second national director at the top, supported the general commissioner. The civil administrator was not represented on the staff of the *Armeeabteilung.*[5] Coordination with the other branches of the Wehrmacht - the commander had no Wehrmacht powers - was ensured by a strong liaison detachment from both the Luftwaffe and Navy.

The *Armeeabteilung Narva* took over the Panther Line from the northwestern edge of Lake Peipus (junction with Eighteenth Army at Tammispaeae) to the coast of the Gulf of Finland, as well as the coastal defense as far as Tallinn exclusively; out of a total front of more than 330 kilometers, approximately 290 kilometers fronted on water.

The Panther Line

The section of the Panther Line falling within the area of *Armeeabteilung Narva* lay along the eastern border of Estonia. There were three sectors in the land front of the army, which at first was approximately 130 kilometers in length. The right sector, characterized by the water front of Lake Peipus, which extended more than 200 kilometers and included Lake Pskov, was at first not an absolute obstacle. The ice on the lake was traversable by all weapons and vehicles. Because of the exceedingly swampy forest territory on the eastern shore of the lake - which extended almost as far as the old Leningrad front - the *Armeeabteilung* did not expect large-scale crossing attempts of the enemy. Reconnaissance raids across the lake, of course, had to be expected at any time. Unfortunately, it had not been possible to bring all the water craft to the near bank in time, or to destroy it during the withdrawal. There was little vegetation on the shore. The dunes were fairly high, and offered a good field of fire. When visibility was clear, the range of observation reached as far as the vicinity of Gdov, the main port on the eastern shore.

Along the Lake Peipus front, the *Armeeabteilung* was able to limit itself to organizing a system of strongpoints. Echeloning in depth was impossible in the completely swampy forest territory. Heavy infantry weapons and artillery were hence necessarily employed at and along both sides of the Mustvoe-Timmispaeae-Vasknarva coastal road, the only line of communication in the sector.

North of Lake Peipus the main line of resistance generally followed the course of the Narva River. From the northern tip of Lake Peipus, the exit of the Narva River from the lake at Vasknarva, through Krivasoo and almost as far as the city of Narva, a forest difficult to penetrate covered the entire depth of the main defensive area. It was extremely swampy. To largely eliminate the danger of the enemy infiltrating into the forest, which was difficult to control, an unbroken line of infantry was necessary, with reserves being kept close at hand in strongpoints. The organization of the artillery encountered particular difficulties. For the tactically proper employment of whole battalions there were only few possibilities. In most cases each battery had to be emplaced separately on a small sand dune or on a corduroy road. Long telephone connections could not be avoided.

In the northern sector, the front advanced eastward as far as a line from Narva to Hungerburg.[6] This was the focal point of defense in the front of the *Armeeabteilung*. *Narva* itself remained a bridgehead, and could be held only as such. The old fortress of Ivangorod, situated on a higher level than its surroundings on the eastern bank of the Narva, dominated the river and the adjacent territory on both sides far to the east and west. It remained the target of constant enemy attacks.

Improvement of the Line

Up to the time the troops moved into the Panther Line only the construction of the Narva bridgehead as a field-type position had been concluded. The army group, which had begun construction on the Panther Line in the autumn of 1943, had been obliged - because of the limited engineer and construction forces at its disposal - to concentrate primarily on the establishment of focal points of defense in the total front, at Pskov and south thereof.

After the *Armeeabteilung* had moved into the Line, construction was principally undertaken by the troops in the position. Spadework was feasible only at the shore and in the dunes along Lake Peipus; on the sandy bank of Vask 'narva; and in the northern sector. The swampy forest permitted no spadework. Fortification in depth was hence limited chiefly to the establishment of strongpoints along tracks and beaten paths and in the dunes as well as the reinforcement of positions by means of wire entanglements and dead and live tree obstacles. Emergency huts above the ground served as shelters. Only at the focal defense points, in the bridgehead and the Narva-Hungerburg sector was it feasible to fortify the entire depth of the main defensive area in field-type fashion. In addition to constant reinforcement work, construction of a rear position anchored on the undulating territory of Moisakuela, twenty-four kilometers west of Narva - termed the "Children's Home Position" after the home for children at Moisakuela - was at once begun and driven ahead with all available means. Poor communications face headquarters and troops with considerable difficulties.

The front along Lake Peipus had as its sole suitable communication the coastal road running through the dunes. Its location - almost on the main line of resistance it was at the same time the sole rear and lateral line of communication - was bound to cause considerable difficulties for the troops committed there, especially in the event of an enemy attack. In the organization of the defense special attention had accordingly to be paid to the possibility of flanking fire and the intervention of local reserves.

In the sector north of Lake Peipus rear communications, frequently corduroy roads, were established under great difficulties. As the principal communication for troop movements and supply, a field railroad was built from Jewe, as supply station, through Ahtme (southeast of Jewe) and Kuremae to Agusalu, with a branch at Gorodenka, close behind the main line of resistance, and to Lutki. Construction troops were assigned to the time- and strength-consuming work on a long-term basis. Lateral communications close to the front existed only in the form of beaten paths.

The northern sector had rear communications in the Tallinn-Narva-Leningrad highway. But even this main communication channel was not built on firm ground in the important section from Jewe to Narva, which was close to the front. In the muddy periods of spring and fall it was traversable only by track-laying and horse-drawn vehicles. Substantial relief was provided by the railroad to Narva. It could be operated by night with steam as far as Auvere station. From there to Narva the line was adapted for horse-drawn traffic by means of planks.

The road and track network lacked density depth. Large-scale troop movements and supply shipments used the railroad from Tartu, unless shipment by sea was practicable. Later, after communication through Tartu had been disrupted, the secondary Tamsalu-Fellin railroad was largely used.

Organization in the Narva Front

Only the previously employed troops were, for the time being, available for the defense. They had suffered tremendous losses in personnel and material as a result of the heavy battles since 14 January. Some of them were in such a condition that they could be considered fir for combat only to a limited degree. Their rehabilitation was urgently necessary. But the situation admitted of no rest for the troops behind the front. Rehabilitation had to be effected on and closely behind the front. Rehabilitation of the 9th and 10th Luftwaffe Field Divisions, which had already been combined, no longer seemed possible. The highly qualified personnel and material still available could considerably facilitate and expedite rehabilitation of the remaining units.[7]

The only staff available for the time being was the staff of the III SS Panzer Corps. It had been assigned to the bridgehead and to the Narva-Hungerburg front. The remainder of the front was controlled directly by the *Armeeabteilung.* Later, the staffs of the XXVI and XXXXIII Corps were assigned there. The XXVI Corps took over the southern sector adjoining the Eighteenth Army, and the XXXXIII Corps the central sector.

Organization of Estonian Units

As the front approached Estonian territory, the anxiety of the Estonians for their country had again entered an acute stage. The general desire of the Estonians to participate actively in the defense of their country was understandable. Since there was no data for a systematic mobilization, the latter was conducted a a pure improvisation. It was carried out by Estonian agencies with the support of the German civil administration.

Three infantry regiments were initially activated. Difficulties in the procurement of weapons and equipment delayed their employment.[8] A Citizen Guard, as a rule varying in strength from a squad to a platoon, had already been formed by the civil administration to provide security. These protective measures, as well as the attitude of the population in general, greatly relieved the burden of the *Armeeabteilung* command. There never was much fighting against partisans.

Defense of the Coast (Cooperation with the Navy)

A new task was the defense of the coast of the Gulf of Finland. This meant an additional front of more than 200 kilometers from the mouth of the Narva River at Hungerburg to - but not including - Tallinn. The coast was decidedly flat, except for a strip north and northwest of Jewe. Here there are cliffs averaging ten meters in height, but easily ascendable. Along the coast, the land is open to view from all sides. When the weather is clear, the range of visibility extends as far as the northern tip of the headland north of Narva. During the period of occupation, there was only a thin chain of observation and signal posts of the German frontier supervision service, the VGAD,[9] and a patrol service of the Estonian Citizens' Guard.

After the *Armeeabteilung* had moved into the Panther Line, coastal defense had to be reorganized from the bottom. The *Armeeabteilung* was entrusted with the defense proper - combat operations on land - while combat operations against sea targets and naval warfare itself was exclusively a matter for the Navy. The missions were naturally closely interwoven. Close cooperation was a prerequisite for successful overall organization of coastal defense. In charge of the Navy was the Rear Admiral Burchardi, "Admiral, Eastern Baltic Sea," with his headquarters in Tallinn. For surveillance assignments and fighting on the sea, he had - so far as the *Armeeabteilung* knew - only light units at his disposal. Medium-heavy and heavy units did not put in an appearance.

For operations against sea targets only little naval coast artillery had been moved into position in comparison with the extent of the coast, and this artillery consisted for the most part of light and medium calibers. They were controlled by an "area commandant," who was subordinate to the Admiral, Eastern Baltic Sea. Local infantry protection of the coastal artillery was ensured by units of the Navy.

A special coastal defense staff, *Stab* Gerok, was assigned to the *Armeeabteilung*. Its qualifications were those of a commander of field forces. Special units for coastal defense were not available. Field units could not be released from the tautly stretched Narva front. The *Armeeabteilung* had to fall back to a large extent on rear services and trains and employ them on the coast under assignment to the coastal defense staff. The necessity of their performing their proper functions, such as maintenance and supply, caused friction. This was overcome by activating *alarmenheiten*,[10] which were constantly at the disposal of the coastal defense staff. In the event that the enemy attempted a landing, employment of the reserve of the *Armeeabteilung* and of available local reserves of field units was contemplated. Possibilities of employment were explored, maneuvers were undertaken. Newly arrived Army coastal artillery was employed in cooperation with the sea commandant.

Large-scale landing operations were not anticipated, since the Russian command had neither the necessary means for undertaking them, nor could procure such means in the foreseeable future. In the western section, from Kunda Bay to Tallinn, such operations seemed impracticable altogether, since the coast did not permit the formation of beachheads. Raids, however, particularly in the vicinity of the front, had to be expected at any time. But even they stood no chance of being expanded so long as sufficient forces were available for defense.

Fronting the coast were the islands Tytarsaari and Hogland. Tytarsaari, which was in German hands, was controlled by the Navy, while Hogland had a Finnish garrison. On Lake Peipus, after the lake had thawed out, the Navy employed a flotilla of eight to ten small ships to provide protection and surveillance. The port from which the ships sailed was Mustvoe. The ships had no armor plating, and were only in part equipped with guns. The use of these ships remained exclusively a Navy matter.

The Defensive Battles of *Armeeabteilung Narva*

Battles in the Northern Sector
from 2 February 1944 to the Beginning of April 1944

From the march column the enemy attacked the left sector in its entire breadth as early as 22 February. As a result of substantial losses, all attacks collapsed at the bridgehead. At Taervala, eight kilometers northwest of Narva, and hard south west of Narva, the enemy was able to cross the Narva River and establish small bridgeheads. He was, however, attacked by the troops moving into the position and was at once thrown back across the Narva in a counterattack. At the bridgehead, the enemy attacked again and again. He was evidently endeavoring to prevent the *Armeeabteilung* from establishing itself securely and to force a breakthrough. After systematic attacks during the following days had failed also, the enemy discontinued his attacks. The Narva front had passed the first battle test. The III SS Panzer Corps had achieved a defensive success, the total effect of which was not to be underestimated.

The main body of the troops was still on the way to the main line of resistance. As far as possible, strong mobile advance parties had been launched. It was a race with the enemy, who approached the Panther Line from the east along the shortest route, while the friendly troops had to make a detour through Jewe on account of the terrain and move into the position from the rear. In this situation the enemy crossed the Narva River at Krivasoo, twenty kilometers southwest of Narva, in a surprise move. Repelling local advanced covering forces, he pushing into the center of the front, which was in the process of organization, and pushed on through Nustajoee in a westerly and northwesterly direction and past Kaerokonna toward the north. Only by rapidly committing the approaching *Feldherrnhalle* Panzergrenadier Division and the newly arrived reinforced regiment of the 58th Infantry Division, and by turning from their march columns all troops that were available, was it possible to stop the enemy in bitter fighting.

It had to be anticipated that the enemy would attack again shortly to get the operation against the Narva front under way again, and to expand the penetration into a breakthrough. Through his surprise success, he had achieved the essential prerequisite for this purpose. Two spearheads appeared in the penetration zone, which was more than twenty kilometers broad and over nine kilometers deep. The eastern spearhead approached the railroad and the Rollbahn, the rear communications of the bridgehead, while the western part of the penetration zone in the forest west and northwest of Krivasoo was not yet under full control. If the enemy managed to achieve a breakthrough to the north, the bridgehead would be cut off. If the enemy veered west there was no foretelling the consequences. There were no more strategic reserves available. If the enemy gained the open territory at Jewe, he could roll up the Narva front, and through Tartu push into the flank of the Eighteenth Army, which would then be open; but he could also push on toward Tallinn and past it into the rear of the army group.

Counterattacks which had been launched everywhere, with a view to narrowing down the penetration zone, had failed at the outset. The strength of the troops was no longer sufficient. A renewed counterattack, even after a hasty assembly, promised no success, and would merely lead to unnecessary and irreplaceable losses. The troops had been over-strained by constant action, and personnel and material had been so weakened in the last defensive and retreating engagements that they were incapable of making an attack for the present. Only a unified, systematic counterattack with fresh troops promised to be successful. Although shortly afterward it was possible to again release a division, it had to remain in the hands of the *Armeeabteilung* to be able to cope with any unexpected development in the situation. Disengagement of further forces seemed impossible. The *Armeeabteilung*, in view of the still generally obscure situation, could not open up a new gap in the still-unconsolidated front and stake everything on one card. The *Armeeabteilung* therefore resolved to establish strong HQ reserves to shift to the defensive at the penetration zone, while preparing a systematic attack in order to eliminate all further danger from this zone. The situation and the plans were transmitted to the army group, and assignment of additional forces requested. The shift to defense at the penetration zone lengthened the front by more than twenty kilometers and tied up troops. But these drawbacks had to be taken into the bargain.

The counterattack required the use of at least two divisions. The possibility of ironing out the penetration zone to its full extent in a single counterattack was not to be taken into consideration even at the beginning. The troops necessary for an action on this scale could be neither freed, nor could it be expected that they would be assigned.

The eastern part of the penetration zone, referred to as the "eastern bag," was the most dangerous one. Here a continuation of the attack had to be primarily anticipated. The enemy was still in unfavorable terrain. So far only a few tanks had appeared. The important point was now to recognize and smash any preparations for an attack as soon as possible. In the western part of the penetration zone, referred to as the "western bag," the enemy - as well as our own troops - had to contend with considerable terrain difficulties. There were only few possibilities for support by heavy arms. Here it had to be assumed that the enemy would continue to use his notorious infiltration procedure. This could be counteracted only by occupation of the front in a continuous line.

Hitler had interfered in the meantime. The holding of the Narva front was not only of pure military significance, it also had economic and political importance. For instance, if the enemy was able to enter Estonia, he would gain an important base for naval warfare in Tallinn and Paldiski. If the enemy succeeded in interrupting communications with Finland, this would influence the further fighting of the Finns, who were still tying down considerable forces. The enemy, moreover, would also have access to the Baltic Sea, and would be in a position to interfere considerably with the shipment of ore from northern Sweden to Germany. Hitler accordingly urged elimination of the danger. Support was promised.

Contrary to expectations, the enemy did not start a systematic attack from the penetration zone. Scattered thrusts remained the order of the day.

The enemy attacked the bridgehead again and again, but although he repeatedly succeeded in achieving minor penetrations, so that the enlarged bridgehead was gradually reduced to its original proportions, he achieved no decisive success. The scattered, increasingly weak enemy thrusts indicated that the enemy was apparently no longer capable of making a full-scale attack with his Second Shock Army. He had to admit that he had been unable to prevent the shift to a systematic defense, and that a breakthrough could now be achieved only by a new systematic breakthrough attack that would have to be prepared with all available means.

The deadline for undertaking the breakthrough attack initially depended exclusively on the procurement and transport of troops capable of making such an attack, but was also gradually influenced to a great extent by the condition of the terrain. Whereas the Germans had so far been obliged to fight with considerable difficulties in the swampy territory because of the thaw, these difficulties now had to be overcome by the Russian troops in their attack. Everything, therefore, depended on seizing the moment when the terrain would again be sufficiently traversable and would also allow tank movements to a certain extent, and to do this before the Germans did.

On 5 March the 11th Infantry Division arrived in the sector of the *Armeeabteilung* from the Eighteenth Army, and shortly afterward the bulk of the 58th Infantry Division arrived from army group reserve. They were assigned to the XXXXIII Corps, which was now able to complete the preparations for assembly for the counterattack. An armored unit could not be made available. The *Armeeabteilung* depended on the small number of tanks and assault guns which had been in its sector since the retreating engagements. They were combined as *Panzerverband* "Strachwitz."[11]

For a successful execution of the counterattack, a thrust through Kaerokonna to Krivasoo seemed to hold out prospects for a decisive action. Such a thrust would disrupt the penetration zone and hit the enemy at his most vulnerable point: the rear communications. Reverberations through the entire penetration zone could be expected. For this thrust one division was committed, reinforced by *Panzerverband* Strachwitz, while the other two attack forces were to break open and clear the eastern part of the penetration zone from the east and northeast. The western part of the penetration zone was to be tied down in its entire extent by fire and local operations.

On 26 March the XXXXIII Corps started its counterattack. In heavy battles the main attack group, screening itself toward west and east, broke through to a point just north of Krivasoo. Because of the extraordinarily strong anti-tank defenses, which caused considerable losses, it was impossible to penetrate to the crossing point. The completely swampy terrain, with a water level of up to fifty centimeters, prevented the recapture of the Narva River as a main line of resistance. The enemy had been deprived, however, of a chance to assemble his troops on the near side of the Narva River.

After the forces had been regrouped, the counterattack against the western part of the penetration zone began on 6 April. On the basis of the reconnaissance results available - the terrain was almost impassable - another postponement of the date for the beginning of the counterattack had at first been intended. Hitler, however, which also had requested an oral report on the intended conduct of the attack, insisted on immediate execution of the attack. A unified counterattack did not materialize. Support by tanks, artillery, and heavy infantry weapons was practicable only to a limited extent as a result of the tremendous terrain difficulties. Hence, it was possible to break up and clear the enemy out of the penetration only in piecemeal fashion. The attacking force sent froward from Gorodenka at the main line of resistance made no headway. In the thickly covered terrain, the counterattack disintegrated more and more, and was finally stopped in the swamps and the water. Relinquishing the Narva River as a main line of resistance, the *Armeeabteilung* had to build up a final front on the dunes and the gently rolling ground. The counterattack made it clear that from this area a major operation of the enemy was not to be expected. The enemy attacked the bridgehead again and again, but was unsuccessful.

On the remaining front, particularly near the penetration zone at Krivasoo, a strength-consuming guerilla warfare developed. Although there were no gaps in the front, the enemy, favored by the terrain, was able to infiltrate again and again. There were often as many as 400-500 Russians behind the front. Although it was possible in most cases to stop the enemy at the front line and to destroy them, a trifling local withdrawal of the front could frequently not be avoided.

While the situation in the left sector of the army was being straightened out, the situation of the Eighteenth Army had continued to develop. The main effort of the enemy offensive was directed against the Eighteenth Army, which withdrew in heavy battles by way of intermediate lines to the Panther Line. Step by step the left flank corps, the XXVI Corps, yielded the eastern shore of Lake Peipus and Lake Pskov from north to south. The enemy did not attempt a large-scale crossing of the lake. He had merely occupied the island of Piirissaar in the southern part of Lake Peipus, located only a scant 100 meters from the western shore, the island was a good stepping-stone for the enemy. Its capture, therefore, seemed necessary. On 24 February, the

Eighteenth Army regained possession of the island and was able to hold it against all counterattacks.

By 1 March, the Eighteenth Army had been able to reach the Panther Line. The front had thus again been closed along its entire extent. The inner flanks of the Eighteenth Army an the Narva front met at Mustvoe, behind the Lake Peipus front, which could be regarded as secure. The land fronts themselves were widely separated by the lake, which was more than 200 kilometers in length. If the left sector of the Eighteenth Army was ruptured at Lake Pskov - and if it proved impossible to restore the situation - it seemed likely that the Eighteenth army would have to withdraw westward to anchor itself on the southern tip of Lake Virts. In the land front a hole would then be torn between Lake Pskov and Lake Virts, which would give the enemy full freedom of movement toward the north. Thereupon a threat would arise far outside the sector of the *Armeeabteilung,* the effect of which on the deep open flank of the Narva front could be foreseen.

The development of the situation at Pskov had, therefore, to be watched continuously and closely by *Armeeabteilung Narva.* As early as 4 March the enemy had again started an attack near Pskov. By 12 March, except for insignificant penetrations, he had not been able to achieve his objective: the hill territory northwest of Pskov.

With the resumption of fighting in the Eighteenth Army sector, combat activity also flared up again in the sector of the *Armeeabteilung* . At many points on the front, primarily along the northern sector, the enemy conducted local attacks. Apparently the enemy was endeavoring to clear up and contain the situation. On Lake Peipus all was quiet. A partisan brigade did however cross the ice by surprise, although the ice was already cracking, just south of the right boundary of the *Armeeabteilung* . On 12 March it broke through the thin security line of the 207th Security Division[12], entered the rear area, and shifted to the sector of the *Armeeabteilung.* In cooperation with the 207th Security division, the XXVI Corps was able to neutralize the brigade within a few days. Estonian units and the Citizens' Guard had a special share in the rapid clean-up of the rear area.

Development of the Situation on other Fronts and Its Effect on the Narva Front.

Undoubtedly time was working for the *Armeeabteilung* in that it was possible to improve the organization of the defense with vigor, and make progress in rehabilitating and consolidating the troops. On the other hand, time was also working for the enemy. He not only had full freedom of action, but also had the means to prepare and carry out decisive operations. The question was only when and where he would attack; he had not revealed his cards yet.

Primarily a large-scale offensive against Army Group Center was expected. If the Russian command, starting out from the Vitebsk area, succeeded in splitting the front between the Army Groups Center and North, a strength-consuming battle on the flank of Army Group North was bound to result. This potential large-scale offensive of the Russian command only indirectly touched the *Armeeabteilung*. It was to be expected that in such a case forces would have to be released.

There was no doubt that the Russian command, in addition to - or in conjunction with - this large-scale offensive, would cling to its former strategic intent of pushing through to Riga and the Baltic. If the enemy achieved a breakthrough at Pskov, which undoubtedly was and remained on of the principal points of main effort, then he could at once veer north to bring about the collapse of the Narva front by a thrust through Tartu. Every unfavorable development of the situation at Pskov hence affected the *Armeeabteilung* and might necessitate new decisions.

In the sector of the *Armeeabteilung* the northern sector remained the focal point. Provided the enemy gave the *Armeeabteilung* enough time, it would be able to consolidate the front to such an extent that it would be equal to any attack. The *Felherrnhalle* Panzergrenadier Division and the 170th Infantry Division were ready as reserves of the *Armeeabteilung*. The disengagement of the 225th Infantry Division had been prepared.[13]

Unfortunately, *Führer* Order No. 1, which provided that no one was to know and learn more than what concerned him directly, had not only a disturbing but often a detrimental effect. As a result, even the information concerning the situation of the adjacent unit remained inadequate. The *Armeeabteilung*, however, had to know what was going on. Only then would it be in a position to collaborate in accordance with the ideas of the upper command levels and take the necessary measures in time. The *Armeeabteilung* hence had to organize its own information procurement.

Continual reconnaissance operations of its own, evaluation of radio reconnaissance and statements by prisoners of war rounded out the picture of the enemy situation. For the present, the enemy on its front showed no offensive intentions. In the middle of June, nine further enemy divisions were identified on the line. Eleven more divisions, apparently in the process of being rehabilitated, were suspected of being behind the front, and this was in part confirmed. The Second Shock Army itself remained inactive. During the following days, too, there was quiet on the front, aside from the normal amount of fighting.

Nevertheless - something was impending.

NOTES

[1]This division had just been raised—nominally—from brigade status. The Estonian SS Brigade had consisted, in late December 1943, of only four infantry battalions containing roughly 1,050 men. The brigade appears to have been utilized primarily in anti-partisan operations during the retreat to the Panther Line. Now that the army group was defending the eastern border of Estonia, Himmler made the decision to have the organization expanded by conscripting Estonian *volksdeutsche* and former NCOs from the Estonian Army. By 8 March 1944 this process had barely begun; headquarters, III SS Panzer Corps, reported that it would require an additional 343 officers, 1,810 NCOs, and 12,000 men to build a full-strength division. This would have to be augmented, if the division were to be exposed to combat, by a replacement and training brigade of 70 officers, 300 NCOs, and 3,500 men. The *Hohere SS und Polizei Führer* for the Baltic States was charged with "recruiting" the necessary men, a task which he undertook with such gusto that the division's ranks were in fact filled within about two months. The calibre of those "volunteers," however, left a lot to be desired. *Heeresgruppe Nord, Zustand der Divisionen,* Operations Abteilung/III, 19 December 1943, T-311, Reel 70; *III SS Panzerkorpskommando,* Ia, no number, 8 March 1944, T-311, Reel 73; Ready, *Forgotten Axis,* p. 305.

[2]This list, compiled from memory, manages to account for the main divisional units in the *Armeeabteilung,* but omits several important non-divisional units. These included *Kampfgruppe* Böhrendt, built around the *Führerbegleit* Battalion and an armored contingent of twelve Pzkw. Mark IVs and five StG IIIs; Tiger Battalion 502 with twenty-three Pzkw. Mark VIs; and Assault Gun Battalion 184 (technically a part of the Army Group North reserve, but operationally available at the beginning) with thirty-two StG III. *Heeresgruppe Nord, Panzermeldungen,* 10 February 1944, T-311, Reel 73.

[3]This was Grenadier Regiment 209, probably reinforced with an artillery battalion. *Armeeoberkommando 18,* Ia, 732/44, 5 February 1944, T-311, Reel 70.

[4]Note in original: "More precisely: 'headquarters of an *Armeeabteilung*.' Since the term '*Armeeabteilung*' was not listed in the T/O, the T/O strength of the staff of an

army headquarters minus certain unnecessary elements was taken as a basis for the staff to be formed."

[5]This is a rather apologist description of the organization and development of *Reichscommissariat Ostland.* See the discussion in Chapter One of Theo J, Schulte, *The German Army and Nazi Policies in Occupied Russia.* (New York: St. Martin's Press, 1989).

[6]Note in original: "On the map, Hungerburg is shown as Narva Joesun."

[7]The bulk of the infantry and combat support units of the 9th Luftwaffe Field Division was assigned to the 126th Infantry Division, those of the 10th Luftwaffe Field Division to the 170th Infantry Division. Field Marshal Model offered first crack at staff and support units to *Reichsführer* Heinrich Himmler for use in building up the foreign volunteer units assigned to the III SS Panzer Corps. The newly organized 20th SS Estonian Waffen Grenadier Division received the administrative troop from the 9th Luftaffe Field Division and the division supply commander of the 10th, plus three heavy truck columns. The 11th SS *"Nordland"* Panzergrenadier Division took six truck columns, the 4th SS *"Nederland"* Panzergrenadier Brigade received three and a supply staff. The corps headquarters itself benefitted by three truck columns and one light flak column. Luftflötte 1 retrieved most of the flak batteries from the two divisions for its own use, while Model then offered the remaining "small staffs" to any unit which felt a need for them. *Armeeoberkommando 18*, Ia, 472/44, 23 January 1944; *Heeresgruppe Nord*, Ia/Id, 1425/44, 14 March 1944; *Heeresgruppe Nord*, OQu/Qu I, 6567/44, 5 April 1944; *Heeresgruppe Nord*, OQu/Qu I, 6967/44, 10 April 1944; *Heeresgruppe Nord*, Ia/Id, 4076/44, 19 April 1944; *Heeresgruppe Nord*, Ia/Id, 4063/44, 21 April 1944; *Heeresgruppe Nord*, Ia/Id, 4201/44, 21 April 1944, T-311, Reel 72.

[8]As a result of the shortage of weapons, the table of organization eventually accepted for these regiments was extremely light. Each regiment carried—at full strength—only ten light machine guns per company and regimental support weapons consisting of eleven heavy machine guns, seven 81mm mortars, five captured Russian 61mm mortars, and four French 37mm or 47mm anti-tank guns. *Armeeoberkommando 18*, Ia, 2493/44, 19 June 1944, T-312, Reel 931.

[9]Note in original: "Verstaerkter Grenzeufaichtadienst (Reinforced Border Control).

[10]Note in original: "Emergency alert units were organized from temporarily dispens-

able personnel of the rear services."

[11]The number of available tanks and assault guns was in fact larger than Recihelt recalled: there were at least 75 available when *Panzerverband* Strachwitz was organized. *Heeresgruppe Nord, Panzermeldungen*, 10 March 1944, T-311, Reel 73.

[12]The "thin screen" to which Reichelt refers would have been thin indeed: by this time the 207th Security Division had been reduced to a "total present strength"—including all support troops—of 2,580 men. *Armeeoberkommando 18*, Ia, 1064/44, 21 February 1944, T-311, Reel 70.

[13]This would have represented a significant decrease in infantry strength. The *Armeeabteilung* had an infantry strength of 14,584. The 225th Infantry Division was the strongest of these divisions, with a frontline strength of 3,646 (25%). *Heeresgruppe Nord*, Ia, no number, 22 February 1944, T-311, Reel 70.

CHAPTER 6

The Battles of *Armeeabteilung Narva,* June-September 1944

Paul Reichelt

In the beginning of June a large-scale offensive of the Russian command had begun at the Finnish front. Liquidation of the Finnish question had long been overdue, as far as the Russian command was concerned. The Finnish front still tied up considerable forces. The headquarters of the Second Shock Army also appeared there. This confirmed its removal from the Narva front. It was not possible, however, to identify troops from the previous units of the Second Shock Army in Finland. Hence, their continued presence at the Narva front had to be assumed.

The large-scale offensive expected at the German eastern front began on 22 June, and in a short time led to a strategic breakthrough just south of the boundary between Army Groups North and Center. The more forces the enemy moved to the scene, the more the southern flank of Army Group North had to become a southern front, unless the ruptured contact between the army groups was restored. The situation would then also affect the *Armeeabteilung,* even though it was not directly concerned.

The *Feldherrnhalle* Panzergrenadier Division had already been dispatched to Army Group Center at the beginning of June. The 170th Infantry Division had to be shipped off with great speed from 28 June on. The Russian breakthrough was now headed for Daugavpils. The 225th Infantry Division was disengaged from the front, as a new reserve of the *Armeeabteilung.* Unfortunately, the Eighteenth Army also had been obliged to give up its last strategic reserves. To what extent it was in a position to organize new reserves remained unknown. Behind Pskov, the flank which was of interest to the Narva front, there was nothing.

In the meantime, it became clear to the *Armeeabteilung* that the army group on its right was hard-pressed. The flank was "suspended in mid-air."

The forces which the army group had at its disposal - or could make available to remedy the situation - had to remain inadequate means in view of the masses of mobile enemy forces. It was to be foreseen that the Sixteenth Army would have to be bent back, and that further forces would have to be given up by the Eighteenth Army. The *Armeeabteilung* offered the 225th Infantry Division to the Army Group. Its transfer seemed necessary in view of the overall situation, and possible in conformity with the appraisal of the situation of the *Armeeabteilung*.

For the purpose of furnishing the *Armeeabteilung* with a new reserve, the disengagement of the 61st Infantry Division was prepared by assembling local reserves. Along the shore of Lake Peipus it was feasible to weaken the front still further. The weaker occupation of the remaining part of the front had to be put up with, and consequently also the potential local aggravation of the situation as a result of enemy infiltration. On 2 July the transfer of the 225th Infantry Division was ordered, and simultaneously the transfer of the the staff of the XXVI Corps. The local reserves held in readiness were committed, and the 61st Infantry Division was made available as the new reserve of the *Armeeabteilung*.

In the course of an oral report on the situation in the *Führer's* headquarters on 3 July, to which General Friessner had also been summoned, the command of the *Armeeabteilung* changed hands. General Friessner assumed command of the army group; General of Infantry Anton Grasser, the commanding general of the XXXXIII Corps, assumed command of the *Armeeabteilung*. In the mission - defense of the present front - there was no change.

An estimate of the situation prevailing at the time showed that if the enemy, contrary to expectations, was to undertake an attack, the *Armeeabteilung* was capable of meeting it despite the fact that it had been weakened. The endangered left sector had been given special attention in all the regroupings of forces necessitated by the transfers, and had been weakened only to a limited extent. All measures necessary for defense had been taken. Preparations had been taken by assembly of the local reserves - and other reserves kept close at hand in the hands of the *Armeeabteilung* - and through strong fortification of the depth of the main defensive area. Acute danger to the German front did not exist.

As the situation of the army group continued to grow worse, the firm connection with the Eighteenth Army increased in significance. There would be a new focal point for the *Armeeabteilung* if the left flank of the Eighteenth Army were torn away. Protection of the deep right flank by friendly

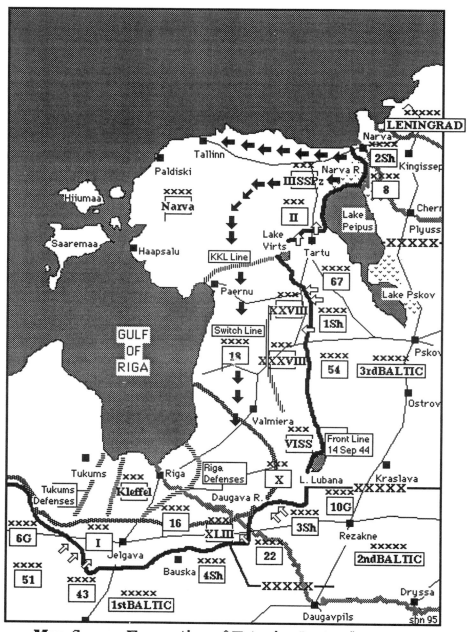

Map Seven: Evacuation of Estonia, September 1944

forces might then become necessary surprisingly soon. To this end, only the Kma River sector on both sides of Tartu could be taken into account. Although this sector lay in the area of the adjacent army, reconnaissance of opportunities for blocking and commitment of troops was initiated, and - by way of precaution - a highly mobile local reserve was organized behind the front (in addition to the reserve of the *Armeeabteilung*) to "fight the fire." Its nucleus was formed by the very strong panzer reconnaissance battalion of the III SS Panzer Corps.[1]

If the development of the situation required the transfer of further units - the mission of the army remaining unchanged - then the front on the northern sector would have to be shortened. A shortening of the front, however, inevitably meant the abandonment of the Narva bridgehead, and the Narva-Hungerburg main line of resistance, protected by the Narva River. The *Armeeabteilung* was aware that every withdrawal would mean a new shock to the Finnish front. The fronts on both sides of the Gulf of Finland would be driven further apart with every step backwards. Therefore, only limited reduction of the front was possible. In determining the alignment of the new position, from the tactical point of view everything depended on giving the enemy as few opportunities as possible for concentration and assembly close to the front. The Narva River had to remain largely under German control. Furthermore, an effort had to be made to eliminate the menace to the flank from the south, out of the old penetration zone.

The "Children's Home Position," already fortified, met these requirements. A withdrawal of the front to this position would reduce the front by more than twenty kilometers. A whole division could then be saved as a reserve. The *Armeeabteilung* accordingly proposed the withdrawal of the left flank and at the same time offered to release the 61st Infantry Division, the army reserve. The army believed to be best able to help the army group in this manner, and at the same time to be able to cope with any situation arising in the new position. The army group approved the situation estimate and the intention of the *Armeeabteilung*, but the shortening of the front was refused by the supreme command for political reasons. The 61st Infantry Division had to be released without a reduction in the length of the front. It ceased to be a part of the *Armeeabteilung* on 9 July.

On 11 July, SS Panzer Reconnaissance Battalion 11 of the III SS Panzer Corps was also demanded on short notice by the army group. The mobile tactical reserve which had just been established was thus disrupted. At the same time, the *Armeeabteilung* had to make available another division as reserve. The army decided to disengage the 58th Infantry Division.

So far it had always been possible to establish reserves by lengthening the sectors of individual divisions. Now improvisation had to be resorted to in order to close the gaps created. The *Armeeabteilung* fell back on Estonian units. The three Estonian infantry regiments already existing were combined under the "300th Special Administrative Division Staff" and employed in the central sector - the less endangered part of the front.[2] In the meantime, activation of three more Estonian regiments was under way. Lack of clothing and equipment had delayed their activation. Platoon by platoon they were employed on the front along Lake Peipus, relieving German units. Inadequate training, and in part the absence of training, as well as the lack of any battle experience had to be accepted.

Up to that point it had been possible to veil all the necessary arrangements, and to maintain the old picture of the front - including that of artillery - by deceptive measures. It was now to be expected that the enemy would become aware of the changes made, and would seek to obtain clarity by means of attacks. The *Armeeabteilung* had to be prepared for all eventualities.

Further withdrawal of the southern sector of the army group had by then become necessary. The enemy, who apparently had become of aware of the retreat, had pushed into it on 10 July, and had hit the 15th and 19th Latvian SS Waffen Grenadier Divisions. The divisions were in no way equal to a situation presenting such difficulties. This made it doubtful whether, in the event of an enemy attack on the *Armeeabteilung*, the Estonian units would be able to hold. They occupied a front which had up till then been occupied by almost two German divisions. As a precaution, a few German units were kept ready as a support behind the 300th Special Administrative Division Staff.[3]

Particular difficulties were caused by the necessity of replacing the division artillery, which had been moved out together with the the divisions to which it belonged. Army artillery was available only to a limited extent. It had to remain employed on the left, and - moreover - its transfer also had to be expected. The army therefore fell back on two Army coastal artillery battalions, thereby weakening the defense of the sea coast, and in addition moved captured guns into position to the extent that ammunition was available.

O 14 July the battle-tested 126th Infantry Division was pulled out of the left sector of the Eighteenth Army. This measure greatly weakened the bastion upon which the holding of the Lake Peipus front depended. On account of the further unfavorable development of the situation on the southern front of the army group, the army group also ordered the transfer of the

58th Infantry Division, which had just been disengaged. Simultaneously, a withdrawal to the shortened position was again expressly forbidden. In all probability, the reason was another *Führer* order. To mitigate the effects of the transfer, which was undoubtedly necessary, the assignment of Navy personnel and men on furlough who had been intercepted was promised; they never arrived. Establishment of a new strategic reserve was no longer feasible. On 15 July the first elements of the 58th Infantry Division were already on their way. The staff of the XXXXIII Corps dropped out on 18 July, and with it all the construction troops still in the *Armeeabteilung* area. The III SS Panzer Corps took over the sector as far as Putki, consequently also assuming command of the 11th Infantry Division. On the remainder of the front, the *Armeeabteilung* again exercised control itself.

In the meantime, the enemy had also started to attack the Eighteenth Army, and on 20 July had broken through at Ostrov, aiming west. The Eighteenth Army believed that it could master the further development of the situation only by withdrawing its left flank to Walk. *Armeeabteilung Narva* was to make elements available in time to provide flank protection for the Eighteenth Army in a line from Lake Virts to Paernu. Nevertheless, its main body was to remain in its position until the Eighteenth Army had completed its withdrawal. It was not to be expected that the army group would issue this suggestion of the Eighteenth Army as an order. Otherwise the enemy would largely have determined the further conduct of the *Armeeabteilung*, as soon as the left flank of the Eighteenth Army had withdrawn from Lake Peipus. It would then have to be the principal task of the *Armeeabteilung* to block the isthmus between Lake Virts and Lake Peipus in order to cover the northern flank of the Eighteenth Army and simultaneously the deep right flank of the *Armeeabteilung*, which would then be unprotected.

On 20 July the immediate disengagement and transfer of the 227th Infantry Division, too, had been ordered. As a replacement, the 122nd Infantry Division was promised. This division - coming from Finland - was expected. The supreme command was again requested to permit withdrawal to the shortened position (Children's Home Position). For the time being, only elements of the 227th Infantry Division could be disengaged, and this by employing the last local reserves. The *Armeeabteilung* had so far deliberately refrained from an appreciable weakening of the bridgehead. The disengagement of the 227th Infantry Division, however, was possible only if the strength of the bridgehead was radically reduced. This reduction now had to been undertaken, and the resulting additional strain would have to be taken into the bargain. Additional Estonian units were also committed. Most of them reached the front with only half of their strength.[4]

The transfer of battle-worthy units from the German front had gradually put such a strain on the troops and the *Armeeabteilung* that it could no longer be borne. Of the nine infantry divisions, two had been disbanded, six transferred elsewhere. In addition to the SS units, only one division remained in the army. The III SS Panzer Corps was stretched far to the southwest. The 11th Infantry Division was situated at the bend in the front, adjoining the III SS Panzer Corps. The area in which the 11th Infantry Division was employed had been selected by the *Armeeabteilung* because - in the event of an enemy breakthrough - it intended to have this division withdrawn to the Children's Home Position and try to intercept the enemy there. At the remaining sectors of the front there were Estonian troops, whose value in battle was dubious. Responsibility for holding the Narva front, for the defense of the present position, had remained. To the concern for this position, however, was added the concern for the right flank. There was growing danger, and this could enter an acute stage at any moment.

On the front of the *Armeeabteilung* all was quiet. The *Armeeabteilung*, however, had to take into account the fact that the enemy was in all probability aware that the front had been weakened. If the enemy attacked in this situation, the army had to endeavor to prevent - as long as possible - the army group from being affected.

Reduction of the Front on the Left Flank, and Engagements in the New Position from 23 July

In this situation the activity of the enemy on the left flank of the army increased suddenly. Increasing reconnaissance raids, increased artillery activity, and heavy enemy air reconnaissance indicated that an attack was about to start. It was clear from the enemy's conduct that new units were involved. It was also to be assumed that the enemy would attack in very great strength. It was possible that he had already been able to release forces on the Finnish front. On the basis of this development of the situation, withdrawal to the shortened line - the Children's Home Position - was finally ordered on 23 July.

The withdrawal had long since been prepared in all detail.[5] The circumstances had become considerably worse in view of the impending enemy attack. The purpose to be fulfilled by the position, which was the release of forces, no longer applied. Despite the shortening of the lines by approximately twenty kilometers, it was impossible to release any strategic reserves. Fortification of the new position had made excellent progress. Its value now depended alone on the performance of the troops - that is to say, on the units of the III SS Panzer Corps and the 11th Infantry Division.

Because of the potential development of the situation, the movements had to be accelerated. Only through speed could time be gained for preparations in the new position. The main body of the III SS Panzer Corps had to withdraw to the shortened position in a single movement during the night of 23-24 July. It would immediately have to again prepare itself for defense. A battle-worthy rear guard had to be left in contact with the enemy. It was to disengage itself only when ordered to do so, and had to delay the advance of the enemy in case he attacked.

In the middle of the withdrawal the enemy attacked. By 24 July he had pushed forward in a northwesterly direction from the section of the front which had been pressed in at the end of March, and between Auvere and Arumace - just south of the railroad - he blocked the path of a retreating SS regiment. Immediate attempts to relieve the regiment failed. The situation, however, required the withdrawal to be continued. On 25 July the enemy attacked the bridgehead and the front as afar as Hungerburg with heavy infantry and tank forces. The rear guards disengaged themselves from the enemy. After crossing the Narva River, the enemy followed rapidly, and was still able to attack elements of the 20th Estonian Waffen Grenadier SS Division. This division suffered considerable losses.[6]

In spite of the large and small mishaps brought about by the development of the situation - which it was impossible to avoid - the III SS Panzer Corps was able to withdraw and gain a lead. On the morning of 25 July, the *Armeeabteilung* was in the new position.

If the enemy was to act correctly in this situation, he would have to take up pursuit immediately. On the basis of the overall situation, he had to assume a general withdrawal of the Narva front. The Russian Eighth Army had appeared in the strength of two tank and ten rifle units. Everywhere the enemy now crossed the Narva River. Places where bridges were being built were identified. In dense columns, the enemy approached the position. In many cases these columns were identified by ground observation and brought under fire by artillery. At the Children's Home Position, the forward elements of the enemy were stopped. Nevertheless, the enemy might still have assumed that the troops confronting him were merely rear guards. In such a case he would attack without systematic assembly. The German troops were fully prepared for this.

In the early morning hours of 29 July, the enemy attacked the Children's Home Position. The attacks collapsed, and the enemy sustained very serious losses. From the march column the enemy again and again fed new forces into the battle. A brief crisis arose when the dominating Children's home hill was lost. A resolute counterattack there threw the enemy off it again. During the noon hours, masses of tanks rolled forward against the position, but they were unable to open up the way either; the enemy lost 113 tanks. Not until dark did the enemy discontinue his attacks. This was a defensive success of decisive significance which the weakened front of the *Armeeabteilung* had gained. It was solely due to the exemplary way in which the troops of the III SS Panzer Corps and the 11th Infantry Division had conducted themselves. In addition to the Eighth Army, the Second Shock Army, the XXX Guards Rifle Corps, and an tank task force were identified. With these forces the enemy had tremendous superiority in numbers. A total strength of at least twenty divisions was to be expected, not all of which, however, had put in an appearance as yet.

The front continued to be active, but contrary to expectations the enemy attacked neither on 30 July nor in the following days. The elation over the great defensive success was unfortunately overshadowed by the news that the enemy had reached the Baltic Sea at Tukums, so that the army group was encircled. It was to be expected that the enemy would now prepare for a systematic breakthrough attack. But the attack did not come. It was possible that because of the numerous losses he had suffered, the enemy still assumed the *Armeeabteilung* to be in its full strength, and hence had made completely new decisions. If the enemy acted correctly, he would have to abandon his intention to attempt a breakthrough, rearrange his forces, and reinforce the point of main effort at another already weak spot in the army group front. He was bound to arrive at the justified conclusion that he could bring about the collapse of the Narva front without attacking it directly. Holding attacks were to be anticipated.

The 122nd Infantry Division, coming from Finland, and which had been promise to the *Armeeabteilung*, meanwhile moved through the army sector to the adjacent unit.

Engagements in the Deep Right Flank, at and South of Tartu on 13 August

In the course of the heavy battles continuing since 10 July on the right flank of the army group, the Sixteenth and Eighteenth Armies had to be puled back considerably. It was merely a matter of time before battles would begin to affect the left sector of the Eighteenth Army. It was not a good sign that the supply for the Narva front no longer used the railroad from Tartu. The *Armeeabteilung* depended on shipments by sea, and on the use of the narrow-gauge Tamsalu-Fellin railroad.

On 12 August the enemy attacked the left flank of the Eighteenth Army. On 13 August the army engaged in a hard defensive battle southwest of Pskov. The enemy had penetrated south of Voru, but apparently had also pushed past Voru on the east in an advance on Tartu. There was no longer a possibility of assuming that the Eighteenth Army had contact with Lake Pskov.

No fundamentally new decisions for the conduct of operations were to be expected on the part of the *Armeeabteilung*. On the basis of the overall situation in which the army group found itself, it could not relieve the *Armeeabteilung* of its concern for its right flank, and the Eighteenth Army could not reestablish a firm connection with the lake. The *Armeeabteilung* had to assure the protection of the deep flank itself, and that without delay. Under a provisional SS brigade staff, a blocking force was at once made ready to march.

Composition[7]
Two battalions of the 11th Infantry Division, semi-motorized.
One battalion of the 20th Estonian SS Waffen-Grenadier Division, semi-motorized.
(Both of these units had hitherto been the corps' reserve.)
Two motorized engineer companies, hitherto at the disposal of the *Armeeabteilung*.
One armored reconnaissance company from the III SS Panzer Corps.
One staff of an anti-tank battalion, with two anti-tank companies, from the III SS Panzer Corps.
One artillery battalion with three batteries of light field howitzers from the III SS Panzer Corps.

Only these troops were available, or could be quickly disengaged from action. In addition, the 300th Special Administrative Division Headquarters had to release two Estonian battalions and assign them to the blocking force. The force's only mission was as follows:

First, to reach the Kma River sector without delay, and thereupon to establish connection with the left flank of the Eighteenth Army an seek contact with the enemy. Second, to delay the enemy advance on Tartu, and by blocking the Kma River sector to prevent further advance by the enemy across the Kma River. Deception of the enemy as to German strength through mobility and by flexible and heavy fire was of special importance.

An estimate of the situation, intentions, and measures taken was transmitted to the army group. The army group approved the decision, and ordered the isthmus between Lake Peipus and Lake Virts to be blocked. The sector on both sides and in front of Tartu was assigned. Thus, another task had been given the *Armeeabteilung*. With the forces available, it seemed unlikely that this task could be accomplished. The sector of the *Armeeabteilung* had so far been 130 kilometers long, in addition to the lake shore. Now over 100 kilometers of coastal front along Lake Peipus, and a completely new land front of approximately eighty kilometers were added.

On the morning of 14 August, the blocking force began its mission in spite of the as-yet completely unclarified situation. Neither the situation of the Eighteenth Army - particularly that of its left flank - nor the enemy situation - were known even approximately. On 15 August, the army group gave the following order: "*Armeeabteilung Narva* will close the gap between itself and Eighteenth Army." The following line was designated as the new boundary with the Eighteenth Army: Oiu Port (northwestern corner of Lake Virts)-Tamme (eastern shore of Lake Virts)-Kiva-Poslva-Sabelda (twelve kilometers of southern tip of Lake Pskov); these villages belonged in the area of the Eighteenth Army.

It was initially not possible for the *Armeeabteilung* to establish contact with its blocking force. But soon it became clear that the left flank of the Eighteenth Army was not to be found at the new boundary; it was withdrawing westward. Thus the gap broadened, and it was impossible to close it with the forces available. Since on 15 August also, the situation of the blocking force remained unclarified, the army placed an advanced command post at Hp.Sootaga, fifteen kilometers north of Tartu, and itself intervened in the control of the blocking force.

Development of the Situation from 16 August

In the vicinity of Ahja, twenty-five kilometers southeast of Tartu, contact was successfully established with the 207th Security Division. According to the information available, the enemy had crossed the lake in the early morning hours at Mehikoorma (near the narrow passage between Lakes Pskov and Peipus) and at Jospera (just north thereof). The division had immediately undertaken a counterattack with local reserves, but it was unsuccessful. Further enemy forces were observed crossing the lake. Effective artillery action was impossible because the contacts with the observation posts had been disrupted. The Navy could not intervene with its units located at Mustvoe. The Island of Piirissaar, north of the narrow passage between the lakes, was again in enemy hands. For the unprotected units to pass it seemed impossible. They were moved up to the mouth of the Kma River to prevent surprise attacks by the enemy. The *Armeeabteilung* took over command of the 207th Security Division.

The launching of a new counterattack with the available security troops and Estonian units - and without the possibility of support by battle-worthy troops - seemed futile. Elements of the blocking forces could not be reached, and besides they would come too late to intervene effectively. Moreover, it was not permissible to tie them down in this situation. The security division hence received orders to delay a further enemy advance in the Ahja sector, and to block it, securing the protection of the southern flank of the sector along the Tartu-Pskov railroad. Immediately south of the railroad, at Poelva (twenty-seven kilometers southeast of Tartu) enemy forces had already been observed in undisclosed strength. A battalion of the 11th Infantry Division, situated in the vicinity of Voenna (twenty kilometers southeast of Tartu) - accordingly in a location favorable to the situation of the security division - was left there as tactical reserve at the disposal of the *Armeeabteilung.*

The Tartu-Elva road to the southwest was clear of the enemy. At Otepaeae, contact was successfully established with elements of the XXVIII Corps, which were retreating westward. The situation of the forward elements, that is, of the left flank of the Eighteenth Army, was not clear and could not be ascertained at the front. In the meantime, enemy forces with tanks were identified on the Tartu-Pskov road south of Liiva. In the undulating territory on both sides of Rebase (fourteen kilometers south of Tartu), a thin blocking line was therefore established with the bulk of the blocking forces. A continuous front before Tartu, by establishing contact with the left flank of the Eighteenth Army - for example to Otepaeae - was impracticable with the forces available. The Eighteenth Army had to manage alone on its left. It could also be assumed that it would retreat immediately with its left flank to Lake Virts. By 17 August it was no longer possible to establish contact with the Eighteenth Army.

The estimate of the situation was as follows: after the enemy had been able to cross the narrow passage between Lakes Pskov and Peipus (the Russian CXIV Rifle Corps had been identified here) and contact with the left flank of the Eighteenth Army had been disrupted, the enemy had become aware of the situation and had veered north. But it was evident that he advanced with hesitation; the reason was not clear. It was possible that he continued to employ his entire strength against the left sector of the Eighteenth Army, and could commit only part of his forces in an attack north. The Russian Sixty-seventh Army, which hitherto had attacked the left portion of the Eighteenth Army front, had been identified. Perhaps, however, the enemy overestimated the power of the Eighteenth Army and was concerned about his own flank in the event of a thrust northward.

The situation for the *Armeeabteilung* and for the blocking force was clear. The blocking force could no longer concern itself with the difficulties of the Eighteenth Army. The only thing was to prevent a thrust north by the enemy, aimed at cutting off the Narva front or to envelop the Eighteenth Army from the north around Lake Peipus. If the blocking force was tied down by the enemy south of the Kma River, the danger would arise that no more forces would be available to block the decisive sector on the Kma River itself, and that the enemy would reach this sector simultaneously with the blocking force. Only a mobile conduct of operations promised success in this situation, with the main points of effort on both sides of the main advance route of the enemy at the Tartu-Pskov road, and with the employment of mobile flank security, which - owing to the "repellent force of fire" - was in a position to inflict losses upon the enemy, to stop him again and again, and to delay him. The *Armeeabteilung* had to count on a vigorous enemy attack at any moment. The estimate of the situation was transmitted to the army group. On 19 August, it issued the following order: "The *Armeeabteilung* will fight its way back to the Kma River sector and hold it." The enemy meanwhile had advanced along the road as far as the blocking line at Rebase. He was stopped by the fire of the Germans. The blocking force withdrew.

The 207th Security division, whose southern flank had already withdrawn from the Ahja sector, retreated to the Kma River, its right sector extending as far as - and including - the Kma River crossing nine kilometers east of Tartu. The Estonian units and the Citizens' Guard on the Kma River were assigned to the 207th Security Division. Tartu remained a bridgehead for the time being, and this was no simple task for two battalions. In front of Tartu and along the Joeesuu (northeastern corner of Lake Virts)-Puhja-Roehu-Tartu road advanced covering parties were to be left. They were to withdraw as soon as the enemy attacked. In the meantime, another battalion of the 11th Infantry Division had been drawn out of the Narva front and brought up. A very strong and seasoned Estonian battalion arrived from the Finnish front.

Occupation of the Kma River on an unbroken line was not possible. It was essential to establish deep obstructions at the crossings - particularly at Joeesuu (northeastern corner of Lake Virts), at Katsvere (twelve kilometers northwest of Tartu) and in Tartu itself. It was here that the enemy's point of main effort was to be anticipated. The Kma River had an average width of 100 meters. The swampy depressions between Lake Virts and Tartu, and at the junction of the Kma River with Lake Peipus, were passable only with great difficulty, but unfortunately they were very hard to cover with observation posts. Tartu was evacuated by the large number of rear services of the Eighteenth Army - to the extent that they were not needed for the blocking force. At the airfield on the northeastern edge of Tartu there was still a fighter unit of the Luftwaffe, which engaged in indefatigable action until the field came under long-range artillery fire.

Contrary to expectations, on 20 August an order arrived the discontinue the withdrawal to the Kma River. This meant that the *Armeeabteilung* would have to defend the present blocking line, from which - however - the bulk of the blocking force had already withdrawn. The *Armeeabteilung* was certain that if the once-issued order was not basically changed, this could only result in severe reverses, and would have to be paid for with a loss of security on the Kma River. The order of the army group had apparently been motivated by the fact that *Panzerverband* Graf Strachwitz, which had reestablished an overland connection at Tukums with the Zone of the Interior, was now at the disposal of the army group for employment. It was to advance east of Lake Virts toward Tartu, and establish contact between the left flank of the Eighteenth Army and the blocking force.

On 21 August the enemy attacked again. The weak elements of the locking force left in contact with the enemy withdrew. The enemy was approaching Tartu. Whereas it had been possible so far, under the favorable conditions prevailing, to deceive the enemy as to the true strength of the friendly forces, these conditions no longer existed on the Kma River. For a defense of the Kma River, the strength of the blocking force was inadequate. The forces were in no position to repel a heavy thrust. What had previously been concern for the left flank of the Eighteenth Army would then be replaced by an acute threat to the rear of the army group.

At Taru and on the Kma River east of Tartu, the *Armeeabteilung* believed it could make out with its own forces for a limited period. In the sector west of Tartu as far as Lake Virts, however, the burden of the *Armeeabteilung* would have to be relieved. The army group promised immediate help through assignment of the 87th Infantry Division, *Panzerverband* Strachwitz, and the staff of the II Corps.

The blocking force had until 23 August to prepare itself. The enemy approached only hesitantly. He had apparently been alarmed by the thrust of *Panzerverband* Strachwitz east of Lake Virts. It was impossible to establish contact with the panzer unit. On 24 August the enemy pressure increased considerably. The blocking force was no longer in a position to influence the conduct of the enemy. Although it was possible to intercept the enemy successfully at the southern edge of Tartu at the Voriku railroad station, on 25 August the enemy upset all calculations. In the swampy territory east of the railroad and southeast of Tartu, which was covered with vegetation, offered poor visibility and had been reported impassable, Russian infantry forces advanced as far as the Kma River bridge in Tartu. The bridge was blasted by the security detail. Subsequently it became known that the Russians were led by a native Estonian officer, in the service of Russia. The section of Taru situated south of the Kma River had to be abandoned. The elements of the blocking force still on the southern bank of the Kma River withdrew across the railroad bridge north of Tartu.

At the same time, however, the Russians had also attacked west of Tartu. They overran the Estonian units at Pihva and Tuki, and made a surprise appearance at the Katevere bridge (thirteen kilometers northwest of Tartu). As a result of confusion in the chain of command and the brainlessness of the local German commander, the enemy captured the bridge in an undamaged condition, and at once formed a local bridgehead. Although it was possible to seal off the bridgehead at the most important points, the enemy immediately infiltrated into the forest north of the bridge.

In the meantime, the forward elements of the 87th Infantry Division were approaching. They had to make a detour through Potsamaa. *Panzerverband* Strachwitz followed; the staff of the II Corps had also arrived. It relieved the army battalion and assumed command of the sector. Before the new forces could become effective, the enemy entered the northern part of Tartu on 26 August, and immediately pushed on in a northerly and northeasterly direction. Employing the forward elements of the 87th Infantry Division, the II Corps succeeded in stopping the enemy by the evening of 27 August. The Russians had formed a substantial bridgehead. It was to be expected that the enemy would start a new attack at once. Troops from seven divisions of the Russian Sixty-seventh Army had so far been identified. Completely unclarified was the situation in the forest north of the Katevere bridge. The enemy appeared at the edge of the forest southwest of Voldi, nineteen kilometers north of Tartu, controlled the Tartu-Tallinn road with his fire, and exerted pressure on the advanced command post of the *Armeeabteilung*. On 28 August, however, the enemy did not attack. It was probable that he was moving up artillery, rearranging his forces, and assembling his troops.

The German front had to be stabilized. This was possible only if the enemy were deprived of the opportunity of assembling his forces north of the Kma River. If the enemy was in the process of regrouping his forces, this weakness had to be exploited. The *Armeeabteilung* resolved to attack with the aim of compressing the bridgehead. On 29 August the II Corps began a counterattack with the 87th Infantry Division, elements of the 563d Volksgrenadier Division which had arrived in the vicinity of Potsamaa by air[8], the old blocking force, and *Panzerverband* Strachwitz. It hit the enemy by surprise. By 31 August, the forces had been able to press in the bridgehead considerably. Only the territory immediately north of Tartu and the airfield remained in the enemy's hands. Elements of the II Corps launched an attack along the road leading from Potsamaa to Katevere bridge, pushed through as far as the bridge, and cut off the enemy forces that had advanced into the woos north of the bridge. The II Corps captured twelve enemy batteries and considerable materiel here.

During the following days the enemy endeavored repeatedly to expand the local bridgehead. But the attacks remained scattered, and it was possible to repulse them. On the basis of information derived from prisoners, it could be inferred that the enemy was again regrouping his forces. The Sixty-seventh Army had apparently been disengaged, and the Second Shock Army had been committed. Its removal from Narva was thus confirmed.

For more than two weeks the *Armeeabteilung* had fought with extremely weak forces against greatly superior numbers, and had retarded the enemy's advance. It was possible to prevent a disastrous turn in the critical situation in front of Tartu by the timely arrival of reinforcements. The II Corps had restored and consolidated the situation. In the meantime the Eighteenth

Army too had reached the line which had been specified, and which was anchored on Lake Virts. The situation had quieted down.

Withdrawal of *Armeeabteilung Narva* from the Narva Front from 16 September

A stabilization of the situation then existing on the front of the army group was not to be expected. At the fronts of the *Armeeabteilung* the following situation arose in the beginning of September 1944:

The Russian Second Shock Army was assembling at Tartu. The Russian Eighth Army stood at the Narva front. The employment of the Second Shock Army indicated the intention of the enemy to attempt a breakthrough. It was to be expected that the bulk of the Second Shock Army would immediately advance in a northwestern direction on Tallinn to cut off the Narva front, while some elements would perhaps also advance north roughly in the direction of Rakvere to attack the army near to the front. The Second Shock Army had to try and capture Tallinn rapidly. Only then could it prevent evacuation by sea of elements of the Narva front. It would then also quickly obtain a base for naval warfare, which was important to the Russian high command.

On the Narva front itself, the *Armeeabteilung* saw no danger of a breakthrough. After he had failed to achieve a breakthrough in the first attempt on 29 July - despite employment of the Second Shock Army in addition to the Eighth Army - the enemy had drawn off forces. True, the Russian Eighth Army was capable of achieving a breakthrough alone in view of its great superiority in personnel and material, but the *Armeeabteilung* did not expect it to try. Strong holding attacks by the Russian Eighth Army were to be anticipated to tie down forces on the Narva front. It could therefore be assumed that the Russian command, while tying down units on the Narva front, desired to put the *Armeeabteilung* into its power through an attack by way of Tartu.

At the Kma River - on a front more than eighty kilometers long - the II Corps faced the Russian Second Shock Army with the 87th Infantry Division[9], the 563d Volksgrenadier Division, *Panzerverband* Strachwitz, the remnants of the 207th Security Division, and the Estonian units. Two battalions of the 11th Infantry Division from the old blocking force remained assigned to the II Corps for the time being. With these forces the corps - especially with respect to materiel - was outnumbered by the Second Shock Army several times over. Although the corps, in its front-line organization, had taken into consideration the fact that the focal point of the defense would presumably be situated at Tartu, it could neither stand up to a breakthrough attack nor prevent a breakthrough.

The forces in the northern sector, in the Children's Home Position, were weak but seemed fully able to defend themselves against the holding attack expected to take place. A cause of anxiety was the sector on and north of Lake Peipus. the weak forces - chiefly Estonian units - employed here on an extended front under the 300th Special Administrative Division Headquarters, seemed unequal even to holding attacks.[10] Assignment of reinforcements to this front was not possible. If a mishap should occur in this sector, new decisions affecting the entire Narva front might become necessary. The mission for the *Armeeabteilung* - defense of the old position - remained unaltered.

The *Armeeabteilung*, however, might at any time face a situation necessitating completely new decisions and immediate action. The possibility of having to face an unexpected situation had existed for a long time. It might have arisen after the left flank of the Eighteenth Army had retreated from Lake Pskov, and it actually would have arisen if the enemy had vigorously exploited this opportunity. The result would have been encirclement of the *Armeeabteilung*. This possibility would again exist unless new orders for the conduct of operations arrived, or the *Armeeabteilung* itself made a new decision. If the *Armeeabteilung* were encircled, it would tie down only few enemy forces. The breakthrough subsequently necessary through the encirclement would be accompanied by the usual contingencies; men and material, however, were irreplaceable as far as the army group was concerned. Accordingly, an encirclement had to be prevented.

The *Armeeabteilung* sooner or later expected a decision from Hitler to abandon Estonia, and consequently it expected an order by the army group to disengage itself from the enemy, and to seek contact with the army group. But the *Armeeabteilung* also expected that such an order would arrive only after the danger was already impending, and without previous warning. To meet this possibility, the *Armeeabteilung* had taken steps a long time before. The removal of the *Armeeabteilung* by sea from Tallinn and the Baltic ports was out of the question in the opinion of the *Armeeabteilung*. the enemy would have immediately followed a withdrawal. Aside from the fact that removal by sea, under enemy pressure from the land and under the action of enemy air and naval forces, would have caused high losses, it could be assumed that the enemy would at once push past Tallinn into the rear of the army group. To prevent this had been - and now remained - the task of the *Armeeabteilung*.

In utmost secrecy as far as the field forces and the Estonian population were concerned - and even with respect to the army group in order not to involve the latter in any action running counter to the *Führer* order - all measures necessary for a withdrawal had been explored, tested in local reconnaissance, and arranged by an extremely small circle since the end of July. The execution required the *Armeeabteilung* to undertake a movement of tremendous proportions, from the eastern frontier of Estonia to a line drawn from the northern tip of Lake Virts to Paernu, involving a wheeling movement of ninety degrees, and simultaneously a movement of the forces employed on the Kma River to protect the flank, involving a wheeling movement of 180 degrees.

March Routes

The left flank of the *Armeeabteilung* had to cover the greatest distance. For the time being, the motorized and horse-drawn elements depended on the Narva-Joehvi-Rokvere road which was the sole rear communication in the sector. This made things considerably more difficult. Only after passing Vaekuela, thirteen kilometers east of Rakvere, was it possible to continued the movement on two roads:

A. Rakvere-Topa-Paide-Paernu road: This road was passable for all weapons at any time. This was the road the motorized elements had to use. Total distance from the front was 300 kilometers.

B. Vaekuela (thirteen kilometers west of Rakvere)-Kiltsi-Koigi-Voehma-Viljanci road: Only parts of this road had a firm surface. A few sections were passable for motorized traffic, but only to a limited extent. This road was suitable for horse-drawn movements. To bypass the defile at Viljandi there was an alternate through Suure-Jaani-Suure-Kospu. Total distance from the front to Viljandi was 200 kilometers.

For smooth progress of the movement on the left flank, it was accordingly important to have horse-drawn march groups start out early and gain a lead so that they could leave the road for motorized movement at Vaekuela (thirteen kilometers east of Rakvere) before the motorized elements arrived. In the central sector north of Lake Peipus there was also no more than one rear communication route available in the beginning, and this was the shore road along Lake Peipus by way of Mustvoe-Joegeva-Potsamaa. It was passable for all weapons. Distance from the front to Viljardi was 165 kilometers.

The disadvantage of this road was its proximity to the front, parallel to the Kma River. The army accordingly built a makeshift road from Kisaku to Tudulinna to obtain a juncture with the route of the horse-drawn elements through Avimura-Paesvere (just south of Muuga)-Noavere-Rakko. By this measure the route to be covered was increased to 210 kilometers, but this had to be taken into the bargain.

Alternate routes to the Baltic ports for use in an emergency were designated as follows:

1. Through Tallinn to Haapsalu opposite the island of Vormai and from Tueri to Virtsu opposite the island of Saaremas. These communications were at first designated only for trains and columns no longer needed by the army, but open also for refugees and stragglers.

2. The narrow-gauge Tamsalu-Viljardi railroad would facilitate the movement if it were possible to make available rolling stock in sufficient numbers.

In the overall preparation for the withdrawal, the *Armeeabteilung* was in a dilemma. On the one hand, it had to see to it that the troops remained solely and unconditionally concerned with the defense of the present position; on the other hand, the *Armeeabteilung* - in order not to lose valuable personnel and materiel in case there was a surprise change of the situation - had to start at once with preparations for a withdrawal. The first task was an immediate evacuation behind the front.

All wounded and sick were shipped off, unless they were likely to become fit for front duty again in a short time. Stocks of material and supplies which were not absolutely necessary were shipped out; large trains and rear services were transferred far to the rear to service the rear area; ammunition and rations were unloaded along the march routes and in part maintained on a mobile basis. The combat trains were dispersed in the depth of the main defensive area, while the combat vehicles were kept close at hand under cover.

To ensure speed in the withdrawal, the *Armeeabteilung* seized whatever vehicles it could in order to move the army largely by motor transportation. Motor vehicles - except for those that were used for the supply of the *Armeeabteilung* - were combined in columns and kept available in the vicinity of the front. It was possible to secure the required fuel.

Nothing had changed in the preparations and the intended progress of the movement through the employment of the II Corps on the Kma River. Flank protection of the Narva front was ensured. The execution could be affected adversely only if the II Corps was surprised by the Russian Second Shock Army and thrown into the withdrawal movement in a northern or northwestern direction. Only by rapid progress of the movement of the left flank could such a danger be to a large extent averted.

Since the General Grasser had no Wehrmacht and no territorial functions all preparations had to be limited to the *Armeeabteilung* itself. However, by way of precaution all possibilities were orally discussed with the Admiral Burchardi. It was important to the *Armeeabteilung* to ascertain the time required by Admiral Burchardi for an evacuation from Tallinn. The strength of the attack to be launched on Tallinn depended on the time required. The consensus of opinion was that, if a withdrawal should become necessary by surprise, only the most valuable items could be evacuated, aside from the troops and refugees, whose transportation must remain ensured at all events. Eight to ten days were fixed as the time necessary.

In a map exercise conducted in the first days of September 1944 - in the presence of General Schörner - all necessary measures for a withdrawal of the *Armeeabteilung* were once again gone over, and the conduct of operations and the movement of the Narva front and the II Corps coordinated. As a guiding principle for the preparations and the time required for the movement, General Schörner issued the following deadlines:

1. Three to four weeks for the evacuation by the army group of material to be salvaged.

2. Advance announcement of the withdrawal and three days time to start the movement.

3. Two weeks for the movement to the Estonian-Western position[11] itself and seven more days for the movement to the "Wendish" position.[12] The *Armeeabteilung* was expected to save three days in the movement if possible.

The *Armeeabteilung* gave itself the following combat mission: "The *Armeeabteilung* will disengage itself from the enemy and gain the Estonian-Western position. It is necessary that the *Armeeabteilung* should early be at the disposal of the army group with fresh forces. Operations are to be conducted in such a way that strong enemy forces are tied down 'in the wrong direction.'" A rapid start and speed while the movement was under way, as well as deception of the enemy, was accordingly aimed for.

On the northern flank there was no doubt that the Russian Eighth Army would attack as soon as it detected signs of a withdrawal. Its advance had to be delayed from the outset in order that distance might be gained. Thereafter, everything would depend on drawing the enemy off to Tallinn by applying appropriate tactics, while the bulk of the *Armeeabteilung* flowed off to the southwest. The forces employed in the southern flank had to prevent a breakthrough by the Russian Second Shock Army, and - when the withdrawal began - to delay the enemy advance in such a manner that any thrust he made would not affect the *Armeeabteilung*. Conduct of operations was not easy. While clinging obstinately to their pivot on Lake Virts, the troops had to retreat first northward and then gradually to the southwest.

The movement of the northern flank and the southern flank was synchronized by setting lines to be reached by a certain time, the *Armeeabteilung* reserving for itself the right to hold certain lines longer or to omit them entirely. On the basis of previous calculations, and according to the stage reached by the preparations, the *Armeeabteilung* believed that it would be able to reach the Estonian-Western position in ten days.

Combat Missions

For the II Corps, the former mission of defending its sector had to remain unaltered. But the corps was to be prepared soon to receive an order to withdraw. The task then was to delay the advance of the enemy toward Tallinn and Potsamaa, while continually reinforcing the pivot on Lake Virts. Points of main effort were to be established along these roads. If the situation remained normal, the II Corps was to join in the withdrawal from Line "C" on. All dispensable trains and rear services were to be removed behind the Estonian-Western position at once.

The plan for the Narva front was that the III SS Panzer Corps, with the 11th Infantry Division assigned to it, would disengage itself from the enemy twenty-four hours after receiving the code word, leaving mobile rear guards in its old position, while its main body tried to gain distance. The preparations had to be carried out in such a manner that all horse-drawn elements, except those shipped by motor transportation, could start out not later than four hours after arrival of the code word.

Strong *kampfgruppen*[13] under the former coast defense staff were to be committed early east of Rakvere and east of Taba. After the III SS Panzer Corps had passed, they were to draw the Russian Eighth Army off toward Tallinn in delaying resistance. Until all of the motorized elements had passed through Taba, the coast defense staff was assigned to the III SS Panzer Corps. In the central sector it was important to see to it that the 300th Special Administrative Division Headquarters rapidly passed the forest territory, which was difficult to traverse, and the bottleneck between Lake Peipus and the Muraka Swamp north of Tudulinna, and that its main body reached the Tudulinna-Avinurme-Rakke road. To avoid friction, the division was assigned to the II Corps for the movement.

Development of the Situation
from 2 September 1944: Finland Gives Up

The Finnish government, whose situation at the front was completely hopeless, had accepted an ultimatum which, as the prerequisite for an armistice, demanded the evacuation from Finland of German troops. On 4 September hostilities had ceased. In the expectation of a large number of refugees, the army group established a collecting point in Tallinn.

The surrender of Finland brought about a certain danger to the sea flank of the army. True, the island of Tytarsaari was in German hands, but the occupation of the island of Suursaari by Russian forces was to be expected. This would have opened up the sea route for the Russian naval forces. In June it had already been intended to occupy the island, or at least share in its occupation. For political reasons, this intention was dropped. Since the collecting point in Tallinn was hardly utilized, and political reasons now no longer existed, the supreme command ordered the capture of the island of Suursaari. The operation had been prepared in all its details. A regimental staff, an infantry battalion, an engineer company of the 23d Infantry Division, and the 531st Coastal Artillery Battalion from the coast defense of the Narva front were assembled in Tallinn.

After a friendly visit on 14 September, the operation was undertaken under the command of Admiral Burchardi during the night of 14 September. The enemy reached the island and was able to start disembarking. Contrary to expectations, a heavy engagement developed, which ended with the operation being broken off as unsuccessful.

On the fronts of the *Armeeabteilung*, at the Narva from and at Tartu, all was at first quiet. It was possible to improve the organization of the defense everywhere. The preparations for a withdrawal were to a certain extend concluded.

Since 10 September there had been an increase in the tempo of fighting on the enemy's side, and an increasing activity behind his front at Tartu, although as yet there was no sign of an impending attack. The picture changed after 14 September, with the beginning of the new Russian offensive against the Sixteenth and Eighteenth Armies. From the bridgehead at Tartu, the enemy repeatedly thrust forward in local operations. He was apparently endeavoring to clarify the situation. Through the swampy territory between Lake Virts and Tartu and near the mouth of the Kma River the enemy attempted to infiltrate in large numbers. Adjustment fire by new batteries and increased enemy air reconnaissance suggested that an attack was about to begin at Tartu.

On 14 September, as expected, the enemy had started new attacks against the Sixteenth and Eighteenth Armies. Within a short time critical situations arose. There were also great losses of materiel. Everywhere the army group had to patch things up as well as it could, but many points could be sealed off only in an emergency fashion. The situation south Lake Virts took a dangerous course. The enemy was able to penetrate and cross the Kma River south of Lake Virts. A breakthrough at this point was bound to separate *Armeeabteilung Narva* from the army group.

The army group could not expect assignment of new forces in view of the strained situation of Germany both in the East and in the West. The strength of the army group's front had been reduced to the limits of possibility. Combat strength had shrunk; the last reserves ere being employed. Pointing out the seriousness of its situation, the army group again requested permission from Hitler to withdraw to the Wendish position and abandon Estonia. Only thus would it be possible to obtain new forces. In this situation, the code word for the withdrawal arrived about 1800 hours on 16 September. The beginning of the withdrawal movement was set for 18 September. General Grasser was simultaneously appointed Wehrmacht Administrative Commander, and had to assume the territorial authority of such a commander.

Course of the Withdrawal

The code word was passed on according to the prepared plan. Admiral Burchardi had already received the necessary orders through his channels. The Commissioner General received orders at once to assemble the civil administration agencies in Tallinn. The Todt Organization and the police, to the extent that they had not been previously withdrawn by the army group, were dispatched toward the Baltic Islands. During the past days, the *Armeeabteilung* had already placed the means of transportation at the disposal of the III SS Panzer Corps so that no special movements were necessary. The extent of available transportation was such that it was deemed possible to move the entire army by motor transportation.

Although the beginning of the movement had been set for 18 September, the *Armeeabteilung* had to adhere to its old plan, which provided for the departure of the horse-drawn elements four hours after the arrival of the code word. Only in this manner could the movement progress smoothly.

Development of the Situation from 17 September

In the early morning hours of 17 September, the Russian Second Shock Army - after heavy artillery preparation and with the use of a large number of ground attack airplanes - attacked the II Corps.

The II Corps had to retreat at Tartu and on the left flank to avoid being beaten, and in the early evening hours it stood approximately where the former bridgehead had been, with its left flank at Varnja. The corps requested an acceleration of the movement of the Narva front so that it could withdraw to the Line "D" during the night of 17 September. General Hasse, the commanding general of the II Corps, believed this to be the only way in which he could ensure protection of the flank. In the opinion of the corps, the enemy had attacked with at least eight to ten rifle divisions and strong tank formations. East of Tartu, in front of the 207th Security Division, the Russian XXX Guards Rifle Corps had been identified. Its removal from the Narva front was thus confirmed.

Estimate of the Situation

While the Russian Second Shock Army could be retarded in its advance, it certainly could no longer be stopped. Hence the task of the *Armeeabteilung* was to accelerate the movement of the Narva front to such an extent that it could at least avoid encirclement. To avoid the necessity of diverting strong elements toward Tallinn, Admiral Burchardi would have to accelerate the evacuation. As evacuation of economic goods was out of the question, Admiral Burchardi believed it would be possible to complete the evacuation in five to seven days. Inquiries at the III SS Panzer Corps and at the 300th Special Administrative Division indicated that these units could start at any time. The troops were rested, so that - accordingly - high demands could be made upon them.

The *Armeeabteilung* therefore decided to disengage itself from the Narva front on 17 September and reach the Estonian-Western position in a single movement. The III SS Panzer Corps was accordingly ordered to withdraw speedily after disengaging itself from the enemy, to begin the motorized movement at once, and to reach the Estonian-Western position in one movement. To ensure unified and clear chain of command during the withdrawal, and to have whole units available early in the new position, the 11th Infantry Division was to act as a rear guard from Line "B" on. The horse-drawn columns already on the move were to keep moving without regard for losses sustained during the march, and to reach the road designated for the movement of the horse-drawn elements. The 300th Special Administrative Division was emphatically admonished to accelerate its movement, its attention being drawn to the situation of the II Corps. It was told to complete the crossing of lines "C" and "D" not later than the evening of 19 September. A large truck column, totaling sixty tons, was assigned to the division at Avinurme.

Development of the Situation in the Northern Sector

On 17 September, with the fall of darkness, the III SS Panzer Corps disengaged itself from the enemy and, by the morning of 18 September, the leading elements began their motorized movement. On 18 September, the 11th Infantry Division reached Line "B." The further development of the situation in the II Corps sector necessitated another change in the execution of the plan, since there existed the danger of a breakthrough.

Since the Russian Eighth Army had not attacked on the Narva front, and withdrawal of the III SS Panzer Corps went off smoothly, the 11th Infantry Division, which was to act as rear guard from Line "B" on, was moved up immediately behind the III SS Panzer Corps. The rear troops, which were still in the old position, received orders to disengage themselves from the enemy and seek contact with the 11th Infantry Division. Unless there were special difficulties, it seemed that it would be possible to get through with the troops of the Narva front. From 18 September on, the way for the Russian Eighth Army was open.

From Joevi on, one company of SS Panzer Reconnaissance Battalion 11 of the III SS Panzer Corps, reinforced by anti-tank personnel, acted as a rear guard. The task of this combat force was to let the enemy come up, fire at him, and disengage itself in time. At noon of 18 September the movement had already proceeded through Rakvere to the southwest. The forward elements of the III SS Panzer Corps reached Line "K" on the evening of 18 September, while the main body of the corps arrived at the Estonian-Western position during the day on 19 September, and the 11th Infantry Division on 20 September. The 11th SS *"Nordland"* Panzergrenadier Division was employed in an expanded bridgehead around Paernu in order to keep the port open for use. The 4th SS *"Nederland"* Panzergrenadier Brigade was immediately employed in the Estonian-Western position, while the 11th Infantry Division was assembled around Moisakuela at the disposal of the *Armeeabteilung.*[14]

The horse-drawn elements, which had started out on the evening of 16 September, had passed Vaskuela (road fork thirteen kilometers east of Rakvere) ahead of the motorized elements, and had by noon of 18 September reached the Tartu-Tallinn railroad in a forced march of 120 kilometers without substantial losses. From Tamsalu on, it was possible to transport substantial elements on the narrow-gauge railroad.

Development of the Situation in the II Corps Sector

On 17 September, it was possible to hold the line north of Tartu until evening. The 207th Security Division had to withdraw its left flank to Line "D." Contact with Lake Peipus was lost. On 18 September, the corps was pressed back in heavy battles to Line "E." The corps was obliged to collect into combat forces along the roads. Breakthroughs off the roads, particularly by tanks, could not longer be prevented. The pressure of the enemy increased continuously, particularly on and along both sides of the road to Tallinn, and on the left flank of the corps, which had meanwhile been completely disrupted.

Up to the evening of 19 September, the corps was able to prevent any breakthrough on the road to Tallinn, immediately south of Joehva (Line "F"), but then the road had to be given up. The weak security forces at Torma and Kustvee were no longer capable of offering resistance, and were moved up to the II Corps. The II Corps now disengaged itself from the enemy, and by 22 September had gained the Estonian-Western position. After Line "G" had been passed, the pressure of the enemy decreased, and after Line "H" had been abandoned it ceased entirely. The main body of the enemy forces was evidently advancing in a northern and northwestern direction.

Development of the Situation of the 300th Special Administrative Division

The division comprised elements of the 20th Estonian SS Waffen Grenadier division[15], four Estonian infantry regiments, and weak German units. All material had been drawn piece by piece from the sector except for captured guns, which it was impossible to move. As a result, it was impossible to prevent the Estonian units from becoming aware of the preparations for the withdrawal, and from forming their own judgment. They had already experienced one Russian occupation, and only for this reason had they volunteered to defend their country. In this they had fully discharged their duties, and substantially relieved the burden on the *Armeeabteilung*. They now realized the new danger. A large percentage of them went home or remained in the woods.

When the order for the withdrawal had been issued, the 300th Special Administrative Division had also begun to move. The bulk of the Estonian units, however, were not equal to the demands of such a withdrawal. Only weak elements, including one battalion that had remained whole up to the last, could be moved back into the Estonian-Western position. On 21 September, the large truck column assigned to the division arrived. It had been cut off through an advance of the enemy from the south toward Avinurme, but the column commander, taking with him a security battalion, had made a detour from Avinurme through Tudulinna-Tudu-Viru-Poela and had succeeded in getting through without encountering enemy forces.

Development of the Situation and Evacuation of Tallinn

After the order for the withdrawal had been issued, the coast defense staff had immediately assembled all forces at Rakvere and east of Tapae. The mobile coast artillery of the Navy and the Army coast artillery employed on the coast had already been withdrawn respectively by Admiral Burchardi and by the army. The permanently emplaced guns were demolished.

On the afternoon of 19 September the combat force came into contact with the leading elements of the Russian Eighth Army. The Russian Eighth Army had apparently moved up immediately after the rear troops. There was no special pressure, however. After the rear troops had passed, the combat force retreated past the intermediate lines. The Russian Second Shock Army had not yet put in an appearance, and the Eighth Russian Army followed only slowly.

The garrison commander at Tallinn had only a few security battalions at his disposal. A defense of Tallinn was not planned, since the completion of the evacuation by Admiral Burchardi was to be expected soon. The evacuation proceeded smoothly. Although enemy air forces appeared in limited strength above the port, they did not substantially hamper the evacuation. In Tallinn itself there was unrest. Alongside of an Estonian national government, a "Red" government had been formed. Brief street battles developed. With the concurrence of the *Armeeabteilung*, the garrison commander negotiated with both parties, with the result that the battles were discontinued, and both parties helped with the evacuation in the port. During the night of 21 September the evacuation was completed. The last ship with the last troops left the port just as the Russians hesitantly entered the fully illuminated town.

At the time the order for the withdrawal had been issued, the *Armeeabteilung* had also informed the Estonian authorities with whom it had dealings - these authorities had always been loyal to the *Armeeabteilung* - and had given them a chance to be evacuated. More than 20,000 refugees made use of this offer, and were taken aboard the transports by Admiral Burchardi.

Meanwhile, another threat to the progress of the withdrawal had arisen. On 17 September, the enemy had expanded his bridgehead south of Lake Virts, and pushed north and west of the lake toward Mustia. The *Armeeabteilung* had to intervene and seal off the enemy south of Mustia with some of its forces to keep the way through Viljandi open. On 22 September, the withdrawal was completed with the arrival of the II Corps in the Estonian-Western position, as was the evacuation of Estonia in cooperation with Admiral Burchardi. The enemy did not probe the new position until 24 September.

Final Situation of *Armeeabteilung Narva*

The II Corps was in the Estonian-Western position. The 11th SS *"Nordland"* Panzergrenadier Division started out for the Sixteenth Army on 21 September; on 22 September it was followed by the staff of the III SS Panzer Corps with corps headquarters troops and the 11th Infantry Division. Simultaneously, the 4th SS *"Nederland"* Panzergrenadier Brigade was withdrawn from the bridgehead at Paernu and assigned to the Eighteenth Army. On 24 September, the staff of *Armeeabteilung Narva* was committed to another location.

Conclusion

In the winter offensive which began in January 1944, the Russian command at the Leningrad Front pursued the strategic objective of brining about the collapse of Army Group North and opening the way to the eastern frontier of Germany. In addition to the destruction of the Eighteenth Army, the Russian command had set itself the primary task - once a breakthrough had been achieved south of Leningrad and out of the Oranienbaum pocket - to push on immediately with part of its forces in the direction of Narva and across the Narva River into Estonian territory. The fact that the Second Shock

Army was committed in this attack shows the significance which the Russian command attached to this task. In addition to reasons of pure prestige, political reasons such as the isolation of Finland, and the intention to clear the way for Russian naval forces may have been decisive. Since the Russian command did not follow up the Second Shock Army with any further forces, it does not appear likely that it planned from the beginning to make a sweep west of Lake Peipus and expand the success by a thrust into the rear of the army group.

The Russian command succeeded in very quickly rupturing the front of the Eighteenth Army, which had been weakened by transfers. After a few days, the Russian Second Shock Army had split off the northern sector of the Eighteenth Army and battered it to such an extent that the Russian Army was able to start pursuit. The withdrawal of the northern elements of the Eighteenth Army could no longer be regarded as wholly orderly and systematic.

The Narva River was reached in the beginning of February. After the Second Shock Army found it impossible to cross the Narva River by the shortest route from the march column, it pushed into the Panther Line, after lunging south of Narva. It was only through the employment of the newly arrived *Feldherrnhalle* Panzergrenadier Division and of elements of the 58th Infantry Division that it was finally possible to prevent a Russian success, the potentialities of which were unpredictable. It now turned out that the Second Shock Army no longer had the strength to start the operation moving again. Thus it had missed its one and only chance.

By the beginning of March the Eighteenth Army also had been able to move into the Panther Line, so that the army group presented a closed front. Here the enemy had also failed to achieve his primary objective. The Eighteenth Army had not been destroyed. The enemy had brought about the successive collapse of the various sectors of the Eastern front, ending with that of Army Group North. But again and again the German command had succeeded in organizing a closed front. Success was due to the fact that the troops - although depleted and overstrained by uninterrupted fighting - were still intact. The cost of a withdrawal forced by the enemy and proceeding under enemy pressure did not allow the establishment of any substantial strategic reserves at any point, even after the front had been shortened.

With the beginning of the Russian summer offensive in June 1944, which disrupted the front at the boundary between Army Groups Center and North, the attack affected Army Group North and in its further development directly hit the Sixteenth and Eighteenth Armies. *Armeeabteilung Narva* necessarily began to be weakened as a result of the transfer of units to the critical points. In all transfers and the subsequently necessary regrouping of forces the *Armeeabteilung* had to bear in mind to avoid decisively weakening the left sector, which was the focal point of defense on the front of the army group. When individual divisions were transferred, the adjacent divisions had to be shifted laterally. Such transfers could be expedited by early, far-sighted assembly of local reserves. Owing to their proportions, these transfers became a problem that could only be solved by improvisation - such as the employment of Estonian units, of coast artillery, and of captured guns. Possible consequences had to be borne in mind. The Estonian units - they were interested only in protecting their own country - fought well. They substantially relieved the burden of the *Armeeabteilung*, and made possible the large transfers.

On the Narva front eight out of nine infantry divisions had to be transferred elsewhere; that is, more than two-thirds of the total effectives, aside from the transfer of GHQ troops and independent units. As far as is known, there has never been a draining off of forces to this extent. The mission, however, remained unchanged. This is the typical example of how fronts were ruthlessly weakened in order to patch up other points, and how they then collapsed as a result. That the Narva front did not collapse must be attributed solely to the tenacity of the troops and to the circumstance that the enemy did not press his advantage until a final decision had been obtained. The large proportions of transfers necessitated great encroachments upon the defensive power of the focal point to close the gaps, and at last led to a reduction in the length of the front.

In the course of the withdrawal to the shortened line, which began on 24 July, it turned out that the enemy was in the process of concentrating with very great forces. The thrust made by the enemy on 24 July from the south showed that he had become aware of the withdrawal, but he had not expected it. There was no vigorous assault along the whole line. Thus it was possible to withdraw the left flank without substantial losses. Apparently the enemy assumed this to be a general withdrawal of the Narva front. Only thus is it understandable that he threw all available units into battle from the march column one after the other without adequate reconnaissance.

The employment of the Second Shock Army and the XXX Guards Rifle Corps, in addition to the Eighth Army, showed that the enemy had retained his former intention of fighting his way into Estonia. Whether it was still correct to adhere to this strategic plan at that time need not be debated. The overall situation would undoubtedly have been considerably and rapidly influenced if the enemy had conducted a vigorous pursuit and forced a breakthrough. It was difficult to understand why the enemy broke off the battle on 30 July, and without exploiting the opportunities afforded him by the strong forces he had at his disposal entirely regrouped his forces. The defensive battle on 29 July shows that if the defense is properly organized, tenacious resistance even by weak forces may achieve extraordinary successes.

As the Russian summer offensive progressed, it was only a matter of time before the fighting extended to the left flank of the Eighteenth Army. The enemy would have acted correctly if he had made the focal point opposite the left flank of the Eighteenth Army so strong from the very beginning that he could - in one blow - have forced a breakthrough at Lake Peipus and a passage south of Lake Virts. In this manner he would not only have cut off the Narva front, but would also have maneuvered the army group into an extremely critical position. But to accomplish this he would have had to assemble the necessary forces and follow up with them.

After the left flank of the Eighteenth Army had been dislodged from Lake Peipus, the enemy had at first judged the situation correctly. He had turned part of his forces northward to Tartu. These forces, however, he had had to take away from the Sixty-seventh Army. As a result, the Sixty-seventh Army was so much weakened in its offensive power in the main direction of the thrust west that it could achieve neither one nor the other objective. What was missing here was the Second Shock Army, which had lost time as a result of the discontinuation of its attack on the Narva front, and which now arrived too late. Only the dispersion of the strength of the Sixty-seventh Army can explain the exceedingly hesitant advance on Tartu.

The way the blocking force conducted the battle no doubt deceived the enemy as to its strength. The enemy could and should have obtained clarity as to the situation through appropriate front-line reconnaissance and an energetic thrust. By the time he had found out the weakness of the blocking force and the Second Shock Army had appeared it was too late, at least for some time. The phase in the fighting from 13 July on demonstrates that even weak forces may achieve successes in flexible combat operations against strong forces if they carry out their task fearlessly. This is a telling example of a battle of weak forces against greatly superior numbers, although it must be said that the numerically inferior side was lucky, too.

The intermission in the fighting in the first half of July 1944 indicated that the Russian command needed time to restore order in its units and to rehabilitate them before it could strike new blows. In order to able to conduct a decisive operation aiming westward on the Eastern front, it had to eliminate Army Group North. The army group tied down strong Russian forces and could menace the flank if the Russians pushing westward passed them on the south. There could, hence, be no doubt that the Russian command would for the time being cling to its old plan of clearing out the German troops in the Baltic countries and forcing an access to the sea.

On the basis of the previously existing distribution of forces, a thrust by the First Baltic Front toward Riga from the Bauska area appeared likely, with the objective of encircling the army group. The Second and Third Baltic Fronts would have to split up and compress the army group. A breakthrough by the Third Baltic Front, which had been launched south of Lake Virts, was to separate the Narva front from the army group. If the enemy acted correctly, he would - while tying down the Narva front - situate his point of main effort opposite the Sixteenth and Eighteenth Armies. The forces of the Narva front would have fallen into his lap like ripe fruit. Their destruction would have been merely a matter of time.

The Russian Second Shock Army was being concentrated near Tartu. Opposite the Narva front stood the Russian Eighth Army. The fact that these strong forces were left to face the *Armeeabteilung* showed, however, that the Russian command was by no means content with the idea of tying down the enemy, but continued to adhere to its plan to immediately fight its way into Estonian territory. It can only be assumed that at Tartu the enemy - by launching an attack by the Second Shock Army, the XXX Guards Rifle Corps, and strong armored units - wanted to gain possession of Estonia rapidly, to encircle the Narva front directly, and at all events prevent the removal of forces from Tallinn. Political reasons no longer existed.

The enemy had succeeded in capturing Estonia, but in the planned encirclement of the Narva front he had failed. The *Armeeabteilung* was able to avoid encirclement. This was due chiefly to the timely and detailed preparations which made a rapid withdrawal possible. But it was also due to the failure of the Russian Eighth Army to become aware of the withdrawal and to begin to move in time. Thus there was no tying down. It became possible to accelerate the movement itself. Owing to the absence of strong enemy air reconnaissance, the Russians did not know the direction of the withdrawal. As a result it became possible to draw the enemy off in the wrong direction by skillful maneuvering.

After its quick retreat, the *Armeeabteilung* was again at the disposal of the army group, without having suffered losses of personnel and materiel. At first the *Armeeabteilung* itself had not considered that it would be able to withdraw so rapidly.

While the Russian command reported the encirclement of the Narva front in radio broadcasts, the army group was able to prevent critical situations south of Riga and at the Eighteenth Army with the forces of the *Armeeabteilung* which had arrived. But the time approached when the situation could no longer be mastered by improvisation and a hand-to-mouth existence. A solution on a large scale was required. If no basically new decisions were made, the continual critical situations were bound to turn into catastrophes sooner or later.

NOTES

[1]Reichelt continually refers to this unit throughout his manuscript. It appears, however, from a systematic combing of the records of *Armeeabteilung Narva*, that the III SS Panzer Corps did not possess a reconnaissance battalion in its corps troops. *Gruppenführer* Steiner in March or April permanently appropriated SS Reconnaissance Battlion 11 from the 11th SS "*Nordland*" Panzergrenadier Division. Subsequent references in the text have been so emended.

[2]This division staff was created from the staff of the disbanded 1st Luftwaffe Field Division.

[3]These units included Marine Battalion "Malchow," *Jagdkommando* 227 (an antipartisan group smaller than a battalion), Panzer Company (captured) 285, and I and II/SS Artillery Regiment 20 from the 20th SS Estonian Waffen Grenadier Division. *Armeeabteilung Narva*, Ia 1170/44, 27 June 1944, T-312, Reel 1632.

[4]The author is, if anything, generous in his estimation of the strength of the Estonian units. Although created with an authorized strength of 2,337 men each, by early July desertion had led to a dramatic decline in the combat strength of these regiments. For example, Estonian Border Guard Regiment 4 reported on 8 July a combat strength of only 870 men; Regiment 5 deployed 1,213; and Regiment 6 had 1,036 men in the line. *Armeeoberkommando 18*, Ia, 2575/44, 8 July 1944, T-312, Reel 946.

[5]One detail of the preparation which Reichelt omits here is that an ad hoc subordinate command, *Gruppe* Reymann (under Lieutenant General Helmuth Reymann, former commander of the now defunct 13th Luftwaffe Field Division) was given control of the 11th Infantry and 20th SS Estonian Waffen Grenadier Divisions. *Armeeabteilung Narva*, Ia, 1170/44, 22 June 1944, T-312, Reel 1632.

[6]Aside from its mediocre personnel, materiel, and leadership, one of the reasons that the 20th SS Estonian Waffen Grenadier Division suffered so heavily in the retreat is that many of its organic units had been attached out to other divisions. Each of its infantry regiments was operating with one battalion missing, the füsilier battalion was detached, and two artillery units were assigned elsewhere as well. This had the effect of seriously weakening an already less than formidable division. It also accounts for the fact that the 20th SS seems to get mauled or completely destroyed in this manuscript several times, only to miraculously reconstitute. *Armeabteilung Narva*, Ia 1170/44, 27 June 1944, T-312, Reel 1632.

[7]The force had actually been organized in late June as Division "Wagner," under *Standartenführer* Jürgen Wagner of the 4th SS *"Nederland"* Panzergrenadier Brigade. Designating the force as an ad hoc division appears to have been a counterintelligence manuever; it never had more than brigade strength. German records are slightly more precise on its composition than Reichelt is able to be from memory. The force included Grenadier Regiment 23 and II/Artillery Regiment 11 (from 11th Infantry); III/SS Infantry Regiment 46 (from 20th SS); SS Reconnaissance Battalion 11 and SS Assault Gun Battalion 11 (from 11th SS); II/SS Artillery Regiment 54 (from 4th SS Brigade); and the following assorted fragments: SS Battalion "Wallonie," *Kampfgruppe* Railer (engineers), *Kampfgruppe* Mann (anti-tank), Füsilier Battalion 31, and II/Artillery Regiment 227. *Armeeabteilung Narva*, Ia, 1170/44, 27 June 1944, T0312, Reel 1632.

[8]The 563d was one of the first Volksgenadier Divisions created on the new, reduced establishment of late 1944. It infantry strength, even before combat, was considerably lower than its designation would suggest. By 16 September, after only moderate fighting, the division reported its combat strength as follows: Volksgrenadier Regiment 1147 had 885 men; Regiment 1148 had 1,078 men; Regiment 1149 had 1,303 men; and Engineer Battalion 1563 had 443 men, for a total infantry combat strength of just 3,709 men. *Armeeabteilung Narva*, Ia/Id, 298/44, 21 September 1944, T-312, Reel 1634.

[9]The 87th Infantry Division, on 16 September, was weak, even by the standards of the German Army in late 1944. Each of its three grenadier regiments had been reorganized as a single battalion. Of the 7,208 men present, the infantry strength of the division was only 1,946—and this figure included both the field replacement and engineer battalions, as well as the heavy weapons troops in the regiments. The actual strength of the three remaining line infantry battalions was a mere 1,028. *Armeeabteilung Narva*, Ia/Id, 298/44, 21 September 1944, T-312, Reel 1634.

[10]The 300th Special Administrative Division had, on paper, one of the largest establishments in the Army Group, reporting 10,268 men present on 16 September, of which fully 6,017 men were assigned to Estonian Border Guards Regiments 2, 3, 4, and 6, or Estonian Field *Polizei* Battalions 286, 288, and 289. Unfortunately, morale and experience were nonexistent, the infantry armaments were either obsolete or captured, and the division completely lacked any organic artillery, being forced to depend on two weak battalion of the 20th SS. Furthermore, the only German units available to stiffen the Estonian resistance were an engineer platoon (40 men); a field replacement "battalion" (19 men); an "alarm" company made from artillerymen whose guns had been lost in previous engagements (44 men); an improvised tank destroyer detachment (91 men); and an improvised infantry company (131 men)—totaling just 325 men. *Armeeabteilung Narva*, Ia/Id, 298/44, 21 September 1944, T-312, Reel 1634.

[11]Note in original: "Estonian-Western position ran from the northern end of Lake Virts to Uulu."

[12]Note in original: "'Wendish' position ran approximately 100 kilometers south of the Estonian-Western position."

[13]Note in original: "A term loosely applied to improvised combat units of various sizes."

[14]Steiner's III SS Panzer Corps was reasonably strong in terms of such a limited defensive mission. The 11th Infantry Division, minus one battalion still with the II Corps, had 9,753 men present (a combat strength of 3,951 infantry); the 11th SS had 9,643 men (2,731 infantry); and the 4th SS Brigade had 4,968 men (1,932 infantry—if attached improvised units are counted). In addition, III/SS Grenadier Regiment 47 (251 infantry) as well as III and IV/SS Artillery Regiment 20 (both of the 20th SS) were attached to the 11th Infantry Division. The 4th SS Brigade had tactical control of of I/SS Grenadier Regiment 47 (171 infantry) and SS Flak Battalion 20. *Armeeabteilung Narva*, Ia/Id, 298/44, T-312, Reel 1634.

[15]By this time, the 20th SS had been so depleted by combat and detachments to divisions in the II Corps and III SS Panzer Corps that of the 10,923 men who were supposedly present for duty, only 6,727 were under the division's control, of which only 1,836 were battle-ready infantry. The few German units at the disposal of the 300th Special Administrative Division headquarters (aside from those already mentioned in note 9 above) were Security Regiment 113 (1,394 present; 1,072 infantry)

and Marine Battalion "Eichstädt" (282 present; 240 infantry). *Armeeabteilung Narva,* Ia/Id, 298/44, T-312, Reel 1634.

CHAPTER 7

The Defensive Battles of Army Group North From 22 June to 9 July 1944

Wilhelm Heinemeyer

Introduction

The large-scale attack of the Red Army against Army Group North in January and February 1944 was intended to bring about the collapse of the northern sector of the German eastern front. It was simultaneously directed against both flanks of the army group – on the south against the Sixteenth Army with the Second Baltic Front, aiming at a breakthrough into the Baltic countries; on the north against the Eighteenth Army with the Volkhov and Leiningrad Fronts attacking from the areas of Novgorod, Leningrad, and Oranienbaum, aiming at splitting up and destroying this army. The Soviet Army, both in personnel and materiel far outnumbering the Germans, achieved tremendous military and political success with the final liberation of the city of Leningrad; the chief strategic objective, however, was not attained, for Army Group North finally did succeed in withdrawing its troops, who fought with unprecedented bravery, to the well-fortified Panther Line just in time to save them from disaster. The Panther Line allowed the troops to repel the pursuing Soviet forces and definitively thwart the strategic plans of the enemy in the heavy defensive battles during the months of March and April.

In the ensuing defensive battles, STAVKA realized that the positions of Army Group North, which had been finally occupied on 1 March 1944, could not be gained despite the great superiority and the energetic thrusts of the attacker. It thus confirmed the opinion held by the army group in the fall of 1943, according to which the strength of the army group was inadequate at that time to hold the extended front from Nevel to Oranienbaum, but suffi-

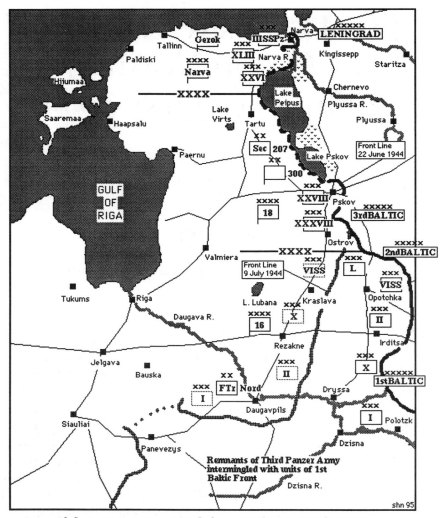

Map Eight: Army Group North from 22 June to 9 July 1944

cient to hold the substantially shorter Panther Line. The Soviet command discontinued its attacks against Army Group North and greatly relaxed its points of main effort.

But at the same time it confirmed the correctness of Hitler's concern in the fall and winter of 1943 that the withdrawal of the front from Leningrad would have calamitous political and military effects on the Finnish ally, and demonstrated the strategic situation in which the army group had been in having to perform a mission of much political moment without adequate forces. As a result of the liberation of Leningrad, the previous pressure of the left flank of Army Group North on the Soviet front on the Karelian Isthmus had been eliminated. Thus the prerequisite for a final solution of the Finnish question in accordance with Soviet ideas.

The Soviet command planned its large-scale attack against the Finnish southern front for the beginning of June 1944. For this purpose, by 22 June it had drawn off no fewer than twenty rifle divisions, eight tank units, and one artillery division from the front of Army Group North and transferred them to the new area of main effort on the Karelian Isthmus and on the Gunus Isthmus. Among these units were the Guards Rifle Divisions of the XXX Guards Rifle Corps, which had earned special distinction as attacking units. Added to these forces were the XXXXIII, XCIX, CVII, CIX, CXV Rifle Corps, the Second Shock Army, and the Fifty-ninth Army. In June 1944, the large-scale attack of the Red Army began – which in September was to result in the elimination of Finland as a German ally.

At the same time, the Soviet command prepared its formidable summer offensive against Army Group Center. The objective was first to break through the German defenses on a broad front and then to envelop and destroy the bulk of Army Group Center – the Ninth Army east of Bobriusk, the Fourth Army on both sides of the motor highway west of Smolensk, and the Third Panzer Army on both sides of Vitebsk – in a double envelopment. In conjunction with the operation against Army Group Center, the southern flank of Army Group North which then would be without protection was to be enveloped preparatory to a Baltic Sea operation aiming at Polotzk, Daugavpils, and Riga, for the purpose of encircling the German northern front and "throwing it into the Baltic Sea."

The Third White Russian Front led the large-scale attack against the German Fourth Army and against the right sector of the Third Panzer Army. For a reinforcement of its sector of main effort on the motor highway west of Smolensk, the Eleventh Guards Army (which up to then had been employed in front of the right sector of Army Group North) was attached to it. With this attack army and the likewise newly attached Tank Force Bodin, the Soviet army group was in a position to build up a formidable point of main effort for its attack on the far inferior German armies.

Northwest of Vitebsk, the First Baltic Front exercised control under the command of Army General Bagramyan, with Major General Khlebnikov as Artillery Commander and Brigadier General Kosarev as Engineer Commander of the front. It used the Thirty-ninth Army to form a main point of attack northwest of Vitebsk opposite the Third Panzer Army; the Sixth Guards Army (which had previously been located opposite the central sector of the German Sixteenth Army) formed a main point of attack opposite the boundary between Army Groups Center and North. The Thirty-ninth Army received the order to encircle Vitebsk. The Sixth Guards Army – under the command of Major General Chistakov, had been reinforced by the strategic force of mortar units, which likewise had been previously employed on the front of the Sixteenth Army. The mission of this army was to drive a wedge between Vitebsk and Orsha simultaneously with the large-scale attacks of the Third White Russian Front east of Orsha and south of Vitebsk, and of the Thirty-ninth Army north of Vitebsk. After the breakthrough south of the boundary between Army Groups Center and North had been successful, the Sixth Guards Army was to turn northwest in the direction of Polotzk in order to envelop Army Group North in its southern flank. The task of the Forty-third Army was to push on westward together with the I Tank Corps, which was attached to it, and protect the left flank of the Sixth Guards Army. The task of the Fourth Shock Army was to join the Sixth Guards Army in a frontal attack westward. The Second Baltic Front, together with the Third Baltic Front, had as its mission to continue to tie down Army Group North through local attacks at the previous points of main effort, namely on the left flank of the Sixteenth Army, and between Ostrov and Pskov in the sector of the Eighteenth Army.

The First Baltic Front had for months been comprehensively and thoroughly preparing its large-scale attack against the extreme left flank of Army Group Center, south of the army group boundary. The preparations began with a tactical briefing, continued with practical exercises in carefully selected terrain resembling the front – seventy kilometers behind the main line of resistance – and were climaxed by a "final rehearsal," which was undertaken with the combined action by all arms with live ammunition. There were systematic exercises for overcoming any obstacles, particularly rivers and lakes, without any aids, a thing which was of utmost importance in the terrain selected for the attack, since it predominantly consisted of swamps and lakes.

Special importance was attached to concealing movement of the troops into the areas of attack and to assembling them there. Any use of the telephone, telegraph, and radio was prohibited. Reconnaissance of the terrain was carried out very carefully, each unit reconnoitering its own position. All commanders up to the highest level had to participate in this. during these preparations, the cooperation of all arms of the service was also worked out. For purposes of camouflage, the trial firing of the artillery was done from the field emplacements of the position artillery. The strategic plan provided for reconnaissance in force on the right Soviet attack sector, south of the German army group boundary. It had been carefully prepared, was skillfully supported by artillery and achieved full success. It rapidly developed into an attack, and during the first two days pushed thirty-five to forty kilometers into the depth of the German defenses.

Since the unsuccessful push across the Volkhov River aiming at Tikhvin in the fall and winter of 1941, the combat mission of the German army group in the northern sector of the eastern front had remained the same: to hold the captured positions. Nor had it been changed when the ratio of strengths in front of Leningrad had changed fundamentally in the fall of 1943, and when finally it had barely been possible to avert complete disaster by moving into the Panther Line in February 1944.

The German troops, greatly weakened by the heavy retreating engagements, had been rehabilitated as quickly as possible during the following months by the allotment of replacements and new materiel. At the beginning of the defensive battles for the Baltic countries, Army Group North – under the command of General Lindemann – controlled three armies: the Sixteenth Army under the command of General Hansen; the Eighteenth Army under General Loch; and the *Armeeabteilung Narva* under General Lindemann, with a total of ten corps (Sixteenth Army: I, X, II Corps, VI SS Infantry Corps, L Corps; Eighteenth Army: XXXVIII, XXVIII Corps; *Armeeabteilung Narva*: XXVI, XXXXIII Corps, III SS Panzer Corps) and a total of thirty-three infantry divisions or brigades, and one panzer division (12th Panzer Division) as mobile reserve. Out of these units, the two Latvian and the two Estonian SS volunteer divisions had to be regarded as reliable only to a limited extent. On 1 June 1944, Army Group North had reached the following strength:

> **Sixteenth Army:** 265,432 soldiers and 5,867 vacancies; 12,450 volunteer auxiliaries.
>
> **Eighteenth Army:** 195,305 soldiers and 3,269 vacancies; 13,563 volun-

tary auxiliaries and 16,699 vacancies.

Armeeabteilung Narva: 156,942 soldiers and 1,429 vacancies; 10,089 volunteer auxiliaries and 7,888 vacancies.

Units of the army group, directly attached: 77,850 soldiers and 5,937 vacancies; 19, 396 volunteer auxiliaries and 4,256 vacancies.

Army Group North total: 695,527 soldiers and 55,495 voluntary auxiliaries.[1]

The above-mentioned regrouping of Soviet forces on the front of the army group must have resulted in immense movements up to the middle of June 1944. Air reconnaissance, however, brought in no information pointing to a shift of major forces. Bad weather in the last weeks, the constantly increasing air defense employing enemy fighter planes and anti-aircraft guns, and especially the small number of reconnaissance planes and the necessity of saving fuel were the chief causes for the lack of an adequate air reconnaissance. Ground reconnaissance on other fronts or radio reconnaissance gave the first information, when changes had already been accomplished.

In front of the left sector of Army Group North, the *Armeeabteilung Narva*, it was assumed as late as 17 June that there were nine Soviet divisions on line, and eleven divisions in reserve. Hence an estimate of the situation was bound to be to the effect that the Soviet command still clung to its objective of passing through to the coast and seizing Narva. In front of the Eighteenth Army, the Soviets unmistakably continued their preparations for an attack at the former points of main effort, west of Ostrov and southeast of Pskov. The strength available, however, permitted the army group to look forward without apprehension to any attack at the old points of main effort.

It is an historical fact that Army Group North very early became aware of the preparations of the Soviet First Baltic Front for an attack against its southern flank, despite all attempts at concealment, and that it took the necessary countermeasures in time. By 25 May it pointed out that there was a possibility that the enemy would conduct an attack against its southern sector in which he would combine the strengths of the Fourth Shock Army, the Sixth and Eleventh Guards Armies (twenty-seven divisions) and the newly attached units, with the objective of pushing through by way of Polotzk-Daugavpils-Riga. Although the Eleventh Guards Army was committed at the Smolensk-Orsha motor highway, this early picture of the enemy was nevertheless confirmed at the beginning of the attack through the units of the Fourth Shock and Sixth Guards Armies. The signs of an impending attack increased during the following weeks until on 19 June "the possibility of an attack against the southern sector of this army group in conjunction with an attack developing on both sides of Vitebsk" had to be taken into account.

Thus, for the third time in the course of the Russian campaign, Army Group North was threatened with a Soviet breakthrough at the boundary with Army Group Center. The measures the OKH took to protect this boundary were limited, and the tendency of Army Group Center ever since the beginning of the campaign to contract toward the center because of its diminishing strength was a calamity. The Soviet command, as a result, was aware of the boundary and of the opportunities it offered. In January 1942 the attacking units of the Soviet Kalinin Front had succeeded in making a broad breach in the front at the army group boundary and in encircling the right flank of the Army Group North in the area of Demyansk. In October 1943 the Kalinin Front, using locally combined forces of the Third and Fourth Shock Armies, had captured the important communications center of Nevel at the army group boundary, and in the course of the battle had expanded the successful attack in conjunction with the armies of the Second Baltic Front into a vast offensive, which had shifted the point of main effort of Army Group North from the Leningrad front to the southern sector. From the army group headquarters to the Sixteenth Army headquarters and the I Corps headquarters (controlling the right sector), "the specter of Nevel" frightened the German command. And its preparations for defense and its subsequent countermeasures were make in a clear recognition of the immense strategic significance of the impending Soviet large-scale attack for the fate of the entire northern front. On the other hand, at the same time there were certain doubts as to whether the German units employed on the left flank of Army Group Center had clearly and timely recognized the preparations for attack undertaken by the Soviet forces northwest of Vitebsk, and whether Army Group Center had attached the proper significance in this attack with respect to the other points of main effort on its front. The definitive judgment on this point must be left to military history.

The Defensive Battle at Polotzk (22 June-6 July 1944)

On 22 June 1944 the Red Army began a decisive attack against Army Group Center.

On the first day, the Third White Russian Front succeeded in breaking through the front of the Third Panzer Army in the left sector of Army Group Center, and approximately fifteen kilometers east-southeast of Vitebsk. Two days later, on 24 June, the Thirty-Ninth Army of the First Baltic Front had encircled the German LIII Corps in the Vitebsk area. The attacker rapidly reinforced himself in the gap between the two adjacent corps: the VI and the XI Corps; by 26 June he had expanded it to roughly fifty kilometers. On the other hand, the attempts of the encircled German forces to break through to the west, west-southwest of Vitebsk at Ostrovono remained unsuccessful for the time being.

Using the attack units of the Sixth Guards Army, supported by the strategic group of mortar units, by tanks, and by ground attack airplanes, the First Baltic Front directed its main effort against the IX Corps – the left flank corps of the Third Panzer Army, south of the boundary between it and Army Group North. The Sixth Guards Army, succeeded in breaking through the left flank division of the Third Panzer Army (252d Infantry Division), with about seven or eight units, immediately south of the army group boundary, and at first achieving a penetration approximately eight kilometers in length and width. Here the terrain was far more favorable for the Russian attackers, who were by nature close to soil, than for the German defenders. The German positions were situated in narrow passages between swamps which were considered impassable. As a result, the German defenses were bypassed, rolled up, and thrown back.

With a view to diverting and tying down forces, the armies of the First and Second Baltic Fronts, after heavy artillery preparation, simultaneously attacked the front of the Sixteenth Army at numerous points in battalion strength, and to some extent supported by tanks. These attacks were for the most part repulsed. Aside from the local defensive measures of the Sixteenth Army and the I Corps, the army group had the 24th Infantry Division at its disposal as a reserve in Polotzk; the disengagement of another division, the 290th Infantry Division, from the right sector of the army had been prepared. The Eighteenth Army and *Armeeabteilung Narva* also each had a division in reserve, and as a mobile reserve the 12th Panzer Division – which was the only panzer division of the army group – was in the rear of the Eighteenth Army, ready to be shifted to any given point of main effort.

On the other hand, as a result of the success of the Sixth Guards Army south of the army group boundary a situation had arisen which resembled that prevailing at Nevel in October 1943. Even now the left flank regiment of Army Group Center and the right sector of Army Group North hung in the air. The situation of the Third Panzer Army was serious. The defensive power of the artillery of the left flank corps, the IX Corps, was weak, because artillery had been moved to other points of main effort before the beginning of the battle. The only reserves that the army was able to round up consisted of a single battalion, while the only force that it had to seal off the enemy was a regiment that had been employed in guerilla warfare.

The command of Army Group North realized at once that the situation could be mastered only with the use of its forces and, in addition, that the destruction of Army Group Center would have unpredictable consequences for the northern sector of the eastern front also. Hence, it acted quickly and resolutely. It continuously and voluntarily furnished units to the OKH in order to give the Third Panzer Army a chance to close the gap in the north and support the defensive battles of the adjacent army group at other points of main effort. At first it furnished its reserve; later it furnished units which had been disengaged from the front. Both Field Marshal Busch, the commanding general of Army Group Center, and Colonel General Zeitzler, the Chief of the Army General Staff, greatly appreciated the help given by the commanding general of Army Group North.

The shifting of the points of main effort to the right and the transfer of units to other sectors of main effort of the adjacent army group had necessarily weakened the defensive power of the army group. This had started a development which, in January of that year, had led to the collapse of the Leningrad front.

With the penetration of the Sixth Guards Army at the extreme left flank of the adjacent army group, Army Group North had lost the protection of its right flank. In response to the army group's urgent request, the OKH – in order to eliminate the penetration – on the first day of the attack ordered the 24th Infantry Division (which had been established as a reserve in Polotzk), together with an assault gun battalion, to be moved to the extreme left flank of the Third Panzer Army. On the following day, 23 June, the OKH took the same measure with regard to the 290th Infantry Division, which had meanwhile been disengaged from the right sector of the Sixteenth Army. Meanwhile the only mobile reserve, the 12th Panzer Division – on orders from the army group – was moved to the hard-pressed adjacent army group to be committed at another point of main effort. As a result, it was possible to extend the southern flank of the Sixteenth Army.

Although it proved unable to recapture the former positions, the heroic defensive battles of these divisions and of the units of the I Corps of the Sixteenth Army frustrated the attempt by the Russian Sixth Guards and Fourth Shock Armies to separate the right flank from the Sixteenth Army. The attacks of the Soviet forces, conducted with greatly superior forces, with tank and mortar support and with a crushing air superiority, failed. The German front was again consolidated in this sector.

Although the two newly arrived divisions had been attached the Army Group Center and the Third Panzer Army, the I Corps of the Sixteenth Army had been obliged to assume command over them for local reasons. Since the OKH could not see its way to changing the boundary between the army groups, and thus placing them in the gap, Army Group North formally resumed command of its two former divisions on 25 June.

The left flank of the Russian Sixth Guards Army had meanwhile succeeded in breaking through the front of the Third Panzer Army also in the central sector of the IX Corps, and in throwing the defenders back behind the Daugava River. As its attempt in the Obol sector at achieving a decisive breakthrough opposite the I Corps of the Sixteenth Army had failed, it prepared to shift its point of main effort farther southward, although for the time being it maintained the frontal pressure on the I Corps with its right flank, and in conjunction with the Fourth Shock Army, if for no other reason than that of tying down the corps' units.

The commanders of Army Group North and the Sixteenth Army immediately recognized that these units were about to be unhinged south of the Daugava River. Hence, by way of precaution it ordered the third division destined for the southern sector, the 81st Infantry Division, which in the meantime had likewise been disengaged from the front of the Sixteenth Army, to be moved into the area south of Polotzk. The idea of letting the 212th Infantry Division – which was being transferred to the scene from the Eighteenth Army – attack from the south through the Third Panzer Army in order to restore contact with Army Group North had to be dropped, because the OKH had this division unloaded much further to the west, at Globoki.

The enveloping maneuver of the Russian Sixth Guards Army led to success on 27 June. Its units again broke through the German defenses in the left sector of the third Panzer Army and began to outflank Polotzk. South of the Sixth Guards Army, the I Tank Corps of the Forty-third Army advanced into the area on both sides of Lepel (28 June). As a result, the First Baltic Front had achieved freedom of action on a broad front. It made use of this freedom by rapidly pushing westward with strong forces and turning northward with the Sixth Guards Army for an envelopment of Polotzk.

The situation of the Third Panzer Army had taken a critical turn as a result of this development. Its commanding general, General Reinhardt, had to report on 28 June that his troops no longer had the strength to resist, and that no resistance could be offered any longer north of the Smolensk-Orsha motor highway and as far as the army groups boundary. The simultaneous directive issued by the OKH to Army Group Center, according to which the Third Panzer Army had to hold or fight clear its present positions, and was under no circumstances to allow itself to be pressed farther back, did not change the situation (28 June).

This development in the left sector of Army Group Center had also decisively changed the situation on the southern flank of Army Group North. In its opinion (28 June) there was no longer any prospect of reestablishing the hitherto-existing contact with Army Group Center, now that the remnants of the Third Panzer Army had been unable to stop the advance of the Russian forces. Any troops that might be moved to the scene would come too late to restore a lasting contact with the present southern flank of the army group. As yet it was impossible to judge whether the enemy aimed at exploiting his successes by a thrust through Vilna and Kovno to Königsberg (in conjunction with a large-scale Baltic Sea operation) or, pivoting earlier through Polotzk and Daugavpils to Riga (small-scale Baltic Sea operation). He had adequate forces at least for the small-scale operation.

Its successful execution would mean the encirclement of the army group. But in whatever way the enemy continued his operations, the army group would in any case be obliged to protect its completely open southern flank with its own forces. Even now the flank, from the previous southern limit of the army group east of Polotzk, was open to the west for a distance of sixty kilometers. As the enemy advanced, an ever-expanding southern front would develop, which could to an increasing extent become the main front the more the enemy pivoted north or northwest in force.

On the basis of this situation estimate, Army Group and Army acted quickly and vigorously on 28 June. Whatever forces were available were moved up to fortify the new southern front in the direction of Daugavpils. The Eighteenth Army received orders to assemble a motorized blocking force and at once dispatch it to Polotzk. The Sixteenth Army disengaged one more division, the 132d Infantry Division, from its eastern front and moved it to Dzisna, while the 170th Infantry Division was transferred to Daugavpils by *Armeeabteilung Narva*. The army received orders to block the Dzisna River crossings in the Szarkovs Zsyjena-Dzisna sector by means of Latvian regiments, and assumed command over all security forces, administrative headquarters, and police forces in the area of the Wehrmacht Administrative Commander for the Eastern Territories east of a line from Ydziai to Daugavpils and south of the Daugavpils-Polotzk railroad. The Eighteen Army finally received orders on 30 June to pull the 215th Infantry Division out of the front immediately, and shift it to the southern sector. To free further forces for the extension of the southern flank west of the Daugava River, the I Corps – comprising the 290th, 24th, and 205th Infantry Divisions, situated east of Polotzk – had withdrawn to a shorter line by the morning of 30 June. The forces released as a result were to be speedily shifted to Dzisna. And finally the army group, on the basis of the experience gained at Army Group Center, ordered all roads as far as fifty kilometers behind the front prepared for demolition as a countermeasure against potential quick breakthroughs. The army providently issued orders to the 3d Engineer Staff Commander to build a personnel-saving switch-line west of Polotzk – from the Dzisna River to the southern tip of Lake Neshcherda, known as the "Geiger Line."

As a result of the developments on its southern flank, the overall situation of Army Group North had taken a turn for the worse. General Lindemann mentioned this in his report dated 29 June, which was still based on the situation prevailing on 28 June. This report stated that – all in all – the eastern front of the army group had been divested of eight divisions. As a result the occupation of the front had become so thin that even attacks by the enemy units now facing the eastern front – provided they formed local points of main effort and committed the numerous reserves at their disposal – could lead to breakthroughs, for the elimination of which no reserves were available. If the enemy moved up forces from other sectors to form a strategic point of main effort, decisive Russian successes would not be preventable either. For the present, Army Group North comprised a total of thirty-two divisions, of which five were either engaged in battle on the southern front (outside of the prevailing army group boundary) or under way. With respect to the twenty-seven divisions remaining at the disposal of the eastern front, special attention should be drawn to the inferior combat value of the two Latvian divisions, as compared to the German units.

On the basis of this situation, the commander-in-chief considered it his duty to report to the Führer that the forces of the army group were no longer sufficient to carry out the mission of holding the present line under all circumstances. Hence he requested new orders for the further conduct of operations. Above all, he needed full freedom of action on the right flank of the Sixteenth Army so that he could obtain new forces for the defensive battle by occupying a shorter line, and if necessary by abandoning the strongpoint of Polotzk. The same held true for the Narva front, where he needed the authority to occupy the shortest line at any time he considered opportune, in order to make the disengagement of forces possible.

Both the Chief of the Army General Staff, General Zeitzler, and Field

Marshal Model (who, in addition to his Army Group North Ukraine, had taken over command of Army Group Center from Field Marshal Busch on 28 June) fully concurred with this estimate of the situation.

The overall situation of Army Group Center, meanwhile, had continued to deteriorate. On 29 June it was as follows: the Second Army, which had not seen much fighting, was still available. The Ninth Army, with its units encircled in Bobriusk, had apparently been destroyed. The Fourth Army, greatly endangered on its flanks, was just fighting its way back toward the west. The Third Panzer Army was to be regarded as substantially destroyed, except for the 212th Infantry Division, which had been newly assigned to it by Army Group North. Out of thirty-three divisions, nineteen had been destroyed; Minsk was threatened from the south by strong enemy forces advancing from Bobriusk toward Slutsk, which was occupied only by weak forces, and from the north from the direction of Lepel. Field Marshal Model therefore demanded the immediate attached of two divisions of Army Group North to the Third Panzer Army. With these forces, added to the four divisions which he was moving up from Army Group North Ukraine, and in conjunction with other makeshifts, he believed that he could venture an attempt to organize a line running in the general direction of "MARDER" (planned) – "BIBER" (planned), anchored to Army Group North at the Daugava switch line. According to his directive, it was to be possible to obtain the two divisions by immediate abandonment of Polotzk. Only if the divisions were quickly moved up would it be possible to execute the plan. Thereupon the Chief of the Army General Staff ordered the 170th Infantry Division – which was being shipped to Daugavpils – to be immediately sent through Vilna to Army Group North in the direction of Minsk; it was impossible to furnish another division until the Polotzk salient had been abandoned.

During 29 and 30 June the situation of Army Group Center and Third Panzer Army continued to deteriorate. The gap between Slutzk and Minsk represented a tremendous danger. With the Third Panzer Army there was no longer a continuous front. Thus Army Group Center had to report on the afternoon of 29 June that the only way it could establish contact with Army Group North was through Glebokie. This was due to the fact that the Third Panzer Army was trying to reassemble its forces on a line thirty kilometers southwest of Vetrino, east of the Beresina River. Field Marshal Model was aware that forces could be obtained only from Army Group North, and then only by withdrawing the southern sector and abandoning Polotzk. Hence, he informed Army Group North on 30 June that he would undertake all steps to induce the OKH to make a speedy decision in favor of withdrawing the souther sector of Army Group North. He feared that otherwise the measures would come too late.

The situation of Army Group North also had changed decisively on 29 June. Strong motorized Soviet forces had – as expected – advanced farther west in the Third Panzer Army area southeast of Glebokie; other heavy motorized forces were pivoting west of Polotzk in the direction of the Daugava River crossing at Dzisna; and at the same time an enemy railroad assembly northeast of Polotzk had been identified. Thus the encirclement of Army Group North was clearly foreshadowed.

The estimate of the situation made by Army Group North on the previous day had been confirmed; the defensive measures taken had anticipated the attack. The Sixteenth Army was putting everything into the effort to organize a new front in the Daugava Valley. Elements of the 132d Infantry Division sent ahead by motor transport established the backbone of the defense from Dzisna westward. All artillery that was not indispensable was moved westward from the southern sector, and orders were issued to likewise move in that direction the battalions of the three divisions being disengaged as they became available as a result of the withdrawal of the I Corps. The II Corps headquarters was pulled out of the eastern front of the Sixteenth Army and placed in charge of the new forces. At the same time orders were issued to prepare to withdraw the front to the Geiger Line.

This adverse development of the situation induced the commander in chief of the army group to address a request to Hitler on the evening of 29 June that he be given freedom of action in the southern sector of the army group, including the strongpoint of Polotzk. Although the opinion of the Chief of the Army General Staff coincided with that of the commander in chief of the army group, Hitler – during the night of 29 June – agreed merely to preparations being made for withdrawal of the front arc from Polotzk to a chord, which for the time being was to include Polotzk, and to speedily fortify the Dzisna-Drissa-Lake Neshcherda line (Geiger Line). The Forty-third Army of the First Baltic Front had reached the Glebokie area, and continued to advance in a general west-northwest direction. With the bulk of the Sixth Guards Army it had pivoted north, and had moved to this army the I Tank Corps of the Forty-third Army. On the morning of 30 June, the left flank elements of the Sixth Guards Army succeeded in entering the southern part of Dzisna with tanks and motorized infantry. Army Group North sought to continue to forestall envelopment by the First Baltic Front by ordering the Eighteenth Army to disengage the 215th Infantry Division from the front immediately, and move its elements into the Daugavpils area as they became available. At the same time the General Lindemann requested Hitler to give him freedom of action – that is, permission to evacuate Polotzk. The Chief of the Army General Staff agreed with this move and advised Hitler accordingly; the commanding general of Army Group Center, Field Marshal Model, made known that he would take all steps to induce the OKH to arrive at a speedy decision to withdraw the southern flank of the army group; he feared that otherwise the forces released as a result of the withdrawal would come too late to improve the situation of Army Group Center. Hitler's answer arrived on the afternoon of the same day; he permitted the freedom of action requested by the army group in the Polotzk area, but only up to a line which included the town. He ordered all available forces to be immediately committed in a compact counterattack in a southwesterly direction in order to reestablish contact by the shortest route with the northern flank of the Third Panzer Army, and to cut off the enemy forces which had advanced to the northwest. To support this attack, a ground attack and anti-tank wing of three groups was at once ordered into the Polotzk area.

Both Army Group North and the Sixteenth Army repudiated Hitler's order to counterattack. According to General Lindemann, the I Tank Corps of the Soviet Forty-third Army was attacking the Third Panzer Army and while the Soviet Sixth Guards Army struck at the southern sector of his army group. If the order to attack were carried out his own forces, presumably consisting of the two divisions now becoming available, would be sent to certain death, especially since it was impossible to close the sixty-kilometer gap to the Third Panzer Army with these forces and because – in addition – Army Group Center held out no promise that the Third Panzer Army would be able to hold. Field Marhal Model sent word that he would make every effort to prevent Hitler's intention from being realized. He pointed out in practice the Third Panzer Army was hardly more than a *kampfgruppe*, consisting of the 212th Infantry Division and an assault gun battalion.

During the night of 30 June, the Chief of the Operations Branch of the OKH managed to persuade Hitler to give up the idea of a penetration, but the latter continued to believe that, whatever happened, an attack must be undertaken from the Polotzk area, aiming southwest to prevent the enemy from advancing on Dzisna, and also because the shift of the two divisions which were becoming available at Polotzk into the area southwest of Daugavpils would be feasible only if an attack was first made from the area southwest of Polotzk. The present attack was to be considered a relief and holding attack necessary for shifting the forces from Polotzk to Daugavpils. Hitler agreed to the proposal of the army group to assemble the two divisions in the area of Daugavpils.

Two hours later General Lindemann, in a telephone conversation at 0015 hours again tried to make Hitler change his mind. He expressed the fear that an attack with the two divisions southwest of Polotzk would not be fully successful, and that the divisions would be tied up, and could not soon be available again. The greatest threat would lie in the direction of Daugavpils. The position at the Daugava River would hold; it would be possible to shift the two divisions into the area south of Daugavpils, and then conduct a compact thrust with four divisions from Szarkovs Zsyjena in the direction of Glebokie. Hitler, on the other hand, held the position that the divisions would not be able to reach the Szark area; the assembly would take place in the Daugavpils area, and Army Group Center would as a result be unhinged. The enemy would quickly advance with tank spearheads so that the contemplated force would have to be thrown into battle. An attack from Polotzk southwest and from Szark into the rear and flank of the enemy would stop the attack and advance of the enemy. We were going through this experience along the entire front: we came too late everywhere because we made no flank attacks. Hence he gave orders to conduct the scheduled attack with all available forces and assault guns – that is, to attack with two to three divisions from Polotzk in the general direction of Glebokie, and with another group from Szark; the first group was to be supported by fifty assault guns, while the other force would be supported by an assault gun brigade from Denmark.

After its commander had been repudiated by Hitler, the army group ordered the Sixteenth Army to hold a line in front of Polotzk, which it had reached during the withdrawal on the morning of 1 July, and to assemble the two divisions (24th and 87th Infantry Divisions) which had become available as a result of the occupation of this line, as well as all available assault guns, west of Polotzk and south of the Daugava River for an attack on 3 July by the left flank along the Polotzk-Molodetczno railroad. This was to be done without waiting for the arrival of the combat force advancing through Szark. The 132d and 215th Infantry Divisions were to be assembled in the area north of Szark for an attack against the Glebokie-Plissa line.

In the meantime, the heavy resistance battles on the southern front of the army group continued. In order to further envelop the open flank, armored reconnaissance forces of the Russian Sixth Guards Army and the I Tank Corps pushed on westward across the Dzisna River. The bulk of the Sixth Guards Army, which meanwhile had veered north, started an attack on Polotzk with approximately six units and additional elements of the I Tank

Corps on the evening of 1 July, while, in the east the Fourth Shock Army moved up to attack. Deep penetrations in the front south of Polotzk forced General Haase, the commanding general of the I Corps, to report that it was no longer possible to hold the Polotzk area. General Hansen, the commanding general of the Sixteenth Army, concurred with this report: an attack with the two divisions in accordance with the Führer order was no longer practicable in view of the newly arisen situation; both divisions would be lost if they were committed in an attack there. During the night of 1 July, General Lindemann reported the change of the situation to Hitler in a telephone conversation, and expressed his anxiety that the attack of the two divisions south of Polotzk might be unsuccessful. Hitler persisted in his previous contention that the attack had to be undertaken to stop the westward advance of the Russians. He pointed out that otherwise there would be a danger that the army group would be thrown back to the Daugavpils-Riga line, and that it was out of the question to allow this to happen. He persisted in his order to attack.

A little later General Lindemann informed Field Marshal Model that permission to abandon Polotzk had been refused. The latter concurred with the opinion that it was impossible to stop a whole enemy army with two divisions, and promised a conversation with Hitler to again warn against making the attack. His argument was that Army Group Center needed the forces requested to meet the critical situation in the Minsk-Molodechno area, and that – however desirable the planned blow by Army Group North from Polotzk in a southeastern direction would be, he would therefore have to apply for further divisions to be speedily moved behind the 170th Infantry Division, toward Molodechno. He was fully aware of the significance of this renunciation, but he saw no other way of mastering the crisis in view of the reported condition of Army Group Center and the gravity of the situation.

On 2 July, the Russian First Baltic Front began its decisive attack on Polotzk with the bulk of the Sixth Guards Army attacking from the south, and the Fourth Shock Army striking from the east. In the morning, the Sixth Guards Army managed to take a dominant height at Polotzk, and thus to flank the entire attack terrain. General Haase of the I Corps reported to General Lindemann that an attack would constitute a wasteful sacrifice of manpower. The prerequisites for such an attack no longer existed. Even an attack on a smaller scale was impracticable, since the losses suffered would outweigh whatever success was achieved. As a result, General Lindemann cancelled the attack by the two divisions.

On the afternoon of that day, the situation in the southern sector of the army group became critical. The Russian Fourth Shock Army started its anticipated attack east of Polotzk with about four units, the main effort being directed against the 205th Infantry Division of the I Corps. After a heavy barrage it achieved a breakthrough as far as the area north of Polotzk, in spite of the heroic resistance of the decimated German troops. Since the town was now endangered from the north, and was threatened with the fate of Vitebsk, General Lindemann cancelled the status of Polotzk as a "fortified position," and designated the town as a "local strongpoint." He justified this measure to Hitler by arguing that, as a result of the destruction of roughly 900 tons of ammunition in air raids during the past few days, the town lack sufficient ammunition to fulfill its mission as a "fortified position," and that as a result of the the development of the situation (the penetration north of Polotzk and the open flank of the army group) the two divisions contemplated as garrison were no longer available to defend the town.

On 2 July, General Lindemann also reported to Hitler that the attack south of Polotzk had not been successful. He estimated the situation as follows:

1. The right flank of the army group was suspended in mid-air.

2. The attempt to cut off the enemy spearheads by an attack in accordance with the Führer order had failed. An attempt to do so did not promise any success in the future either, since no further forces could be made available for this purpose, whereas the enemy was following in force, and had also achieved a deep penetration from the east into the rear of Polotzk, as far as Vashchaki. Moreover, the distance to the flank of the Third Panzer Army was steadily increasing as a result of its withdrawal.

3. The eastern front of the army group – which had not been attacked – had been weakened so much as a result of the transfer of nine divisions and numerous special arms that it was not equal to an attack of locally combined enemy forces.

General Lindemann therefore saw only the following possibilities for a continuation of operations:

1. Reinforcement of the forces in the area southeast of Daugavpils to protect the endangered depth of the flank, if possible by an attack (attachment of two divisions).

2. The only way of obtaining forces for this purpose was b immediately abandoning the bulge in the line at Polotzk, in favor of the Dzisna-Lake Neshcherda chord.

To this proposal of the army group, Hitler agreed.

Thereupon the army group, during the night of 2 July, ordered the Sixteenth Army to withdraw to the northern bank of the river those elements of the I Corps that still stood south of the Daugava River, and thereafter to withdraw its southern flank – sector by sector – to a general line from Dzisna to the souther tip of Lake Neshcherda (Geiger Line) and to begin the final defense there. During the withdrawal, two divisions were to be made available and assembled in the area southeast of Daugavpils. In order to fortify the new front at Daugavpils, the army group ordered *Armeeabteilung Narva* to disengage a further division and the XXVI Corps, and to transfer these units to Daugavpils. By way of precaution, the army group gave orders to the 3d Engineer Command Staff to fortify the "Latvian Position" in a line running from Drysviaty through Kraelava, Ludza, and Krasenyi to the Latvian chord.

The evacuation of Polotzk had come three days too late. The aggravation of the situation on the southern flank, which meanwhile was expanding into a western flank, forced the army group to shift the two divisions becoming available into the area southeast of Daugavpils. The purpose which Army Group Center had pursued in its energetic request for evacuation of Polotzk – the gaining of forces for the heavy defensive battle impending – had not been achieved.

The Russian First Baltic Front continued its advance westward, although hesitantly. Presumably for the time being its principal objective was to eliminate the left flank of the Third Panzer Army. Hence it sent elements of the I Tank Corps against the northern flank of this army, which was under attack by the Forty-third Army. The Sixth Guards Army joined the attack with its elements on the left, advancing in the general direction of Daugavpils, and protected this area by attacking toward the north in the area southwest of Dzisna (from 3 July). As a result of this surprise thrust toward the Daugava River, on 3 July a dangerous situation arose for Army Group North, constituted by a new threat on its flank even before the units which had become available had been shifted to Daugavpils.

The army group issued orders to the Sixteenth Army to eliminate this great danger to the further conduct of operations, using all means to mount an attack. The right flank of the Russian Sixth Guards Army and the Fourth

Shock Army meanwhile continued their heavy actions against the front at Polotzk.

On the basis of the development of the situation, on the afternoon of 3 July the army group gave the extreme right flank of the Sixteenth Army the objective of stopping the enemy forces advancing on Daugavpils as far ahead of this city (which was vital to the army group) as was possible, and of establishing contact with the Third Panzer Army in the area north of Pistavy. To this end the forces arriving in Daugavpils were to be moved forward to a line from Lake Bogin to Lake Drysviati without waiting for them to assemble. Ground had to be gained so long as it was possible to do so without a battle – or against an enemy who was still weak. After this line had been reached, the forces arriving subsequently were to be combined in a strong group capable of conducting an attack in the depth of the flank of the army group.

In the opinion of Army Group North and the Sixteenth Army, the development of the overall situation at both army groups made a large-scale strategic operation imperative. Army Group Center shared this opinion. On 3 July Minsk was captured by the enemy, and Vilna was in great danger, according to that army group. Its manpower situation required quick assignment of new forces. These could only be obtained from Army Group North. Hence, Field Marshal Model requested that further forces be made available for re-employment by a movement of Army Group North. Hitler, however, brusquely refused to draw the inevitable conclusions from the prevailing situation; he repudiated any idea of the Daugava Line. The army group merely received orders, which it had already issued to the Sixteenth Army, to reestablish contact between the Third Panzer Army and the I Corps of the Sixteenth Army with the greatest possible speed in an offensive operation from the area southeast of Daugavpils, and as planned to move the 225th Infantry Division to Daugavpils. For this purpose the assignment of three battalions and one light SS parachute battalion from the Zone of the Interior was promised the army group. In addition, orders were issued to do everything to reinforce the widely extended front of the army group at those points where enemy attacks might be expected, and then to move up all available forces (security and frontier battalions) and hold them in reserve immediately behind the threatened sectors.

During the night of 4 July, Hitler replaced Colonel General Lindemann as commanding general of Army Group North with General of Infantry Friessner, formerly the commanding general of *Armeeabteilung Narva*. The latter received a clear-cut order from Hitler to hold the present positions of the army group under all circumstances, and to reestablish contact with the

Third Panzer Army.

On the basis of this order, during the night of 4 July General Friessner reported his intention to organize a defensive front in a general line from Koziany to Kraslava, which would prevent the enemy spearheads from advancing westward, and at the same time would establish contact with the Third Panzer Army in the area south of Koziany. South of the Kraslava-Drissa-Daugava sector, he intended to assemble a strong force with a view to preventing the enemy from advancing further westward by a thrust into the depth of his flank in the direction of Szarkovazczysna. The II Corps received orders to establish contact with the Third Panzer Army, using the reinforced 215th Infantry Division, and to establish a blocking line from Koziany by way of Lake Bogin to Lake Drysviaty. To begin with, the 81st and 290th Infantry Divisions were to attack the enemy forces that had penetrated southwest of Drissa, and subsequently the 81st Infantry Division was to be combined with the 225th and 205th Infantry Divisions to form an attacking force behind the 132d Infantry Division for an attack southward.

In contrast to this plan, the Sixteenth Army made another estimate of the situation on 4 July: in the enemy attack against the thin security line of the army it saw the beginning of a thrust into the depth of the army's flank. The available forces were unable to stop this thrust. They could only delay it. The enemy attacked at three bridges: the II Corps feared that the 81st Infantry Division would not be able to fight effectively at the Dzisna bridgehead and proposed that an enemy thrust against the Daugava River be delayed with the forces situated south of the river, and that a rear line be organized behind the Daugava River, with the 81st and 205th Infantry Divisions. The planned attack of the 225th and 205th Infantry Divisions could not take place, according to a report from the army, before 10 July. The army, however, needed further forces.

The opinion of the commander of the army group was, in addition, contradicted by the situation estimate of Army Group Center, which the commander of this army group sent to Hitler and made known to Army Group North on 4 July. According to the estimate, Army Group Center still had a total of eight battleworthy formations at its disposal, compared to 180 enemy battleworthy formations, along a front of 350 kilometers. After the enemy had been able to enter Minsk – and from there was advancing west and northwest with tank forces, the question was whether the army group would be able to stop the enemy until the second half of July, by which time the three divisions fighting in other theaters would have arrived. It had to maintain its request for assignment from Army Group North of a division for the Vilna area, and immediately thereafter for assignment of another division. The *kampfgruppen* of the Third Panzer Army, which in practice included only one division – the 212th Infantry Division – would be able to carry out its task of blocking the narrow passage between Lakes Narocz and Dsizna only if it received further forces from Army Group North. It would be able to execute that task most effectively through an early attack by elements of Army Group North from the Daugavpils area. The uncertainty as to whether the missions could actually be carried out by the armies against a far superior and mobile enemy made it necessary to move up at least one division each from Slonim, Lida, and Vilna, to act as a second wave. Only if these units arrived before 10 July was there a chance of stopping the enemy, in spite of the unusually great numerical inferiority, by exploiting the short intermission in operations which was now to be expected of the Russians, and by conducting further attacks with a limited scope.

Field Marshal Model, however, was convinced that in the long run the additional forces absolutely necessary for a restoration of the situation in the center could only be gained by a withdrawal of the northern half of Army Group North to the Ostrov-Daugavpils line. In his opinion, only quick action could result in a satisfactory and permanent solution, since in the foreseeable future nineteen divisions would be facing 180 enemy combat formations on a front of 350 kilometers. In accordance with this estimate of the situation, the commander of Army Group Center asked the commander of Army Group North to assign the 225th Infantry Division to his army group, and left it up to him to move into the aforementioned line, which had been proposed to Hitler: "Otherwise, once the Russians are in Vilna, the whole thing is of no use to you!"

Meanwhile, the commander organized the "ruthless employment of all forces and the extracting of the last fighter and the last weapon" from the Communications Zone, both from the area of the Wehrmacht Administrative Commander for the Eastern Territories and from the rear units and service troops of the GHQ units, to build a line of security from Koziany to Kraslava. As planned, on 4 July the 215th Infantry Division attacked south, from the area southeast of Daugavpils, to reestablish contact with Army Group Center.

However, on the following day – 5 July – Army Group Center requested the OKH to issue orders for Army Group North to immediately discontinue its attack on the southern sector and to withdraw. In the evening, the commander of Army Group North reported to the Führer, as Commander-in-Chief of the Army, that according to a personal inspection undertaken on that day of the southern front of the Sixteenth Army, he was able to report that the mission assigned to him would be executed, although the contemplated thrust into the depth of the flank of the enemy was no longer practicable. The situation, which had changed since he had last been present at the Führer's headquarters, and the continued withdrawal of the hard-pressed *kampfgruppen* of the Third Panzer Army, no longer permitted the execution of a thrust in this direction. But he intended to use the 225th Infantry Division, whose leading elements were arriving in Daugavpils, to establish contact with the Third Panzer Army southeast of that city, and thus ensure a compact defensive front facing toward the east. Since he knew the situation at Army Group Center, he offered to give it four of his divisions, which he could release if Hitler gave the order. He proposed to shorten the front of the Sixteenth Army by taking it back to the Latvian Line (general alignment: Drysviaty-Kraslava-Ludza-Krasnenty; the Latvian chord).

These reports from the two army groups were commented upon by Hitler during the night of 5 July as follows: "The proposed withdrawal would not result in a saving of four divisions, since the proposed new position was not fortified, and the divisional sectors would have to be kept much narrower than they were in the present fortified location. The withdrawal would lead to considerable losses of personnel, since the Russians would at once push into the movement, overtake the withdrawing units along side routes, and lie in wait for them. According to the experience gained in recent times, it was unfortunately to be feared that such measures on the part of the Russians would have far-reaching consequences in respect to the coherence and fighting power of the German units. The withdrawal would lead to considerable losses of materiel, since a systematic shipment of the materiel to the rear would be impossible, and especially since large stores of unloaded ammunition and stationary artillery could not be moved." Hence, Hitler requested precise reports on the time schedule and on the intermediate lines.

Despite this refusal on Hitler's part, at noon of 6 July, the commander of Army Group Center, after he had assured himself of the concurrence of the commander of Army Group North, renewed his request to Hitler for assignment of four divisions from Army Group North, the front of which was to be simultaneously withdrawn to the Latvian position, and for immediate assignment of the 225th Infantry Division to plug the hole between the army groups. The request now had the status of a "cabinet question" for Field Marshal Model: in agreement with the commander of Army Group North he reported that by now the crisis of Vilna and Daugavpils had reached a climax which forbade further deferment of the requested decision. The following steps had to be ordered without delay:

> 1. Assignment of the 225th Infantry Division to the Third Panzer Army in order to meet the great tactical danger here for the southern flank. The Vilna-Daugavpils area had already been penetrated by enemy tank forces at Podbrodzie, according to recent reports.
> 2. Withdrawal of the southern flank of Army Group North to the Latvian Line for the purpose of freeing the divisions absolutely necessary for further operations on the strategic level, in view of the fact that the enemy was constantly reinforcing himself in front of the Fourth Army and Third Panzer Army. If contact between the two army groups was not to be permanently ruptured, and if Vilna was not to be exposed to great danger, the decision had to be made not later than at 1400 hours. Further delay would necessarily result in great damage to the troops involved, and consequently to the overall situation.

In a very pointed manner on 6 July, Hitler again refused to allow occupation of the Latvian position. He termed the idea of disengaging four divisions during the withdrawal "stupidity and ill will." He merely permitted a retreat to the following lines (from the left) from the Velikaya sector east to Opotulka to Sebosh, while taking the greatest possible advantage of the Panther Line; thence to Lake Ossea, while taking advantage of the lakes; thence to the Daugava River bend at Ustje, to the northern bank of the Daugava River as far as Oruja, and southwest to the lakes at Braskov. In doing this no division was to be allowed to be released for Army Group Center; on the contrary, denser occupation of the position was to be achieved. The purpose which the two army groups pursued with the request withdrawal was thus defeated from the very beginning. Nothing was gained by the movement into the new position; instead the previous good position was abandoned. Only one division as to be assigned to Army Group Center, the 225th Infantry Division.

The order given by the army group to the Sixteenth Army during the night of 6 July to withdraw into the aforementioned position provided for the movement to take three days by way of intermediate lines (Operation "SCHILDKROETE"). Contrary to Hitler's order, according to which no division was to become free, the army group ordered the army to disengage the three divisions occupying the new position; one of these divisions was to be employed at an endangered point, and two were to become army reserves. At the same time, by way of precaution, the army group caused the

Latvian position to be fortified as a rear support.

During the night of 2 July, the I Corps began to withdraw to the Dzisna-Lake Neshcherda line (Geiger Line), abandoning Polotzk. On 4 July, the divisions which had been fighting heavily for days south of the Daugava River were systematically withdrawn to the northern bank from the front of the Russian Sixth Guards Army, and in the face of strong pressure by the Russian Fourth Shock Army from the east. Polotzk was abandoned after a heavy attack by the enemy, supported by tanks, heavy artillery, and ground attack airplanes had been repulsed. In the morning of 6 July, the I Corps had moved into the Geiger Line.

Thus the defensive battles at Polotzk had come to an end. Since the beginning of the Soviet large-scale offensive on 22 June, the I Corps of the Sixteenth Army, under the command of General of Infantry Hilpert, had faced two Soviet armies – the Sixth Guards and Fourth Attack Armies, with at least fifteen divisions and five tank brigades. Numerically far inferior to the enemy with respect to personnel and material, the corps had contained these forces by an active conduct of battle, partly in dense, pathless forests and swamps. Only after the gap leading to the adjacent units of the I Corps on the right – as a result of the withdrawal of the left flank of Army group Center – had become so great that it could no longer be closed as intended by an attack by the weak I Corps elements, and the danger constantly increased that the I Corps (which was echeloned far ahead) would be enveloped and cut off by the enemy, did the divisions retreat to the Geiger position in compliance with orders. The losses of the Soviets in the battles for Polotzk from 22 June to 6 July 1944 were estimated at approximately 13,000 men killed and wounded; seventy-three tanks had been destroyed; and thirty-three planes shot down from the ground alone.

NOTES

[1] The discrepancies of 2 and 3 respectively in the final totals are reflected in the original figures.

CHAPTER 8

The Defensive Battle at the Eastern Border of Latvia From 10-31 July 1944

Wilhelm Heinemeyer

Hitler's order for the movement into the new position expressly emphasized that this line was definitely to be held, and that "any thought of a further withdrawal by commanders and troops was to be ruthlessly resisted with the most severe means." In contrast, the commanders of the two army groups and their chiefs of staff appraised the situation to the effect that the overall situation called for withdrawal of Army Group North behind the Daugava River. In this opinion the Chief of the Army General Staff and the Chief of the Operations Branch of OKH concurred. The latter were of the opinion that the movement would take approximately one month, and hence had to be started immediately. Although both exerted their power to reach this objective, they did not succeed in inducing Hitler to change his mind. After their efforts also failed, on 8 July they consideered it necessary to have the commanders of the army groups report their views in person to Hitler on 9 July.

According to the calculations of Field Marshal Model, the enemy would be situated on the Brest-Grodno-Kovno line by 17 July, at which time the reinforcements promised were to arrive at the army group. So far, Army Group Center had lost five corps and twenty-nine divisions, making a total of 350,000 soldiers. The object of greatest concern remained the Vilna-Kovno area. At least four infantry divisions and one panzer division were necessary to defend it. Hence, Field Marshal Model proposed to Hitler to withdraw Army Group North without delay to the Latvian position, to disengage four divisions in this movement, and to assign these divisions as quickly as possible to his army group in the area of Kovno – thus blocking the enemy's route to the Baltic Sea. He requested Hitler to seize this one-time chance to stop the enemy offensive by a really effective measure. But again Hitler pointedly refused to authorize the withdrawal of the front to the Latvian position. In his opinion, any major retreat was bound to lead to a collapse both in the case of Army Group North and in the case of Army Group Center; the experience of Army Group Center had shown that the enemy pushed through any gap in the line; splitting the front up and destroying it. Hitler considered a systematic retreat possible only in winter, since then troops were bound to roads far more than in summer, when the enemy could move forward in any terrain. The sole opportunity for establishing effective barriers lay in the narrow passages between lakes. Besides, he considered the Latvian position to be too close to the Ostrov-Daugavpils road and railroad which was the only route for shifts of the army group. From 17 July on a large number of divisions would be available.

Field Marshal Model in turn pointed out that these divisions would come too late. Only the immediate assignment of four divisions could help. These divisions could most quickly be provided by Army Group North. General Friessner was also of the opinion that haste was required. On Hitler's question he agreed to take the risk of freeing the four divisions rquired by Army Group Center for the "REIKER" movement, Hitler himself stipulating that these divisions had to be replaced by OKH, so that only a critical period of seven days would have to be overcome until the arrival of the first division. Hitler decided that Army Group North would give four divisions to Army Group Center in the "SCHILDKROETE" withdrawing movement, and set 17 July as a deadline for the divisions contemplated as replacements.

Upon the renewed request of Field Marshal Model for quick assistance, General Friessner resolved to offer the 69th Infantry Division, which was already being shipped to the Daugavpils area. As one of the next divisions, he offered the 93rd Infantry Division, which was to be disengaged from the front in the "SCHILDKROETE" movement after 9 July, and which was to be moved with the utmost speed to Kovno to Army Group Center.

The ideal of a withdrawal to a Daugavpils-Riga line was repudiated by Hitler. Such a withdrawal wold have meant for the troops a retreat of over 400 kilometers, requiring a period of at least one month. These units would have come too late anyway in the present situation , hence help could not come through a shortening of the front, but by the assignment of units from the Zone of the Interior, in other words, of the fifteen blocking divisions in the process of activation. In the opinion of the Grand Admiral Karl Dönitz, commander-in-chief of the Navy, the Narva front with the northern coast of Estonia was of decisive significance in the blocking of the Gulf of Finland and the political and economic consequences involved therewith in the Scan-

Map Nine: Withdrawal of Army Group North, 10 - 31 July 1944

dinavian areas. However, Admiral Dönitz simultaneously emphasized that the entire Estonian area would become useless once the Soviets succeeded in gaining possession of the coastal sector at Liepaja, from which the Baltic Sea could be controlled from the air bases which would subsequently be stabilized.

Since the beginning of the defensive battles for the Baltic countries (22 June) the Russian First Baltic Front had operated against the inner flank armies of Army Groups Center and North. Its Thirty-ninth Army had encircled Vitebsk. Its Forty-third Army had constantly applied pressure in pursuit of the Third Panzer Army, while attempting again and again to simultaneously envelop it from the north and the south. Its Sixth Guards Army had tried to envelop and crush the flank of the Sixteenth Army, which was suspended in mid-air. Its Fourth Shock Army had attempted, in a frontal attack, to sever the flank from the Sixteenth Army.

The Third Panzer Army had succeeded in frustrating the constant attempts to envelop it by the Forty-Third Army by always withdrawing in time during the night. The corps encircled in the Vitebsk area had been able to fight its way back westward. As a result of the two weeks march with an average daily coverage of thirty kilometers, the German troops were greatly exhausted; their uniforms were torn and some of the troops were without boots.

To fight off the enemy pressing in pursuit, the army had lacked fresh troops that could be quickly shifted to the successive focal points. Only the subsequently assigned 212th Infantry Division had made it possible to do this, and it had put up an excellent fight each time. During the enire withdrawal, the army had constantly pushed the unscathed service troops of nine infantry divisions ahead of it. It had continuously combed the countryside to intercept stragglers, refugees, and soldiers which the trains could dispense with to rehabilitate the combat troops. Since the beginning of the retreat, a total of 6,000 men had thus been obtained.

Continuous withdrawal had saved the Third Panzer Army from encirclement and destruction, but at the same time the gaps between it and the adjacent units – the Fourth Army in the south and the Sixteenth Army in the north – which had been made soon after the beginning of teh Soviet large-scale offensive, could not be closed. Now, around 8 July, the Soviet Fifth Tank Army pushed south-southwest into the southern gap toward Grodno. It had turned off the III Guards Mechanized Corps northwest against Vilna, which since 6 July was controlled by the Third Panzer Army as a fortified locality. On 8 July the Soviet units reached Vilna and on the following day they encircled it. Elements of the Thirty-ninth Army – which had constantly lagged behind ever since the encirclement of Vitebsk – had now come abreast on the left of the Forty-third Army, and furnished infantry support to the III Guards Mechanized Corps.

The Thirty-ninth Army, the Foirty-third Army, the Sixth Guards Army, and the V and I Tank Corps of the First Baltic Front resumed the attempt to expand the gap in the Third Panzer Army sector, and at the same time to envelop the southern flank of the Sixteenth Army. As early as 9 July the Forty-third Army blocked the highway from Daugavpils to Kovno, pushed itself between the two German army groups, in spite of counterattacks by elements of the Sixteenth Army (205th Infantry Division), and again on 9 July forced the Third Panzer Army to withdraw its left flank in the face of an impending envelopment. The Sixth Guards Army meanwhile had turned over its frontal sector at Polotzk to the adjacent unit on the right (the Fourth Shock Army) and had shifted its units westward in the direction of Daugavpils. While the army – with one rifle corps and the bulk of the I Tank Corps attacking – established the necessary flank protection from Druja-Orissa to the Daugava River, it formed a strongpoint of main effort south of Daugavpils with two infantry corps, which later were joined by the I Tank Corps. In this manner the First Baltic Front, with four armies (Thirty-ninth, Forty-third, Sixth Guards, and Fourth Shock) and with two tank corps (V and I Tank Corps) prepared a thrust in a general westerly direction toward Kovno and in the northwest toward Daugavpils. On 9 July it resumed the strong break-through attempts northwest of Polotzk with eight divisions of the Fourth Shock Army, five of which were concentrated in a point of main effort. The losses opposite the German I Corps, however, were so heavy that the army had to suspend its attack on the following day.

On the evening of 10 July, it could be seen that the consolidation of the right sector of the army group south of the Daugava River (and in particular the establishment of a firm contact with the left flank of the Third Panzer Army) had not been successful. The divisions, which had been moved to the scene in good time for this task (170th, 225th, and 69th Infantry Divisiosns) had had to be turned over to Army Group Center. With approximately seven divisions the enemy succeeded in breaking through the widely spread-out right sector of the Sixteenth Army from the northern flank of the Third Panzer Army, which had been withdrawn about ten kilometers with the knowledge of Army Group North, to the southeast of Daugavpils. The army group ordered a rear line to be organized. Since it was impossible to let the four battalions of the 205th Infantry Division fighting southeast of Duagavpils – which were to establish contact with the Third Panzer Army – remain in place without exposing them to destruction, they were withdrawn. Thus a gap of twenty-five kilometers came into being between Army Group North and the Third Panzer Army.

The army group moved further forces to the scene: a Latvian-Estonian police *Kampfgruppe*; the 61st Infantry Division (whose disengagement from the Narva front it had ordered on 9 July); and the 81st Infantry Division, which was to be south of Daugavpils with its main elements by 13 July. However, despite all efforts to accelerate their movements, these forces could not reach the Daugavpils area before 14 July. According to the opinion of both the army groups and the Sixteenth Army, they were in all events too weak to attack in order to close the existing gap, which by then would have contained new enemy forces. They were perhaps sufficient to delay a further enemy advance toward Daugavpils or stop the impending envelopment of the western flank of the Sixteenth Army. The three divisions released from the "SCHILDKROETE" movement, the 93d, 263d, and 87th Infantry Divisions, were destined for Army Group Center. It was, however, doubtful even at that time whether these divisions would get on the move in time, in view of the anticipated enemy pressure. Thus General Friessner felt obliged to report to Hitler on the evening of 10 July that the army group – in view of the present development of the situation – was no longer able with the forces left to it to perform its mission of establishing firm contact with the Third Panzer Army and of holding the line specified in the order.

Upon the news that Army Group North had not only discontinued the attack with its right sector, but had even withdrawn its spearheads so far that a gap of more than twenty-five kiometers existed between the two army groups, Field Marshal Model reported to Hitler that this had changed the situation between the Memel and Daugava Rivers to a particularly threatening degree, as the enemy was already crossing forward there with considerable forces – namely one tank corps. The assembly of the first wave of the Kovno force, consisting of the *kampgruppe* of the 6th Panzer Division and of the 69th and the 93d Infantry Divisions, could be completed no earlier than 17 July. By this time the gap between the two armies would have to be closed. This task Army Group Center was unable to accomplish with its own forces. A decision would soon have to be arrived at by OKH concerning the combat forces of Army Group North, which would both ensure the arrival of the divisions promised Army Group Center, and permit resumption within the shortest possible time of the attacking aiming north. Field Marshal Model held the opinion in view of the present situation that the southern division of those envisaged for Army group Center – the 87th Infantry Division – under the control of the II Corps together with the 225th Infantry Division, had to continue the attack through Utena to close the gap withutmost speed and the greatest possible concentration of its forces, since no other possibilities existed for the time being. The particularly serious threat to East Prussia and consequently to Army Group North permitted no delay of the decision.

On 11 July Field Marshal Model assigned the Third Panzer Army the mission of preventing an extension of the Baltic gap. The army was to conduct the fight at and southeast of Kovno in such a manner that Kovno, Janov, and Vikomir were held. Contact with Army Group Center was to be established by fitting the IX Corps firmly into the army front after it had achieved and maintained contact westward.

Upon the requst of the two army groups, during the night of 11 July, Hitler decided as follows: the gap between Army Group North and the Third Panzer Army was to be closed as fast as possible by an attack by Army Group North. For this purpose it was to retain two divisions destined for Army Group Center (87th and 93d Infantry Divisions). In addition to the 61st Infantry Division, another division was to be disengaged from the eastern front to serve as a reinforcement soutwest of Daugavpils. Army Group Center was to organize a combat force in the Kovno area, which would be in a position to stop the enemy advance on East Prussia. For this purpose it was to receive two divisions from Army Group North, the 69th and 263d Infantry Divisions, and two additional divisions from the Zone of the Interior.

To stabilize the situation on the right flank of the army group, Army Group North had given orders on 11 July to *Armeeabteilung Narva* to disengage the extremely mobile and very seasoned 11th SS Panzer Reconnaissance Battalion and shift it to the right sector of the army group. On the following day it ordered the Sixteenth Army to organize *Gruppe* Kleffel on its right, using the 225th and 61st Infantry Divisions and the 11th SS Panzer Reconnaissance Battalion (assignment of still another division was planned) in order to establish contact with the northern flank of the Third Panzer Army by means of an attack. The 11th SS Panzer Reconnaissance Battalion was to reconnoiter in the direction the gap between the two army groups as soon as possible, to make contact with the Third Panzer Army, and to retard a potential enemy advance. At the same time, the *Armeeabteilung Narva* received orders to disengage one more division.

During the night of 10 July, the withdrawal of the Sixteenth Army and of the extreme right flank if the Eigtheenth Army (L corps) to the "REIKER" position ("SCHILDKROETE" movement) began. It led over two intermediate lines, and was to be completed in three days. Three divisions (93d,

263d, and 87th Infantry Divisions) were freed during the course of the withdrawal.

On the day preceding the start of the withdrawal (10 July), probably because they had dicerned the intentions of the enemy, Soviet units conducted locak thrusts against the extreme left of the Sixteenth Army, in the sector of the VI SS Volunteer Corps. They managed to achieve a local success, and in exploitation of this success managed to push through the German front to a depth of twelve kilometers, thus interfering with the systematic beginning of the "SCHILDKROETE" movement. By following up this success with tank units and infantry forces on the next day they threw the Latvian divisions, the 15th and 19th Latvian SS Waffen Grenadier Divisions, out of the first intermediate line prematurely. There were a number of reasons for the failure of the two divisions, which had suffered decisively as a result of great losses of men and materiel, and which now dropped out of the operations of the army group. These reasons included the attack by concentrated enemy forces, who knew of the planned withdrawal, inadequate training, the lack of an officer corps, the lack of a desire to fight, the lack of German cadres, and the employment of the two units next to each other. The army assigned the two divisions to their adjacent divisions, the 15th Latvian SS Division to the 23d Infantry Division and the 19th Latvian SS Division to the 93d Infantry Division, so that the adjacent divisions had to take over the sector in the "REIKER" position intended for the two Latvian divisions. Despite continued heavy attacks it was possible to draw together the two German divisions, including the remnants of the Latvian divisions, in the "REIKER" position prematurely on 12 July. In the morning of 13 July, the "SCHILDKROETE" withdrawal into the "REIKER" position had been successfully completed, despite heavy enemy pressure.

As expected, the Russian First Baltic Front had begun an attack with strong forces against the defensive flank of the Sixteenth Army on 10 July. Of the Forty-third Army, a force of two divisions had initially been observed in the Utena area; it apparently pursued the intention of of attacking from the southeast toward Daugavpils. The Sixth Guards Army, with a focal attack group of seven divisions, supported by the I Tank Corps, likewise engaged in an attack from the southeast aiming at Daugavpils with its left flank.

On 11 July the Sixteenth Army expected – in addition to the Forty-third Army, approximately twenty-five other units to appear south of the Daugava River within the forseeable future. With these units the enemy was likely to be in a position not only to envelop the present defensive flank of the army from the front and the west to push it in and throw it back to the Daugava

River, but also to start a strategic envelopment with strong forces from the depth aiming in a northwesterly direction. In view of this presumable development of the situation it no longer seemed possible to release the forces freed as a result of the "SCHILDKROETE" movement. On the contrary, everything depended on concentrating them speedily in the area southwest of Jekabpils to stop the pending large-scale envelopment offensively or defensively, depending upon the situation. A new aggravation of the situation appeared on 12 July on the western flank of the army group southeast of Daugavpils when the Sixth Guards Army, supported by the I Tank Corps, succeeded in breaking through the 215th Infantry Division, whose front was forty kilometers long on a narrow sector fifteen kilometers deep. Although it was possible to close the new defense line by means of a counterattack, it had to be expected that the Sixth Guards Army and the I Tank Corps would exploit the situation for a decisive thrust on Daugavpils.

General Friessner drew the conclusions from the situation as it presented itself on the evening of 12 July: he tried to induce Hitler to seek a large-scale, strategic solution. He once again gave an account of the course of events since his assumption of command on 4 July. The continual movement of forces against the northern flank of the Third Panzer Army, which had made itself increasingly felt, had caused Army Group Center to withdraw its northern flank more and more to the west. The result was an increasing danger of the gap between the inner flanks of the army groups being enlarged. All measures which he had taken from his first hour of his command to close the gap between the two army groups at Daugavpils, at the very latest, were unavailing because of the transfer of the forces assembled for this purpose (especially of the 225th and 69th Infantry Divisions) to stabilize the situation of Army Group Center. He therefore decided to move up new forces – the 61st Infantry Division and the 11th SS Panzer Reconnaissance Battalion – for the same purpose of closing the gap. *Gruppe* Kleffel, organized with these forces, however, could not begin an attack southward before 14 July, and then only if there was no major interference with the front of the army group through enemy attack or partisan actions designed to delay the movements. Now that Army Group North had already been weakened by the transfer of twelve divisions to Army Group Center, and its front had had to be lengthened by 200 kilometers owing to the development of the southern sector or from a thrust into its flank, its defensvie capacity – even with the forces moved up – had decreased so much that a stable defense both on the eastern and southern front was no longer ensured.

To feed a decisive conduct of operations on the southern flank, General

Friessner had also ordered the 126th Infantry Division to be disengaged from the Pskov bridgehead. As a result, the withdrawal of the forces situated there in the almost fortified Irboska position would perhaps become necessary. Even in respect to *Armeeabteilung Narva*, which had orders to release one more division, he had to reserve for himself the right of withdrawing the salient of Narva to the tactically well-fortified Children's home position.

In conclusion, General Friessner regarded the situation as follows: the enemy would with all his might attack to maintain the westward direction (Kovno) of his thrust. This would in practice mean that Army Group North was cut off. As a secondary action, the enemy was already attempting to push forward to Daugavpils and Kraslava with major forces. By doing so, the enemy would disrupt the structure of the eastern front of the army group. The German forces necessary for an appropriate defense were no longer available, in view of the superior enemy forces, attacking with heavy tank forces. If the armies of the army group were to be saved, the decisive thing – in his opinion – was to withdraw the armies in the following manner after leaving strong rear detachments to fight delaying actions: *Armeeabteilung Narva* to Tallinn, with shipment by sea to Riga, Liepaja or Memel depending on the situation; the Sixteenth and Eighteenth Armies to the Kovno-Riga line. It could not be said with certainty whether the withdrawal was still feasible, in view of the development of the situation south of the Daugava River. But it would be the last chance to save Army Group North from encirclement and destruction, as clearly and unmistakeably could be seen.

This proposition was also rejected by Hitler (13 July). The previous orders were to remain in force. In a personal conference with the commanders and chiefs of staff of both army groups at his headquarters on 14 July, he maintained his basic standpoint that the Baltic countries were not to be abandoned under any circumstances. The situation of Army Group Center was becoming stable, and it was to be hoped that the Soviet thrust would be absorbed in the present line. The movement of new divisions to the scene permitted a bolstering of the entire front of Army Group Center to be expected.

Hitler offered the prospect of providing a panzer army for a thrust through the gap between Army Groups North and Center in the general direction of Daugavpils. The beginning of its attack could be expected in six to seven days. This critical period had accordingly to be overcome by both army groups in order that the assembly could proceed undisturbed and the attack be launched as soon as possible.

This conception of Hitler's reached the ears of the public. On 13 July the spokesman of the Wehrmacht High Command [*Oberkommando der Wehrmacht* – OKW] had deprecated "certain plans regarding an alleged straightening of the front in the Baltic countries. A straightening or shortening of the front in the Baltic area is completely out of the question. If south of the Baltic countries, in the vicinity of Polotzk, the German front had been somewhat rounded off, this was done only to establish a contact with the new line in the central sector and thus be in a better position to ensure the protection of the Baltic countries. The Baltic countries belong to Europe. The German Wehrmacht will defend and hold this European territory, both in the south and in the north of the Eastern Front, under all circumstances."

The attacks of the Russian Sixth Guards Army and the I Tank Corps southeast of Daugavpils continued to intensify on 13 July. General Hansen reported that there were signs that the front would collapse unless new forces were immediately moved to the scene. The enemy apparently intended to smash the German forces at the Daugava River to gain increased freedon of movement in a northwesterly direction. The mission of preventing this, however, could in the long run not be unertaken unless new forces were provided. the army group hence felt obliged to release the 61st Infantry Division (which it had been contemplated to employ in *Gruppe* Kleffel) for employment with the II Corps, southeast of Daugavpils. Thus the organization of this attacking force with which contact with the Third Panzer Army was to be reestablished, had failed. Now that it consisted only of the 225th Infantry Division and the 11th SS Panzer Reconnaissance Battalion, it had to limit itself to taking over protection and reconnaissance on the right flank of the army group, and to delay a potential enemy advance toward the northwest. The Sixteenth and Eighteenth Armies received orders to be ready to withdraw to the Latvian position as soon as the signal was given. The army group had to report to OKH that a release of forces was no longer possible. Since the Russian Sixth Guards Army, on 13 July, had succeeded south of Daugavpils in breaking through the front of the severely decimated German troops at several points, and in gaining ground locally, and since the fighting power of these German troops had dropped noticeably in the past days, the army group – upon request – had to release the 87th Infantry Division to the Sixteenth Army for its southern flank. This measure, however, at the same time increased the new and serious danger to the northern flank of the Sixteenth Army.

The Russian Second and Third Baltic Fronts had learned prematurely of the withdrawal of German troops to the "REIKER" position. Hence, they had followed up the withdrawal everywhere with their forces. By 13 July they had already attacked the new position. While the attacks were repulsed by the I and X Corps, the Soviets succeeded in pushing into the "REIKER" position on a front of almost forty kilometers with superior infantry and tank forces (approximately nine rifle divisions and three tank units) east of Opotchka in the sector of the VI SS Volunteer Corps, in which the 23d and 93d Infantry Divisions had been driven together as a result of taking over the sectors of the two Latvian divisions.

The danger of a gap between the Sixteenth and Eighteenth Armies threatened. The Sixteenth Army believed itself to be no longer in a position to prevent this, since the 87th Infantry Division was urgently needed in the southern sector. *Gruppenführer* and Lieutenant General of Police Karl von Truenfeld, the commander of the VI SS Volunteer Corps reported that he was unable to hold his position beyond evening; if the old order remained in effect, the remainder of his forces – including the weapons – would be lost. In the opinion of the Eighteenth Army, the Soviet command also pursued the intention of disrupting the army group front at the army boundary, and in addition was preparing attacks against the Eighteenth Army itself. The army placed the first *Regimentsgruppe* of the 126th Infantry Division, which had been disengaged at Pskov, behind the army boundary. On account of the critical development of the situation, the army group felt obliged during the night of 13 July to withdraw the inner flanks of both armies.

The strong pressure against the Eighteenth Army continued on the following days. Greatly superior enemy forces struck against the German front again and again with tank units in the points of main effort south of Daugavpils, north of Drissa as far as Lake Lissno, and between Sebash and Opotchka. The fighting power of the German divisions, who fought on overextended fronts, dropped rapidly. South of Daugavpils it was possible to avert the danger for the time being by the employment of the 87th Infantry Division. South of Lake Lissno, the situation became very critical during the day on 14 July. The enemy attacked three German divisions with fifteen divisions, and achieved a penetration ten kilometers in depth. An equally deep penetration was achieved opposite the VI SS Volunteer Corps; the 23d Infantry Division was split up into isolated gorups. Thus the X Corps was threatened with a double envelopment from the south and north. While it was possible to seal off the southern penetration in bitter battles, the enemy achieved a deep penetration on a front of thirty-five kilometers between Sebash and Opotchka on the following days. The 23d and 93d Infantry Divisions, which had taken over the sectors of the Latvian divisions a few days before, had to be regarded as having themselves been defeated.

Again the army group was threatened with being split up at the boundary of both armies. The Sixteenth Army was at the end of its strength. In the conviction that only the Eighteenth Army could free forces to stabilize the situation, the army group assigned the sector of the VI SS Volunteer Corps to this army and gave it the 126th Infantry Division and the available remnants to seal off the penetration further westward, and to reestablish a firm contact with the left flank of the Sixteenth Army. Up to that time, the Sixteenth Army was to hold the shoulders of the penetration zone with all available means. In addition, Hitler approved the intention of the army group to disengage another division, the 58th Infantry Division, from the Narva Front. A withdrawal of this front to the Children's home position and the abandonment of Narva was to be avoided for military and political reasons. In order that the division might nevertheless be disengaged, 5,000 men of the Navy and 3,000 men returning from leave were promised to the army group for employment at the Narva flank.

The danger that the front between the two armies would be ruptured permanently had by no means been averted. The Russian Third Shock Army and the Tenth Guards Army, supported by an operational tank group, attempted to force a breakthrough in the penetration area southwest of Opotchka with about ten rifle divisions and four to five tank units. The Tenth Guards Army pushed forward with motorized forces to a point ten kilometers east of Ludsa. The measures designed to seal off the breakthrough, however, were at first only partly effective.

On 16 July the Eighteenth Army estimated the situation to the effect that the enemy would continued his strong attacks here with the aim to break through by way of Ludsa in the direction of Rezekne, with elements advancing from Krassny in the direction of Abrene. The enemy pressure west of Opotchka forced the army, with the consent of the army group, to withdraw its previous southern sector to the Latvian position in order that further forces coul be gained for the battle in the penetration zone. South of the former army boundary, any enemy advance east of the Latvian position was to be checked as long as possible under any circumstances, and brought to a standstill along a continuous front with a firm contact with the Sixteenth Army, to prevent the army group from being split. Whether the army would succeed in preventing the thrust toward Luiza, however, remained doubtful. At the same time – on 16 July – there was danger that the northern flank of the Sixteenth Army would be enveloped by two enemy divisions. The army group had to approve the request of the army to withdraw its northern flank to an intermediate line between the present main line of resistance and the

Latvian position, in order to gain definite contact with the Eighteenth Army. General Abberger, the commander 3d Engineer Staff, by way of precaution, received orders from the army group to employ the construction troops currently in the Latvian position in the construction of the Marienburg position immediately upon arrival of the combat troops.

In conclusion, the army group estimated the situation on 16 July as follows: the operations of the army group were in part influenced decisively by the continuing deterioration in the situation of the adjacent unit on the right, the Third Panzer Army, whose northern flank – threatened with envelopment – had to withdraw further from the right flank of Army Group North, and by the decrease of the forces on its own front. In conformity with Hitler's orders, the operations were conducted using every means available, with toughness and admirable efforts on the part of officers and troops. It had to be regarded as a miracle that the Soviets had not yet moved up major forces for an envelopment of the western sector of the army group in the direction of Riga. Except for weak blocking forces, the army group had nothing to line up against them. Nevertheless, penetrations could not be avoided, owing to the great length of the sectors, continuous losses, and the fatigue of the troops – who had been fighting continuously for four weeks. On 16 July, the army group had been barely able, with the last division disengaged from the front (the 126th Infantry Division) to close the gap caused by the complete collapse of the Latvian corps. From the next day on, the 58th Infantry Division – arriving with its initial elements on the evening of 18 July in the vicinity of Rezekne – was at the disposal of the commander as a last reserve. General Friessner had to report to Hitler that with its employment all available resources to conduct operations were exhausted: "The last alert units, the last arms-bearing men are already fighitng in the lines of the units committed. After 20 July I shall have no more means to prevent breakthroughs, let alone to eliminate them. A rupture of the army group front must then be expected."

The same conception was voiced by General Friessner to Hitler in a personal conference on 18 July in the Führer's headquarters. On the basis of the situation, he asked the Führer for directions regarding his further operations which would make allowance for the potential development of the situation, and for a decision as to whether the focal point of the defense of the arm group were to be located in the Daugavpils area or in the Ostrov area. The forces of the army group were no longer sufficient for both points of main effort. Hitler admitted that the simplest solution would be to occupy the Daugava line. This, however, was impossible because of the unending consequences. Abandonment of the Eastern countries would have the following results: the surrender of Finland and thus the loss of the sole source of nickel; loss of Sweden with an annoual amount of 9,000,000 tons of ore; access of the Soviets to the Baltic Sea; and the end of the entire program of submarine training. Such measures could subsequently result in the loss of the war. An example for this was the Crimea Peninsula. Its abandonment had caused the desertion of Turkey. Through Turkey's change of attitude, the attitude of Bulgaria had been greatly influenced, and this could not remain without effects upon Rumania and Hungary. In the event of a collapse of these allies, it was superfluous to point out the effect on the Balkans as a whole, and the consequences for the overall conduct of operations. Hence, the mission of Army Group North had to remain the holding of the present front by all means, and with all conceivable makeshifts. By 1 August it would be possible to assemble three panzer divisions in the northern sector of Army Group Center for the purpose of closing the gap. Up to then operations in the gap must be conducted in a flexible manner to delay the advance of the enemy.

On the basis of these considerations, OKH on 18 July ordered the two army groups to prevent an advance of the enemy through the gap in a western or northwestern direction with mobile units in flexible operations, while absolutely holding the present positions of the flanks, and to close the gap as soon as possible. Army Group North concentrated its forces in the extreme western sector, under the command of the XXXXIII Corps headquarters, which had been disengaged from the Narva front.

Meanwhile the heavy attacks of the Russian Sixth Guards Army and the I Tank Corps south of Daugavpils against the II Corps of the Sixteenth Army had continued unabated. The strategic intention of the Soviet command to break through from the penetration zone of the 81st and 132d Infantry Divisions toward Daugavpils, however, was frustrated by the bravery and tenacity of these divisions, which were supported by elements of the 61st and 87th Infantry Divisions. Five rifle divisions, one mechanized and one tank corps attacked in vain here until 18 July. The Sixth Guards Army realized the impracticability of its intention, disengaged its attack forces, and regrouped them toward the west.

The Soviet command at first refrained from pushing on further in the gap between the two army groups. Instead it directed its efforts to smashing the western sector of the Sixteenth Army by heavy attacks of the Forty-third Army, supported by tank formations and ground attack aircraft. It was also getting ready for a decisive breakthrough toward Daugavpils through new attacks of the Sixth Guards Army, consisting of seven rifle divisions and the

I Tank Corps, after shifting its point of main effort further west. In the face of the clearly recognizable enveloping movements against the right flank, the army group felt it necessary – on 20 July – to commit the 61st Infantry Division there. The 58th Infantry Division was likewise moved there from *Armeeabteilung Narva*.

The withdrawal of the inner flanks of the Sixteenth and Eighteenth Armies had started during the night of 16 July. The Soviets followed with concentrated rifle and tank units, and established pronounced points of main effort. Unmistakably the objective was to smash the eastern front of Army Group North with the armies of the Second and Third Baltic Fronts. North of the Daugava River, the Fourth Shock Army supported by the V Tank Corps was engaged in an attack on Krslava and Daugavpils; adjacent on the north was the Twenty-second Army.

In the area on both sides of Ludza the Second Baltic Front still maintained a particularly heavy point of main effort at the inner flanks of the Third Shock Army and the Tenth Guards Army, which comprised numerous tank units of a mechanized operational group, all ready for a thrust toward Rezakne and Jekabpils. Another point of main effort was situated on the right of the Tenth Guards Army east of Krassny, ready to veer west of it toward Rezakne from north to south. The Fifty-fourth Army of the Third Baltic Front, reinforced by units of the Sixty-Seventh Army, had formed a new point of main effort west of Lake Vele, as far as Ostrov. The intention of this army was, with the eight divisions employed here, to veer north through Abrene and Vilska in the direction of Irboska, and toward Lake Pskov, in order to roll up the Eighteenth Army from the south. In view of the danger threatening the entire front in the northern sector, the army group instructed the Eighteenth Army to fight in its present positions, but in case the army was thrown out of them to do everything to withdraw west and southwest, and in no case to allow itself to be pushed north. The far superior Soviet forces achieved penetrations of menacing proportions northeast of Ludza, west of Krassny, and west of Lake Vele; sealing them off could only be attempted in the depth, and by greatly weakening the sectors that had not been attacked. On 18 July, in view of this development of the situation, General Loch realized that the solution lay in retreating to the Daugava River, while putting up a delaying action.

The far superior forces of the Soviets, which were supported by tanks, succeeded in breaking through westward in the area north of Ostrov on 20 July. To avoid a major breakthrough and free another division for use on the endangered sector of the front (which was that of the 32d Infantry Division) the Eighteenth Army felt it necessary to withdraw the front south of Pskov, including Ostrov, during the night of 20 July, and Pskov itself during the following night – withdrawing from the Panther Line to a chord. The army group felt obliged to disengage another division from the Narva front, replacing it by Estonian units, and thus accept another reduction in strength. The continued unfavorable development of the situation caused the Eighteenth Army to point out to the army group on 21 July that without assignment of fresh forces it would no longer be equal to the enemy pressure, and hence considered necessary the quick initiation of a movement which, with the northern tip of Lake Lubanas as a pivot, would have to begin with turnign the left sector of the army toward the vicinity of Walk. The Lake Lubanas-Walk line could be reached in a week. For this movement of the Eighteenth Army it was important to hold the Narva front until the left flank of the Eighteenth Army had reached Walk. At least some elements of *Armeeabteilung Narva* would have to be withdrawn in time to a general line from Lake Virts to Paernu.

The situation on the eastern front of the Sixteenth Army was similar. General Hansen had reported on 20 July that, if the enemy continued his heavy attack against the eastern front of the army on the following days, the army would face collapse. The divisions were decimated, and their condition would become worse by the hour, so that there was no longer any chance of holding the present positions. Unless something was done, the army would collapse on the next day.

According to the opinions of the army group and the two armies (21 July) the situation was characterized by the envelopment of the right flank which was clearly taking place, by the deep penetration north of the Daugave River and east of Daugavpils (I Corps), by the deep and broad penetration of the eastern front south of Ostrov, and by the steady draining of forces. General Friessner sent his chief of staff, Major General Eberhard Kinzel, to the OKH to report personally to the Chief of the Army General Staff that naturally the order of Hitler to hold the present line would be carried out, but that there were no longer any reserves to seal off the penetrations. Thus, if an attack was made to carry out the present mission, the destruction of the army group could be expected in the foreseeable future. Then Hitler would not only lose two armies, but the eastern countries also. If the mission were changed, it would seem possible to gain substantial forces to close the "Baltic Gap." The new Chief of the Army General Staff, General Guderian, turned down these suggestions in a most pointed manner. He stated that in the event of a catastrophe General Friessner was man enough to issue the necessary orders.

As an episode occurring on the northern front on 20 July, the day of the attack on Hitler's life, the telephone call made by Colonel General Ludwig Beck to the chief of staff of the army group may be mentioned. Assuming Hitler to be dead, Beck had asked General Kinzel whether it would be possible for the army group to fight its way back to East Prussia. When told that this was still possible, he issued orders for the retreat, giving as his reasons that there must be no second Stalingrad, and that the army group was needed for the defense of the frontiers of Germany.[1]

The situation of the army group continued to get worse daily. The Russian First Baltic Front continued the envelopment of the eastern front in a menacing manner. Since the northern flank of the Third Panzer Army had again had to be withdrawn considerably on 22 July, the already existing gap between the army groups was enlarged. Now as ever, the army group was of the opinion that forces to close this gap could only be freed by a speedy withdrawal of the front to s shorter line. It was evident that the Russian forces on the Eastern front of the army group were attempting a breakthrough simultaneously with three strong groups of forces – north of the Daugava River with seven divisions in the direction of Daugavpils; likewise with seven divisions (plus four brigades and tank units) in the direction of Rezakne; and with fifteen divisions and five to six tank units between Kraslava and Ostrov. The long-expected attack against the Narva front seemed to be about to begin.

The operations of the army group pursued the aim of maintaining the continuity of the front between the Daugava River and Lake Pskov or – where it had been lost as a result of a deep breakthrough – of reestablishing it. Like the armies, the army group believed that this could only be achieved if it withdrew the front to a line further west ("SONNENVOGEL" movement). Nor did the command of the army group indulge in the illusion that even this line, which was already endangered, could be held; it had to gain time by further retreats to restore order in the troops and to prepare them for an effectual defense. Hence it ordered the armies to prepare (by way of precaution) for a further withdrawal to the following line: Lake Drysviaty-eastern edge of Daugavpils-northern edge of Daugavpils as far as Lievenhof-Lake Lubanas-Rugaji-Kaceni-northern part of the Irboska chord. General Friessner felt obliged to report to Hitler that it would not be possible to hold even this last-mentioned chord in the long run against a far superior enemy. But if it once became necessary – and this would be the case in the foreseeable future – to abandon the front along Lake Peipus, a further withdrawal behind the Daugava Line would become vital.

On 23 July, Hitler strictly refused the request of the army group to withdraw further westward. Because of the development of the situation, however, the armies considered it necessary to continue the "SONNENVOGEL" withdrawing movement. The army group was also of this opinion. General Friessner again made this request to the OKH. The answer, on 24 July, was in the form of the replacement of the commander, General Friessner, by Colonel General Ferdinand Schörner, and of the chief of staff, General Kinzel, by Colonel Oldwig Natzmer.

General Schörner was vested with extraordinary authority by Hitler, an authority far more inclusive that that his predecessors had held. He had the power to employ all available combat forces and means of the Wehrmacht and Waffen SS, as well as the organizations and forces outside the Wehrmacht – the Party and civil authorities – to repulse the enemy attack, and to hold the eastern countries. The entire zone of jursidiction of the army group became the zone of operations, and the Wehrmacht Administrative Commander for the Eastern Countries was placed under the authority of the army group in every respect. Thus the commander of the army group had finally received Wehrmacht authority.

At the same time, on 24 July, a new directive was issued for the conduct of operations on the Eastern Front. According to it, Army Group Center was to organize the forces in its northern sector in such a manner that it could reestablish contact with Army Group North in an attack from the area northeast of Kovno. Army Group North was to hold its previous positions, and to establish a point of main effort on the right, in order to close the gap to Army Group Center through an attack from the Rokiskis area aiming southeast. Improvised mobile forces were to be organized without delay and employed to this end. From 26 July the long overdue replacements for the units of the army group, most of which had been compeletely decimated, were to be shipped to the scene. Beginning with 27 July, it was intended to move up into the gap between the army groups two divisions being activated in Wehrkreis I.[2]

The favorable development of the situation on the Finnish theater of war had meanwhile permitted the Soviet command to resume the attacks which had failed in the spring against the German Narva front. The significance of the Narva front in the fate of the Baltic countries and the development of overall operations called for this attack just as much as did the prevailing situation in the north of the Eastern front, since Army Group North faced the simultaneous danger of being encircled on the south and split up by a breakthrough in the central sector. The successful breakthrough into Estonian territory was bound to lead into the rear of the Eighteenth and Sixteenth Armies, and be conducive to the capture of Tallinn and Pabliski, and possibly even to the capture of the Baltic islands and the elimination of the port of Riga.

The Russian Leningrad Front, under the command of Marshal Govorov, which controlled both the Russian troops on the Narva front and those on the Karelian Isthmus, began to assemble strong forces on the Narva front approximately in the middle of July. It shifted a large number of units – particularly tank units – from the area of the Soviet Twenty-first Army on the Karelian Isthmus toward the west, and forces of the Thirteenth Air Army from Leningrad into the Kingissepp area.

On the one hand, the Leiningrad Front established a strong point of main effort in the sector of its Eighth Army; on the other hand, the front of *Armeeabteilung Narva* had been almost completely divested of German troops, owing to the Soviet large-scale attacks against the other two armies of Army Group North. The last battleworthy German unit was the 11th Infantry Division; it was supported by the volunteer units of the III "Germanic" SS Panzer Corps (SS Panzergrenadier Division "*Nordland*" and SS Panzergrenadier Brigade "*Nederland*"). The Estonian units employed in the front were not experienced in battle, only in part equipped with heavy weapons, and – although they were fighting for their own country – unreliable. A large number of Estonian soldiers had already deserted during movement to the front, and many more deserted at the front itself.

In view of this tremendous difference in size between the German and Soviet forces, *Armeeabteilung Narva* and the army group had for a long time before requested freedom of action to give up – if necessary – the Narva bridgehead, which consisted of unfavorable terrain, and which demanded additional forces, and to move into the Tannenberg ("Children's home") position. This request had hitherto been turned down by Hitler out of regard for the Finnish ally. But once the Finnish High Command had given its consent, Hitler gave the army group a free hand. This withdrawal took place on 22 July. By the morning of 26 July the position had been occupied in an orderly manner.

On 24 July the Soviet Eighth Army conducted strong reconnaissance thrusts southwest of Narva. On the following day it shifted its point of main effort into the area between Narva and Narva Joesuu. On a broad front its units – in superior force and vigorously supported by by the action of the air force – succeeded in crossing the Narva River, inflicting severe losses on the

20th SS Estonian Waffen Grenadier Division, and in crushing it completely on 26 July. In the penetration zone, the Eighth Army employed no fewer than ten rifle units and two tank brigades. Nevertheless, *Armeeabteilung Narva* succeeded in completely restoring the situation.

As yet the combined attack of all available forces of the Leningrad Front had not begun. The attacking forces were constantly reinforced by new troops shipped to them from the Karelian Isthmus. Alongside of the Eighth Army, the Second Shock Army was again employed. Each of the two armies had four rifle corps with at least twenty-one rifle units at their disposal on 27 July. The vast number of tank units were combined under the unified command of a mechanized operational force. The Thirteenth Air Army moved two ground attack divisions, one fighter division, and one bombardment division to the scene of action. Finally, the XXX Guards Rifle Corps, which had had an outstanding record for years, was moved up from the Karelian Isthmus.

On 29 July, the large-scale attack began on the Narva front, with the objective of a breakthrough toward Tallinn. On the first day of attack the two Soviet armies committed thirteen rifle divisions and approximately six tank units. But despite all efforts they did not succeed in breaking through the thin front of one German division and two volunteer units. *Armeeabteilung Narva* achieved a brilliant defensive success. In view of the high losses – on the first day alone 113 tanks had been disabled – the Soviet command discontinued the attacks.

It was to be regarded as a miracle that the First Baltic Front had still not pushed through to the Baltic Sea in the gap between the two army groups to permanently interrupt the overland connection with the German Zone of the Interior. At first it seemed possible to trace the interruption in the advance to the circumstance that the motorized units of the enemy had attained the limit of their technical capacity, and need to be rehabilitated. Undoubtedly there were also supply difficulties at times. But the decisive point most probably was the fact that the Soviet command consiered its present forces as insufficient both for the large-scale attack (in the direction of East Prussia) and for the limited attack (in the direction of Riga). Hence, it had resolved to move strong additional forces to the scene and reorganize the chain of command. Previous attacks in the gap etween the army groups evidently had merely pursued the purpose of preventing a closing of the gap and a freeing of routes of advance.

The First Baltic Front turned over the army on its left flank, the Thirty-ninth Army, to the adjacent unit on the left, the Third Belorussian Front. By pivoting the adjoining army – the Forty-third Army – toward the north, and by concentrating its forces, sufficient space was gained to insert two new armies, which had becone free on the Crimean front: the Second Guards Army was insert on the right beside the Thirty-ninth Army (with its attack direction toward Siauliai) and the Fifty-first Army (with its attack direction toward Jelgava or Riga). In addition to the two mobile corps that had been previously assigned to the front – the III Guards Mechanized Corps in the area of the Second Guards Army and the I Tank Corps in the sector of the Sixth Guards Army – two more mobile corps were moved to the scene: the VIII Guards Mechanized Corps and the II Guards Tank Corps. The Sixth Guards Army rearranged its forces and faced them west by taking over the right sector of the Forty-third Army.

On 22 July the Russians attacked the northern flank of the Third Panzer Army with greatly superior forces, and again threw it back. The army was obliged to retreat step by step in order to protect its northern sector (comprised on the IX Corps) from destruction. With elements of the Second Guards Army and the III Guards Mechanized Corps, the Russian First Baltic Front advanced toward the important traffic center Siauliai to envelop the Third Panzer Army from the north. Army Group North did not have at its disposal the forces to protect Siauliai. Army Group Center, in spite of repeated requests submitted to the OKH, had not been furnished with the necessary forces. In the additional gap between the army groups the Soviet forces continued for the time being to display little activity.

While the attack of the two German divisions against the right flank of the enemy in the gap south of the Daugava River was still being continued to "force the right shoulder forward," although it encountered increasing resistance, the new army group command – which had been appointed on 24 July – was with great energy building a blocking front in the gap, beginning from the north. It assigned all the blocking and reconnaissance forces employed there – elements of the Army, the Luftwaffe, the Waffen SS, and the Navy – to the *Gruppe* Kleffel headquarters, and after 26 July to the army group directly, in order to achieve a unified command. Since the army group could no longer extract forces from the other fronts, the latter being themselves engaged in defensive battles, this new front remained a thin reconnaissance screen, which would possess no adequate power of resistance in the event of an enemy breakthrough attempt.

In the meantime a severe crisis had developed for the army group in the sector around Daugavpils. The Russian Sixth Guards Army had been able to achieve a penetration six kilometers deep with five rifle divisions and one tank brigade south of Daugavpils on 23 July, for the elimination of which a division freed as the result of the withdrawal (the 132d Infantry Division) had to be employed. There was no doubt that the Soviet command, by means of a double envelopment from the south and north was endeavoring to quickly cpature Daugavpils and the Daugava River crossings there, to disrupt the contact still existing in the center of the Sixteenth Army owing to these crossings, and accordingly would continue to exert pressure on both sides of the Daugava River.

General Hansen was of the opinion that north of the Daugava River the enemy – shaken off by the withdrawal – would follow up in the previous main direction, and that it would not be possible to repulse the immediately impending large-scale attacks in the intermediate position which had been occupied on the night of 22 July. Therefore, it had to be feared that within twenty-four hours the present front south of Daugavpils would have been subjected to such a strain and probably broken through or ruptured at places that a systematic continuation of the "SONNENVOGEL" operation, with the Daugava sector in the rear, would be no longer possible. He accordingly requested permssion to continue the "SONNENVOGEL" operation no later than in twenty-four hours.

The actual events took a different course. As expected, on 24 July the Second Baltic Front managed to produce a gap north of Daugavpils with the tank units of the V Tank Corps and to push toward northwest with elements of the Fourth Shock Army, across the Daugavpils-Rezakne railroad. The following day a concentric attack was made by the Sixth Guards Army in the south, and by the Fourth Shock Army – together with the V Tank Corps – in the north against Daugavpils. Whereas in the southern point of main effort the breaktrough attempts of the Russians failed, they managed to advance further from the penetration zone north of the river, and despite initially successful counterattacks to extend the deep penetration into a breakthrough halfway between Daugavpils and Livani by simultaneously turning south toward Daugavpils and north toward Riga. As a result, the situation of the army group was decisively aggravated. It felt constrined to abandon Duagavpils and to withdraw to the Marienburg position over three intermediate lines. Through this movement two divisions were at the same time to be disengaged for active operations in the "Baltic Gap."

Thus, during the night of 26 July, the city of Duagavpils was evacuated, after all installations important for warfare had been destroyed. By the morning of 31 July it had been possible, despite heavy attacks by superior enemy forces west of Abrene and west of Ostrov, to occupy the Marienburg position. The simultaneous intention of the army group, by means of this movement, to build a continuous front of the Eighteenth Army west of Ostrov, despited the heavy enemy attacks with tanks and air support which had been in progress for several days, had for the time being been realized.

On 26 July the First Baltic Front began to advance north into the gap between the army groups. With a tank formation of the III Guards Mechanized Corps and elements of the Second Guards Army it pushed forward in the manner described above, against the important traffic center of Siauliai. An attack by weak elements of *Gruppe* Kleffel, designed to relieve the garrison of Siauliai failed because, in addtion to other reasons, of the mutiny of the Latvian troops used. The brave garrison received orders to break out toward the west, and prevent an advance of the enemy toward the vital port of Liepaja. The breakout was accomplished during the night of 27 July.

The right portion of the Russian Fifty-first Army and the bulk of the Forty-third Army – the units adjacent to the Second Guards Army on the right – attacked on 27 July on a broad front with seven to eight rifle divisions and two to three tank units (probably belonging to the VIII Guards Mechanized Corps) in an attempt to break through toward the north and northeast. At the same time, elements of the III Guards Mechanized Corps enveloped the western flank of the army gorup farther to the north, and entered Jelgava on 28 July. As a result, the last rail connection of Army Group North with East Prussia was disrupted. On the following day Russian tanks reached the Baltic Sea north of Tukums; Army Group North was encircled.

For the army group everything depended on building a solid defense front west and southwest of Riga before the arrival of major enemy forces. The Wehrmacht Administrative Commander for the Eastern Countries was placed in charge of fortification, security, and defense in the Riga bridgehead, and in the advanced local stongpoint of Jelgava. All elements employed in front of the bridgehead were assigned to *Gruppe* Kleffel. At the same time, the army group began to move the divisions becoming free in the Marienburg position – the 215th and 93d Infantry Divisions and the 281st Security Division – to the right sector, and to build a solid front with them. On 28 July *Gruppe* Kleffel was again assigned to the Sixteenth Army, and all elements of this army north of the Daugava River (X Corps) were assigned to the Eighteenth Army.

To push into the eastern flank of the enemy forces advancing toward Jelgava, the Eighteenth Army received orders to attack on 28 July from Bauska west toward Kleja. As soon as sufficient forces were available in the Bauska area, the attack westward was to be continued. Further intentions were to close the gap between the army groups through an attack in cooperation with the Third Panzer Army. According to the opinion of the army group, the preparatory attack toward the west was necessary because the defensive ring of Riga was manned only by weak elements, and the loss of this city and its port would have grave consequences. The subsequent attack was to be undertaken – after a concentration of forces – with a strength of three and one-half divisions on or about 31 July from the Bauska area, and was to aim first southeast, then north against the Seduva-Panevezys line in order to close the gap above the Third Panzer Army southwest of Panevezys. The time and place of the attack as selected by Army Group Center corresponded to the intentions of Army Group North: Attack by two panzer divisions on 1 August from the Kedainisi area in the direction of Seduva. In contrast to these intentions, Hitler (probably with the concurrence of General Guderian) ordered the assault forces – which were to be made available – to launch an attack immediately on Panevezys in order to close the gap between the two army groups by the shortest route. Army Group Center was to move three panzer divisions to the scene for the purpose. The Memel River was to be protected temporarily in the East Prussian position by battalions of replacements and anti-tank forces.

On the basis of the experience gathered in attempts to close the gap since the beginning of the Soviet large-scale offensive, the Sixteenth Army remained skeptical about these plans. It doubted that the Third Panzer Army would be able to concentrate enough forces this time to attain the desired end. The army advocated a closer objective for the planned attack on the right flank of the army – that is to say, the elimination of the immediate menace to Riga as the result of the enemy breakthrough, preventing the enemy from crossing the Daugava River southeast of Riga and appearing in the rear of the Eighteenth Army, and also reopening the railroads to East Prussia.

On 29 July, Army Group North issued orders to the Sixteenth Army to attack from the Birzai area to the souhwest on the morning of 2 August with at least three divisions, support by the stongest possible artillery as well as assault guns, with the objective of establishing contact with the northern flank of Army Group Center south of Panevezys.

On the evening of 31 July, the situation of the army group was as follows: the enemy had encircled the army group in a line from Bauska to the Gulf of Riga, but only with weak forces for the time being. He had been unable to realize his intention of enveloping the western flank of the army group with the rifle units following behind. This was due to the fact that his attack had each time encountered units which had been moved up just in time. It had to be assumed that the Russians, with the tenacity natural to them, would cling to their intention of pushing concentrically toward Riga from the area of Jelgava, north of Daugavpils, and west of Ostrov. As a result of the shortening of the front west of Daugavpils, they had freed rifle units, with which they could replace and disengage the mobile units still tied down on the encirclement front. The mobile units, comprising four mechanized or tank corps, would then be free to either force a breakthrough toward Riga or to push against the coastal sector of Liepaja-Irben highway. Since the further operations of the army group depended entirely on the control of the Baltic Sea, supply by sea would at any rate be rendered exceedingly difficult. The mobile units could also be committed for a thrust into East Prussia, and thus for the envelopment of the northern flank of Army Group Center. For Army Group North the decisive point was to prevent the enemy from advancing further in the direction of the Liepaja-Irben highway, and from moving additional forces into and westward through the Baltic gap, while continuing to hold Riga.

This task had to be solved quickly, before reinforcements arrived, and could only be solved by an attack at the narrowest point, in other words from the Birnai area in the direction of Panevezys. The attack, however, promised to be successful only if sufficient forces were committed from the northern sector of Army Group Center with the same objective, and if possible simultaneously. If no attack by Army Group Center was made, the last forces of Army Group North, which had been drawn together from all parts of the front at great risk, would be sacrificed without a prospect of success, and the overall situation of the army group would become grave.

Although the army group had, in time, prepared itself for receiving supplies across the Baltic Sea, the supply situation was aggravated immensely in these days. The lack of fuel had assumed such proportions that all operations and supply threatened to stop. The weapons of the troops had been decreased so much as a result of losses which had never been made good that in many cases combat missions could no longer be carried out. Equally inadequate was the supply of ammunition. On the other hand, the long overdue replacements of combat personnel were gradually arriving to cover the great losses which had arisen in the continuous six-week struggle. The losses sustained during the period 22 June to 26 July 1944 totaled 49,498 men (Sixteenth Army: 33,020; Eighteenth Army: 12,158; *Armeeabteilung Narva*: 4,320 men).

As anticipated by the Sixteenth Army, the prerequisite for the attack by Army Group North to reestablish contact with the adjacent army group was also lacking this time. This was an attack by Army Group Center, while simultaneously holding its previous positions. On 29 July the Soviet large-scale attack on both sides of Kovno had begun. At the same time, the assault units of the Red Army, turning northwest in front of Siauliai, continued the enveloping movement against the left flank of the Third Panzer Army. Mechanized reconnaissance forces pushed forward to a point thirty kilometers northeat of Tauroggen even on the first day of the attack. The Third Panzer Army was again forced to withdraw westward. Since the necessary attack forces of that army continued to be tied down in battle, on 3 August Hitler ordered Army Group North to suspend the attack for the time being to maintain its fighting power, and through attacks with limited objectives to prevent an attack by substantial enemy elements in the direction of East Prussia. Thus, for the time being, the army group was encircled. An attack designed to liberate it had to be postponed until necessary forces could also be committed from the south.

NOTES

[1] For a more complete description, see Peter Hoffmann, *The History of the German Resistance, 1933-1945* (Cambridge MA: MIT Press, 1977), p. 497.

[2] Note in original: "Military area."

CHAPTER 9

The Defensive Battles of Army Group North From 30 July-27 September 1944

Wilhelm Heinemeyer

The Defensive Battle at Birzai, North of the Daugava River, and at Modohn (30 July-31 August 1944)

The Russian First Baltic Front meanwhile increased its pressure from the southwest against the Daugava River; at Birzai with the Forty-third Army and the I Tank Corps, at Bauska with the Fifty-first Army, and at Jelgava with the Second Guards Army and the III Guards Mechanized Corps. To prevent the impending breakthrough by the Forty-third Army and the I Tank Corps toward the Daugava River in the direction of Friedrichstadt, the Sixteenth Army threw all available forces into the battle at Birzai – among others two additional divisions (215th Infantry Division and 281st Security Division) – and began a counterattack. Although the Russians moved up reinforcements from other sectors, the attack made good headway, and on 1 August Birzai was recaptured. The success achieved by the Fifty-first Army, the Second Guards Army, and the III Guards Mechanized Corps between Jelgava and Bauska, however, forced the army group to discontinue the successful counterattack in the Birzai area on 2 August. As a result, it was possible to free a division to eliminate the deep penetration northwest of Bauska. For use against the enemy penetration east of Jelgava, the Sixteenth Army had to disengage another division on its left.

In heavy battles the army succeeded in eliminating the deep penetrations at Jelgava and Bauska. On 6 August, the Russian Forty-third Army, supported by the I Tank Corps, managed to rupture the German defensive front southeast of Bauska between Saliciai and Birzai. After the failure of the battle-worn troops employed there, it was no longer possible to close the

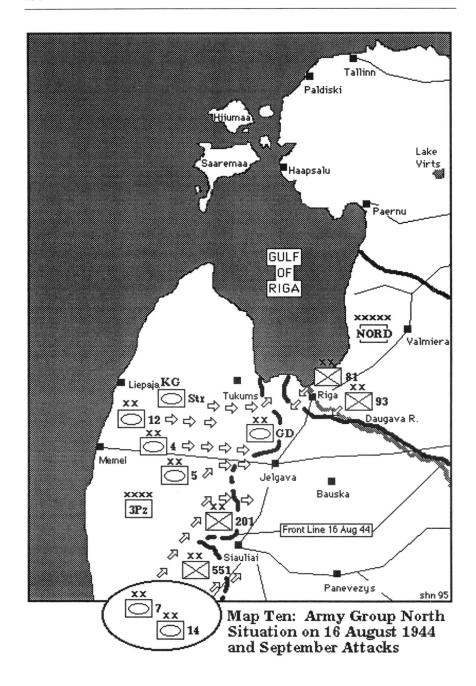

Map Ten: Army Group North
Situation on 16 August 1944
and September Attacks

front by an attack. Thus the only remaining possibility, especially as the situation on the right flank of the Eighteenth Army had also become critical, was to withdraw the left flank of the Sixteenth Army to the Bauska-Trentelberg line in order, as a result of the reduction of the length of the front, to disengage a unit for the Eighteenth Army "HEUSCHRECKE" movement.

The STAVKA regarded the previous attack by the Sixteenth Army as an attempt to force a breakthrough to East Prussia along the shortest route. The First Baltic Front, therefore, reinforced its main point of attack there by transferring to the Forty-Third Army – which up to that point had been supported northwest of Birzai by the I Tank Corps (four tank and motorized brigades) – the XIX Tank Corps (five brigades), three rifle divisions of the Sixth Guards Army, units from the eastern sector of the Forty-third Army and the Fourth Shock Army, artillery of the Fifty-first Army, and the entire 21st Artillery Division of the Sixth Guards Army, into the area southwest of Birzai. Finally, twelve rifle divisions and two tank corps were facing the decimated units of the I Corps of the German Sixteenth Army, which waged a truly heroic fight on which the fate of the army group at this decisive sector of the front depended.[1] Deep breakthroughs forced the army to start the "HEUSCHRECKE" movement prematurely during the night of 7 August. It was completed the following morning according to plan. The enemy discontinued his heavy attacks and regrouped his forces.

Simultaneously with the battles described above, in the sector of the Sixteenth Army the Russian Second and Third Baltic Fronts had resumed their attacks against the Eighteenth Army with the aim of pushing through to Riga and smashing Army Group North. Directly north of the Daugava River, at Rivani, the Second Baltic Front had formed an unusually strong focal point with eight rifle divisions of the Fourth Shock Army and the left flank of the Twenty-second Army and the V Tank Corps. Its intention was to push through first to Krustpils and then to Riga.

The German troops were greatly outnumbered by the enemy; in the course of the battles on 3 August twenty Soviet units were assumed to be engaged opposite three German units of the X Corps. The Germans were also short of weapons, fuel, and ammunition. The lack of men made itself particularly felt in the forest fighting.

The attacks began on 30 July north of Livani by the Russian Fourth Shock Army, units on the Twenty-second left flank, and the V Tank Corps. There were considerable penetrations, and at length the enemy breakthrough on the entire front of the X Corp forced the Eighteenth Army to withdraw the front here toward the west on 2 August. But even on the following day the situation had taken a turn for the worse: the units in the right sector of the Twenty-second Army and the Third Shock Army managed to achieve a deep penetration in the central and left sectors of the X Corps. Simultaneously the Tenth Guards Army, which had been returned by the Third to the Second Baltic Front, formed a point of main effort south of Lake Lubanas.

With the bulk of four armies and one tank corps, the Second Baltic Front sought to form a breakthrough between Livani and Lake Lubana to the Stockmannshof-Modohn railroad. The Eighteenth Army and the army group each moved one division (32d and 24th Infantry Divisions) to the hard-pressed right sector of the army. Nevertheless, on 5 August the greatly superior Soviet units managed again to thrust through the front, just as it was being fortified. The situation had become extremely critical, especially as the right flank of the Tenth Guards Army had already thrown back the German front ten kilometers over a breadth of twenty kilometers in the area north of Lake Lubanas on 3 August, and thus had also provoked a crisis in the adjacent corps sector, Here also the lack of men and weapons in the wooded battle terrain made itself decisively felt.

On 6 August the army group was caught in a severe crisis. As has been described above the enemy had ruptured the front between Saliciai and Birzai in the left sector of the Sixteenth Army, southeast of Bauska. Thus there was no chance of closing the front through an attack. With the Eighteenth Army the critical situation could not be mastered either, despite the support of three newly arrived divisions. The eastern front of the army group was threatened with a breakthrough. It had to give the enemy the desired freedom of action, which would lead inevitably to the splitting up of the army group. The personnel and materiel situation was extremely strained, Hence, the only remaining possibility of obtaining the forces necessary for the Riga bridgehead and the Eighteenth Army was to withdraw the inner flanks of the two armies to the line from Bauska through Trentelberg, and the Aiviekste position, to the Modohn position by 10 August over two intermediate lines, and in so doing free further forces in the Sixteenth Army sector for the defensive operations. Providentially, on 7 August the army group issued orders to the Eighteenth Army to fortify the Walk position, and to General Abberger, the 3d Engineer Staff commander, the fortify the Wendish position.

The army group advised the OKH that unless it received additional forces, and the attack by Army Group Center was started soon, it would be unable to keep up the defensive in the long run. It could then only receive the mission of itself reestablishing the overland connection with the adjacent army group through an attack southwest, after abandoning a part of the territory now held, and maintaining its combat strength. To this end, *Armeeabteilung Narva* would have to be withdrawn to a bridgehead position around Tallinn and transported by sea. At the same time, the Eighteenth Army, while maintaining the position of its right flank, would have to withdraw its left flank westward first to an approximate line from Jaunjelgava through Ashof to Walk, and later to an extended bridgehead position around Riga. It would then be the task of the army group to undertake attacks west and southwest while the east and north front yielded – with a view to reestablishing contact with Army Group Center. A new defense front could subsequently be organized approximately in a line running from northwest of Kovno-east of Siauliai-Bauska-the sector of the Lielupe River as far as north of Sloka. Time benefitted the enemy in that he could steadily increase the strength of his defensive organization in the encirclement front. Accordingly, with every passing day, the breakthrough became more difficult. These plans would become a necessity if the political situation in Finland changed. Continuation of the battle of the army group under the present conditions depended on the further supply service; the present one, especially with respect to ammunition, was inadequate.

While the Second Baltic Front was undertaking its heavy attacks with the objective of a strategic breakthrough to Riga (since 30 July), the Third Baltic Front had regrouped its forces. The army on the right, the Forty-second Army, had been disengaged for other employment as a result of the reduction in front length. Its sector had been taken over by the Sixty-seventh Army, as the adjacent unit of the left. Between this army and the Fifty-fourth Army, the First Shock Army (which had become free earlier in the course of the German withdrawal) had been reinserted. With the Fifty-fourth Army and the First Shock Army the Soviet front had formed points of main effort south of Marienburg, and on both sides of Laura with the intention of interrupting the Riga-Pskov Rollbahn through an attack toward the north and northwest. On 2 and 3 August, the heavy attacks had begun. Although the attacker achieved penetrations in both zones of attack, he was unable to achieve a successful breakthrough, and this was due in great part to the poor spirit of the Soviet troops, who at some places had to be forced forward at the point of a gun.

Defensive Battle Between Pskov, Walk, and Tartu (10 August-28 August) and Continuation of the Defensive Battle at Birzai, North of the Daugava River, and at Modohn, 30 July-31 August 1944

The remarkable habit of the Soviet command of continuing with great tenacity to pursue a once-set objective in spite of repeated failures also became apparent here. It did not give up its strategic goal, consisting of a breakthrough to Riga and the Baltic Sea, and the destruction of the Eighteenth Army. The Second and Third Baltic Fronts prepared a simultaneous attack against both flanks of the Eighteenth Army. The main thrust of the former was directed, with six to eight rifle divisions in the southern sector, and approximately six rifle divisions in the eastern and northern sectors, concentrically against Modohn. The units of the V Tank Corps again provided support. The Third Baltic Front gave up the previous point of main effort south of Marienburg in favor of the point of main effort of the First Shock Army at Laura, and formed another point of main effort on both sides of the Riga-Pskov Rollbahn with the Sixty-seventh Army, reinforced by units assigned from the Narva front. According to German estimates, the two armies initially had a total of seventeen rifle divisions, approximately four tank units and eight to ten Guards mortar units, with about 250 automatic guns at their disposal. The main thrust of the First Shock Army was directed from the south against Voru with the intention of pushing on from there to the west to Walk, while the Sixty-seventh Army intended to advance on Voru from the east.

The simultaneous withdrawal of the inner flanks of the Sixteenth and Eighteenth Armies (Operation "HEUSCHRECKE") was completed on the morning of 10 August. As a result, it became possible to assign to the Eighteenth Army a division from the left sector of the Sixteenth Army, the 398th Infantry Division. The army regrouped its right flank units, exchanged battle-worn units as far as possible against those that had been disengaged from less heavily attacked sectors, and placed the entire zone of main effort on both sides of Modohn under the command of the L Corps. The penetration zone west of Laura was turned over to the 122d Infantry Division, which had been shipped to Finland in June and had just returned. For the German command there was no doubt that the Soviets would shortly resume the attacks, which up to then had been unsuccessful. But despite the careful defensive measures taken, the paralyzing shortage of combat troops, of ammunition, and of fuel continued to prevail in this as well as in all other sectors of the army group.

On 10 August there began the joint large-scale attack of the Second and Third Baltic Fronts with superior forces against the two flanks of the Eighteenth Army. Penetrations and a shortage of forces constrained the army to withdraw the front at its right flank to the edge of the town of Modohn on the night of 11 August, and to a shortened line west of the town on the following night. Thereby a few forces could be gained. Without attaining further successes, the exceedingly heavy attacks of the Soviets subsided temporarily during the following days. The enemy command altered its chain of command and regrouped his forces for a new attack.

Simultaneously with the Second Baltic Front, the Third Baltic Front had started its expected large-scale attack against the two divisions in the left sector of the Eighteenth Army on 10 August with at least twelve rifle divisions and one to two tank units of the First Shock Army and the Sixty-seventh Army. A heavy barrage smashed the German defenders, large numbers of ground attack aircraft hindered their movements, while the defense itself was hampered by a constantly increasing shortage of ammunition from the very first day on. Hence the Soviet units managed to rupture the front in a depth of more than ten kilometers even on the first day, and to achieve a deep penetration toward the northwest.

The only effective relief brought to the two intensely struggling German divisions, the 112d and 30th Infantry Divisions of the XXVIII Corps, was that of the Luftwaffe, which since 11 August had been permitted to employ its whole strength without regard for the fuel situation. The army group had no choice in dispatching new defence forces to the army. During the night of 11 August, the First Shock Army succeeded in breaking through north of Voru on a breadth of ten kilometers and a depth of twenty kilometers, with two rifle divisions supported by tanks. Army group and army tried to round up partial units, and with this stop this enemy force, which was now attacking north of the Rollbahn in a westerly direction.

The situation had become very grave. The flank attacks designed to close the gap failed, as no more than one weal battalion was available for each. Through simultaneous penetrations by elements of the Sixty-seventh Army on the extreme left, the contact with Lake Pskov had already been partly lost. The German infantry fought very bravely, but the weak combat forces of the two divisions on the left were unable to stand up to the superior enemy attacking units. According to the opinion of the army group, everything now depended on preventing an expansion of the gap. To this end it was necessary to hold the positions of the inner flanks as bastions. In addition, the pivot at Voru had to be held, and the penetration zone somehow sealed off. General Loch did his utmost to ensure that every available man, every available gallon of fuel was brought to the scene. He made it clear to the army that, primarily for political reasons, any departure from the old mission was out of the question.

At the same time General Loch submitted an estimate of the situation to the OKH. Pointing to the strong enemy pressure south of Voru, the unsuccessful counterattack, the very high losses on the German side, and the fact that accomplishment of the large-scale withdrawal to Riga was already jeopardized, he reported that unless panzer forces pushed through to Bauska on 13 August for an attack on Voru, withdrawal to Riga (involving abandonment of the Narva front) was unavoidable. On the same day, however, Hitler forbade a withdrawal to Riga. He ordered the enemy breakthrough intercepted by exhausting all available means. On the following day, the army group received the 31st Grenadier Division by air transport, as well as a unit of Luftwaffe anti-tank personnel. In addition, the army group urgently requested the OKH to accomplish the planned thrust to Riga from the west as soon as possible, in order that after its successful completion, one of the panzer units could immediately be pulled through to the Eastern front. The earliest date, however, that General Guderian was able to set – in view of the fuel shortage – was 15 August.

Thereupon the army group issued orders to the Eighteenth Army on 12 August to prevent the enemy from breaking through in the direction of Walk and Riga with a flexible – and if possible, offensive – operation, while maintaining the left sector in its present positions. For the penetration zone, forces were to be freed by reductions of the front length, and further elements were to be disengaged from the army front. For the army group, everything depended on preventing a deep breakthrough of the enemy and a splitting of the front until the announced measures could produce effects – in other words, approximately until 17 August. The Sixteenth Army received orders to immediately establish a fully motorized tactical reserve force, and to dispatch it to the Eighteenth Army.

To gain at least two more battalions, the central front of the Eighteenth Army withdrew to a shortened line on both sides of Marienburg during the night of 12 August. At the suggestion of the army group, the Eighteenth Army headquarters on 13 August turned over the tactical command of the three corps in the southern part of the army front to the L Corps as *Gruppe Wegener*, in order to be able to devote itself with its operations staff solely to the conduct of operations in the endangered northern sector. *Luftflotte* One was requested to intervene in the battles, again without regard for the fuel situation.

Before these defensive measures could become effective, the situation in the penetration zone had again worsened for the German troops in the last few hours. The objective of the Third Baltic Front was, as mentioned before, the splitting up and destruction of the Eighteenth Army by a thrust to the Gulf of Riga. Hence the northern flank of the First Shock Army struck at Voru from the south with the intention of pushing on from there in a westerly direction to Walk. The Sixty-seventh Army was engaged with its southern forces in an attack from the east toward Voru; its northern elements pushed past Voru on the east in the direction of Tartu. Split up into small combat forces, enveloped from several sides, their command posts like islands in a vast flood, the German divisions stood in a tough, bitter battle with a total of twenty rifle divisions, four tank and ten Guards mortar units, Voru was lost on 13 August. West of the town a dangerous gap was torn open. Contact with Lake Pskov was lost.

It could be foreseen that a breakthrough by the right sector of the Sixty-seventh Army toward Tartu would lead to a collapse of the Narva front. To prevent this, the army group assigned the sector on both sides and in front of Tartu to *Armeeabteilung Narva* and ordered it to speedily block the narrow passage between Lake Peipus and Lake Virts. Alongside of the local forces, mostly consisting of Estonians who had been assigned at the same time, the *Armeeabteilung* had to build up the front with elements of units which it disengaged from the Narva front on 13 August. The Eighteenth Army, at the same time, was assigned the mission of giving up contact with Lake Pskov and of trying to stop the enemy in the Voru by flexible operations, and – if this did not succeed – of bringing him to a standstill at the latest in a line from Walk through Lake Virts to the Tartu blocking line, With the two divisions moved up by air and from the Sixteenth Army (the 31st Grenadier Division and the 87th Infantry Division) a new front had gradually been built east of Walk since 13 August. The II Corps, moved up by the Sixteenth Army, assumed the unified command in the penetration zone west of Tartu.

Particularly critical was the development of the situation in the following days in the left sector of the Eighteenth Army (XXVIII Corps). The front had dissolved into a number of small strongpoints. The German forces were being shattered more and more. They were unable to hold their positions in the face of incessant attack and envelopments by the greatly superior enemy rifle and tank units. At length there was nothing left but to slowly bend the left flank of the army to the southwest. But thereby a gap was of necessity created between it and *Armeeabteilung Narva* through which the enemy pushed forward toward the north and northwest. No forces were available to close this gap. The crisis was further aggravated by a Soviet rifle corps – the CXIV Rifle Corps – with three rifle divisions and one tank unit, which crossed the narrow passage between Lake Pskov and Lake Peipus at Mehikoorma on 15 August. The counterattacks immediately launched by *Armeeabteilung Narva*, which were designed to eliminate this beachhead were without avail. The Soviet forces pushed westward from the bridgehead to join with the elements of the Sixty-seventh Army pushing northwest between the German armies.

Thus the only thing to do was withdrawal *Armeeabteilung Narva* to the Ahja sector as far as the mouth of Kma River, and order it to establish contact with the northern flank of the Eighteenth Army and keep mobile forces ready behind the specified line to attack immediately any penetrating enemy, throw him back, and under all circumstances prevent a breakthrough of enemy forces toward Tartu. The forces employed there were to be reinforced as far as was permitted by the situation on the Narva front, for which the old combat mission remained in effect. Thus the *Armeeabteilung* found it possible to move only a few German battalions to the scene. The bulk of the defense was formed by the Estonian frontier guard regiments. These had hitherto proved increasingly unreliable. By hundreds they left the troops, deserted into the forests and went home, thus contributing to the increasing shortage of men.

The Russian First Shock Army and Sixty-seventh Army made every effort to break through toward the northwest to Lake Virts and toward the north to Tartu. The former launched a new double envelopment against Walk. With seven rifle divisions it attacked the II Corps (employed in the center of the penetration zone) and through gaps in the front achieved several penetrations westward. Against the left flank of the Eighteenth Army, and against the southern front of *Armeeabteilung Narva*, the Sixty-seventh Army closed in on a broad front. On 19 August, there were new breakthroughs in the central sector of the penetration zone. Soviet forces advanced westward primarily between the left flank of the Eighteenth Army and *Armeeabteilung Narva*. The XXVIII Corps employed there was threatened with an envelopment on both flanks. Since there was no longer any prospect of closing the gap between the two armies, the army group found it necessary to order the Eighteenth Army to withdrawal its left flank, and to have the southern flank of the *Armeeabteilung Narva* withdrawn likewise, so that on the whole the Walk-Lake Virts-Kma River position was occupied.

This move had already been approved by Hitler on 18 August in the event of heavy attacks. In giving his permission, he had primarily stressed that the Narva front must not be divested of too many forces, for the holding of Estonia still had great political significance, in view of the situation in Finland. Finland could be kept in line only if the continued defense of the Narva front was successful, and if the Soviet advance toward Tartu could be halted. Hitler's plan was, after the "certain" and full success of the attack by the Third Panzer Army, to pull a panzer corps through, and by having it attack perhaps along the Riga-Pskov Rollbahn, and advance to the southern tip of Lake Pskov, to eliminate the enemy penetration west of the lake, and to destroy the enemy thus encircled.

The order issued by the army group on 19 August was also made necessary by the development of the situation in the right sector of the Eighteenth Army.

The STAVKA had by no means abandoned its intention of braking through north of the Daugava River toward Riga, simultaneously with the breakthrough attacks of the adjacent unit on the right aiming at Walk and Tartu with the objective of pushing through to the Gulf of Riga and the Baltic Sea. The heavy losses which the Second Baltic Front had suffered here in the last battles had induced it to make an extensive regrouping of its forces. The Fourth Shock Army had come under the control of the First Baltic Front, and in line with its general shift westward had now been employed south of the Daugava River on a defensive mission. In the previous zone of main effort from the Daugava River to north of Modohn, the Third Shock Army and the Tenth Guards Army regrouped their forces. They received reinforcements both from the Fourth Shock Army and from the Twenty-second Army. The V Tank Corps was also available again.

On 17 August, the Second Baltic Front started a new large-scale attack in the aforementioned zone of main effort with a total of nineteen rifle divisions and with tank and air support. Numerous enemy penetrations and the quick decrease in combat strength forced the Eighteenth Army to withdrawal the front on both sides of Laudona, even on the first day of the attack. But despite the employment of no fewer than twenty-two units, a defensive success was denied to the Third Shock Army and the Tenth Guards Army, because of the bitter resistance which the German troops offered, although they had been weakened by high losses. On 18 August, the Second Baltic Front committed the V Tank Corps, which it had up to then kept in reserve, with seventy to eighty tanks in an attack between Laudona and Modohn. It succeeded in breaking through with twenty tanks and with infantry spearheads as far as the important traffic center of Ergli, and with the bulk of the tanks and strong infantry forces into the area west and southwest of Lake Ealu.

Thus a situation had come about for the German command which was far more dangerous than that at Walk and Tartu. For, whereas at these places there was still a chance of withdrawing to the Walk position, the thrust here was directed straight toward Riga, the heart of the army group, while a renewed withdrawal was impossible. The Eighteenth Army could not oppose strong forces of the V Tank Corps, attacking in conjunction with the Third Shock Army. The army group had to limit itself to employing the entire air force in its area against the penetrating enemy fores in order to smash the spearheads, since the weak German battalions were insufficient. The construction forces of General Abberger received orders to occupy the Wendish position, and thereafter to prepared the Segewold position as a permanent position.

The critical aggravation of the situation on both flanks of the Eighteenth Army had induced the army group to issue the aforementioned order on 19 August. Only through further withdrawal could forces be gained for the heavy defensive battle of the army group. Everything depended on preventing another enemy advance in the direction of Riga on the boundary of the Sixteenth and Eighteenth Armies, the latter of which turned over its right corps sector (X Corps) to the adjacent unit on the right – effective immediately – and on withdrawing the left flank of the Eighteenth Army and the southern flank of *Armeeabteilung Narva* to the Walk-Lake Virts-Kma River position, and on holding this position. The flanks, which had remained intact on both sides of the penetration point at the new boundary between the Sixteenth and Eighteenth Armies, were to be held in their present position. The withdrawal on the left flank of the Eighteenth Army was to lead approximately to the Sangaste-Otepaa-Elva line during the night of 19 August, while the army group reserved for itself the right of giving the signal for a further withdrawal to the Walk position (Jaunjelgava sector to Pargla). *Armeeabteilung Narva*, on the other hand, while fighting a delaying action. was to withdraw step by step to the Kma River position on both sides of Tartu. The mission for the Narva Front, however, did not change.

Immediately south of the new boundary between Sixteenth and Eighteenth Army, the Soviet attack units were being continuously reinforced. They veered southeast, thus increasing the danger that the corps in the left sector of the Sixteenth Army would be enveloped and destroyed. To prevent this, the army felt constrained to withdraw this corps northwest toward Ergli, with a pivot at Trentelberg. With the forces thus freed, the army intended to strengthen the left sector, with a view to reestablishing contact with the Eighteenth Army, which was attacking south with one division. During the night of 19 August, the Sixteenth Army started a counterattack designed to recapture Ergli. The following days brought exceedingly heavy battles in this sector. The army fed them with forces which it disengaged from sectors south of the Daugava River and moved up to the battlefield at Ergli. The German troops attacking from the west and north at last succeeded in recapturing Ergli, and in reestablishing contact between the armies. But there could be no doubt that the Soviet command would resume the large-scale attack in the direction of Riga as soon as it had moved up replacements, and perhaps even new forces.

On the right flank of the army, the "HEUSCHRECKE" withdrawal, which was completed on the morning of 10 August, had meanwhile induced the STAVKA to undertake an extensive regrouping in the form of a general westward shift, and had at the same time afforded it a chance to considerably consolidate its forces opposite the extreme right flank of Army Group North. The army on the extreme left of the First Baltic Front was the Second Guards Army, in the Siauliai area; to reinforce it, the I Tank Corps was dispatched to the right sector from the former point of main attack of the Forty-third Army. The army, facing west, stood opposite the left flank of Army Group Center. The adjacent unit on the right was the Fifty-first Army with a rifle corps in the Dobele area facing westward, and two rifle corps from the coast to the area halfway between Jelgava and Bauska, facing eastward. Adjoining them was the Forty-third Army, together with the III Guards Mechanized Corps. The Sixth Guards Army, together with the XIX Tank Corps, formed a new point of main effort in the old zone of main effort of the Forty-third Army, north of Birzai. The adjacent unit on the right, the Fourth Shock Army, had crossed the Daugava River in a southerly direction, and from the Second Baltic Front it had been placed under the command of the First Baltic Front. The fight front boundary of the latter now ran along the Daugava River. The commander of tank and mechanized troops of the front, Brigadier General Skornjakov, controlled a total of four mobile corps.

On 15 August, the First Baltic Front attacked – for the third time – aiming at a breakthrough to Riga in the sector of the I Corps of the Sixteenth Army. Concentrating its forces after a heavy artillery preparation, the Sixth Guards Army – supported by a large number of tanks and ground-attack aircraft, advancing from the former zone of main effort of the Forty-third Army, attacked the two German divisions – which despite their great numerical inferiority had frustrated all previous breakthrough attempts. The excellent conduct of operations of the I Corps and the outstanding bravery of the two divisions again caused the strategic intentions of the Soviet command to fail after three days of heavy battles. One hundred and eight Soviet tanks were disabled in these three days. Then the German attack from the west (from the sector of the third Panzer Army) caused the First Baltic Front to discontinue the attack of the Sixth Guards Army and the XIX Tank Corps in order to move reinforcements (including the XIX Tank Corps) westward from the Eastern front.

On 16 August the attack on the left flank of Army Group Center, long desired by Army Group North, had begun with the aim of reestablishing contact with the encircled army group. The OKH had issued orders to Army Group Center on 9 August to concentrate all available mobile divisions on the northern flank of the Third Panzer Army against the enemy forces in the Baltic gap, and in smashing the enemy forces to reestablish contact with Army Group North. The operation was to launched in such a manner that the German forces, utilizing the Courland territory, would make a sweep west of the Tauroggen-Jelgava road, and in a very short time push toward Jelgava through the enemy forces there, which were not yet very strong. After establishing contact with Army Group North, it was the task of the Third Panzer Army to turn south, and with the combined strength of the panzer divisions to push through Seduva and Panevezys in the direction of Kovno into the enemy forces fighting on both fronts, and to destroy the enemy facing the eastern front of the Third Panzer Army. The task of Army Group North was to contain the enemy on the southern front until contact had been established, and then to join in the southward attack of the panzer forces in order – in this manner – to establish a firm contact with Army Group Center on the south. The first objective of the joint operation of the army groups was to reach the Kovno-Vilkonir-Anyksiai-Pokiskis-Akmiste line. If circumstances were favorable, a decisive operation was planned by the OKH. Hitler's ideas further provided for a panzer corps to be included in the Army Group North area, with which the penetration west of Lake Pskov could be eliminated through a thrust along the Riga-Pskov Rollbahn in the direction of the southern tip of Lake Pskov, while the enemy thus encircled could be destroyed.

The attack of the southern force had been set for 16 August, and that of the northern force for the following day. The deterioration of the situation of the army group as a result of the Soviet large-scale attack against the Eighteenth Army (since 10 August) induced the army group to address an urgent request to the OKH for acceleration of the attack. But an earlier launching of the attack was impossible, because the necessary fuel would not be available sooner. Besides, the army group had to insist that, immediately upon completion of the breakthrough, an adequate panzer force would be pulled through to the eastern front. It was the opinion of the army group that only in this manner could the situation there be consolidated again. The shortage of manpower did not permit it to push from the east to meet the attacking units of Army Group Center, as would have been urgently desirable.

The final plan of the attack provided for the organization of the attack forces (the XXXX Panzer Corps with one panzer, one panzergrenadier, and one infantry division and the XXXIX Panzer Corps with five panzer divisions and *Panzerverband* Graf Strachwitz). The task of the XXXX Panzer Corps was to push forward through Siauliai toward Jelgava; the task of the XXXIX Panzer Corps, attacking on the same day, was to push forward through Autz and capture Jelgava. *Panzerverband* Graf Strachwitz received the mission to cover the northern flank of the two attacking forces until they had completed their assembly, and later – pushing forward through Sloka or Jelgava – to establish contact with Army Group North. Its attack was to be supported by the 2d Naval *Kampfgruppe* (Force *"Prinz Eugen"*). The Sixteenth Army received the mission from the army group of undertaking a westward attack with the forces on the right flank to meet *Panzerverband* Graf Strachwitz halfway; to form bridgeheads between Bauska and Sloka; and to push westward as soon as the attack of the panzer units made itself felt.

On the morning of 16 August the two forces simultaneously attacked in the direction of Siauliai and north thereof, with the elements that had arrived by that time. The Soviets offered heavy resistance. The First Baltic Front reacted very quickly by shifting its point of main effort to the western front. It moved the XIX Tank Corps out of the area of the Sixth Guards Army (as a third mobile corps), organized heavy additional artillery reinforcement on the west, discontinued the attack of the Sixth Guards Army in the Birzai area on 18 August, and then shifted the Sixth Guards Army front the front south of the Daugava River to the west in order to insert it between the Second Guards Army and the Fifty-first Army – whose point of main effort it likewise turned around. In addition, it moved the Fifth Guards Tank Army from the south closer to the new point main defense. Thus, the Soviet army group opposite the left flank of the Third Panzer Army controlled three tank corps and a tank army.

Nevertheless, the OKH continued to entertain the idea of a large-scale operation designed to establish the broadest possible overland connection between the army groups (18 August). The first objective of the attack was to recapture the road and railroad to Jelgava, in order subsequently to reach the Raseinen-Seduva-Varkai line as an intermediate goal, and with a strong right flank. The further goal – the line running Memel-east of Jurbakas-Kedainiai-Panevezys-Birzai-Radviliskis – was to be retained.

The attack by the two panzer corps made only slow headway in the face of the increasing resistance of the Soviets. In an increasing measure they had to combat enemy counterattacks. On 19 August, *Panzerverband* Graf Strachwitz started its breakthrough attack. By the following day, it managed to capture Tukums and establish contact with the attack groups on the right flank of the Sixteenth Army, which had taken Kemmern by assault. The attack was effectively supported by the *"Prinz Eugen"* with two destroyers firing from the Gulf of Riga. Desirable as was the suggestion of the Sixteenth Army to clear up the Tukums area with *Panzerverband* Graf Strachwitz and then turn this force south in order to push the other panzer units of the Third Panzer Army forward by this strategic thrust, the army group regarded it as absolutely necessary to incorporate the panzer force at once in its area, and to move it to the eastern front, for the situation at Tartu had meanwhile degenerated into a crisis.

In the following days, the newly established overland connection between the two army groups was consolidated in mopping-up operations, and a line of security was organized facing south, which in the following days was reinforced with artillery and armor-piercing weapons because of the extraordinary strategic importance of the overland bridge in the fate of the army group. The attack by the two panzer corps on the left of the Third Panzer Army was continued for some time, the forces being regrouped several times, but fell short of the desired success because of the very heavy Soviet resistance. On 27 August, it was discontinued. Although the final objectives had not been attained, the attack of the two panzer corps had still made it possible in heavy battles with three Soviet tank corps, ten rifle divisions, and seven other units to reestablish the overland connection through Tukums to Army Group North; had brought decisive relief to the Sixteenth Army in its heavy defensive battle; and had also had effect on the situation in front of the Third Panzer Army north of the Memel River, from which the Russian Fifth Guards Tank Army had been withdrawn.

The reestablishment of the overland connection with German territory, and the prospect of being able to employ *Panzerverband* Graf Strachwitz at the eastern front within a short time, induced the army group to discontinue the withdrawal at the inner flanks of the Eighteenth Army and *Armeeabteilung Narva* to the Walk-Kma River position on 20 August. The situation here was threatening. There were sure signs that the Soviets were forming a new point of main effort opposite the left flank of the Eighteenth Army with a view to resuming the large-scale attack in the area around Voru on one of the very next days. Equally certain was it that the thinly occupied front here could not be held against a strong attack of the enemy. The southern front of *Armeeabteilung Narva* was peculiarly jeopardized. Its weakness lay in the entirely inadequate combat value of the Estonian frontier guard regiments. The *Armeeabteilung* hence had requested permission to retreat to the Kma River position, while holding a bridgehead around Tartu; it considered its forces insufficient to hold the sector west of Tartu.

The Third Baltic Front, which was under the command of Army General Maslennikov, had meanwhile actually formed a new strategic point of main effort between the Voru-Walk railroad and road, with the right sector of Fifty-fourth Army, which had extended its sector as far as Voru, and the First Shock Army under the command of Major General Sakhvatsev. The Sixty-seventh Army, under the command of Major General Romanovski, evidently had the mission of fighting the right flank free by undertaking an attack on Tartu. For Army Group North, the strategic danger was situated in the sector north of Walk, but because of its reduced strength its greatest danger was at Tartu.

On 21 August, the new heavy attacks of the Third Baltic Front against the left flank of the Eighteenth Army, and against the southern flank of *Armeeabteilung Narva*, began. The Fifty-fourth Army and the First Shock Army achieved no noteworthy success opposite the Eighteenth Army. The Sixty-seventh Army, however, succeeded in pushing through the weak security front of the Estonian units employed with *Armeeabteilung Narva*, using three rifle divisions heavily supported by tanks and ground-attack aircraft, and in breaking through toward Tartu. The army group ordered the *Armeeabteilung* to prevent an advance of the Russians north and northwest in the gap in the Eighteenth Army sector by means of flexible operation, and to hold the bridgehead at Tartu (23 August). To this end *Panzerverband Graf Strachwitz* was sent forward from the area east of Lake Virts toward the northeast in the direction of Tartu, with the intention of pushing into the rear of the enemy attack forces. It did not achieve a decisive success (24 August).

Instead, the Sixty-seventh Army, which was now quickly trying to exploit the original secondary operation by moving up reinforcements, managed to break through northward (west of Tartu) and subsequently to form a bridge-head across the Kma River. As a result, the left flank of the Eighteenth Army was again threatened with envelopment. This flank had meanwhile been able to frustrate all attempts of the enemy to force a breakthrough toward the southern tip of Lake Virts with ten rifle divisions, five tank units, a large number of ground-attack aircraft, and strong artillery forces. The army group thereupon decided to withdrawal the left flank of the Eighteenth Army to an intermediate line during the night of 24 August, and to the Walk position on the following nights, In this manner, new forces could speedily be freed for *Armeeabteilung Narva* (87th Infantry Division and *Panzerverband* Graf Strachwitz). The command of the Kma River front was consolidated by the assignment of the II Corps Headquarters from the front east of Walk.

Against *Armeeabteilung Narva* during these days, the Sixty-seventh Army had employed two rifle corps with seven divisions, supported by tanks and assault artillery. For days it had been faced, on a front of sixty kilometers, by a combat force fighting hard and flexible, whose backbone consisted of three weak German infantry battalions and one weak security regiments, in addi-tion to Estonian units and forces without combat value. West of the Tartu bridgehead stood only Estonian citizens' guard units. On 24 August, the *Armeeabteilung* believed it would be able to hold the Kma River position for a limited period with its forces and the additional forces promised to it, but also believed that a decisive attack upon Tallinn by the Russians was to be expected once they had moved up their artillery and completed their assem-bly. The *Armeeabteilung*, which had already greatly weakened its Narva front, would then be unable to decisively defend the Kma River position with its own forces for any length of time. After assignment of *Panzerverband* Graf Strachwitz, the position would have sufficient strength for long-range defense only if the large gaps in the front were closed by a newly moved-up German division, and if the presently employed forces were able to organize reserves.

The situation continued to deteriorate. On 25 August, Tartu was lost up to the Kma River, despite the brave resistance of the German soldiers. In addition, Soviet attack units managed to cross the Kma River northwest of the town in the strength of one to two divisions with tanks, and to form a bridgehead, which it was impossible to eliminate with the German forces available. On the following day, the northern part of Tartu was also lost, and the Russians were able to considerably enlarge their bridgehead northwest of the town.

On 25 August the overall situation of the army group underwent an-other critical aggravation.

In the old penetration zone north of the Daugava River, the Sixteenth Army had hitherto continued its counterattack. The Second Baltic Front, however, had by no means abandoned its intention of breaking through westward to Riga. It had rehabilitated the two attacking armies – the Third Shock Army and the Tenth Guards Army as well as the V Tank Corps – with new replacements, and had received further reinforcements, among them several units from the Narva and the Finnish fronts. On 25 August, the Second Baltic Front resumed its breakthrough attack on the boundary between the Sixteenth and Eighteenth Armies. Although the Sixteenth Army made every effort to bolster its endangered left flank, for example by dispatching a Tiger tank battalion to it, the shortage of men was again the greatest danger, particularly at the right flank of the Eighteenth Army. The only possibility of remedying this shortage for the time being was the withdrawal of the entire Eighteenth Army to the Walk position. The hope of the army group to receive the panzer corps promised by Hitler had not materialized so far.

The worsening of the situation north of the Daugava River and on the Kma River induced the army group to submit a situation estimate to Hitler. In its opinion, everything depended on furnishing new forces quickly to the army group or on making new decisions. Every hour lost augmented the danger.

But neither of the alternatives was accepted. Thus, the army group felt constrained to arrive at a decision on its own. On 20 August, it ordered the Eighteenth Army to withdraw its central sector to the Walk position, beginning on the following night, and completing the move by the morning of 28 August. In this movement, one division – the 122d Infantry Division – was to be freed and placed behind the right flank of the army, to be employed there in the event of an impending enemy breakthrough. On the same day, 26 August, the Second Baltic Front, attacking with eight divisions, tanks, and ground-attack aircraft, succeeded in breaking through the extreme right sector of the Eighteenth Army. Not before the afternoon could a holding line be organized. The left flank of the Sixteenth Army had to be bent backward to maintain the connection.

This development induced General Schörner to make a personal report to Hitler at the Führer's headquarters on 27 August. The mission of the army group was not changed. The practical result of the conference was the transfer of the 14th Panzer Division from the left sector of the Third Panzer Army to the area of the army group, and the promise of the 563d Grenadier Division and one further engineer battalion, of which at least one regiment and the divisional engineer battalion could be flown to the scene at once.

Although the Second Baltic Front, in the course of the battle which had been resumed on 25 August, had received considerable reinforcements from other sectors of the front – among them five divisions from the Narva front alone – it again failed to achieve the decisive breakthrough to Riga. The Eighteenth Army, which, on 28 August, resumed command of the extreme left sector of the Sixteenth Army, had withdrawn to the Walk position according to plan by morning of that day. It was in a position to start a counterattack on its right with the 122d Infantry Division, which had been freed by the withdrawal. On 30 August, the Second Baltic Front discontinued its futile attacks.

On the Kma River front, the extremely costly battles of the past days had exhausted the strength of the Sixty-seventh Army. The Luftwaffe, in particular, had contributed in inflicting very heavy losses upon its units. On 28 August, the Third Baltic Front discontinued its attacks, and shifted to the defensive. It made every effort to hold the bridgehead northwest of Tartu, into which it had meanwhile dispatched four divisions. Thereupon, the German defenders started a counterattack. The German command expected it to stabilize the situation on the Kma River. In heavy battles, which caused numerous losses on both sides, the Russian units were gradually pressed back. On 31 August, it was even possible to eliminate the enemy bridgehead northwest of Tartu. On a broad front, the 87th Infantry Division, which had been moved up a few days ago from the Eighteenth Army, reached the Kma River. Thereupon, the army group on 31 August ordered *Armeeabteilung Narva* to also eliminate the enemy bridgehead at Tartu by an attack from the northeast and east and south of the Kma River toward the west, in order to regain the Kma River position including the town of Tartu.

The defensive battles at Birzai, north of the Daugava River, and at Modohn as well as between Pskov, Walk, and Tartu, were at an end.

The Defensive Battle for Livonia and Estonia, The Retreating Engagements Toward the Riga Bridgehead, and the Baltic Islands (14-27 September 1944)

The STAVKA clung to the idea of clearing the Baltic countries of German troops. Army Group North, bruised but by no means defeated or smashed, constituted a constant menace to the planned Soviet operations from the central sector of the entire front against the General Government of Poland, and against East Prussia. This menace from the depth of the right flank first needed to be eliminated. In doing so, the Baltic ports would be freed of the enemy, the Baltic Fleet would obtain access to the Baltic Sea and could assume the protection of the depth of the right flank of the Soviet front. Accordingly, the Soviet command prepared a new large-scale attack against Army Group North.[2] The strategic objective was again encirclement and destruction of the northern sector of the German Eastern front.

The forces available for this operation were the armies and mobile corps of the four Soviet fronts previously employed in the northern sector, to which, in the course of the battle, major reinforcements from other fronts were added.[3] The First Baltic Front, under the command of Army General Bagramyan, received the mission of forcing a breakthrough from the Bauska area to Riga, the vital nerve of the German defense, and thus once again to encircle Army Group North. To this end, it employed two armies on its extreme right – the Fourth Shock Army and especially the Forty-third Army, which was reinforced by assignment of the III Guards Mechanized Corps and the "Strategic Force of Mortar Units." At the same time the bulk of its tank units between Siauliai and Dobele were still at the disposal of the First Baltic Front both for defense against a German attack on the left flank of Army Group Center, and for a thrust in a western or northwestern direction.

The Second and Third Baltic Fronts, under the command of Army Generals Yeremenko and Maslennikov, again received the task of splitting up the German front by means of simultaneous attacks from the areas west of Modohn and Walk, and of encircling and destroying the individual *kampfgruppen* after having pushed them away from the major ports. For this purpose, the Second Baltic Front again formed a very strong point of main effort with the Third Shock Army, the Tenth Guards Army, and the V Tank Corps. The Third Baltic Front considerably strengthened its point of main effort south of Lake Virts by moving the Sixty-seventh Army from the Kma River front west, and employing this army south of Lake Virts immediately right of the First Shock Army.

The Leningrad Front, under the command of Marshal Govorov, received the mission of fighting its way into the depth of the Estonian territory, with its left flank advancing from the Tartu sector in a piecemeal attack after the large-scale attack on the other sectors had begun, in order to separate the German Narva front from the rest of the front, push it away from the ports, and destroy it. For this purpose it had disengaged the Second Shock Army from the Narva Front – after this army had turned over its sector to the Eighth Army – and with it had taken over the old sector of the Sixty-seventh Army on both sides of Tartu. Very strong air forces, which were reinforced by units assigned from other fronts, such as the Crimea, were available for the main points of attack.

The mission of Army Group North had remained unchanged. It consisted of defending the position it held. This mission was maintained even after the military and political reasons for it had vanished.

The large-scale Soviet offensive on the Finnish front, which had begun in June, had broken the resistance of the Finnish ally. Hence, on 25 August, the Finnish Government had addressed a query to Moscow through Stockholm as to the conditions of an armistice, a conclusion of peace, or both. On 29 August it received the answer, given in concurrence with the United States and Great Britain, that a prerequisite for such negotiations was the rupture of relations with Germany and the departure of German troops from Finland within two weeks (but no later that 15 September), or else disarmament and "extradition" of the German troops. The ultimatum handed over by the Soviet Union on 1 September expired at 2400 hours on the following day. Thus, the Finnish Diet felt obliged on 2 September to accept a proposal by the government to fulfill these terms, and to make the public statement demanded by the Allies. Thereupon, Minister President Mackzell said in a radio address, that Germany was expected to prove itself a comrade-in-arms by recognizing the desire to have the German troops leave, and by complying with the aforementioned terms. The Finnish foreign minister pointed out to the German ambassador that owing to several years of comradeship-in-arms, the government of Finland hoped for a sympathetic understanding on the German side of the difficulties under which it was striving to ensure future freedom for Finland (2 September). In the morning of 4 September, hostilities ceased along the entire Finnish front.

The loss of Finland did not induce Hitler to change the mission for Army Group North. On the contrary, he pointed out that the political significance of holding the present main line of resistance of the army group remained. The point was to encourage those Finns who did not wish to follow the government's course, and also to influence the political attitude of Sweden. The army group, therefore, opened a collecting point for Finnish volunteers in the vicinity of Tallinn. It was unsuccessful. Hitler made allowance for these considerations by ordering, on 12 September, the execution of Operation "TANNE."

The Island of Hogland, situated in the Gulf of Finland between the Estonian and Finnish coast, together with the mines sown by the Navy, constituted the protection of the left flank of Army Group North. The island was occupied by Finnish troops. A previous offer by the army group to par-

ticipate in the occupation of the island had been refused for political reasons. With the surrender of Finland, the danger arose that the island would
be occupied by Soviet troops, and thus would constitute an extraordinary
menace to the left flank of Army Group North. To eliminate this menace,
Rear Admiral Burchardi, received orders from Hitler to carry out Operation
"TANNE," in other words, to gain possession of the island. For this purpose, elements of the 23d Infantry Division, stationed on the Baltic Islands,
were assigned to the Navy. The landing operation, which was undertaken in
the morning of 15 September, ended in complete failure. A fight took place
with the Finnish garrison of the island, whose commander, contrary to expectations, did not "cooperate," and considerable losses were the result. The
absurdity of this operation is evident alone from the fact that on the following day the withdrawal of the Narva front was ordered, so that the German
troops – even if Operation "TANNE" had been successful – would have had
to be again picked up at once.

The opinion of the General Guderian in estimating the situation of Army
Group North did not agree with that held by Hitler. In the former's opinion,
an evacuation of the Baltic countries could not be avoided in the long run;
besides, the units of the army group would certainly very soon be needed at
other points on the Eastern front. He endeavored to convince Hitler of the
necessity of evacuating the Baltic countries. By way of precaution, General
Guderian issued oral orders to the army group on 5 September to make
preparations for the execution of this decision on all sectors, within the scope
of the Wehrmacht authority held by General Schörner, stating that every
minute that passed without being utilized was lost. Since the army group
had, some time before, prepared the withdrawal in the form of a map exercise (code name "KÖNIGSBERG," later "ASTER"), preparations for its
execution could begin immediately.

The "ASTER" map exercise was concerned with the withdrawal of the
army group to the Wendish position. According to the final version, it was
the task of the Sixteenth Army to hold the present main line of resistance
against the heavy enemy attacks to be expected on the entire army front, and
especially against a breakthrough attempt on the "land bridge" to the north,
or in the Jelgava-Bauska sector toward Riga. The Eighteenth Army was to
hold its present front against enemy attacks until *Armeeabteilung Narva* had
reached the Estonian western position, and was then to withdraw speedily to
the Wendish position. *Armeeabteilung Narva*, beginning with the withdrawal
of the Narva front on the third day (according to "ASTER"), and while bending the southern and Peipus fronts back in time, was to retreat to the Esto-

nian western position with the greatest possible speed. From this time on, the *Armeeabteilung* was to be under the control of the Eighteenth Army. On the roads leading westward, the *Armeeabteilung* had to retard the advance of the enemy toward Tallinn and the ports on the western coast of Estonia by means of a sufficiently strong *kampfgruppe*. Troops and refugees from these ports were to be shipped to the Baltic islands. On "ASTER" day, General Grasser was named Wehrmacht Administrative Commander for the Eastern Countries, with authority over the three branches of the Wehrmacht, the Waffen SS, the civil administration, the police, and Organization Todt.[4] For the conduct of operations of the *Armeeabteilung*, everything depended on preventing an encircling maneuver in pursuit by the enemy by means of speed of mobile detachments, rear guards, and flank security parties, and thoroughly prepared obstructions and demolitions at points of main effort, and providing protection for the open northern flank.

Luflötte One was to support the defensive battle at the stationary front of the army group as well as flexible conduct of operations by fighter and ground-attack plane action at the points of main effort. It was to undertake continuous reconnaissance, and was particularly to protect the traffic bottlenecks in and around Riga by means of flak forces.

Rear Admiral Burchardi was requested to keep the available offensive forces ready to repulse an enemy landing launched in an encircling maneuver in pursuit of the *Armeeabteilung*, to employ security forces for the surveillance of the endangered sea areas, and to ensure the evacuation of troops, materiel and refugees from the western ports of Estonia between Paernu and Tallin.

Preparation for the troop movements required three days; the orderly evacuation of the materiel which could be salvaged, three to four weeks; withdrawal to the Estonian western position (roughly 210 kilometers by air), approximately twelve days; from the present main line of resistance to the Wendish position (roughly 350 kilometers by air), approximately twenty-one days. Under the most favorable circumstances the army group believed itself to be able to save a maximum of three days for the entire movement. With the arrival in the Wendish position, new plans for further operations would have to be prepared.

Although the military and political situation in the eastern Baltic Sea had changed fundamentally as a result of the surrender of Finland, General Guderian – pressed for a basic decision by Army Group North – despite all his efforts could not obtain an order for the execution of the withdrawal.

When the enemy attacks subsided during the last days of August, the army group advanced the opinion that either the land bridge had to be expanded so that both railroads from Riga toward the west could be used, or permission had to be granted to abandon the Baltic countries. But neither decision was made, although as mentioned above General Guderian exerted himself in favor of the latter decision.

As well as possible under the circumstances, the army group used the intermission which had occurred in the fighting to restore order in its units, and to bolster the sectors threatened by the new Soviet points of main attack which were clearly taking shape. In view of the change of the situation in the Gulf of Finland – caused by Finland's surrender – and in view of a potential execution of Operation "ASTER" it caused the depleted 23d Infantry Division to be withdrawn from the right sector of the Eighteenth Army, and to be shifted to the Baltic Islands to protect the latter.[5]

The few reserves at the disposal of the army group, which had now been moved to the enemy points of main attack which had been identified, appeared in no way sufficient. On 10 September, the Sixteenth Army therefore, realizing the weakness of its infantry, and in view of the anticipated strong Soviet attacks against the land bridge on both sides of Bauska and against the right sector of the Eighteenth Army (in other words into the depth of its own left flank), requested the assignment of one division, one personnel replacement transfer battalion for each division of the I Corps deployed at Bauska, reinforcement of the GHQ artillery, and the moving up of mortars. The army correctly pointed out the importance of its mission within the overall operation of Army Group North. Thereupon the army group had the Eighteenth Army disengage the 263d Infantry Division, which it then assigned to the Sixteenth Army for employment in the zone of main effort of the I Corps. In so doing, the Eighteenth Army made use of the permission granted it to withdraw its front to the Tirza position. On the morning of 13 September, this movement was completed.

In addition, the army group provided the Sixteenth Army with heavy artillery and sufficient ammunition for employment on the land bridge. To induce the Soviet command to draw off its forces from the point of main effort at Bauska, the OKH on 13 September ordered Army Group Center to prepare an attack from the Siauliai area and south thereof, and to consider disengaging another panzer division. By way of precaution, Army Group North was ordered to speedily fortify the Lielupe River position facing east, and another position on both sides of Tukums, as well as along the boundary between the army groups.

With superior forces and tremendous amounts of materiel, the Red

Army started its large-scale attack against Army Group North on 14 September with six to eight rifle divisions and two tank units in the anticipated areas near Bauska; with eighteen rifle divisions, elements of the V Tank Corps, and elements of four to five other tank units west of Modohn; and with thirteen rifle divisions north of Walk. Deploying its last reserves, and ruthlessly stripping the sections of the front that had not been attacked, the army group managed to prevent a decisive breakthrough by the Soviets on the first two days of the attack. But there were numerous penetrations, some of which it was possible to seal off only in an emergency fashion.

North of Bauska, the situation took a most critical turn. Although it was possible to prevent a breakthrough toward Riga, it was not possible to build a continuous blocking line. Weak Soviet forces were able to push north beyond the Jelgava eastern position. It was known that strong forces were following behind the leading enemy elements. An enemy success in the direction of Riga was bound to tremendously aggravate the overall situation of the army group.

In the penetration zone west of Modohn, further substantial successes by the Soviets were prevented only by the action of the 14th Panzer Division and reinforcements moved up from other sectors. Nevertheless, on the evening of the second day of the attack, the Russians managed to achieve a narrow, deep penetration, which did not permit the immediate disengagement of the "emergency unit" of the army group, the 14th Panzer Division. Attacks with forces concentrated locally, north of this point of main effort, tied down additional German troops.

On the left flank of the Eighteenth Army, the Soviets were able to establish a bridgehead south of Lake Virts, which they continually reinforced. It could be foreseen that an enemy breakthrough at this point would force the German troops to withdraw from the lake, and in the further course of the battle would result in the separation of *Armeeabteilung Narva* from the army group.

The German troops fought bravely to the point of self-sacrifice against an enemy who outnumbered them several times, employed immense amounts of materiel, and who was supported by ground-attack aircraft in previously unknown strength. Losses among the infantry divisions committed at the point of main effort amounted from one third to one half of the combat strengths employed even during the first two days. At Bauska, there were heavy losses of materiel in the artillery, which maintained its positions up to the last. Substantial relief was again brought by the units of *Luftflotte* One.[6]

The army group anticipated that the attacks of the Soviets would continue for some time with unabated force. The enemy had sufficient reserves at his disposal in all the sectors of main effort to feed the attacks. In addition, it expected heavy attacks to begin during the next days at Dobele against the extreme right sector of the Sixteenth Army and at Tartu against the southern front of *Armeeabteilung Narva*. All available reserves – and large additional numbers of engineers, construction engineers, and *alarmeinheiten* – had already been committed. The stripping of sectors of the front which were not under attack had reached the extreme limit. The decrease of the combat strengths of the infantry made itself especially felt, since the amply forested combat territory required a great many men. Long-term feeding of the battle at the focal points of defense was impossible.

As a result of this situation, on 15 September – the second day of the attack – the commanding general of the army group requested that General Guderian try to obtain an immediate order for Operation "ASTER" before the danger of a split of the army group made its execution impossible. The defensive battle of the army groups had become a fight for existence; unless it was withdrawn at the last moment, it was doomed to be destroyed. In response to an oral report by General Schörner, Hitler resolved, on 16 September, to issue the order for the withdrawal of the army group to the Wendish position – with the significant limitation that the order might be rescinded within two days.

A prerequisite for a successful withdrawal was that, for the time being, the Sixteenth and Eighteenth Armies held their positions. The Sixteenth Army, for instance, was defending the main supply artery of the army group south or Riga. If the Russian First Baltic Front here achieved the desired breakthrough to Riga with the Forty-third Army, elements of the Fourth Shock Army and the III Guards Mechanized Corps, the army group would be thrown back to coast north of Riga and destroyed, since an attempt at embarkation on the flat beach was bound to spell disaster. By the second day of attack, the Soviets had been able to press back part of the German units committed at Bauska to the Jelgava eastern position, and even to break through them at one point.

On the basis of the permission granted by Hitler to move into the Wendish position, on the evening of 16 September the army group ordered the Sixteenth and Eighteenth Armies to withdraw to the Jelgava eastern position, the Daugava line, and to the northern part of the Wendish position by the morning of 18 September. As a result of this movement, it became possible to free a few forces for the I Corps, which was struggling hard at Bauska, and these forces the army was able to move up speedily from the extreme left of the army, since it had recognized that the enemy was shifting the Fourth Shock Army employed there to the point of main attack of the Forty-third Army and the III Guards Mechanized Corps. The Sixteenth Army, to which the 14th Panzer Division was dispatched after 17 September, received orders to stop the enemy attack in the Jelgava eastern position, and to close the already existing gap by means of an attack. The move into this position constituted the last chance of withdrawal for the Sixteenth Army.

The situation south of Riga also remained exceedingly strained in the following days. It was typical of the extremely intense battles that the weak German infantry was helplessly exposed to the enemy fire and enemy air raids because of its lack of ammunition and aircraft fuel. Nevertheless, it was possible to prevent the enemy breakthrough to Riga. On 12 September, however, another critical deterioration of the situation arose. Concentrating their units, some of which had been newly moved to the scene, the Soviets managed to extend their breakthrough considerably toward the north. A decisive thrust to the Daugava River, on the other had, was again denied them this time. With the first elements of the 11th SS *"Nordland"* Panzergrenadier Division, which had been withdrawn from the Narva front in the "ASTER" movement on that day, the enemy was halted. But the army group felt it necessary to also commit, south of Riga, the 11th Infantry Division, which was just returning from Estonia. With the employment of these divisions – under the command of the III SS Panzer Corps, the danger to the life-thread of the army group could be regarded as removed for the time being.

The situation of the Sixteenth Army was rendered difficult by the fact that for some time it had had reason to expect heavy enemy attacks from the Dobele area against its extreme right flank, and against the land bridge. Here the First Baltic Front had formed a new point of main attack with the Sixth Guards Army, the Fifty-first Army, and strong tank forces. To relieve the Sixteenth Army and draw the enemy attack forces at Dobele south, units of the XXXIX Panzer Corps of the Third Panzer Army had been attacking south thereof in the direction of Jelgava since 16 September. According to the order that the OKH issued on 20 September regarding the further operations of Army Group Center, the Third Panzer Army had the mission of waging battle in the zone of attack of the XXXIX Panzer Corps, meanwhile tenaciously holding its defensive front, and of smashing and tying down very strong enemy forces, and thus facilitating the defensive battle of the Sixteenth Army. On 21 September, the Third Panzer Army was assigned to Army Group North.

As had the First Baltic Front at Bauska, the Second and Third Baltic

Fronts fell short of achieving a decisive breakthrough at Modohn and Walk. No fewer than twenty rifle divisions of the Third Shock Army and the Tenth Guards Army, as well as six tank units, conducted the attack in the Modohn area, and fourteen rifle divisions and five tank units of the First Shock Army and the Sixty-seventh Army in the Walk area. Simultaneously with the left flank of the Sixteenth Army, the right flank of the Eighteenth Army had withdrawn to the northern part of the Wendish position during the evening of 16 September and the morning of 18 September. Although the Second Baltic Front had been employing the V Tank Corps since 17 September, it did not manage, during the following days, to achieve any success beyond some minor penetrations. The attempts to break through to the west were frustrated in very heavy fighting.

The decisive task of the Eighteenth Army was to ensure the retreat of *Armeeabteilung Narva*, set for 16 September, by holding its left flank firmly in its present positions at Lake Virts. Withdrawal from the southern tip of the lake was bound to result in certain destruction of the *Armeeabteilung*. With newly assigned forces, supported by continuous ground-attack air actions, the Soviets managed on 17 September to thrust through the blocking position built there, and to throw back the weak German troops, which had continued to fight only in strongpoints and around the command posts. The army did not consider it possible to maintain contact with Lake Virts on the following day, and hence requested permission to withdrawal its left to Lake Vels. The army group had to refuse this request. It dispatched to the left flank of the army the advance elements of *Armeeabteilung Narva*, which had been motorized in an emergency fashion, and ordered them to remain in contact with Lake Virts, and to prevent a thrust by the enemy in the direction of Fellin or westward, since such a thrust might endanger the movements of the *Armeeabteilung*. Thus the army had to resist for at least three long days the breakthrough attempts which the enemy conducted with massed forces, until the troops of *Armeeabteilung Narva* had been pulled through from the Narva Front. The heavy defensive battle of the army was characterized by the waning combat strength of the infantry caused by losses and fatigue; the adverse ammunition situation which became more and more critical with every passing day; and the limited extent of the territory in which the army had to operate. In the north there was no chance of withdrawing; in the south there was only a slight chance. On 19 September, the army reported that by 22 or 23 September its artillery ammunition would be exhausted. After that it would have to march!

On 16 September, Hitler had ordered the army group to withdraw to the Wendish position. The movement from the Narva front to this position led over a distance of 350 kilometers, and according to schedule was to have been completed in twenty-one days. The beginning was set for 19 September. All along, the army group was aware that a withdrawal undertaken in this form would not influence the situation at Riga. The course of events on the southern flank of the *Armeeabteilung*, and on the Kma River front, however, necessitated another schedule and a considerable acceleration of the operation.

Here the Leningrad Front had started to attack northward, north and east of Tartu on 17 September. Greatly superior forces – nine rifle divisions and three to four tank units – supported by ground-attack planes in great numbers, were committed by the Second Shock Army. East of Tartu, the XXX Guards Rifle Corps, supported by a tank unit, succeeded in breaking through the thinly occupied German lines, and in bringing about the collapse of the entire front of the Estonians employed there, whose battleworthiness was limited. It was out of the question for the weak German forces to stop the advance of a whole enemy army into the depth of Estonian territory. It was to be expected that the Second Shock Army would push into the flank of the German troops withdrawing from the Narva front split up *Armeeabteilung Narva*. Thus the army group saw itself faced with the decision of leading the *Armeeabteilung* back to Tallinn – which would have meant the loss of the entire stocks of equipment and very likely also of large numbers of troops (especially that of the II Corps employed on the Kma River front) – or of ordering the entire III SS Panzer Corps, employed on the Narva front, to mount their vehicles and move at one stroke through Paernu toward the south, and the II Corps to make a speedy turn around the northern tip of Lake Virts. The army group decided in favor of the latter solution. On 17 September, it ordered *Armeeabteilung Narva* to bring as far as Paernu the III SS Panzer Corps in a continuous motorized movement from the evening of 18 September to 20 September, as well as the trains and horse-drawn elements to Tallinn or – depending on the transport situation – the Baltic islands. The infantry of the 11th Infantry Division was to be included in the motorized movement up to the last man. The II Corps was to be withdrawn speedily around the northern tip of Lake Virts, and to the Estonian western position.

On the evening of 18 September, the withdrawal of *Armeeabteilung Narva* from the Narva front began abruptly, and in one stroke. Although a certain amount of industrial and other commodities had been removed from Estonia during the past months, such measures had had to be limited in order not to alarm the Estonian population. In all the measures taken, allowance had to made to maintain the morale of the Estonian troops, since they had to hold the larger part of the front in Estonia, and keep the population well-disposed in order that the present state of order and security behind the front, which was undisturbed by partisan activities, might be maintained. A large majority of the Estonian soldiers of the 20th SS Waffen Grenadier Division and in the frontier guard regiments, however, no longer possessed the necessary will to resist. The Estonian citizens' guard units were utterly unreliable, according to the experience gained in the battles at Walk and Tartu. Hence, at the Narva front the *Armeeabteilung* had already embarked upon a policy of reorganizing the Estonian units as German-Estonian *kampfgruppen*. Thus no actual evacuation in the economic field had been undertaken.

At the beginning of the month, the army group had point out to the *Armeeabteilung* that the three weeks considered necessary by the latter for a systematic evacuation would under no circumstances be available. As a result, a large part of the population would not be evacuated, the livestock would not be moved away, and a large number of other measures would not be carried out. During the period 1-15 September, only 4,500 Estonians had let themselves be evacuated to Germany. But it was estimated that approximately 100,000 Estonians would be able to escape the Red Army by fleeing west during the withdrawal.

In the northern sector of the Narva front, the Coastal Defense Staff, Tallinn, received orders as *Kampfgruppe* Gerok to retard an enemy advance on Tallinn from the east and southeast through delaying action, and to defend Tallinn and Paldiski until the evacuation was completed. *Kampfgruppe* Gerok, consisting of units of the Navy, Estonians, GHQ troops, elements of the 11th Infantry Division, and the III SS Panzer Corps, withdrew systematically to Tallinn in a leap-frog movement, while fighting a delaying action.[7] The movement lasted three days over three intermediate lines, and along the Rakvere-Tallinn road, and by the morning of 22 September the *Kampfgruppe* had embarked at Tallinn, after all agencies and supply installations had been transported away, and all strategic installations had been destroyed. The motorized and horse-drawn vehicles which were no longer need had previously been assembled into columns and dispatched to Paernu, on order to be shipped over to the Baltic islands.

In accordance with its order, the III SS Panzer Corps withdrew west from the Narva front on the evening of 18 September, and led its two motorized units, the 11th SS *"Nordland"* Panzergrenadier Division and the 4th SS

"Nederland" Panzergrenadier Brigade, the motorized GHQ troops, and the 11th Infantry Division (which had been motorized in a makeshift fashion), through Estonia and back to Paernu in one movement. The 4th SS *"Nederland"* Panzergrenadier Brigade received orders to protect the bridgehead at Paernu in such a manner that use of the port remained possible for the loading of valuable items that were being evacuated. The 11th SS *"Nordland"* Panzergrenadier Division was, as mentioned above, dispatched to the Sixteenth Army for employment in the area south of Riga. The 11th Infantry Division led its units, although they were poorly motorized, into the assembly area southeast of Paernu in an exemplary motorized movement. After the evening of 2 September, elements of the division arrived continually. As far as possible, the horsedrawn elements of the division had previously been dispatched to the assembly area on 17 September. In view of the fact that the combat elements of the division were disengaging themselves quickly from contact with the enemy on 19 September, the march group had to endeavor to place some distance between themselves and the possibly pursuing enemy as fast as possible, and at the same time it had to avert a threat to its flank from the left – from the Tartu area where the Soviets had achieved their breakthrough. In 19 and 20 September, the endangered area had, therefore, to be crossed in a speedy forced march. By morning of 20 September, the horsedrawn elements of the division had succeeded in doing so, after a daily maximum performance of 126 kilometers, Despite the haste and despite the immense effort, the progress, order, and discipline of the march remained faultless up to the time of junction with the division. On the morning of 22 September, the East Prussian 11th Infantry Division moved by motor transportation into the Riga area, to be employed in the Sixteenth Army area.

To move southwest the troops employed in the right sector of the Narva front (300th Special Administrative Division with four Estonian frontier guard regiments and the 20th Estonian Waffen SS Grenadier Division), *Stab* Höfer was formed (headquarters of the 300th Special Administrative Division).[8] With the beginning of the withdrawal, the *kampfgruppe* was assigned to the II Corps, which was employed on the Kma River front. On the afternoon of 18 September, it received orders to shake off the enemy by moving with the utmost speed. At the same time everything depended upon pulling through the *kampfgruppe* from east to west before the enemy started to press north from the Kma River front. The protection of the left flank from the forces of the Second Shock Army, which had broken through from the Kma River front northward, and which consisted of two rifle corps and three tank units, was to be assumed by elements of the II Corps withdrawing from the Kma River front.

Nevertheless, the Soviet units succeeded in overcoming the weak German covering parties from the south and in blocking the retreat route. As a result, the bulk of the Estonian frontier guard regiments and elements of the 20th SS Estonian Waffen Grenadier Division were cut off, and to the extent that they had not already disbanded themselves of their own accord, they were crushed. The horsedrawn artillery, which had covered 120 kilometers in thirty-six hours in forced marches, managed to escape the enemy's strangle hold in time. The II Corps had drawn *Kampfgruppe* Höfer into its right flank by the morning of 21 September, and speedily withdrew it southward to the Estonian western position during the following two days. On 21 September, *Armeeabteilung Narva* was placed under the command of the Eighteenth Army.

Up to this point, the withdrawal of *Armeeabteilung Narva* had been successful. The development of the overall situation of the army group, however, drifted toward disaster. In the Dobele area, on the extreme right of the army group, the attack of the First Baltic Front with two armies and heavy tank forces was, it appeared, immediately impending. South of Riga the Soviets achieved a deep breakthrough toward the north. In the right sector of the Eighteenth Army, they managed to make a large number of deep penetrations; on the evening of 21 September only a disconnected line composed of battery positions and command posts existed here. At the eastern front of the army, the Soviet command had by now recognized the intentions of its enemy.

To cut off the German troops withdrawing from Estonia, the Third Baltic Front shifted its point of main effort to the main highways from Pskov to Riga, and from Walk to Nolmar, and fed its heavy attacks at these points by continuous assignment of fresh forces. On 22 September, using greatly superior units, it forced a deep breakthrough west of Walk through the thinly occupied German front, which consisted only of strongpoints. This breakthrough jeopardized the further movements of *Armeeabteilung Narva*. Forces needed to restore the situation were lacking. An extreme speed-up of the further withdrawal became necessary. The attempt to withdraw the II Corps of *Armeeabteilung Narva* in time toward the southwest, and maintain contact with the left flank of the Eighteenth Army, succeeded. The 4th SS *"Nederland"* Panzergrenadier Brigade abandoned Paernu, and was employed opposite the enemy breakthrough in the central sector of the Eighteenth Army (23 September). Greatly outnumbered by the enemy, without sufficient ammunition, helplessly exposed to the enemy air force for lack of aviation fuel, the German troops offered heroic resistance.

On the basis of the development of the situation on 23 September, Hitler had ordered the army to continue the withdrawal beyond the Wendish position into the Segewold position. This position was to be defended decisively, and the southern part of this position – which was at present in the hands of the enemy – was to be recaptured.

The infantry divisions which became available, especially those of the Eighteenth Army, including *Armeeabteilung Narva*, were to immediately replace the panzer divisions of the Third Panzer Army, and be assembled for an offensive operation aimed at destroying the enemy forces in the salient southwest of Jelgava, while at the same time capturing the shortest route between Siauliai and the Segewold position. The simultaneous attack of an infantry force from the area north of Bauska was envisaged.

In accordance with the order from Hitler, on 23 September the army group issued a directive to continue the withdrawal to the Segewold position. The mission of the Third Panzer Army (which in view of the subsequent offensive operation had been assigned to Army Group North since 21 September) and that of the Sixteenth Army was to hold their present positions. In addition, the latter was to narrow down the penetration zone south of Riga by means of attacks, to ensure the orderly flow of the troops withdrawing from the area north of the Daugava River through the Riga-Sloka traffic bottleneck to Courland, and to prepare itself to assume command of the entire front north of the Daugava River upon conclusion of the withdrawal to the Segewold position. The left flank of the army had to be withdrawn with the Eighteenth Army – the latter out of the present movement – to the Segewold position while maintaining the continuity of the front. This position and the Baltic islands were to be defended decisively. Rear Admiral Burchardi was requested to keep ready his offensive forces for defense against an enemy landing on the Baltic islands, on the coast of the Gulf of Riga, or on the Courland front. He was to employ naval security forces to protect the endangered areas of the sea now under surveillance, to reinforce the the coastal defense on the Baltic islands with a point of main effort in the Koop Sound and on the Irban road, and to ensure the evacuation of materiel and refugees from the Baltic islands, and from Riga in direct concurrence with Army agencies.

Surprisingly, the First Baltic Front discontinued its attacks south of Riga, first with the Forty-third Army on 24 September, and on the following day with the Fourth Shock Army. It relaxed its point of main effort there, and –

as the German command learned – shifted part of its attack units toward the west. Army Group North at once followed this movement which, as it seemed, was headed for the Dobele area by ending the engagements aimed at obtaining a suitable main line of resistance, and causing the 11th SS *"Nordland"* Panzergrenadier Division of the III SS Panzer Corps to be disengaged and employed in the Dobele area with the 4th SS *"Nederland"* Panzergrenadier Brigade, which had meanwhile become available at the Eighteenth Army. In addition, it inserted the headquarters of *Armeeabteilung Narva*, redesignated as *Armeeabteilung* Grasser, at this point of main effort as a tactical operations staff. The *Armeeabteilung* received the mission to hold the present main line of resistance against the large-scale enemy attack to be expected in a few days and thus to keep open the overland bridge of Tukums.

Even opposite the Eighteenth Army, the Soviets did not after all achieve decisive success. On the right flank, it was possible to occupy the Segewold position according to schedule. Although the Third Baltic Front, as mentioned above, had achieved a deep breakthrough northeast of Nolmar on 22 September, and continued its strong tank advance on the following day, the Eighteenth Army – decisively supported by units of *Luftflötte* One, managed to maintain a loose continuity of the front, and on the whole to continue the movements according to plan. Attended with heavy battles, the withdrawals also progressed according to schedule during the following days; in some cases, of course, the troops had to fight their way back into their own lines. Although the Soviets pressed hard in pursuit with motorized and tank forces, the army was able to move into the Segewold position as planned.

On the morning of 27 September, the army group had reached the Segewold position. Thus the withdrawal ordered on 15 September, and begun on 18 September, was terminated. Made necessary by the Soviet successes in the course of the large-scale attack started on 14 September, the operation had been begun prematurely owing to the breakthrough of the Second Shock Army on the Kma River front. From 17 September on, *Armeeabteilung Narva* was threatened with the danger of being cut off south of Lake Virts. Neither here nor south of Riga and west of Modohn – where the Soviet command strove to achieve a major strategic solution – did its fronts and armies attain the desired success. The breakthrough attempted with a total of 101 rifle divisions, two tank corps, one mechanized corps, at least eighteen independent tank units, and a large number of assault gun regiments, had been denied it. The personnel and materiel losses of the Soviets were high; more than one thousand tanks had been shot out of action. The units of *Luftflötte* One had a very great share in the success of the withdrawal, and in repulsing the enemy attack. The days on which they could not fly for lack of fuel saw the ground troops helplessly exposed to the very strong air forces of the enemy.

The premature beginning and tremendous speed-up of the withdrawal had made high demands also on the Navy. The evacuation shipments from the major ports of Tallinn and Paldiski began on 17 September and were completed on 22 September. During the period of 17-25 September, units under Rear Admiral Burchardi shipped a total of 37,831 soldiers, 13,049 wounded, 20,418 evacuees, and 931 prisoners of war out of Estonian ports. Out of Tallinn alone they shipped roughly 60,000 persons, using twenty-one transports, fourteen merchant ships, and numerous warships; from Paldiski, 10,165 persons, using six military transports. In addition, they shipped roughly 28,000 tons of materiel out of Tallinn. By means of bombing and torpedo attacks, units of the Red Fleet sought to prevent the evacuation. The losses which these attacks inflicted on the German shipments, however, amounted only to a total of 600 men, that is about nine percent of the total number of persons who embarked in Tallinn and Paldiski. During the same period, 17-25 September, the following numbers of men, animals, and materiel were shipped from the continent to the Baltic islands: 22,500 prisoners of war, 16,500 persons, 520 cattle, and 1,000 vehicles. These shipments were carried out in landing craft of the Navy, coastal fish cutters, engineering vessels, and barges of the Army Sea Transportation Battalion from the ports of Rohaukuela and order across the Koop Sound. Evacuation and transportation by the units of the Navy was fully successful.

Once in the Segewold position, Army Group North had reached its terminal position; it was to be defended decisively. The Führer had expressly ordered that Riga be held. The army group, on the other hand, had from the beginning been against holding this position. General Schörner had pointed out to General Guderian as early as 19 September that in view of the present materiel superiority of the Soviet infantry the Segewold position could not be defended successfully in the long run, and that the purpose of its occupation – the disengagement of the mobile forces of the Third Panzer Army for the planned offensive operation – had not been achieved, since the German "divisions" were no more than weak *kampfgruppen.*[9] Maintenance of an expanded bridgehead around Riga was also deprecated by the army group. On 25 September the army group reported to the OKH that the considerable decrease of the combat strengths of almost all divisions of the Sixteenth and Eighteenth Armies (as a result of the successfully waged ten-day defensive battle in conjunction with materiel losses) rendered a saving of effective forces after occupation of the Segewold position impossible. Nor did it seem certain that this position could be held against the anticipated large-scale attack, aside from the fact that a holding of the position depended upon infantry reinforcement of the right sector of the Sixteenth Army, and on the occupation of the Baltic islands, for which no forces were available. Moreover, sufficient forces were not available to eliminate the penetration zone south of Riga, which was a prerequisite for the holding of the Segewold position.

In the opinion of the army group, only the Aa or the Tukums positions could be considered as a holding line after the evacuation of Riga. Nevertheless, this report of the army group resulted in the decision that the Segewold position was to be held under all circumstances. At least the OKH achieved the evacuation of Riga accelerated. Roughly 100,000 tons had to be shipped out, an action requiring three weeks. Again the army group pointed out that the Segewold position would not be able to hold against a serious attack, and that then there would no longer be a chance of withdrawing its forces systematically as it had been possible to do so far. On 27 September, General Schörner emphasized, in a discussion with General Wenck, (who was himself convinced of the necessity of a broad solution) that it was impossible to hold the bridgehead, to repulse the still-anticipated attack against the bridgehead, and to undertake an offensive operation.

NOTES

[1] The author here omits mention of the fact that the First Baltic Front received, for this operation, the support of four Soviet Air Armies, the 3d, 13th, 14th, and 15th. Haupt, *Kurland*, p. 11.

[2] For this offensive the Soviets employed 900,000 men in 125 rifle divisions and seven fortress brigades; 17,480 guns; 3,080 AFVs in five tank or mechanized corps; and 2640 Aircraft. Haupt, *Kurland*, p. 11.

[3] *Fremde Heer Ost* reported on 3 September 1944 that the Soviets had considerable quantities of strategic reinforcement available for this offensive. There were four armies with thirty-two rifle divisions, eight rifle brigades, twelve independent tank units, and thirteen assault gun regiments facing the Finns above Leningrad; ten rifle divisions, six rifle brigades, four tank units, and five assault gun regiments north of Lake Ladoga but preparing to be released to operations against either the Twentieth Mountain Army or Army Group North; and fifteen rifle divisions, two rifle brigades, eight tank units, and eight assault gun regiments already committed to move into the Baltic. Helmuth Forwick, *"Der Rückzug der Heeresgruppe Nord*

nach Kurland," in Hans Meier-Welcker, ed., *Abwehrkämpfe am Nordflügel der Ostfront, 1944-1945.* (Stuttgart: Deutsche Verlags-Anstalt, 1963), pp. 181.

[4] Note in original: "Paramilitary organization of the Nazi party, auxiliary to the Wehrmacht."

[5] The much depleted 23rd Infantry Division, under the command of Lieutenant General Hans Schirmer, was reinforced by the remnants of Assault Gun Brigade 202; Army Coastal Artillery Regimental Staff 1006; Army Artillery Battalions 289 and 810; Naval Artillery Battalion 530; and Naval Flak Battalion 239. Haupt, *Kurland,* p. 50.

[6] The artillery of the I Corps had not been especially strong at the beginning of the fight. The corps reported an artillery strength on 15 September of four light and seven heavy field howitzers in the 290th Infantry Division; twelve light field howitzers in the 215th Infantry Division; four heavy field howitzers in Army Heavy Artillery Battalion 814; and two 210mm mortars in Army Artillery Battalion 636. That the corps gave a solid account of itself in this battle is evidenced by the 240 Soviet tanks destroyed by its subordinate units. Luftwaffe support—both fighters and flak—accounted for the destruction of at least 150 Russian aircraft. This was not achieved without the cost, however, of nearly 3,100 infantry casualties in six days. Forwick, "*Kurland,*" pp. 116, 187.

[7] The "GHQ troops" consisted of an army artillery battalion, and the unit from the III SS Panzer Corps was the panzerjäger battalion. The *kampfgruppe* was commanded by Major General Kurt Gerok, the former commander of the 153rd Field Training Division. Forwick, "*Kurland,*" p. 121; Keilig, *Das Deutsche Heer,* III: 211/p. 99.

[8] The commander was Major General Rudolf Höfer, who would later be captured by the Soviets as the last commander of Stettin. Keilig, *Das Deutsche Heer,* III: 211/p. 138.

[9] An idea of the depletion of the German divisions at this point can be gained by examining the strength of an average infantry division in the Riga area, the 87th, and comparing its combat strength in critical categories to that of a 1944-type division at full strength:

Category	Combat strength	Full strength
Men	5,000	13,656
Artillery (including heavy mortars)	20	75
Assault guns	3	14
Horse-drawn vehicles	462	1,466
Motor vehicles	292	615

Forwick, "*Kurland,*" p. 164; Buchner, *German Infantry Handbook,* p. 143-144.

CHAPTER 10

The Battles in the Jelgava Area from 24 September to the Encirclement of Army Group North in the Courland Area

Paul Reichelt

Preliminary Remarks

For the preparation of this study, the author had his own notes, records of the Third Panzer Army, and maps of the German and enemy situations of the period at his disposal. The study was supplemented from memory.

The author served initially with *Armeeabteilung Narva*, and together with it was enveloped in the Courland pocket.

Withdrawal of Army Group North to the Segewold Position in September 1944

The events in the Army Group North sector after the middle of September 1944, which initially made it necessary to abandon Estonia and withdraw the army group beyond the Wendish position to the Segewold position, later on substantially determined the further development of the situation leading to the final elimination of the army group in Courland.

On 14 September, the Russian command had again, after a brief intermission, begun an attack against Army Group North.

The Russian forces were launched as follows:

The First Baltic Front south of Riga against the Sixteenth Army,
The Second Baltic Front at Modohn,
The Third Baltic Front south of Lake Virts against the Eighteenth Army.

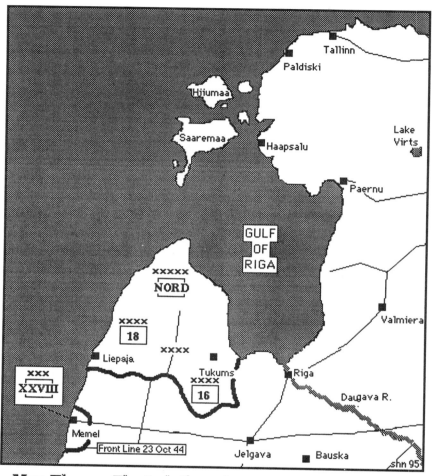

Map Eleven: The Isolation of Army Group North

Against the southern front of *Armeeabteilung Narva*, an attack at Tartu by the Second Shock Army of the Leningrad Front was impending.

The accumulation of forces proved that the Russian command still intended to fight the Baltic countries clear, and to eliminate Army Group North. The manner in which the forces were launched showed that the enemy had thoroughly recognized the weakness of the army group.

The first days of the attack showed that the army group, which had lost a great deal of personnel and materiel, was in the long run no longer equal to the situation on the extended front. It was threatened with the danger of again being encircle and finally eliminated.

On the basis of the development of the situation, the OKH issued orders to the army group on 16 September to withdraw to the Wendish position. At that time, the army group was already engaged in an extremely heavy defensive battle. Hence, the inevitable result was bound to be a movement influenced by the enemy, with all its consequences, and could not bring about the intended reinforcement of the front, despite the reduction in its length. Yet – on that same day – the army group issued the necessary orders.

They began by instigating the withdrawal of *Armeeabteilung Narva* across Estonia to the Estonian western position, while the endangered southern flank was simultaneously bent backward along the Kma River, between Lake Virts and Lake Peipus. In order not to jeopardize the withdrawal of *Armeeabteilung Narva*, it was for the time being absolutely necessary to hold the old positions of the Sixteenth and Eighteenth Armies, particularly those of the left flank of the Eighteenth Army on Lake Virts. This was bound to further aggravate the situation of the Sixteenth and Eighteenth Armies, and could be achieved only at great cost. Everything depended on a rapid progress of the withdrawal of *Armeeabteilung Narva*, which had to cover considerable distance with its northern sector.

The movements of *Armeeabteilung Narva* could take a comparatively free course until it had reached the Estonian western position, and established contact with the Eighteenth Army. For the further withdrawal the movements of the army were harmonized by intermediate lines.

In the right sector of the army group, south of Riga, the Forty-third Army and the Fourth Shock Army of the First Baltic Front had already achieved deep penetrations along the roads to Riga on 15 September, so that here the front had to be withdrawn to the Jelgava eastern position by 12 September, and as a result the inner flanks of the Sixteenth and Eighteenth Armies were also withdrawn to the Daugava River and the southern part of the Wendish position.

To bring relief, the Third Panzer Army had – since 16 September – ben conducting attacks with the XXXIX Panzer Corps from the Autz area toward Jelgava. The attack hit the full defensive strength of the enemy forces employed and assembled there. Although the Third Panzer Army had reinforced the corps enormously by weakening its remaining front, its forces were insufficient in every respect for the mission of containing and destroying strong enemy forces. The attack of the corps hence remained an offensive conduct at a snail's pace, and did not achieve substantial territorial gains. Although the forces of the Third Baltic Front which had not yet been committed had been tied down to a certain extent, the enemy forces engaged against the Sixteenth Army south of Riga were not affected. They retained their full freedom of action.

West of Modohn, the Eighteenth Army in its heavy defensive battle against the Second Baltic Front (which was attacking with the Twenty-second Army, the Third Shock Army, and the Tenth Guards Army) succeeded in preventing – for the time being – a breakthrough toward the west, owing to the action of the 14th Panzer Division which had been attached to it.

South of Lake Virts opposite the left flank of the Eighteenth Army (in other words, on the flank decisive for the withdrawal of *Armeeabteilung Narva*), the Third Baltic Front had formed a new point of main effort by using – in addition to the attacking Fifty-fourth Army and First Shock Army – the Sixty-seventh Army which meanwhile had moved up from Tartu. By 17 September, the Sixty-seventh Army had already succeeded in establishing bridgeheads south of Lake Virts across the Kma River, and in expanding them to such a degree that it was able to turn north toward Mustia (west of Lake Virts). Thus the Eighteenth Army was not only threatened with envelopment of its left flank, but with the danger that the route of *Armeeabteilung Narva* would be blocked.

Against the southern front of *Armeeabteilung Narva* the Second Shock Army had started an assault near Tartu on 17 September. The critical development – a breakthrough was impending – forced the *Armeeabteilung* to withdraw its Narva front the same day in order to gain contact with the army group in the Estonian western position by means of a prepared motorized movement, while gradually bending backward the southern front. Only in this manner did it seem possible to evade the impending encirclement by the Second Shock Army with the forces at the Narva Front. This seemed also to be the only manner in which fresh and combat-ready units could be speedily furnished to the army group.

On the basis of the development of the situation south of Riga and in the Eighteenth Army sector, however, it was already possible to foresee that the forces freed at *Armeeabteilung Narva* could not be saved, but would have to be given up by the army group as soon as they arrived, to avert a breaking up of the army group. For the time being, the front of the Sixteenth and Eighteenth Armies still held. The decrease in combat strengths, particularly in the strengths of the infantry, however, had assumed such proportions that even a withdrawal to the Wendish position could no longer be expected to result in a substantial reinforcement of the front. From this situation the OKH drew its conclusions, and on 20 September ordered the extension of the withdrawal beyond the Wendish position to the Segewold position. Upon the effects of this order the OKH had placed tremendous hopes.

The Segewold position was to be defended as a terminal position. With the forces freed as a result of the withdrawal to the Segewold position, the army group was not only to restore the situation south of Riga, but immediately to replace the panzer divisions of the Third Panzer Army. These divisions were to be assembled for an offensive operation designed to establish communications along the shortest route between Siauliai and the Segewold position. For this purpose the Third Panzer Army was assigned to the army group on 23 September.

In the meantime, the Forty-third Army and the Fourth Shock Army had expanded their penetrations into the Jelgava eastern position south of Riga as far as Baldane. Forces required to restore the situation were no longer available. The army group could hence prevent a breakthrough to Riga only by immediate commitment of the forces first freed as a result of the withdrawal of *Armeeabteilung Narva*; these forces were the III SS Panzer Corps headquarters troops, the 11th SS *"Nordland"* Panzergrenadier Division, and the 11th Infantry Division.

On the left flank of the Eighteenth Army, the enemy had meanwhile shifted his point of main effort, apparently in recognition of the withdrawal. With the Fifty-fourth Army and First Shock Army, the enemy had pushed southwest along the Walk-Riga Rollbahn, and by 23 September had considerably pressed in the front. The resulting critical situation southwest of Walk could be mastered only by commitment of the 11th SS *"Nordland"* Panzergrenadier Division, which had to be withdrawn from the bridgehead at Paernu for this purpose. As a result, all forces of the *Armeeabteilung* had, by 22 September, already been used up, and were no longer available for the missions referred to in the order which the supreme command had issued on 20 September.

The situation called for the immediate and accelerated continuation of the withdrawal of the army group to the Segewold position. The necessary order was issued by the army group on 23 September. On the extreme left, the movement was delayed once again. As a result of the withdrawal of the 11th SS *"Nordland"* Panzergrenadier Division from the Paernu bridgehead, the left flank of the Eighteenth Army had been exposed. To restore a closed front, the II Corps – which had reached the Estonian western position – first had to be taken back to Lake Vela on 23 September, and on 24 September had to be extended westward with its left flank as far as the coast.

It was possible to accomplish further withdrawal to the Segewold position systematically, although there was hard fighting. By 27 September, the Sixteenth Army was in the Segewold position, and on 28 September the Eighteenth Army had arrived in the position. To this position the army group was tied by an order from OKH. The intended improvement in the situation of the army group, however, had not been achieved. The forces of *Armeeabteilung Narva*, freed through the abandonment of Estonia, had already been assigned elsewhere. New reserves could not be formed, and thus the desired disengagement of the panzer divisions of the Third Panzer Army was not feasible.

The Courland Pocket

Ever since the beginning of the withdrawal to the Segewold position, a new point of main effort by the First Baltic Front at the overland bridge southwest of Riga had been taking more and more definite shape. The overland bridge was of immense importances to the army group. In the form of a narrow corridor, it constituted the sole overland communication to the German Zone of the Interior and within the army group itself. Its importance increased in the course of the withdrawal to the Segewold position, as port after port – beginning with Tallinn – was abandoned.

To locate the boundary line between the Third Panzer Army and the Sixteenth Army precisely at this vulnerable point was a great weakness. To ensure a unified control and organization of the defense, the army group decided to assign the sectors on both sides of the boundary between the Third Panzer Army and the Sixteenth Army to a single headquarters, and to entrust this mission to the headquarters of *Armeeabteilung Narva*, which had become free after the completion of the withdrawal to the Estonian western position. On 24 September, the headquarters of the *Armeeabteilung* was appointed a tactical operations staff, with the mission of keeping open the overland contact with Tukums, by defending the old main line of resistance against the anticipated attack. On 26 September, *Armeeabteilung Narva* took over the sector. It was redesignated *Armeeabteilung* Grasser, after its commander.

Situation of *Armeeabteilung* Grasser

According to the picture of the enemy's situation available to the army group, the following units were at the disposal of the First Baltic Front:

The I Tank Corps of the Second Guards Army in the area on both sides of Siauliai.
The Sixth Guards Army, including the XIX Tank Corps and probably also the III Guards Mechanized Corps, north thereof as far as Dobele.
The Fifty-first Army in the Dobele sector and east thereof.
The Fifth Guards Tank Army in a second line in the depth of the area.

As for tank forces, a concentration of roughly 800 enemy tanks was assumed.[1]

The army group primarily expected an attack by the Fifty-first Army and the Sixth Guards Army, with the employment of extremely heavy tank forces. The *Armeeabteilung* had the following picture of the situation: for the time being, only the Fifty-first Army was to be considered in the attack, and it now stood at the overland bridge. It could scarcely be assumed that the enemy could avail himself of substantial elements of the Second and Sixth Guards Armies. The Second Guards Army was tied down opposite the Third Panzer Army, possibly with some elements still in front of the sector of the *Armeeabteilung*. The Sixth Guards Army was still tied down by the latest attack of the XXXIX Panzer Corps in front of the sector of that corps. The only free forces at the disposal of the First Baltic Front were those of the Fifth Guards Tank Army. The tank forces definitely identified were the I and XIX Tank Corps, and the III Guards Mechanized Corps. Their employment was to be expected, unless they were needed as support behind the Second and Sixth Guards Armies. The attack forces of the First Baltic Front were thus primarily the Fifty-first Army, the Fifth Guards Tank Army, and several independent tank units.

The striking power in tank units which the enemy could raise was unusually great, especially since the attack had no distinct strategic objective. Whether the infantry forces were sufficient to encircle the army group after a successful breakthrough to the Baltic Sea – and at the same time build up a defensive flank toward the west – was doubtful Evidently, the enemy did not feel strong enough for a renewed thrust north, if indeed he considered such a move at all. In such a case, it was incomprehensible that he had not attacked earlier, although the forces in this area had been at his disposal for some time.

The first attack of the Third Panzer Army – started on 16 August – which had already resulted in *Panzerverband* Graf Strachwitz reestablishing the overland connection, had forced the enemy to employ the Sixth Guards Army and the XIX Tank Corps between the Second Guards Army and the Fifty-first Army for defense, and by way of precaution to pull up closed the Fifth Guards Tank Army. The attack that the Third Panzer Army undertook with the XXXIX Panzer Corps from 16 September had again hit the enemy hard, and this time at his most vulnerable point if he intended to attack north to the Gulf of Riga.

As terrain for an enemy attack, the territory west of the Courland Aa was out of the question. It was very swampy, and lacked good north-south communications. Hence the enemy had to take the old attack direction from the Dobele area, just as the army group expected. His assembly and concentration area had been greatly narrowed down by the Third Panzer Army. The XXXIX Panzer Corps, of whose strength the enemy was apparently not aware, threatened his flank in any action toward the north.

Contrary to expectations, the First Baltic Front had discontinued the attack south of Riga with its combat forces on the right – with the Forty-third Army on 24 September, and with the Fourth Shock Army on 25 September – although its attack was already well under way. Movements of these armies from the zones of action toward the west had been identified. If the First Baltic Front also moved up this force, an early beginning of the attack was to be expected, provided the Russian command still intended to attack. There were no signs pointing to this possibility.

The general enemy situation at the front was not clear, but there were none of the typical signs that an attack was forthcoming. The enemy did not undertake reconnaissance in force, and no artillery preparation was identified. There were no signs of assemblies or concentrations of forces. Radio reconnaissance offered no clues. Loud motor noise indicated heavy concentrations of tanks, but no more than was usual in front of the XXXIX Panzer Corps. Enemy air reconnaissance was normal. For the *Armeeabteilung* everything now depended on clarifying the situation. Particularly important were observations of the present whereabouts of the Forty-third Army and the Fourth Shock Army, as well as the progress of the reported movements.

To accomplish the mission, only the forces already employed in the sector were available. On the right was the XXXIX Panzer Corps (this was previously the corps on the extreme left of the Third Panzer Army). The corps had shifted to the defensive on 21 September. The organization of the defense had been started by the corps; tanks and assault guns had changed from a purely offensive organization with points of main effort to a loose organization in depth for anti-tank defense. On the whole, the distribution of the corps naturally did not yet correspond to a thoroughly organized defense. Despite the materiel losses in the previous offensive engagements, the corps now had more than 200 tanks fit for use at its disposal in its panzer units, and roughly 200 assault guns in the units and forces under its command. According to the conditions prevailing at the time, this was a tremendous combat strength. It was unnecessary to concentrate and station them at any one point on the defense.

From a purely local point of view, the corps was in a favorable position for a flank thrust. But apart from the extraordinary difficulty of attacking from the defense organization, it was to be expected that the enemy would have organized a strong defensive flank precisely in front of the XXXIX Panzer Corps in the event of a northern thrust, provided he did not include the sector of the XXXIX Panzer Corps in the attack, and that he would have done this if only to tie down the corps. The high degree of flexibility of the striking and defensive power of panzer divisions, the possibility of shifting quickly for employment at another point, was lost in any case. To free the panzer divisions again was, therefore, necessarily a primary task. But a disengagement depended upon the assignment of other units by the army group.

Locally, the left sector of the *Armeeabteilung* was in charge of actually protecting the overland bridge. This was the focal sector. Here *Gruppe* Kleffel (previously part of the Sixteenth Army) was employed on a broad front with only one infantry division and numerous fragmentary units of the Army, the Luftwaffe, and the Navy. Although heavy artillery and anti-tank forces had been furnished to this sector, the strength of the defense was in no way commensurate to the importance of the overland communication to be protected.[2] To consolidate the front, the army group had meanwhile ordered the disengagement of the III SS Panzer Corps and the 11th SS *"Nordland"* Panzergrenadier Division from the Sixteenth Army, and the reassignment of the 4th SS *"Nederland"* Panzergrenadier Brigade as a result of the withdrawal by the Eighteenth Army, and their employment in the Dobele sector.

The weakness of the defense in the left sector of the *Armeeabteilung* had to be overcome until the arrival of additional forces. But an establishment of reserves was possible only by weakening the front of the XXXIX Panzer Corps. The present sector lengths of the panzer divisions, which still corresponded to the length of their attacking fronts, permitted such a move. Hence the *Armeeabteilung* decided to disengage the 5th Panzer Division as a reserve.

Fortification of the Position

No systematic positions existed as yet at any point of the sector of the *Armeeabteilung*. The XXXIX Panzer Corps had dug in wherever it had discontinued the attack. With *Gruppe* Kleffel, fortification had progressed further, especially in the construction of strongpoints and anti-tank obstacles. Fortification in the depth of the main defensive area was not yet commensurate with requirements at any point. Rear positions did not exist.

Since the middle of September, a position at the Courland Aa and another one on both sides of Tukums – both facing east – had been under construction by the army group as a precaution. With respect to supply, the *Armeeabteilung*, which itself had only few rear services at its disposal, depended upon the Sixteenth Army; with respect to tank maintenance, upon the Third Panzer Army. This system of necessity resulted in a certain amount of friction, especially in combat.

Situation of the Third Panzer Army

On the right of the *Armeeabteilung*, the Third Panzer Army stood adjacent to the XXXIX Panzer Corps. Since 21 September, it had been assigned to the army group, and had to defend its previous position. Anchored on Army Group Center, its mission was to protect the communications to Tilsit, the northernmost passage for an invasion of East Prussia, and the highways leading from the Siauliai area to Memel and Liepaja on the whole (in other words, the land communications of Army Group North through Courland to East Prussia).

On a front of almost 200 kilometers, the Third Panzer Army merely had five divisions at its disposal, consisting in part of newly activated units without substantial combat experience, whose equipment was frequently inadequate. Since the Third Panzer Army had concentrated all combat-worthy units and forces in the XXXIX Panzer Corps for the attack it had started on 16 September, it had no combat-worthy unit left and no substantial reserves – especially of tanks and assault guns – after it had turned over the XXXIX Panzer Corps to *Armeeabteilung* Grasser. The weakness of the front of the Third Panzer Army constituted a considerable danger for Army

Group North.

Development of the Situation of *Armeeabteilung* Grasser

Until 29 September, the picture at the front of the *Armeeabteilung* did not change. There were no signs of preparations and plans for an attack on the part of the enemy. There were no indications that the movement from the area south of Riga had reached the sector of the *Armeeabteilung*, although according to calculations the sector of the *Armeeabteilung* should have been reached a long time before. Nor did air reconnaissance produce substantial results.

During the night of 29 September, motor noises both in the depth of the enemy territory and in the vicinity of the front had continue unabated. They far exceeded those of normal motor traffic. Reports from several points of the front pointed to large-scale motor movements in a north-south direction in front of the Third Panzer Army. This report could be of great importance. The possibility that the First Baltic Front was drawing forces from the front of the *Armeeabteilung* had to be taken into account.

The Third Panzer Army had already identified the movements from the sector of the *Armeeabteilung*. In the opinion of the Third Panzer Army something was brewing in front of its sector. Specific conclusions could not be drawn. The army group, on the other hand, saw no change of the situation yet in the enemy picture such as would have pointed to basically new intentions of the enemy, and would have required new decisions. The overland bridge retained its full importance as long as the army group had to hold the Segewold position.

A cause of anxiety to the army group was the necessary disengagement of the panzer divisions of the XXXIX Panzer Corps. After the release of the III SS Panzer Corps with its 11th SS *"Nordland"* Panzergrenadier Division and 4th SS *"Nederland"* Panzergrenadier Brigade for consolidation of the of the front of the overland bridge a freeing of additional divisions of the Sixteenth and Eighteenth Armies from the Segewold position was no yet possible, especially as a redemption of the fighting at the Segewold position had to be expected as soon as the enemy had pulled up his rear units.

If, up to then, a change in the plans of the enemy had not been clearly evident, the situation was now to be surprisingly and abruptly clarified. On 1 October, commitment of a machine gun battalion – a decidedly static unit – was observed northwest of Dobele. This not only confirmed the previous estimate of the situation by the *Armeeabteilung*, according to which no offensive plans on the part of the enemy were to be inferred, but proved that the First Baltic Front had entirely abandoned the idea of an attack against the overland bridge. A change in the conduct of the enemy in front of the XXXIX Panzer Corps pointed to the fact that troops had been pulled out here, too. Departure of the Sixth Guards Army (possibly also of the Fifty-first Army) from the front of the *Armeeabteilung* was to be expected.

The motor noises continuing in the depth of the enemy territory made it appear likely that the enemy was moving past the front of the *Armeeabteilung* with the Forty-third Army and the Fourth Shock Army. Consultation with the Third Panzer Army showed that the latter had observed an enemy assembly in three groups before its front: in the Raseinen area, east of Kelmen, and at Siauliai. The Third Panzer Army expected the enemy to try and break through to Tilsit, Memel, and Liepaja. A particular cause of solicitude to the Third Panzer Army was the weakness of its own front. It was neither in a position to rearrange its forces in order to reinforce the endangered sectors, nor did it possess substantial reserves.

Thus a dangerous, completely new situation began to develop. The Russian command had arrived at basically new decisions. In the execution of its intentions, it had progressed far. It had not only shifted its point of main effort, but was already in the middle of an assembly of heavy forces in front of the Third Panzer Army. A breakthrough in the Third Panzer Army sector was bound to encircle the army group again. But a breakthrough on a broad front also presented the fatal danger that the overland communications of the army group with East Prussia would be interrupted over long stretches, so that its reestablishment would seem almost hopeless.

From the Siauliai area, a thrust at Liepaja was to be expected. Here the Russian command had a further strategic objective: the first port to be free of ice at all times. But this thrust affected the *Armeeabteilung* directly. It laid bare its southern flank, for the protection of which it did not have sufficient forces at its disposal. For the *Armeeabteilung* the mission remained to keep open the overland bridge by defending the old main line of resistance. At the overland bridge, however, the danger was no longer acute.

A cause of anxiety was the situation in front of the Third Panzer Army, and its possible effect on the *Armeeabteilung*. It had to be expected that the XXXIX Panzer Corps, in the course of the new operation of the enemy, would also be attacked frontally, if only for the purpose of tying it down for the time being. To this possibility, and to the potential threat to its southern flank, the army now had to adjust itself. The main elements of the 5th Panzer Division were already at the disposal of the *Armeeabteilung*.

On the basis of the change in the situation, the *Armeeabteilung* decided to thin out the front northwest of Dobele, and through an immediate rearrangement also to extract the Panzergrenadier Division *"Grossdeutschland."* Disengagement of the infantry regiments of the remaining panzer divisions would be possible only after new forces had been assigned. In case of danger, the army could also fall back on corps and divisional reserves – particularly on the panzer reconnaissance battalions, anti-tank personnel, and engineers. Greater concentration of the tanks was ordered as a precaution.

The immediate transfer of the 5th Panzer Division to Army Group Center in East Prussia was unexpectedly ordered on 1 October. On 2 October, the division started out with its forward elements for an overland move through Tilsit. The army group released the 58th Infantry Division, which had been disengaged from the Sixteenth Army, as army group reserve. It was shipped to Army Group Center by sea.

Encirclement of Army Group North in Courland

In the meantime, the situation in front of the Third Panzer Army continued to become more aggravated. On 2 October, the army – again pointing out its weakness – reported to the army group that in its opinion the enemy attack on the right flank of the army at Raseinen might start any time within the next few days from the Kelmen and Siauliai areas. The enemy was expected to employ tremendous forces.

The Russian command was in a position to use the free Fifth Guards Tank Army as well as the Second Guards Army, which was opposite the Third Panzer Army. Efforts to free offensive forces and replace them by static forces were observed. South of Raseinen, the 132d Command District was identified with the 228th, 346th, and 380th Machine Gun Battalions. In front of the *Armeeabteilung,* the Sixth Guards Army could be moved up, possibly also the Fifty-first Army. Appearance of the Forty-third Army and Fourth Shock Army had to be anticipated.

Thus the Russian command had the entire First Baltic Front at its disposal. The units were rested, except for the Forty-third Army and the Fourth Shock Army. Reinforced by the I and XIX Tank Corps, which had already been added to the First Baltic Front, and by the III Guards Mechanized Corps, a tremendous striking power could could thus be employed. In the Fifth Guards Tank Army and the independent tank corps the First Baltic Front had excellent breakthrough forces at its disposal, but it also had strong mobile units for thrusts into the depth against far-flung strategic objectives.

Danger was impending. The army group again requested permission to abandon the Segewold position and withdraw the Sixteenth and Eighteenth

Armies. All measures required for an immediate execution of a withdrawal were now initiated. The army group had providently already initiated the evacuation of Riga in line with the withdrawal, and had greatly thinned out its forces by transferring to Courland all cumbersome services and installations no longer needed for the battle in the Segewold position. Through the employment of a special patrol and traffic regulating service, fluid progress of the movement through Riga and along the sole rear communication through the overland bridge was ensured.

Only through complete abandonment of the Segewold position – and necessarily also through withdrawal from Riga, could forces be gained to bolster the Third Panzer Army.[3] As an immediate measure to bolster the Third Panzer Army, the army group ordered *Armeeabteilung* Grasser to release Panzergrenadier Division *"Grossdeutschland"* and the Eighteenth Army to release the 61st Infantry Division. In addition, the army group took initial steps to extract further forces from the Sixteenth and Eighteenth Armies. On 3 October, the forward elements of Panzergrenadier Division *"Grossdeutschland"* began to move. In view of the fuel shortage, rail shipment had been ordered for the tanks of the division.

Development of the Situation of Third Panzer Army From 4 October

On 4 October, the enemy undertook local reconnaissance thrusts in strength along the entire front of the Third Panzer Army. At a few points – particularly in the middle of the army front, the situation as a result became obscure.

On 5 October the enemy began an attempt to break through on a broad front, employing an unusually large number of tanks. Points of main effort became apparent, as expected, at Raseinen, Kelmen, and Siauliai. Despite strong local resistance by the greatly outnumbered forces of the Third Panzer Army, the enemy was able to achieve deep penetrations at numerous points in his initial attack. At a few points, particularly in the middle of the army front, he had already disrupted the front on the first day of the attack.

On the right flank of the army, continuity of the front could be maintained only by employment of the 5th Panzer Division. This division, on its march to Army Group Center through the army area, had approached Tilsit with its forward elements on 5 October. It was stopped, incorporated in the front north of Tilsit, reassigned to the Third Panzer Army, and employed to bolster the right flank of the army. Through the employment of the 5th Panzer Division, it was possible to maintain continuity of the right flank of the army, and subsequently to bend this flank back toward Tilsit.

The I Tank Corps of the Second Guards Army had been identified. Its objective was undoubtedly Tilsit.

Particularly critical was the development of the situation in the center of the army front. Here the front had already failed to stand up under the reconnaissance thrusts of the enemy on 4 October, so that with the beginning of the breakthrough attack on 5 October the enemy hit a soft spot, and exploiting the situation pushed through at once into the rear. The division employed here, like all the divisions, was greatly overextended, and inadequately supplied with means of communications. Hence, reports on the development of the situation of 4 October reached the corps late and only incorrectly. The development of the situation rapidly assumed catastrophic proportions.

The Forty-third Army had appeared. Its thrust was evidently directed toward Memel.

On the left flank of the Third Panzer Army, the enemy on the first day of attack succeeded in penetrating deeply at numerous points of the front. Parts of the left flank withdrew to the Tryskiai-Vieksniai line while fighting, as well as north to Akmene. Contrary to expectations, the enemy did not turn north, but pushed west. His objective evidently was Liepaja.

Southeast of Telsche, the first elements of Panzergrenadier Division *"Grossdeutschland"* came into contact with the forward elements of the enemy on 6 October. The division, coming from *Armeeabteilung* Grasser, was to be assembled behind the center of the Third Panzer Army. The bulk of the division was being moved there by motor transportation and a few elements – for lack of fuel – by rail. The situation accordingly required a piecemeal employment of the division. Only gradually could the division be concentrated. Against the greatly superior enemy forces, the division could not stand its ground despite the heaviest resistance. It was thrown back upon Memel, which the enemy encircled.

The Fifth Guards Tank Army and the Sixth Guards Army were identified.

Employment of the Panzergrenadier Division *"Grossdeutschland,"* which attracted and tied down strong enemy forces, prevented the enemy from rolling through to Liepaja, and in the last analysis made it possible to intercept him and build up a new front.

Organization of the Front of the Courland Pocket

The complete collapse of the front of the Third Panzer Army along its entire length could not be stopped, and the renewed encirclement of Army

Group North could no longer be averted. Everything now depended on preventing the army group from being rolled up from the south, and the enemy from gaining possession of Liepaja. The withdrawal from the Segewold position, which the army group had initiated on 4 October, was in full swing by then.

All the units and forces already available, particularly all rapid mobile ones (including the temporarily motorized 11th Infantry Division and the 14th Panzer Division), as well as a large number of engineer units, were committed by the army group on 5 and 6 October. *Armeeabteilung* Grasser was at once to disengage the 4th and 12th Panzer Divisions, and place them at the disposal of the army group. The Eighteenth Army headquarters, which was just turning over its sector to the Sixteenth Army, was entrusted with the unified conduct of operations.

Development of the Situation of *Armeeabteilung* Grasser from 4 October

The breakthrough in the Third Panzer Army sector rapidly led to an exceedingly critical development in the situation of *Armeeabteilung* Grasser. By the evening of 4 October, there was no clear picture of the situation of the adjacent unit on the right. On 5 October, the situation developed with extreme result.

A panzer reconnaissance battalion sent south on a reconnaissance mission by the XXXIX Panzer Corps was unable to force its way through. It was no longer possible to establish contact with the Third Panzer Army. On the evening of 5 October, direct contact existed with only a few elements of the Third Panzer Army. South of Papils, the front had apparently fallen apart. Elements of the left flank of the Third Panzer Army retired west, while weak elements withdrew north – behind the front of the *Armeeabteilung*. restoration of contact with the Third Panzer Army was out of the question.

The *Armeeabteilung* no longer had any free forces at its disposal. The 5th Panzer Division had been released to Army Group Center, and had left the army area. Panzergrenadier Division *"Grossdeutschland"* was no longer available, the first elements having moved off on the evening of 3 October, some by rail (the tanks), the bulk on 4 October by motor transportation, and all going south to join the Third Panzer Army.

On 5 October, however, the army group had also ordered the immediate transfer of the 4th and 12th Panzer Divisions to the army group. Disengagement of the infantry fighting at the front, however, was impossible without replacements. Any moment the *Armeeabteilung* had to expect that the XXXIX Panzer Corps would also be frontally attacked. At the suggestion of the *Armeeabteilung*, the army group fell back on the fully motorized III SS Panzer Corps with its SS units, which were strong with respect to personnel and materiel. The corps was soon available; some of its elements immediately. The corps had detached strong reserves, and could hence be freed within a short time through extension of the sector of the 93d Infantry Division, and employment of the now-arriving 389th Infantry Division. Further movement of the 389th Infantry Division to the 4th and 12th Panzer Division sectors would have resulted in a great loss of time. On 6 October, the 4th and 12th Panzer Divisions and the leading elements of the III SS Panzer Corps began to move. The last elements could be disengaged during the night of 7 October.

On 6 October, the breakthrough of the enemy – whose right attack flank was immediately south of the army boundary – began to affect the *Armeeabteilung* directly. During the day the enemy had already undertaken strong reconnaissance thrusts at Kruopiai and southwest of Schagarren. During evening hours an enemy attack supported by tanks, occurred moving northwest through Papils. The right flank of the *Armeeabteilung* was suspended in the air. To prevent an envelopment close to the front, the right flank of the *Armeeabteilung* retreated, and had to be withdrawn behind the brook sector on both sides of Akmene. The roads leading south across the Moscheiken-Vieksniai-Akmene line had meanwhile been blocked by a panzer reconnaissance battalion compose of anti-tank personnel and engineers. Reconnaissance launched toward the southwest and south could no longer get through. Everywhere it encountered small enemy forces, especially mechanized reconnaissance, which had advanced from the south and southeast. Enemy pressure of Vieksniai increased. Here, the 505th Army Engineer Battalion had been committed as a *sperrverband*. A capture of this important traffic center, which was of special importance to the enemy, had to be prevented. The 32d Infantry Division, which had been the first unit to arrive, had therefore to be employed in this sector. With its right flank it had to seek contact with the Eighteenth Army southeast of Moscheiken.

The elements of the Third Panzer Army, which had retreated west and north behind the Tryskiai-Vieksniai line, had meanwhile been reunited. They were again employed between the 32d Infantry Division and the right flank of the army, under the commander of the staff of the 201st Security Division, which had arrived from the Third Panzer Army. thus a continuous front was established as far as Moscheiken. As a result of the withdrawal of the right flank of the *Armeeabteilung*, the salient in the main line of resistance jutting out in the direction of Kruopiai was vulnerable to pressure.

Here the main line of resistance blocked the Schagarren-Papils road, which was important to the enemy. The *Armeeabteilung* could not resist a new strain, however. Hence – with the consent of the army group – it decided to withdraw the main line of resistance to a shorter and substantially more favorable line. After the 21st Luftwaffe Field Division and the 329th Infantry Division had been committed in the new main line of resistance, the old front was withdrawn beyond the new main line of resistance which had been occupied.

Contrary to expectations, the enemy pressed forward only with weak forces, while the bulk was evidently following up behind the Fifth Guards Tank Army and the Sixth Guards Army. The Fourth Shock Army was identified. As the withdrawal from the Segewold position continued, it became possible to gradually consolidate the new front by employment of the divisions which had been moved up.

Development of the Situation of the Eighteenth Army from 6 October

On 6 October, the army headquarters reached the area east of Liepaja. Its command post was at Rudbarzi. It had to prevent the enemy from advancing north into the rear of the army group, and – under all circumstances – to Liepaja. In a situation which was completely obscure, the army had to solve a task from scratch, and the execution of this task depended solely on the timely arrival of German forces. Under the protection of motorized reconnaissance elements, which west of Talsche were still in contact with Panzergrenadier Division *"Grossdeutschland,"* the army was able – for the time being – to build up a thin obstacle line, particularly along the roads leading to Liepaja. On 7 October, the army received the first combat-worthy units and forces. The 4th and 12th Panzer Divisions were approaching from *Armeeabteilung* Grasser. Upon the arrival of the 11th Infantry Division and III SS Panzer Corps, the Eighteenth Army succeeded in intercepting the enemy southwest of Liepaja, and in gradually building up (after additional units had arrived from the Segewold position) a new, though thinly occupied front, while fighting extremely heavy battles, especially south and east of Skuodar and at Vainode.

Development of the Situation at the Sixteenth Army from 5 October (Abandonment of the Segewold position)

With the beginning of the withdrawal, the Sixteenth Army had assumed command of the entire front of the Segewold position. The withdrawal itself began on 5 October. Under pressure of time, the individual divisions were disengaged and dispatched through a forwarding point to the Eighteenth Army and *Armeeabteilung* Grasser. The necessary leaving of rear guards inevitably led to a mingling of units, which could only later be gradually remedied.

It was possible to accomplish the withdrawal without substantial enemy pressure. In front of Riga, which was to be held as a bridgehead upon orders from the OKH in order to permit continued utilization of the port, enemy pressure increased. North of Riga, the bridgehead was pushed in almost as far as the Daugava River. To hold it any longer was impossible for the few forces still at the disposal of the army. The development of the situation necessitated a further withdrawal of the Sixteenth Army behind the Courland Aa. Riga was abandoned to the enemy without any fighting.[4] The Third Baltic Front followed the movement. The First Shock Army and the Sixty-seventh Army were identified. The exceedingly swampy terrain west of the Courland Aa made it impossible to establish a main defensive area organized in depth. Hence, after the Tukums position had been fortified further, the Sixteenth Army was withdrawn to it. As it moved into the Tukums position, it simultaneously assumed the further organization of coastal defense.

Engagements in the Courland Pocket

On the basis of the intention of the Supreme Command to reestablish the overland connection between Army Group North and East Prussia, the panzer divisions were disengaged from the fighting and committed in an attack along the coastal road to facilitate the relief expected from the south. The 4th and 12th Panzer Divisions – and the 14th Panzer Division which had meanwhile arrived from the Sixteenth Army – were available for this purpose. The 4th and 12th Panzer Divisions were again at full strength, after the infantry units arrived from *Armeeabteilung* Grasser. The 14th Panzer Division had lost a great deal of its combat strength in previous fighting in front of Riga.

Under unfavorable conditions, the panzer divisions started their attack. By the second day of the attack, it had become evident that the available forces were absolutely insufficient; the attack was stopped. Undoubtedly, the enemy had already moved strong forces to the scene for the thrust at Liepaja, and had reached the coast with his Fifty-first Army. The violence of the battle and the strength of the enemy was evident along from the fact that the panzer divisions destroyed more than eighty enemy anti-tank guns with the first two days of the attack. This attack was – and remained – the only attempt to reestablish the overland connection.

On the right flank of the Third Panzer Army, the situation had meanwhile developed as follows: As a result of the complete collapse of the center of the army front, the right flank of the army (which had again been bolstered by the 5th Panzer Division) was suspended in mid-air. The Russian Forty-third Army breakthrough to Memel, and the danger of an envelopment by the Second Guards Army, necessitated a step-by-step withdrawal of the right flank toward Tilsit; north of the city an extensive bridgehead was held. The Second Guards Army pushed forward through Skandwil, Tauroggen, and Schilehlen (where the I Tank Corps was located) to Hodekrug, while elements of the Russian Thirty-ninth Army (which formed part of the Third Byelorussian Front) pressed forward from the east to Georgenburg. After 10 October, the Third Panzer Army was again assigned to Army Group Center.

After reinforcements had been moved up, contact by the Tilsit bridgehead with the forces that had been encircled in Memel since 10 October (two divisions under XXVIII Corps Headquarters) was to be reestablished in order that the overland connection with Army Group North might thereupon be restored during continuation of the attack. The forces envisaged for this operation (Parachute-Panzer Corps *"Hermann Göring"*), however, arrived only gradually – approximately from 12 October on – and in such weak combat strength that the attack was soon stopped. On about 18 October, the plan was, therefore, dropped, and the Tilsit bridgehead abandoned. Thus, Army Group North was finally encircled in the Courland pocket.

No sooner had the front of the Courland pocket been formed, that new battles flared up along its entire length. The Russian command evidently intended to destroy the army group in an immediate attack. In front of the Eighteenth Army, the First Baltic Front concentrated the Fourth Shock, Sixth Guards, and Fifth Guards Tank Armies in the Moscheiken-Skuodas area, with the intention of breaking through to Liepaja and cutting off the army group from its last sea communication. Without engaging in time-consuming preparations, the First Baltic Front launched its attack with immense amounts of materiel. A special point of main effort developed from the Vainode area. Although the front was pushed back, the enemy achieved no breakthrough.

In the meantime, the enemy was in full assembly also on the east front of the pocket. The Second and Third Baltic Fronts had followed up the further withdrawal of the army group from the Segewold position. While the Second Baltic Front had closely followed the withdrawal west by using the interior line, the Third Baltic Front was pushing after it by way of Riga.

In the middle of October, signs of a directly impending attack increased in the *Armeeabteilung* Grasser sector. Assembly of the Tenth Guards Army was observed east of Autz, and that of the Third Shock Army and Fifth Guards Tank Army in the Dobele area. On the southwestern front of the pocket, the enemy displayed no aggressive intentions for the time being. Here, static troops (machine gun battalions) were identified.

While the Eighteenth Army was already engaged in an extremely heavy defensive battle, the Second Baltic Front started its breakthrough attack at Autz on 18 October, and at Dobele immediately thereafter. Despite the heavy resistance, Autz was lost on 20 October. West of Dobele, the front was also pressed back to Lake Zebres.

The enemy breakthrough attempts now continued steadily along the entire front. Interrupted only by short pauses, which the enemy required in order to move up new materiel, rehabilitate his units, and often also to shift his local points of main effort, the attacks were made again and again. Often it was possible to smash enemy forces in their assembly areas, or to intercept them early. But it was impossible to prevent the enemy from again and again achieving penetrations, which – for lack of forces – could frequently not be eliminated, so that the front was gradually pushed back as far as Prauenburg. A breakthrough, however, was not achieved by the enemy.

The army group had to endure a hopeless battle in a forlorn post, a battle which could only serve the purpose of tying down enemy forces. Its tasks had to be limited to rapid establishment of main points of defense, and to the elimination of critical situations by a continuous shift of forces, especially of tanks. If the fighting of the army group in the Courland pocket was an unequal one from the beginning, in the course of time, with the aggravation of the supply and food situation, it became an indescribable struggle against greatly superior enemy forces. The will to self-preservation made every last man in the army group give a superhuman performance. Not until March, as the battles in Germany progressed further, did the attacks of the enemy subside.

With the unconditional surrender, Army Group North, too, had to give up its arms.

Conclusion

The army group had early realized the danger with which it was threatened as a result of the Russian large-scale offensive begun on 22 June, which in the end – owing to the collapse of Army Group Center – led to its being cut off. Again and again it endeavored, in conjunction with Army Group Center, to reestablish a solid, continuous front by means of a large-scale, strategic solution. Only through a timely, radical shortening of the front, through an extensive withdrawal could a certain freedom of action be regained. A continuous struggle against the enemy with his great numerical superiority, especially in materiel, hampered as it was by the order "not to abandon an inch of ground," was bound to result in an unfavorable turn in the situation. Thus, by the end of August, the army group had been pushed back to an extended, sensitive front running from the southwest of Riga to the Narva River. This front, in the single overland communication of the narrow isthmus southwest of Riga, had an exceedingly vulnerable spot.

The intermission in the fighting at the beginning of September could not conceal the fact that the enemy would attack again as soon as he had moved up all his units, and rehabilitated and redistributed them. It was certain that the army group, with the few forces at its disposal, was unequal to the situation. Nevertheless, it was bound to this front by an order, even after all the military and political necessities for this order had ceased to exist. As a result, the army group found it necessary, in the extremely critical situation prevailing, to wrench from Hitler the long-overdue decision for withdrawal. It came, as the course of events had shown, only when the fronts had already become mutually entangled and danger was impending. The Sixteenth and Eighteenth Armies were already engaged in an extremely heavy defensive battle which they had to fight until the arrival of the retreating *Armeeabteilung Narva*. Although *Armeeabteilung Narva* was able to complete the withdrawal and establish contact within a very short time, and without interference by the enemy, the situation – which had deteriorated in the meantime – necessitated immediate employment of the forces which had become available. Although it had reduced the length of the front, the withdrawal had at no point fulfilled expectations, since it had had to be undertaken under pressure from the enemy. The continuation of the withdrawal to the Segewold position was unable to bring the required relief.

The withdrawal at first surprised the Russian command at the Narva front. After it had become aware of the movement, however, it followed up immediately, and at first locally, by shifting the point of main effort toward the southwest opposite the Eighteenth Army. As the withdrawal progressed, the Russian command was inevitably forced to arrive at basically new decisions. It could assume that the evacuation of the Baltic countries was in progress. If it still wished to achieve a decisive success, it had to attack the army group at its bases. But since movement toward the south was limited by the Third Byelorussian Front, this could be done only in Courland, in the sector of the Third Panzer Army. Here, the Second Guards Army and the Fifth Guards Tank Army – two fresh units – were available; in addition, the Sixth Guards and the Fifty-first Armies could quickly be drawn to the scene.

South of Riga, the attack of the combat force on the right of the First Baltic Front was well under way, but a decisive success could be achieved only after reinforcements had been moved up. Such a movement required time, however, and every day lost decreased the prospects for success. Logically, therefore, the Russian command was required to rely on the Forty-third Army and the Fourth Shock Army to form a new point of main effort elsewhere, and to make this point a strong one from the beginning. As a result, the Forty-third Army and the Fourth Shock Army discontinued their attack south of Riga on 24 and 25 September, respectively. To Army Group North the sudden cessation of this attack came as a surprise. Movements toward the west were observed. They pointed to a shift to the Dobele area. Here an attack was already anticipated on the basis of the picture of the enemy situation which was then available.

No doubt the enemy had originally intended to encircle the army group again by a thrust north from the Dobele area. But the prerequisites for this were no longer present. While, at the end of July, in exploitation of the situation prevailing at the time, the enemy had managed to push through to the Baltic Sea by way of Tukums, at present – since the reestablishment of the overland communication and concentration of its panzer units (XXXIX Panzer Corps) on its northern flank – the Third Panzer Army menaced his flank. If the First Baltic Front wished to achieve any success at all here, it had to attack immediately. The prospects for success, however, were bound to decrease from day to day.

The further development of the enemy situation in the Dobele area gave no clue to the offensive intentions of the enemy; the Forty-third Army and the Fourth Shock Army did not appear. The shift of the point of main effort of the First Baltic Front against the Third Panzer Army had already been clearly identified by the latter on 28 September; but Army Group North did not yet fully subscribe to this. As a result, the enemy gained a lead, and Army Group North was unable to catch up.

The situation could have been mastered only by a rapid withdrawal of the army group from the Segewold position, by an immediate reinforcement of the front of the Third Panzer Army, and an assembly of a strong tactical reserve. Bound to the Segewold position and depending upon a single rear line of communication, all measures designed to bolster the Third Panzer Army were bound to come too late. The tying down of the panzer divisions of the XXXIX Panzer Corps in the defensive front prevented their quick employment against Russian penetrations in the Third Panzer Army sector on 5 October. The 5th Panzer Division and Panzergrenadier Division *"Grossdeutschland"* were on their way, but the infantry of the 4th and 12th Panzer Divisions were still tied down at the front. The rapid and disastrous development of events in the Third Panzer Army sector was an inevitable result of its weakness (five infantry divisions for a front length of almost 200 kilometers).

The encirclement of the army group could no longer be averted. The resulting situation was similar to that following the collapse of Army Group Center in the summer. An open flank developed, which – with the further advance of the enemy to the west – was lengthened more and more, and became a south front. While the army group then had had to obtain the necessary forces by a ruthless thinning out of the unattacked sectors of the front, at present forces to organize a new front could be obtained only by a complete abandonment of the Segewold position.

The breakthrough disrupted communications with Army Group Center over a long distance. There was indeed an intention of restoring the overland communication through an attack from the south. Army Group North was to have facilitated this attack by a thrust from the north. From the south, things did not progress beyond the intention, and from the north a success was attainable only if the thrust was conducted early, before the enemy had drawn tight the ring around the army group. The forces of the army group were few, and the objective remote. Hence, only an attack with a limited objective could be considered, but even for this circumstances were unfavorable. Thus the battle ended as it had to end. The attack was stopped on its second day. The fate of the army group was sealed.

The Supreme Command was no longer in a position to influence the fighting of the army group, or to fall back upon substantial elements of the army group. Although a few individual units were shipped by sea, such as the headquarters of *Armeeabteilung* Grasser and the XXXIX Panzer Corps, as well as the 30th, 31st, 83d, and 227th Infantry Divisions, the bulk of the army group had to be written off.

Whether the encirclement of Army Group North in Courland could have been prevented by an earlier evacuation of the Segewold position, and whether by transferring these forces to East Prussia the German Eastern front could have been reinforced to the extent that the Russian offensive of January 1945 would have been prevent from resulting in the complete collapse of the Eastern front, must remain an open question.

NOTES

[1] In hindsight the author exaggerated German intelligence estimates of Red Army tank strength. Army Group North intelligence reports for that period pegged Soviet tank strength at the following levels:

5 Guards Tank Army	95
III Guards Mechanized Corps	39
I Tank Corps	6
XIX Tank Corps	85
143st Tank Brigade	21
1021st Assault Gun Regiment	8
Two unidentified tank units	30
Unspecified	30
Total	314

Forwick, "*Kurland*," p. 179.

[2] Commanded by General of Cavalry Phillipp Kleffel, *Gruppe* Kleffel's non-divisional units at this time consisted of one company of Engineer Battalion 181; III/Artillery Regiment 181; Army Artillery Battalion 513; 3./Assault Gun Brigade 912 (six StG IIIs); 4./Flak Battalion 291 (twelve 20mm flak); and detachments from Army Anti-tank Battlaions 666 and 667 (between eix and eight 88mm flak). Forwick, "*Kurland*," p. 108.

[3] The extent to which Army Group North's strength had become dangerously attenuated in critical sectors, while forced by OKH to maintain excessive strength on the Riga front is attested to by the tank and assault gun strength of the army group on 2 October 1944. Of 798 AFVs (410 tanks and 388 assault guns), 409 were concentrated in *Armeeabteilung Grasser* (chiefly in the XXXIX Panzer Corps); 162 in the Sixteenth Army; ninety-four in the Eighteenth Army; and only 133 in the Third Panzer Army. Simply to quote these figures actually creates the appearance of more strength in the Third Panzer Army than there really was. On 3 October the Panzergrenadier Division *"Grossdeutschland"* reported no more than twenty-five

combat-ready tanks and the 7th Panzer Division only ten. The remaining ninety-eight AFVs considered to belong to the army were not yet in the front lines, belonging to units still in transit: 5th Panzer Division, Tiger Battalion 502, and Panzerjäger Battalions 752 and 753. Forwick, "*Kurland*," pp. 135, 147, 153.

[4] The logisitical miracle wrought by Army Group North at Riga is somewhat slighted in this account. As the bridgehead contracted, twenty divisions, one brigade, sixty-eight engineer, construction, or police battalions, 120 flak batteries and their various regimental and battalion staffs, thirteen panzer or assault gun battalions, and twenty-eight army artillery battalions withdrew through the city, along with most of the administrative staff of *Reichskommissar Ostland*—in sum, over 111,000 motor vehicles. Forwick, "*Kurland*," p. 166.

CHAPTER 11

The Tactical Success
of Army Group North

From the fall of 1942, when the last serious consideration of a plan to capture Leningrad had to cease as a result of the Stalingrad debacle, to the beginning of 1944, Army Group North became not only a secondary front but essentially a static one. Though the fighting there was no less fierce and the conditions no less grim than on any other section of the line in Russia, neither Hitler nor Stalin considered the area to be fertile ground for decisive operations. The failure of the Soviets to achieve a strategic success at Nevel in 1943 was due primarily to the failure of STAVKA to project that such a success was in fact possible, and therefore committing inadequate reserves to exploit the breakthrough before the Germans could seal it off.

The Red Army operations beginning in January 1944, although more ambitious (seeking, for example, to destroy the Eighteenth Army in front of Leningrad before it could retreat toward the Panther Line), were still essentially secondary in Stalin's strategy. Between January-October 1944, Soviet assaults against Army Group North were designed to compliment the primary operations against Army Group Center or to further political goals, such as isolating Finland. Both the Russians and the Germans realized, despite all the rhetoric of "unhinging" the northern flank of the German eastern front, that the road to Berlin led through Belorussia and Poland, not the Baltic states and East Prussia. After Army Group North was penned up in Courland, STAVKA was essentially content to let the Wehrmacht feed and supply its own soldiers rather than making the effort necessary to capture them, and the Russians used the backwater to blood new divisions or rebuild shattered ones.

This lack of decisive strategic potential is one of the reasons that the operations in this theater in 1944 have been largely ignored by military historians. Histories of the siege of Leningrad invariably break off as soon as the Germans are driven out of artillery range, and the more comprehensive nar-

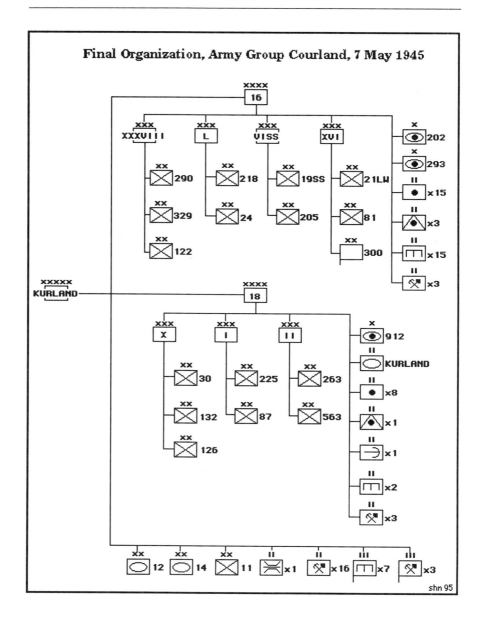

Final Organization, Army Group Courland, 7 May 1945

shn 95

ratives available in English are rarely much better. Albert Seaton combines the battles around Leningrad in early 1944 with the winter battles in the Ukraine into one short chapter, in which the smallest formations mentioned are usually German corps and Soviet armies. Almost as much coverage is given to operations in Finland as to those in the Baltic states by Earl Ziemke (although he does describe the January-February 1944 battles in detail), and the Russian attacks which finally pocket Army Group North in Courland consume only a few pages. Even more striking is the failure of Paul Carell, whose books are known for their tactical detail if not always their objectivity, to cover any of the operations on the Leningrad front after the withdrawal from the Demyansk salient in 1943. Alex Buchner's study of the Eastern front in 1944 also omits the northern theater. Even Wolfgang Schumann and Olaf Gröhler's massive six-volume history of the war devotes not quite three full pages of text to the withdrawal to the Panther Line, and is even more sketchy on operations in the summer and fall. While it is understandable that historians have chosen to limit their coverage of a secondary theater in order to devote more space to "decisive" operations, there are valuable tactical and operational lessons to be learned from a closer scrutiny of the battles fought by Army Group North in 1944.

On a tactical level, Army Group North was the most successful higher headquarters on the Eastern front, and perhaps in the entire German Army during the last half of the war – its only serious competition for this honor being Army Group C in Italy. Despite being outnumbered by 3-1 in divisions, 3-1 in artillery, and 6-1 in tanks, assault guns, and aircraft, the Eighteenth Army avoided encirclement and destruction in January-February 1944, under conditions which led to disasters on other fronts. Without ever having more than part of a single understrength panzer division as a mobile reserve, the Sixteenth Army held its ground against similar odds in the Panther Line and at Polotzk from February to July until the collapse of Army Group Center uncovered its flank. During September, *Armeeabteilung Narva* conducted one of the most successful disengagements in the history of modern warfare. Throughout the period covered in this book, Army Group North, with an average of thirty-five divisions, faced as many as fifteen Soviet armies and five tank or mechanized corps.

The weight of numbers against Army Group North was commensurate with the odds faced by other army groups on the rest of the front. Throughout 1943, for example, the relative weight of numbers against both Army Groups North and Center in terms of soldiers, artillery, and armored fighting vehicles was close to identical (see Table One). Likewise, in the two Soviet strategic offensives aimed at destroying each of these army groups – against Army Group North in January 1944 and against Army Group Center in June – huge numbers of men and weapons were employed. Again, however, the odds against the two army groups were similar (see Table Two). Admittedly, a much larger force of soldiers was kept in STAVKA reserve for the operation against Army Group Center, but that factor should be balanced against nearly a dozen crack German divisions rushed into Belorussia, opposed to the meagre reinforcements accorded to the troops falling back from Leningrad. Only in terms of combat aircraft was the Red Army significantly stronger against Army Group Center, but this is somewhat offset by the fact that at the main point of attack against the Eighteenth Army the Soviets employed local superiorities of 8 or 10-1.

Table One
Relative odds against Army Groups North and Center, 1943

		Soviet forces opposite Army Group North	Soviet forces opposite Army Group Center
July 1943			
	Men	1.7 - 1	1.6 - 1
	Artillery	1.9 - 1	2.0 - 1
	AFVs	11.8-1	3.9 - 1
October 1943			
	Men	1.6 - 1	1.7 - 1
	Artillery	1.5 - 1	2.6 - 1
	AFVs	4.5 - 1	5.7 - 1

Table Two
Relative odds against Army Groups North and Center
at the beginning of Soviet offensives, 1944

	Soviet forces opposite Army Group North, 1/44	Soviet forces opposite Army Group Center 6/44
Men	2.1 - 1	1.8 - 1 (3.5 - 1)*
Artillery	2.0 - 1	2.4 - 1
AFVs	10 - 1	10 - 1
Aircraft	3.7 - 1	6.7 - 1

*including STAVKA strategic reserves

The results of the two operations, however, were drastically different. Although Army Group North sustained heavy losses – 88,847 men in two months (14.7% of its 1 January 1944 strength) – it retreated to the Panther Line as an intact fighting force. Only two of its thirty-nine divisions were so badly mauled as to be permanently disbanded, and the Soviets were fought to a halt at the Estonian border far short of their operational objectives. Army Group Center, on the other hand, was annihilated, losing twenty-eight divisions with loss estimates which began at 350,000 and moved swiftly up from there. The Red Army was not so much halted at the Vistula River in Poland as it simply outran its primitve logistical tail.

It has been argued that by June 1944 Army Group Center had long since been gutted of quality formations. Of its fifty-one divisions, five were security divisions, four were Hungarian, and only three were panzer or panzergrenadier. Yet few of the divisions assigned to Army Group North could be characterized as elite units either. In January 1944 the German order of battle outside Leningrad included forty-one divisions and three brigades. Of these, only one was nominally a mobile division, the untested 11th SS "*Nordland*" Panzergrenadier Division, which was composed of Scandinavian volunteers and deployed fewer than two dozen tanks. The remainder of the SS formations in the army group included a division of Latvians and one brigade each of Dutch and Estonian troops. Four divisions were either security or field training divisions, without heavy weapons, transport, or more than a single regiment of infantry each; another five were Luftwaffe Field divisions, which had earned the reputation of notoriously poor combat units. The differing results in the two campaigns cannot be ascribed either to the odds or the inherent quality of the German divisions.

One obvious advantage enjoyed by Army Group North over its neighbor was in senior leadership during the first critical days of the Soviet onslaught. It was the good fortune of the soldiers who retreated from Leningrad to the Panther Line that Field Marshal Ernst Busch, who had previously commanded the Sixteenth Army, was promoted by Hitler in late 1943 to command Army Group Center. There his rigid obedience to the *Führer's* strident "no retreat" orders lost the battle in less than a week. His counterpart and former superior, Field Marshal Georg von Küchler, fought hard enough against Hitler's wishes that he lost his position but saved his armies. Following his dismissal, Army Group North received competent if hardly inspired leadership for the remainder of 1944 from Walter Model, Georg Lindemann, Johannes Friessner, and Ferdinand Schörner. All four generals were primarily tacticians rather than strategists, which is precisely what the commander of an army group defending a secodnary front needs to be. Two of the four – Model and Schörner – developed reputations as talented if ruthless improvisers, which kept them in Hitler's good graces throught the war. Friessner, a Model protege, had some measure both of the tactical skills and the positive relationship with the *Führer*, but not quite enough to last out a crisis of confidence in mid-summer. Lindemann was an organizer rather than an improviser, and a traditional German officer of the sort who could never evoke warmth from his dictator; his tenure in command was therefore quite brief.

On the lower levels, at army and corps command, the army group was also fortunate. With so many non-Germans in the line, it is important to note that of the few Wehrmacht officers who managed to get along with the Reich's allies two were in key positions in Army Group North. Felix Steiner commanded the III SS Panzer Corps throughout the campaign, the bulk of which from February-September 1944 consisted of Belgians, Estonians, and Scandinavians. Steiner was a competent if not brilliant tactician, but any lack of flair in that regard was more than counterbalanced by his ability to inspire and lead his foreign troops. Likewise, Christian Hansen, who commanded the X Corps and then the Sixteenth Army, had earned a reputation for tactful dealings with the Rumanians two years earlier and developed a respect for the potential fighting capacity of non-German contingents when properly led – a critical quality for a commander whose army's line sometimes depended on the Latvians of the VI SS Corps.

Logistically speaking, Army Group North had a tremendous advantage over the other army groups in Russia in terms of its secure left flank on the Baltic Sea and its relatively safe lines of communication. The Baltic remained a German lake until the last weeks of the war, assuring Army Group North of the safe transport of supplies and the availability of naval gunfire support along the coast at critical junctures. Soviet operations against the islands off the coast of Estonia never became significant strategic considerations for the Germans, and as the summer and fall progressed more and more coastal defense and artillery units were redeployed to the front lines without any consequences. Moreover, Army Group North's road and railroad net through the Baltic states was both physically superior and more secure than that upon which the other army groups had to depend. Only in the area between Lake Pskov and Leningrad did the Germans face a significant partisan problem, whereas Army Group Center was harried by as many as 240,000 irregulars. This meant that Army Group North had the luxury of employing the staffs of its security divisions to supervise quiet sectors of the front and that security and *polizei* regiments could be dragooned into combat duty.

Throughout 1944 Army Group North benefited repeatedly from the best employment of both fixed and field fortifications on the Eastern front. Thanks primarily to the work of Major General Erich Abberger and his 3rd Construction Staff, the Rollbahn position saved two corps of the Eighteenth Army from annihilation in January. The Panther Line provided the necessary foundation to allow the army group to halt the direct Russian advance into Estonia for seven months. Improvised fortifications like the Children's Home position at Narva and the phase-lines for *Armeeabteilung Narva's* retreat allowed Army Group North greater safety and tactical freedom of action than could be found anywhere else in Russia. Those who argue that even without Hitler's irrational influences on strategy and operations that the German Army by 1944 was foredoomed to lose the war against the Soviet Union should study the campaigns of Army Group North very carefully. The Panther Line in Estonia was only the northernmost component of the so-called "Eastern Wall" which the generals wanted to construct. Its success (as well as the success of German defensive positions in Italy) is instructive; while the Wehrmacht certainly could not have laid a continuous line of fortifications across the entire front, a strongly developed fall-back position at the Beresina River in June 1944, for example, might well have saved the entire Ninth Army from destruction.

Fighting from fortified positions and falling back from one such position to another conserved manpower and equipment. Due to the nature of its defensive mission the army group rarely received significant numbers of tanks, but it was well-equipped with artillery and anti-tank guns. Furthermore, combat operations based on strong defensive lines reduced attrition among the artillery and anti-tank units in the army group. Further, a comparison of the nine infantry divisions in the First Panzer Army (Army Group North Ukraine) in March 1944 with those of the Eighteenth Army in June shows that the infantry divisions in the south had had their supporting arms devastated from months of campaigning in open country without fortifications. The nine divisions in the First Panzer Army averaged just three light artillery batteries, one heavy battery, and eight anti-tank guns, while the eight assigned to the Eighteenth Army averaged nine light artillery batteries, three heavy batteries, and – most significantly – sixteen anti-tank guns. Throughout 1944 the ratio of field artillery pieces to soldiers (75mm, 105mm, 150mm and 210mm in divisional and GHQ units, but not including static or naval guns) was consistently higher in Army Group North than anywhere else in Russia.

Yet for all the foregoing, neither leadership, logistics, nor fortifications were the decisive factors in Army Group North's tactical success. The simple fact is that the army group managed throughout 1944 to maintain its divisions at a higher strength than those further south. German records make it difficult to track the strength of individual divisions past the disasters of mid-June, but it is possible to examine what the modern U.S. Army calls the "division slice." The division slice is derived by dividing the combat strength of an army or army group by the number of division headquarters in the organization. This method has the advantage of averaging out the strength of non-divisional combat units into the fighting divisions. When this computation is done for Army Group North from mid-1943 to the end of the war, the resulting figures document that in 1944 the army group was remarkably successful in maintaining its strength (see Table Three).

Table Three
"Division slice," Army Group North, 1944-1945

Date	Total strength	Divisions	Division slice
1 January 1944	602,583	39	15,451
1 March 1944	567,147	43	13,189
1 June 1944	617,677	38	16,254
1 September 1944	510,000	40	12,750
1 December 1944	505,586	34	14,870
7 May 1945	200,000	20	10,000

While the tactical and logistical considerations noted above certainly had an effect on the army group's attempts to maintain its fighting strength, the peculiarities of the German replacement system had an equal hand in keeping up divisional strengths. Throughout the war Army Group North actually received preferential treatment in terms of replacements. Table Four documents the losses and replacements along the Russian front from December 1942-August 1943 (not counting the capitulation of the Sixth Army). Even a cursory glance reveals that Army Group North suffered but 13.5% of the casualties and received 22.3% of the replacements; in point of fact, the army group was the only one which received replacements in excess of its casualties! This situation continued into 1944: the 88,848 casualties incurred during January-February would have been debilitating without the immediate influx of 51,603 replacements before March 1. By June Army Group North was actually stronger by 15,000 men than it had been on January 1 –

even though it had conducted a bloody fighting retreat, a protracted struggle for the Panther Line, and had had at least one division transferred away. No other army group received comparable treatment.

Table Four
German Replacements in Russia
December 1942 - August 1943

Army Group	Losses	% of total losses	Replacements	% of total losses	Net
North	170,922	13.5	211,365	22.3	+40,443
Center	534,174	42.3	350,453	37.0	-183,724
South*	556,917	44.2	386,282	40.7	-170,635
Total	1,262,013	–	948,000	–	-313,913

*"South" here includes Army Groups South, Don, A, and B.

This state of affairs existed because the German replacement system in World War Two – at least until it was turned over to Heinrich Himmler after July 1944 – remained the same decentralized organization employed in World War One, which was itself a holdover from the Prussian Wars of Unification. With neglible exceptions, divisions were raised within the confines of a particular *Wehrkreis* (regional military headquarters) and drew their replacements from the same area throughout the war. This gave rise to the strong regional identifications of most German divisions. Each division initially had its own dedicated *ersatz* regiment composed of battalions corresponding to each of its regiments. As the Wehrmacht expanded rapidly in 1941-1942, the system became overloaded, and instead of creating enough additional *ersatz* regiments, several divisions would be assigned to the the existing ones, which naturally reduced the replacement pool for each division, although it is evident that at least until the beginning of 1944 the "First Wave" divisions (the original divisions of the prewar army) continued to receive preference both in terms of numbers and quality of replacements.

The flow of replacements was also related to the distance the troops had to travel to the front and the frequency with which a division was redployed to different fronts. An infantry division fighting deep in the Caucasus at the end of a supply line consisting of single-track railroads and dirt wagon tracks too attenuated to keep up a steady delivery of ammunition or fuel could hardly expect the same rate of arriving replacements as another division outside Leningrad with secure rail and sea routes of only a few hundred miles back to the Zone of the Interior. Likewise a division remaining endlessly on the march from one crisis point to another often outpaced its own replacements for months at a time, even in a unit such as the Panzergrenadier Division "*Grossdeutschland*" which had its own dedicated replacement organization. On both of these counts Army Group North could be considered fortunate – in January 1944 thirteen divisions, a full third of the divisions in the army group, had been stationed on the Leningrad front since the first day of the campaign, a state of affairs unprecedented anywhere else in the East.

Even more important, seventeen of Army Group North's divisions (43.5%) hailed from the easternmost regions of Germany: East Prussia, Pomerania, Brandenburg, and Eastern Silesia, and nine of those were among the long-service veterans in northern Russia. The replacement organizations in *Wehrkreis* I, II, III, and VIII therefore had superior logisitical connections to deliver replacements to the army group as well as an extremely practical reason for doing so. At least until mid-summer 1944 the inhabitants of those areas would reasonably have seen Army Group North as the part of the front most directly defending their homes. In addition, one SS division and two SS brigades (both later raised to a division) had been recruited in Latvia and Estonia, which meant that the source for their replacements was nearby and under the administrative control of the *Höhere SS undPolizei Führer Ostland,* who himself had a stake in active recruiting since he was often called to the front with his security forces. These divisions, like the western European volunteers of the III SS Panzer Corps which benefitted from the SS replacement system, spent the overwhelming majority of their fighting careers with Army Group North. Thus well over half of the divisions in the army group had access to far better supplies of replacements than the other army groups on the Eastern Front.

Ironically, the successes achieved by Army Group North were detrimental to the German cause, at least in the sense that the disproportionate numbers of reinforcements delivered to a secondary front might have had a more significant strategic effect if directed toward other army groups. The 40,000 soldiers in excess of combat losses sent to the Leningrad front between December 1942-August 1943 might, for example, had made a critical difference to the outcome of the Kursk battles on the central and southern fronts that summer. An examination of German Army records suggests that neither Hitler nor successive Chiefs of the Army General Staff were fully conscious of the high number of replacements being funneled into Army Group North. As Samuel Mitcham has pointed out, the senior commanders spent most of

1942 and 1943 transferring divisions away from the army group.[1]

The successful defensive operations conducted by Army Group North also had another side effect, which was probably unknown to the average *Landser* in the trenches but which could not have been completely hidden from senior officers, especially those who had been stationed around the Baltic for three years. As retreats began on all fronts, *Reichsführer* Heinrich Himmler moved to cover up the evidence of the death camps and systematic genocide in the East. In the Baltic states this took the dual form of deporting to Auschwitz the last Jews who had been suffered to exist in ghettoes in Riga or Siauliai because they worked in war industries and the return of personnel from the original murder squads – the *einsatzgruppen* – to exhume the bodies of their victims and burn them.[2] All of these activities came under the direct control of *Höhere SS und Polizei Führer Ostland* Friedrich Jeckeln, who also supervised the recuitment of Latvian, Lithuanian, and Estonian SS volunteers, conducted vicious anti-partisan activities in the immediate army group rear area, and even led his security units at the front from time to time. While admiring the individual courage of the soldiers and the operational skill with which Army Group North held a numerically superior enemy at bay, it is important to remember the full extent of the horrors those soldiers died defending.

NOTES

[1] Samuel W. Mitcham, Jr., *Hitler's Field Marshals and Their Battles* (Chelsea MI: Scarborough House, 1988), p. 262.

[2] Martin Gilbert, *The Holocaust, A History of the Jews of Europe during the second World War* (New York: Henry Holt), 1985, p. 722.

Order of Battle, Army Group North, 16 January 1944

Field Marshal Georg von Küchler, Commanding

Chief of Staff: Major General Eberhard Kinzel
Engineer Officer: Lieutenant General Gerhard Medem
Quartermaster General: Colonel Otto Rauser
Supply Officer: Lieutenant General Rudolf Schrader
Panzer Officer: Colonel Hyacinth Graf von Strachwitz
       von Gross-Zauche und Camminetz

Eighteenth Army
Colonel General Georg Lindemann

Chief of Staff: Major General Friedrich Foertsch

III SS *"Germanische"* Panzer Corps
    Gruppenführer Felix Steiner

        11th SS *"Nordland"* Panzergrenadier Division
            Brigadeführer Fritz von Scholz
            Operations Officer: Captain von Bock
            SS Panzergrenadier Regiment 23 *"Norge"*
            SS Panzergrenadier Regiment 24 *"Danmark"*
            SS Panzer Battalion 11 *"Hermann von Salza"*
            SS Panzer Reconnaissance Battalion 11
            SS Panzer Artillery Regiment 11
            SS Flak Battalion 11
            SS Assault Gun Battalion 11
            SS Panzer Jäger Battalion 11

SS Panzer Engineer Battalion 11

4th SS *"Nederland"* Panzergrenadier Brigade
    Brigadeführer Joachim Ziegler
    SS Panzergrenadier Regiment 48 *"General Seyffardt"*
    SS Panzergrenadier Regiment 49 *"De Ruyter"*
    SS Panzer Reconnaissance Battalion 54
    SS Panzer Artillery Battalion 54
    SS Engineer Battalion (motorized) 54

61st Infantry Division (-)
    Lieutenant General Günther Krappe
    Operations Officer: Lieutenant Colonel Starcke
    Grenadier Regiments 151, 162, 176
    Staff & III/Artillery Regiment 161
    Füsilier Battalion[1]

9th Luftwaffe Field Division
    Colonel Ernst Michael
    Operations Officer: Lieutenant Colonel Biehler
    Luftwaffe Jäger Regiments 17, 18
    Luftwaffe Artillery Regiment 9
    Luftwaffe Füsilier Battalion 9
    Luftwaffe Panzer Jäger Battalion 9[2]

10th Luftwaffe Field Division
    Major General Hermann von Wedel
    Operations Officer: Lieutenant Colonel Eppendorff
    Luftwaffe Jäger Regiments 19, 20
    Luftwaffe Artillery Regiment 10
    Luftwaffe Füsilier Battalion 10
    Luftwaffe Panzer Jäger Battalion 10

attached units:
    II/Artillery Regiment 397
    I/Artillery Regiment 399 (170th Infantry Division)
    Füsilier Battalion 126 (126th Infantry Division)[3]
    III/SS Artillery Regiment *"Polizei"* (4th SS *"Polizei"* Division)

police/security units:
  1./*Einsatzabteilung "Ostland"*

corps artillery:
  Artillery Commander 138
      Colonel Gustav Hundt
  Artillery Battalions 810, II/58
  Artillery Batteries 4./37, 4./58
  Werfer Regiment 3 (-I)

engineer troops:
  Construction Battalions 121, 156
  1. & 3./Railroad Construction Battalion 565
  Fortress Engineer Battalion 25

panzer troops:
  Panzer Jäger Battalion 752
  1. & 4./Panzer Jäger Battalion 477
  I/Panzer Regiment 29 (12th Panzer Division)

L Corps
General of Infantry Wilhelm Wegener

  126th Infantry Division (-)
      Colonel Gotthardt Fischer
      Operations Officer: Lieutenant Colonel Merkel
      Grenadier Regiments 422, 424, 426
      Artillery Regiment 126
      Engineer Battalion126

  170th Infantry Division (-)
      Lieutenant General Walther Krause
      Operations Officer: Lieutenant Colonel Albinus
      Grenadier Regiments 391, 399, 401
      Staff, II & III/Artillery Regiment 240
      Field Replacement Battalion 240

  215th Infantry Division
      Lieutenant General Bruno Frankewitz

Operations Officer: Lieutenant Colonel Schelm
Grenadier Regiments 380, 390, 433
Artillery Regiment 215
Füsilier Battalion[4]
Field Replacement Battalion 215

attached units:
I & II/Artillery Regiment 161 (61st Infantry Division)

police/security units:
Security Battalion 938

corps artillery:
Artillery Commander 18
Artillery Battalions II/37, 458, 633, 641, 744, 914 (Static)
Artillery Batteries 3./680, 503 (Static)
Werfer Regiment 70

engineer troops:
Engineer Regimental Staff 667
Construction Battalion 707
Engineer Battalion 44

panzer troops:
Panzer Jäger Battalions 563 (- 3.), 667

LIV Corps
General of Infantry Otto Sponheimer

11th Infantry Division
Lieutenant General Karl Burdach
Operations Officer: Major Langenstrass
Grenadier Regiments 2, 23, 44
Artillery Regiment 11
Panzer Jäger Battalion 11

24th Infantry Division (-)
Lieutenant General Kurt Versock
Operations Officer: Lieutenant Colonel Herzog

Grenadier Regiments 31, 32, 102
Staff, II & III/Artillery Regiment 24
Panzer Jäger Battalion 24
Field Replacement Company 24

225th Infantry Division (-)
      Lieutenant General Ernst Risse
      Operations Officer: Lieutenant Colonel Ritter und Edler
                         von Rosenthal
      Grenadier Regiments 333, 376, 377
      Staff, I & II/Artillery Regiment 225
      Engineer Battalion225

police/security units:
      Security Battalion 636

corps artillery:
      Artillery Commander 146
      Artillery Battalions 615, 910 (Static), 928 (Static)
      Army Flak Battalion 292 (-1 battery)

engineer troops:
      Engineer Regimental Staff 690

panzer troops:
      Panzer Jäger Battalion 753 (- 2.)

XXVI Corps
      Lieutenant General Anton Grasser

225th Infantry Division
      Lieutenant General Wilhelm Berlin
      Operations Officer: Lieutenant Colonel Starck
      Grenadier Regiments 328, 366, 412
      Artillery Regiment 227
      Füsilier Battalion[5]

212th Infantry Division
      Major General Dr. Koske

Operations Officer: Lieutenant Colonel Ogilvie
Grenadier Regiments 306, 317, 365
Artillery Regiment 212
Reconnaissance Battalion 212
Panzer Jäger Company 212

attached units:
    III/Artillery Regiment 225 (225th Infantry Division)
    Sturm Battalion, 18th Army

corps artillery:
    Artillery Commander 113
        Colonel Werner Heucke
    Artillery Regimental Staff for Special Employment 818
    Artillery Battalions 153, 507 (Static), 624
    Artillery Battery 1./814

engineer troops:
    Engineer Regimental Staff 574
    Construction Battalions 55, 401

panzer troops:
    2./Panzer Jäger Battalion 753

XXVIII Corps
    General of Artillery Herbert Loch
    Chief of Staff: Colonel Edmund Blaurock

    21st Infantry Division
        Lieutenant General Gerhard Matzky
        Operations Officer: Lieutenant Colonel Schroetter
        Grenadier Regiments 3, 24, 45
        Artillery Regiment 21
        Panzer Jäger Battalion 21
        Field Replacement Battalion 21

    121st Infantry Division
        Lieutenant General Hellmuth Priess
        Operations Officer: Major Hoefer

Grenadier Regiments 405, 407, 408
Artillery Regiment 121
Panzer Jäger Battalion 121
Legion Espaniola de Voluntarios (attached)[6]
    Colonel Antonio Garica Navarro

12th Luftwaffe Field Division
    Colonel Gottfried Weber
    Operations Officer:Lieutenant Colonel Richter
    Luftwaffe Jäger Regiments 23, 24
    Luftwaffe Artillery Regiment 12
    Luftwaffe Bicycle Reconnaissance Battalion 12
    Luftwaffe Panzer Jäger Battalion 12

13th Luftwaffe Field Division
    Lieutenant General Hellmuth Reymann
    Operations Officer: Major Koch
    Luftwaffe Jäger Regiments 25, 26
    Luftwaffe Artillery Regiment 13
    Luftwaffe Bicycle Reconnaissance Battalion 13
    Luftwaffe Panzer Jäger Battalion 13

Kampfgruppe, 4th SS *"Polizei"* Panzergrenadier Division
    Brigadeführer Fritz Schmedes
        Operations Officer: *Obersturmbannführer*
        Pipkorn
        SS *"Polizei"* Panzergrenadier Regiment 3
        Staff, I/SS Artillery Regiment *"Polizei"*

attached units:
    I/Artillery Regiment 31 (24th Infantry Division)
    Regimental Staff for Special Employment 540

corps artillery:
    Artillery Commander 24
    Artillery Battalion 850
    one battery/Army Flak Battalion 292

engineer troops:
        Construction Battalions 95, 101, 503
        Engineer Battalion 657 (-1 co.)

XXXVIII Corps
        General of Infantry Kurt Herzog

        2nd SS (Latvian) Volunteer Brigade
                Stadartenführer Hinrich
                Operations Officer: *Hauptsturmführer* Moldering
                SS Waffen Grenadier Regiments 42, 43, 44
                SS Füsilier Battalion 19
                SS Artillery Regiment 19
                SS Panzer Jäger Company 19
                SS Engineer Battalion 19

        28th Jäger Division
                Lieutenant General Hans Speth
                Operations Officer: Lieutenant Colonel Schaeder
                Jäger Regiments 49, 83
                Jäger Artillery Regiment 28
                Panzer Jäger Battalion 28

        1st Luftwaffe Field Division
                Major General Petrauschke
                Operations Officer: Major Daub
                Luftwaffe Jäger Regiments 1, 2
                Luftwaffe Artillery Regiment 1
                Luftwaffe Füsilier Battalion 1
                Luftwaffe Panzer Jäger Battalion 1

        attached units:
                Grenadier Regiment 503 (290th Infantry Division)
                II/Artillery Regiment 290 (290th Infantry Division)
                I/SS Artillery Regiment *"Polizei"* (4th SS *"Polizei"* Division)

        police/security units:
                Lithuanian Security Battalion 256
                "Ost" Battalions 658, 659

corps artillery:

    Artillery Commander 30

    Artillery Regimental Staff for Special Employment 785

    Artillery Battalions I/106, 289 (Static), 815, 854, 929 (Static)

engineer troops:

    Construction Regimental Staff 32, 77

    Construction Battalions 127, 156, 591, 677, 741

panzer troops:

    2./Panzer Jäger Battalion 477

    4./Panzer Jäger Battalion 478

Army Troops

    Army Rear Area (Korück) 516

police/security units:

    Security Regimental Staffs for Special Employment 605, 730

    Security Battalions 236, 375, 638, II/728

    Ost Battalion (Estonian) 660

    Fortress Battalion 657

    Military Police Detachment 689

army artillery:

    Senior Artillery Commander 303

    Artillery Regimental Staff 802

    Artillery Battalions II/84, 708 (static), 768

    Artillery Batteries 1. & 2./68, 508 (static), 515 (static)

    Railroad Artillery Regimental Staff 802

    Railroad Artillery Battalions 459, 686, 691, 693, 695

engineer troops:

    Engineer Regimental Staffs for Special Employment 32, 71

    Construction Battalions 95, 127, 147, 156, 591, 677

panzer troops:

    Panzer Jäger Battalion 478 (- 4.)

    3./Panzer Jäger Battalion 563

    part of I/Panzer Regiment 29

Sixteenth Army
General of Artillery Christian Hansen

Chief of Staff: Major General Paul Hermann
Army Engineer Officer: Colonel Hubert-Maria Ritter von Heigl

X Corps
General of Infantry Thomas-Emil von Wickede

30th Infantry Division
Lieutenant General Wilhelm Haase
Operations Officer: Major Bach
Grenadier Regiments 6, 46
Füsilier Regiment 26
Artillery Regiment 30
Panzer Jäger Battalion 30
Field Replacement Battalion 30

8th Jäger Division
Lieutenant General Friedrich
Volckhamer von Kirchensittenbach
Operations Officer: Lieutenant Colonel Lorenz
Jäger Regiments 28, 38
Jäger Artillery Regiment 8
Panzer Jäger Battalion 8
Field Replacement Battalion 8

21st Luftwaffe Field Division
Major General Rudolf-Eduard Licht
Operations Officer: Lieutenant Colonel Rüden
Luftwaffe Jäger Regiments 41, 42, 43
Luftwaffe Artillery Regiment 21
Luftwaffe Panzerjäger Battalion 21

corps artillery:
Artillery Commander 19
Artillery Battalions II/2 *Lehr*, 429
Artillery Batteries 2./436, 1. & 2./511

engineer troops:
> Engineer Regimental Staff 519
> Construction Battalions 25, 108, 680
> Engineer Battalions 656, 677

II Corps
> General of Infantry Paul Laux
> Chief of Staff:
>> Colonel Erich Schmidt-Richberg

> 93d Infantry Division
>> Major General Karl Löwrick
>> Operations Officer: Lieutenant Colonel Greiner
>> Grenadier Regiments 270, 272
>> Artillery Regiment 193
>> Field Replacement Battalion 193

> 218th Infantry Division
>> Lieutenant General Viktor Lang
>> Operations Officer: Lieutenant Colonel Picot
>> Grenadier Regiments 311, 346, 389
>> Artillery Regiment 217
>> Mobile Battalion 217[7]

> 331st Infantry Division
>> Major General Heinz Furbach
>> Operations Officer: Lieutenant Colonel Niepold
>> Grenadier Regiments 537, 558, 559
>> Artillery Regiment 331[8]
>> Field Replacement Battalion 331

attached units:
> Grenadier Regiment 374 (207th Security Division)
> Security Regiment 368 (207th Security Division)
> assault gun co./Panzer Jäger Battalion 8 (8th Jäger Division)

corps artillery:
> Artillery Commander 105
> Artillery Batteries 4./2 *Lehr*, 3./577, 1./818

engineer troops:
>   Engineer Regimental Staff 547
>   Construction Battalion 254
>   Engineer Battalion 660

XXXXIII Corps
Lieutenant General Ehrenfried Boege

VI SS *"Freiwillige"* Corps Headquarters
>   *Gruppenführer* and Lieutenant General of Police
>   Karl Pfeffer-Wildenbruch

>   15th SS Waffen Grenadier (1st Latvian) Division
>   *Brigadeführer* Karl von Truenfeld
>   SS Waffen Grenadier Regiments 32, 33, 34
>   SS Füsilier Battalion 15
>   SS Artillery Regiment 15
>   SS Panzer Jäger Company 15
>   SS Engineer Battalion 15

23d Infantry Division
>   Major General Paul Gurran
>   Operations Officer: Lieutenant Colonel Niepold
>   Grenadier Regiments 9, 67
>   Füsilier Regiment 68
>   Artillery Regiment 23
>   Field Replacement Battalion 23

69th Infantry Division
>   Lieutenant General Bruno Ortner
>   Operations Officer: Major Henrici
>   Grenadier Regiments 159, 236
>   Artillery Regiment 169
>   Field Replacement Battalion 168

83d Infantry Division
>   Lieutenant General Theodor Scherer
>   Operations Officer: Lieutenant Colonel Krüger
>   Grenadier Regiments 251, 257, 277

Artillery Regiment 183
Füsilier Battalion[9]
Panzer Jäger Company 183

205th Infantry Division (-)
Major General Horst von Mellenthin
Operations Officer: Lieutenant Colonel Klostermann
Grenadier Regiment 335
Artillery Regiment 205
Füsilier Battalion[10]
Panzer Jäger Company 205

corps artillery:
Artillery Commander 133
Artillery Regimental Staff for Special Employment 787
Artillery Battalions 531 (Static), 639 (Static)
Artillery Battery 2./817

engineer troops:
Engineer Regimental Staffs 35, 504
Construction Battalions 98, 416
one co./Engineer Battalion 566

panzer troops:
Heavy Panzer Jäger Battalion 666 (-1 co.)

VIII Corps
General of Infantry Gustav Höhne

58th Infantry Division
Major General Kurt Siewert
Operations Officer: Lieutenant Colonel Simon
Grenadier Regiments 154, 209, 220
Artillery Regiment 158

81st Infantry Division
Lieutenant General Erich Schopper
Operations Officer: Lieutenant Colonel Krüger
Grenadier Regiments 161, 174

Artillery Regiment 181
Field Replacement Battalion 181

263d Infantry Division
Colonel Hans Wagner
Operations Officer: Lieutenant Colonel Sulzberger
Grenadier Regiments 462, 482, 486
Artillery Regiment 263
Field Replacement Battalion 263

329th Infantry Division
Lieutenant General Johannes Dr. Dr. Mayer
Operations Officer: Major Kuhn
Grenadier Regiments 551, 552, 553
Artillery Regiment 329
Mobile Battalion[11]

attached units:
Grenadier Regiment 353 (205th Infantry Division)
I/Artillery Regiment 132 (132d Infantry Division)
II/Artillery Regiment 207 (207th Security Division)

police/security units:
Security Battalion 663
Latvian SS Police Battalion 319
3./Military Police Battalion 561
Cossack Battalion 443
SS *Polizei* Regiments 9, 26

corps artillery:
Artillery Commander 408
Artillery Regimental Staff for Special Employment 110
Artillery Battalions 536, 626 (Static), 629 (Static), II/814,
I/818 (-1.), 833, 917
Artillery Batteries 1. & 3./636
Werfer Battalion 10

engineer troops:
Engineer Regimental Staff 31

Construction Battalions 413, 510
Engineer Battalion 672

panzer troops:
Tiger Battalion 502
3./Panzer Jäger Battalion 477
one co./Panzer Jäger Battalion 757
one co./Heavy Panzer Jäger Battalion 666

I Corps
General of Infantry Carl Hilpert

32d Infantry Division
Lieutenant General Hans Boeck-Behrens
Operations Officer: Lieutenant Colonel von Kleist
Grenadier Regiments 4, 94, 96
Artillery Regiment 32
Reconnaissance Battalion 32
Field Replacement Battalion 32

122d Infantry Division
Lieutenant General Kurt Chill
Operations Officer: Lieutenant Colonel Weber
Grenadier Regiments 409, 410, 411
Artillery Regiment 122
Field Replacement Battalion 122

132d Infantry Division (-)
Major General Herbert Wagner
Operations Officer: Lieutenant Colonel Geyer
Grenadier Regiments 436, 437, 438
Staff, I & II/Artillery Regiment 132
Panzer Jäger Battalion 132

police/security units:
Gruppe Jeckeln
Gruppenführer Friedrich Jeckeln
Operations Officer: *Obersturmbannführer d.*
Schupo Gol

Estonian SS *Polizei* Regiments 45, 46
Estonian SS *Polizei* Battalion 286
SS *Polizei* Regiment 16
Latvian *Polizei* Regiment "Riga"
three cos./SIPO

Gruppe von Gottberg
 Gruppenführer Kurt von Gottberg
 SS *Polizei* Regiments 2, 13, 24
 SS Jäger Battalion "Panier"
 SS Special Battalion "Dirlewanger"
 Polizei Border Command "Kreikenbom"

Bicycle Security Regiment 2
Security Battalions I/601, 795

corps artillery:
 Artillery Commander 401
 Artillery Regimental Staff for Special Employment 49
 Artillery Battalions 435, 436 (-), 526, 636 (-)

engineer troops:
 Construction Battalions 18, 214, 502
 Engineer Battalion 655

Army Troops:
Senior Artillery Commander 309
 Major General Gerhard Grassmann
Senior Artillery Commander 315
 Lieutenant General Christian Usinger
Army Rear Area Command (Korück) 501
Heavy Artillery Regiment 584
Security Regimental Staffs 85, 120
Security Battalions I/107 (281st Security Division), I/191, 343, 493, 591, II/601, 860, 865, 868, 989
Latvian Security Battalion 231
Cossack Battalion 631
Ost Regimental Staff for Special Employment 753
Estonian *Ost* Company 657

Lithuanian *Polizei* Battalions 5, 13
Military *Polizei* Battalion 567 (-)
Engineer Regimental Staff 16
Construction Battalions 79, 87, 306, 402
Panzer Jäger Battalion 757 (minus one company)

Army Group Reserves

Rear Area Commander, Army Group North
General of Infantry Kuno-Hans von Both

Field Training Division 388
Lieutenant General Johann Pflugbeil
Field Training Regiments 639, 640

207th Security Division (-)/Commandant, Riga and Lake Peipus
Lieutenant General Erich Hofmann
Operations Officer: Major (R) von Below
II/*Polizei* Regiment 9
Ost Cavalry Battalion 207
Panzer Company (captured) 207

281st Security Division (-)
Major General Wilhem-Hunnold Stockhausen
Operations Officer: Major (R) Fischer
Grenadier Regiment 368
II/Security Regiment 107
II/Artillery Regiment 207
Ukrainian Cavalry Battalion 281
III/*Polizei* Regiment 9
Panzer Company (captured) 281

285th Security Division
Lieutenant General Gustav Adolph-Auffenberg-Komarow
Operations Officer: Captain (R) Rauls
Grenadier Regiment 322
Security Regiment 113
I/*Polizei* Regiment 9
III/Artillery Regiment 207

Ukrainian Cavalry Battalion 285

Cavalry Regiment "*Nord*"
    Lieutenant Colonel Karl Prinz zu Salm-Horstmar
Latvian Security Battalions 275, 678, 886
Fortress Battalions 660, III/712
Estonian Militia Battalions 37, 38, 40, 41
Military Police Battalion 697

Under direct Army Group Control:

    290th Infantry Division (-)
        Lieutenant General Conrad-Oskar Heinrichs
        Operations Officer: Lieutenant Colonel Jordan
        Grenadier Regiments 501, 502
        Staff, I & III/Artillery Regiment 290
        Mobile Battalion[12]

    Army Group Weapons School
        Colonel Gustav Schulzen
    3./Security Battalion 636
    Artillery Battalion 509 (Static)
    Artillery Battery 2./929 (Static)

Panther Line

    3d Engineer Staff
        Major General Erich Abberger
        Construction Battalions 505, 906
        Engineer Battalion 676

    Regimental Staff for Special Employment 610
        Construction Battalions 100, 132, 257
        Engineer Battalions 652, 657

    Flak Units in the Army Group North Operational Area
        under the control of Luftflötte 1

2nd Flak Division
> Major General Luczny
> Operations Officer: Major Kramer
> Flak Regiment (motorized) 182 (Narva area)
>> Lieutenant Colonel Meerkötter
>> Light Flak Battalion 833
>>> (4 heavy & 4 mixed batteries)
>>> Captain Wiehe
>> I/Mixed Flak Regiment (motorized) 2
>> (assembling)
>>> Captain Krüger
>> Light Flak Battalion 719
>>> (1 heavy & 2 mixed batteries)
>>> Captain Köstlin
>> Light Flak Battalion (self-propelled) 75
>>> (1 heavy & 3 mixed batteries)
>>> Captain Herke
>> Mixed Flak Battalion 361
>>> (2 heavy & 3 mixed batteries)
>>> Major Dr. Thimm
>> II/Mixed Flak Battalion (motorized) 132
>>> (2 heavy & 2 mixed batteries)
>>> Captain Gemünde
>> II/Mixed Flak Regiment (motorized) 36
>>> (1 heavy & 4 mixed batteries)
>>> Captain Gloger
>> I/Mixed Flak Regiment (motorized) 51
>>> (3 heavy & 2 mixed batteries)
>>> Captain Meÿn
> Flak Regiment (motorized) 164 (south of Leningrad)
>> Lieutenant Colonel Bulla
>> Mixed Flak Battalion 617
>>> (1 heavy & 2 mixed batteries)
>>> Captain Lesch
>> Mixed Flak Battalion 431
>>> (3 heavy & 4 mixed batteries)
>>> Major Fischer
>> Light Flak Battalion 834
>>> (2 heavy & 2 mixed batteries)

Major Marten

II/Mixed Flak Regiment (motorized) 16
   (2 heavy & 2 mixed batteries)
   Lieutenant Strube
I/Mixed Flak Regiment (motorized) 54
   (2 heavy batteries)
   Captain Schafer
Flakgruppe "Sud" (HQ, Light Flak Battalion 766) (Luga area)
Major Bruggerman
Light Flak Battalion 766
   (2 heavy & 4 mixed batteries)
   Major Bruggerman
Mixed Flak Battalion 341
   (1 heavy & 2 mixed batteries)
   Captain Heuer
I/Mixed Flak Battalion 40
   (2 heavy & 1 mixed batteries)
   Captain Hartmann
Flakgruppe "Pleskau" (HQ, Mixed Flak Battalion 214) (Pleskau area)
Lieutenant Colonel Krichler
Mixed Flak Battalion 214
   (2 heavy & 3 mixed batteries)
   Lieutenant Colonel Krichler
Light Railroad Flak Battalion 867
   (3 light railroad batteries)
   Captain Reckzeh
Flak Regiment (motorized) 41 (Dno area)
Colonel Rauch
Mixed Flak Battalion 645
   (3 heavy & 4 mixed batteries)
   Major Knitschko
Light Flak Battalion 843
   (1 heavy & 3 mixed batteries)
   Major Katzinger
Light Flak Battalion 994
   (1 heavy & 3 mixed batteries)
   Major Kuck

6th Flak Division (motorized)
Major General Anton
Operations Officer: Major Dölle
Flak Regiment (motorized) 43 (Postockhka-Idriza area)
Lieutenant Colonel Giebner
Mixed Flak Battalion 127
(3 heavy & 2 mixed batteries)
Captain Oelekker
Light Flak Battalion 753
(1 heavy & 5 mixed batteries)
Captain Frölich
Light Flak Battalion (self-propelled) 92
(3 mixed batteries)
Captain Horn
I/Mixed Flak Regiment (motorized) 291
(3 heavy & 2 mixed batteries)
Captain Sarnitz
Mixed Flak Battalion 294
(6 heavy & 5 mixed batteries)
Major Wolbrecht
Flak Regiment (motorized) 151 (Polotzk area)
Colonel von Ludwig
I/Mixed Flak Regiment (motorized) 411
(3 heavy & 2 mixed batteries)
Major Kruse
I/Mixed Flak Regiment 73
(3 heavy & 2 mixed batteries)
Captain Dirk
II/Mixed Flak Regiment (motorized) 14
(3 heavy & 2 mixed batteries)
I/Mixed Flak Regiment 50
(2 mixed batteries)
Flagruppe "Ostland" (HQ, Flak Regiment 36) (Baltic states)
Lieutenant Colonel Meÿer
Mixed Flak Battalion 215
(4 heavy & 1 mixed batteries)
Major Letterer
Mixed Flak Battalion 219
(2 heavy & 1 mixed batteries)

Lieutenant Emrich
Mixed Flak Battalion 385
(4 heavy & 1 mixed batteries)
Captain Maskow
Mixed Flak Battalion 517
(3 heavy & 3 mixed batteries)
Captain Pelz
Light Flak Battalion 720
(2 mixed batteries)
Captain Dehn

Organizing:

I/Flak Regiment (motorized) 111
(3 heavy & 2 mixed batteries)
I/Flak Regiment (motorized) 36
(3 heavy & 2 mixed batteries)

NOTES

[1] The much-reduced reconnaissance and panzer jäger battalions had been combined into a single battalion, with one bicycle company, one armored car company, and two panzer jäger companies. Keilig, *Das Deutsche Heer,* I: 15/23.

[2] Formerly Army Panzer Jäger Battalion 225; Keilig, *Das Deutsche Heer,* III: 130/8.

[3] As noted for the 61st Infantry Division, with the exception that this battalion contained also a battery of light flak. Keilig, *Das Deutsche Heer,* I: 15/26.

[4] As noted for the 61st Infantry Division, except that in this division the füsilier battalion contained only one bicycle reconnaissance company and one panzer jäger company. Keilig, *Das Deutsche Heer,* I: 15/29.

[5] As noted for the 61st Infantry Division, but with organization: one bicycle reconnaissance company, one motorcycle company, and one panzer jäger company. Keilig, *Das Deutsche Heer,* I: 15/30.

[6] The worsening of Germany's military situation had caused Spain to withdraw its 253d *"Blau"* Infantry Division from the Russian front; all that Hitler could convince Franco to allow him to retain was a small legion of volunteers—essentially a weak regiment of two infantry battalions and a support battalion of engineers, anti-tank guns, etc. The unit was no more than 1,500 men strong at its inception, and was literally decimated during January 1944. The remnants were disbanded and sent home in February. Gerald R. Kleinfeld and Lewis A. Tambs, *Hitler's Spanish Legion, The Blue Division in Russia* (Carbondale IL: Southern Illinois University Press, 1979), pp. 339-343; Pedro V. Roig, *Spanish Soldiers in Russia* (Miami:

Ediciones Universal, 1976), pp. 106-107.

[7] As with 61st Infantry Division, the reconnaissance and panzer jäger elements of this division had been combined into one battalion with two bicycle reconnaissance companies, one panzer jäger company, and one 20mm flak company. Keilig, *Das Deutsche Heer*, I: 15/p. 30.

[8] Two battalions. Keilig, *Das Deutsche Heer*, I: 15/p. 36.

[9] Reconnaissance elements integrated into the Füsilier Battalion, which had two bicycle companies and one armored car company. Keilig, *Das Deutsche Heer*, I: 15/p. 24.

[10] Reconnaissance elements integrated into the Füsilier Battalion, which had three bicycle companies and one armored car company. Keilig, *Das Deutsche Heer*, I: 15/p. 28.

[11] Reconnaissance and panzer jäger elements combined into mobile battalion with three bicycle companies, one armored car company, and one panzer jäger company. Keilig, *Das Deutsche Heer*, I: 15/p. 35.

[12] Reconnaissance and panzer jäger elements combined into mobile battalion with one bicycle company, one 37mm flak company, and three panzer jäger companies. Keilig, *Das Deutsche Heer*, I: 15/p. 35.

Bibliography

Buchner, Alex. *The German Infantry Handbook, 1939-1945.* West Chester PA: Schiffer, 1991.

Catpured German Records, National Archives, Washington DC:
Heeresgruppe Nord
Armeeoberkommando 18
Armeeoberkommando 16
Armeeabteilung Narva
II SS Panzer Generalkommando I
VI SS Generalkommando
Gruppe Sponheimer

Carell, Paul. *Scorched Earth, The Russian-German War, 1943-1944.* New York: Ballantine, 1966.

Conner, Albert Z., and Robert G. Poirier. *Red Army Order of Battle in the Great Patriotic War.* Novato CA: Presidio, 1985.

Erickson, John. *The Road to Berlin, Continuing the History of Stalin's War with Germany.* Boulder CO: Westview, 1983.

Fleming, Gerald. *Hitler and the Final Solution.* Berkeley: University of California, 1984.

Forwick, Helmuth. "*Der Rückzug der Heeresgruppe Nord nach Kurland,*" in Hans Meier-Welcker, ed., *Abwehrkämpfe am Nordflügel der Ostfront,*

1944-1945.. Stuttgart: Deutsche Verlags-Anstalt, 1963.

Hoffmann, Peter. *The History of the German Resistance, 1933-1945.* Cambridge MA: MIT Press, 1977.

Keilig, Wolf. *Das Deutsche Heer.* 3 volumes. Frankfurt: Podzun Verlag, 1958.

Kleinfeld, Gerald R., and Lewis A. Tambs. *Hitler's Spanish Legion, The Blue Division in Russia.* Carbondale IL: Southern Illinois University Press, 1979.

Madej, Victor. *German Army Order of Battle: Field Army and Officer Corps, 1939-1945.* Allentown PA: Valor, 1985.

Madej, Victor. *Hitler's Elite Guards: Waffen SS, Parachutists, U-Boats.* Allentown PA: Valor, 1985.

Newton, Steven H. *German Battle Tactics on the Russian Front, 1941-1945.* Atglen PA: Schiffer, 1994.

Platonov, S. P. *Bitva za Leningrad, 1941-1944.* Moscow : Ministry of Information, 1964.

Ready, J. Lee. *The Forgotten Axis, Germany's Partners and Foreign Volunteers in World War II.* Jefferson NC: McFarland & Co., 1987.

Roig, Pedro V. *Spanish Soldiers in Russia.* Miami: Ediciones Universal, 1976.

Schulte, Theo J. *The German Army and Nazi Policies in Occupied Russia.* New York: St. Martin's Press, 1989.

Schumann, Wolfgang, and Olaf Gröhler, eds., *Deustchland im zweiten Weltkrieg,.* 6 volumes. Köln: Pahl-Rugenstein Verlag, 1981-1985.

Seaton, Albert. *The Russo-German War.* New York: Praeger, 1971.

Thomas, Nigel, Carlos Caballero Jurado, and Simon McCouaig, *Wehrmacht Auxiliary Forces.* London: Osprey, 1992.

Ziemke, Earl F. *Stalingrad to Berlin, The German Defeat in the East.* Washington DC: Center for Military History, 1968.